What is a 21st Century Brand?

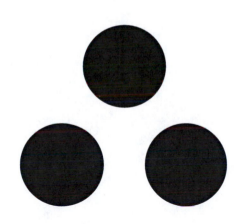

What is a 21st Century Brand?

New thinking from the next generation of advertising leaders

Edited by Nick Kendall

KoganPage

LONDON PHILADELPHIA NEW DELHI

Publisher's note

Every possible effort has been made to ensure that the information contained in this book is accurate at the time of going to press, and the publishers and authors cannot accept responsibility for any errors or omissions, however caused. No responsibility for loss or damage occasioned to any person acting, or refraining from action, as a result of the material in this publication can be accepted by the editors, the publisher or any of the authors.

First published in Great Britain and the United States in 2015 by Kogan Page Limited

2nd Floor, 45 Gee Street   1518 Walnut Street, Suite 1100   4737/23 Ansari Road
London EC1V 3RS   Philadelphia PA 19102   Daryaganj
United Kingdom   USA   New Delhi 110002
www.koganpage.com   India

© The Institute of Advertising Practitioners 2015

The right of The Institute of Advertising Practitioners to be identified as the author of this work has been asserted by them in accordance with the Copyright, Designs and Patents Act 1988.

ISBN   978 0 7494 7262 7
E-ISBN   978 0 7494 7263 4

British Library Cataloguing-in-Publication Data

A CIP record for this book is available from the British Library.

Library of Congress Control Number

2015006669

Typeset by Graphicraft Limited, Hong Kong
Print production managed by Jellyfish
Printed and bound by CPI Group (UK) Ltd, Croydon CR0 4YY

CONTENTS

BACKGROUND

What is the IPA Excellence Diploma?

The IPA Excellence Diploma is the culmination of the series of career-defining qualifications created by the IPA (the Institute of Practitioners in Advertising) for the UK marcomms industry since 2003.

The focus of the Diploma is brands – what are they, what is their value to business, how should ideas be used to build them in today's world, and how must we organize ourselves to do that?

The programme is aimed at those individuals who feel they have reached a level where they have mastered their craft and are searching to *master their own point of view*. The Diploma is designed to stimulate, encourage, even force them to do that.

Delegates are first required to read through the most comprehensive reading and viewing list ever compiled on brands, representing our 'shared texts, learning and case histories'. In short, our collective knowledge and intelligence as an industry.

They then attend 'deep dives' organized around the core questions. These are led by industry figureheads, and are an opportunity to debate and explore with invited experts and, of course, their fellow Diploma delegates.

Critical to the process also, is the mentorship they receive 'back at the ranch' within their own agency support team.

Throughout, they are encouraged to build on the 'shoulders of giants' and voice their own opinions through a series of essays, and the programme culminates in a final 'I believe... and therefore' thesis on the future of brands, brand ideas and communications agencies.

The pieces are marked primarily on the basis of originality and application, as well as clarity, presentation and support of argument.

It is an intensive twelve-month process, rather than an 'exam', and for this reason it has been variously described, by delegates themselves, as a 'brand assault course', and 'the MBA of brands'.

The IPA itself has come to describe the Diploma as its very own 'BrandLabs' initiative – a kind of R&D programme for the business. A programme built from the bottom up by the next generation of leaders vs the current or past generations.

The best of the final 'I believe... and therefore' pieces are published in *Campaign*, the UK ad industry's trade magazine, and offer the industry fresh original perspectives on the future of the business we are in – building brands.

ACKNOWLEDGEMENTS

Nick Kendall

I would like to thank all those who have helped pull this book together, including Jonathan Kemeys, who chased, harried and collated on my behalf, and Patrick Mills and Tessa Gooding, whose idea this book originally was.

I would also like to thank JWT and Sally King for the use of material by Stephen King.

Finally, I would like to thank all those people who have helped put the Diploma itself together over the past 10 years.

Time, they say, is our most valuable resource. Which is why I will always be grateful that these busy people gave theirs so generously. There are many ways of learning, from doing to studying. Learning from others, particularly ones of such quality and pedigree, has been a privilege.

Module editors

Will Collin
Mark Earls
Nick Emmel
Peter Field
Daryl Fielding
Chris Forrest

Wendy Gordon
David Hackworthy
Tom Hampson
Steve Henry
Richard Hytner
Mark Lund

Gerry Moira
Gurdeep Puri
Tony Regan
Jim Taylor
David Wilding

Examiners

Louise Ainsworth
Tess Alps
Paul Bainsfair
John Bartle
Karen Buchanan
Pete Buckley
Alex Dunsdon
Carlos Grande
Colin Grimshaw
David Grint
Janet Hull OBE

Frances Illingworth
Tim Jones
Moray Maclennan
Caroline Marshall
Sophie Maunder-Allan
Craig Mawdsley
Nicola Mendelsohn
Steve Parker
David Pattison
Ian Priest
Hamish Pringle

Leo Rayman
Martin Runnacles
Alan Rutherford
Gideon Spanier
Stuart Sullivan-Martin
Rory Sutherland
Jonathan Taylor
Sue Unerman
John V Willshire
Stephen Woodford

IPA Excellence Diploma Team

Erika Bewers	Libby Foster	Sam Roberts
Kate Bromage	Tessa Gooding	Sarah Shortt
Ann Murray Chatterton	Jonathan Kemeys	Chloe Williams
Felicity Cranfield	Patrick Mills	

FOREWORD

I believe we must professionalize

*Stephen Woodford, Executive Chairman, Lexis, and
IPA President, 2003–2005*

*"I believe the value created by agencies will be greatly
enhanced if we transform how we share our collective
knowledge with future generations of brand and agency
people.*

I recently joined an NHS teaching hospital trust as a non-executive director, and one of the many things that have impressed me is how much effort is put into lifelong learning and sharing of expertise. Obviously, a successful healthcare organization depends on this. It would be unthinkable to have a doctor or nurse caring for patients who had only 'learned by doing', or by mimicking their superiors, or was relying on their natural brilliance as a medic.

Likewise, you wouldn't want an architect, engineer, pilot, accountant, lawyer, or bricklayer for that matter, who hadn't mastered the knowledge of their trade and could demonstrate this through their qualifications.

Not wishing to put branding and advertising in the same category as medicine in terms of its importance in our national life, but it does make a major contribution to the private sector and the tax revenues that fund the NHS and everything else. A recent Deloitte report[1] calculated that every pound spent on advertising generates six in the wider economy, so imagine how much more could be added if we were as rigorous as other professions at sharing our collective expertise.

Despite the decades-long efforts of the IPA, and others, to improve the knowledge and skills base of our industry, that difference is one of the key reasons agency people are not charged at, or earning, the rates of other knowledge-based professions. An audit partner at a Top 20 firm, based in London, would typically charge around £370 per hour.[2] A partner at a Magic Circle law firm could charge up to £850 per hour,[3] whereas a creative, planner or account handler with 10 years' experience at a big London agency is more likely to be charged out at around £200 per hour.[4]

So the professional expertise recognized and paid for when buying accountancy or legal advice is not rewarded to anything like the same degree when buying advertising. Yet advertising contributes much, much more to the firm's growth and sustained profitability.

I believed that we needed to 'professionalize'

The opportunity to 'professionalize' the branding and communications business – to organize the collective wisdom and latest insights of the brightest and best thinkers and practitioners in our trade and pass it on for the next generation to build on – is what inspired me in my term as IPA President 10 years ago.

It was also driven by personal experience, or more accurately, a lack of it. I joined the business as an account manager from a client background and my bosses, not unreasonably, thought I knew what I was doing. Being afflicted with the male mindset of never asking for directions, even when lost, I clattered the first few fences of the account manager handicap hurdles and learnt on the job the hard way, and at the expense of my colleagues and clients.

So from these two sources of inspiration, one perhaps idealistic and the other as prosaic as they come, we set about designing a programme of professional qualifications, launching the first two in 2004.

We started with the Foundation Certificate, aimed at giving new entrants to the industry a broad understanding across the waterfront of marketing and communications.

This was shortly followed by the Excellence Diploma, which this book is rightly celebrating. It was designed to inspire the brightest and best practitioners from agencies and client companies to broaden and accelerate their learning, and therefore their careers. These were to be bookends that would stimulate people in our industry to learn and develop throughout their career.

A further five courses and qualifications have since been added, for example The Eff Test. To date over 10,000 people have passed an IPA qualification, and the IPA now exports these to over 60 countries.

The MBA of brands

The Excellence Diploma has had over 100 people graduate from a course that is undoubtedly the best of its kind in the world. It has had the benefit of Nick Kendall's brilliant design and leadership over the last decade and this book is a tribute to him, to all the tutors and other contributors and, most of all, to the hard grafting and talented Diploma graduates.

The brief Nick and I agreed at the start of the process was based on the 'if I only knew then what I know now' principle. It was to give people in the early part of their career the benefit of many lifetimes of learning from the best thinkers and practitioners from around the world.

We shared a belief that the learning curve in agency careers tended to flatten out after about 8 to 10 years, accelerating again when people reached management positions in their 30s and 40s. If we could keep the learning curve steep through this period and put someone in a position by their 30s to have the breadth of knowledge of someone perhaps 10 or more years further on in their career, the effect would be profound and lasting for them as individuals, and for their clients, agencies and colleagues.

Not that this knowledge would have just been accumulated by more years at the coalface. The key benefit of the course is the distillation of the most relevant and valuable insight and learning that exists around the world, continually updated and refreshed to keep the Diploma at the leading edge of our industry.

Nick took this brief on, with dedicated and diligent support from the IPA – Ann Murray Chatterton, then the IPA Director of Professional Development deserves special credit for this. The potential of the idea, and Nick's tireless energy, secured invaluable contributions from many leading practitioners, writers and academics.

Together they designed the Excellence Diploma programme, a grand tour of the leading edges of branding, creativity, behavioural economics, technology, communications theory and much more.

...and therefore we need to drive wider engagement

Over the last 10 years I've talked to many of the graduates at the dinner that celebrates the end of each programme. The quality of the course seems to fire up their talent and ambition and this has shone through in how their careers accelerate and broaden. All talk in glowing terms about the difference the experience makes to their confidence and desire to make bigger and bolder contributions in their agencies. I think it also breeds a healthy dissatisfaction with the status quo and a hunger to make the business better.

So for me it is now about the numbers. There is no doubt that the Diploma is a great success and makes a huge difference to the careers and the value the graduates generate. One hundred graduates over 10 years is a wonderful milestone to celebrate in this book. Ten years from now I would love to see 100 people a year graduate, and that I believe would truly transform the value agencies create for their clients and the wider economy, and the rewards they get in return.

Notes

1 (July 2012) Advertising pays: How advertising fuels the UK economy, Deloitte LLP, commissioned by Advertising Association, London.
2 Source: Kingston Smith, 2014.
3 Burton, L (26 November 2013) Magic Circle hourly rates hit all-time high of £850, *The Lawyer*.
4 Source: IPA survey data, Spring 2014.

Introduction
How to read this book and some observations

NICK KENDALL
Founding Partner, Bro-Ken and
Former Global Strategy Director, BBH

So often we try and solve problems 'without working on the theory of the thing first'. (STEPHEN KING, 'WHAT IS A BRAND?')

Ten years of the MBA of brands: 20 provocations

The pieces published here on the Diploma's 10th anniversary are the best of the best. They are chosen from the President's Prize winners, and from the delegates who secured the prize for the Most Outstanding Body of Work. I have also taken the liberty of including some of my *personal* favourites from across the years.

By definition, they offer unashamedly subjective points of view. The book is not governed by one theme or answer to the question of the title *What is a Brand?* Rather, the reader is offered multiple windows into the house of brands.

In part, this is the nature of 'a collection of...' book. But also I believe it reflects the truth of what all practitioners know from deep experience. There is no one answer.

'What is a brand?' changes depending on the market, on whether it's a luxury brand or an FMCG brand, on the brand's market position as leader or challenger, on the audience and their needs.

But, most critically, sometimes I think it depends on the brand itself. Every brand, one hopes, is uniquely itself. Like a character in a book or film a truly authentic brand creates its own story, its own role in people's lives , and its own rules of engagement such that the answer to 'what is a brand?' can change even within a market.

Every practitioner knows a brand is not subject to an academic definition that reduces the answer to one glib theme.

Therefore, I am pleased to offer each of these pieces to the reader, each with its personal belief, as *provocations*. I hope and trust the reader will take their own learnings and actions from each.

The structure of the book

The 20 pieces here are arranged into three parts:

- Part 1: What is a brand?
- Part 2: What is a brand idea?
- Part 3: How should we organize to deliver?

These sections reflect the intellectual journey the delegates take through the Diploma.

At the beginning of each section I have invited people who have supported the Diploma over the years to draw their own conclusions from the provocations that follow in that section.

I have also taken the liberty to explore my own overall reactions to the 20 beliefs – first of all later in this introduction. But also I have forced myself to pin down my own brand beliefs as a further provocation for you.

Finally, in front of every essay I have allowed myself to be 'provoked' into three 'brand therefores' around what the individual 'I believe' piece implies for our overall brand thinking, our brand engagement thinking and finally our brand organization and capability.

I have also asked each of the writers to revisit their piece – summarize their POV and, more importantly maybe, asked them to put down their 'personal therefores' and actions as a result of their belief: first in their work, then their careers, and then their lives. After all, what are beliefs without action?

Again all these are provocations and it is hoped this will help you come to your own 'therefores' from the piece.

How to read this 21st-century 'What is a brand?'

The book follows the logic of the Diploma itself and, as Stephen King put it, starts with working on 'the theory of the thing first'. Stephen King was one of the founding fathers of account planning, leader of JWT and pioneer of their famous 'brand planning cycle' approach. But you are not taking the qualification so I would recommend a post modernist reading of this book. By which I mean, pick it up at random and dive into one of the essays and its 'therefore' companion piece for just 15 minutes.

I promise it will stimulate your thinking.

Choose a brand you are working on and apply that belief to that brand.

Choose an idea you have created or inherited and apply the rules of engagement suggested.

Think of the agency you are working for and think what you would change by implication?

Write down what you would do therefore, and I guarantee you will generate a new action.

So do not try and read all the way through. Do not start at the front and finish at the end. Jump around. Read the contents page and let it take you where your interests drive you. Have a short attention span, but have a blank piece of paper next to you, *or your very own 'I believe... and therefore' notebook.*

I believe you will discover what the delegates discovered. There is in the 21st century no unifying single theory, which is why this book offers 20!

But I believe you will discover something more valuable – the Diploma mindset! As Stephen King suggests in the opening quote, there is a unifying and professional model of thinking to allow you to approach any challenge. What is a brand? How should it come alive, therefore? And how should we organize to deliver it as a result?

This is a surprisingly novel approach, I would suggest. Normally, of course, we start with how we are organized, followed by an idea rooted in the capabilities at our disposal, which are in turn rooted in some old, generalized, mostly 20th-century model of brand thinking that shapes our views of what the brand is even before we start.

Try the reverse, and use this book to help you.

What is a brand: 1970 vs 21st century – my own observations

The first text in the delegates' reading is Stephen King's seminal piece 'What is a brand?'

It is a piece I have long admired. A piece I would happily hand out to *every single person* who joins the business, whatever the discipline. A piece I send to people who are thinking about getting into the business.

I do this for three reasons:

- First, it is a reminder of the business I believe we are truly in.
  We are *not* in advertising, or media, or PR or design. We are *not just* creatives, or media planners or digital specialists. These are inputs vs output. We are all *brand builders*.

- Second, I love the way King thinks. Starting from the beginning, vs halfway in, is a very good place to start. A lesson to us all.
- Third, his piece is inspiring. It reminds us our job is not to run around chasing deadlines. Our job is to build one of the 20th century's (or arguably earlier) great inventions – the brand.

Certainly I would recommend readers of *this* book to take a look at Stephen's original piece, if they haven't already. It stands as an interesting companion piece.

Written in 1970, it explored his answer to that simplest of questions: 'What is a brand?' and then goes on to suggest some consequences.

Nearly 50 years later, this collection of pieces acts as a kind of 21st-century set of answers to the same simple question. And the comparisons between Stephen King's answers and the Diploma delegates' is fascinating.

The context of power

In the Stephen King piece the overriding context was the rise of retailer power.

For our 21st-century authors, we quickly recognize that the overall context is the rise of consumer power, enabled and activated of course by the rise of digital and the internet.

All the 20 pieces that follow, in one way or another, start from the truth that the brand owner is no longer in sole control. All explore how to make this an *opportunity* for new forms of relationships between producer and consumer. They do not fear it, but celebrate the potential of new joint ownership.

The workers, as it were, have taken over the the means of production and they love being capitalists apparently. They certainly love the chance to express their autonomy and individual worth through brands.

A brand is...

In the 1970s 'What is a brand?', King goes on to define a brand as a personality, a set of intangible added values that consumers related to, beyond the function:

> What I am saying in fact is that Andrex succeeds as a profit earner because, in addition to its value as a product, the brand has values beyond the physical and functional ones. And those added values contribute to a brand personality.
>
> People choose their brands as they do their friends. You choose friends not usually because of specific skills or physical attributes (though of course these come into it) but simply because you like them. It is the total person you choose, not a compendium of virtues and vices.

In *What is a 21st Century Brand?* the answers are more varied (maybe not least because people are thinking beyond manufacturing and FMCG brands). And you have the pleasure, in what follows, of reading 20 individuals' beliefs, not just one person's.

Again, what I see as joining them is a simple, obvious answer: the brand is us.

And from this the essays quickly explore different ways of involving or connecting us. We live now in a world of what might be called open-source branding. The brand owner issues the code – the consumer uses it and works with it to make it better for them, their friends and the brand owner.

The role of advertising

In his essay Stephen King goes on to consider, as a result of his definition of a brand, what our approach to advertising should be:

> We can recognize that advertising is a totality. A campaign, like a brand, is not just a number of its put together – a claim here, a packshot there, a reason why somewhere else. If we produce it by the atomistic approach, we will end up with a sort of identikit brand. It will be a perfect description of the structure of the brand, as the identikit can describe the contours of the face. But it won't be the same thing. The brand will never come to life.

I suspect the 21st-century authors would agree with much of this. Obviously, we no longer like to use the word advertising, though it is obvious in the quote above that Stephen was thinking way beyond definitions around TV/print/posters, etc. And of course, in these 21st-century answers there is an absolute assumption that we live in a broader 'everything-is-media' world.

The difference may only be that today's writer's instinct would be to build a brand around a brand's *vision* rather than around a personality only – a brand as an idea to live by and engage with, as and when and how they please.

And then, as Mark Earls observes on page 19, our authors quickly move on to what they regard as *the* critical question in the 21st century (interestingly one that Stephen King's quote above only ends on): how to bring the brand alive? Critical for them, I think, because they have an instinctive understanding that the real challenges today are about engagement – how to cut through in a super-saturated world of content; overcoming consumer cynicism in a world of super transparency; commanding consumer attention when there is so much to engage with; managing brand coherence around an idea in such a fragmented world; building longevity in a 'here-today-gone-in-the-next-nano-second' environment.

In these 21st-century answers to 'how to bring a brand alive?' there is the same recognition of the importance of the totality vs the atomistic, for eco-system thinking vs identikit. But then the exploration is of *how* to hold the totality together; how to make the connections, how to join the dots between parts of the brand and its identity, recognizing that the person most often joining the dots, literally clicking and sharing them, is us, the consumer, as both audience and media in our own right.

All of which makes you realize just how much our end is in our beginning, and our beginning is in our end. These essays, with all their bright new thinking, seem to collectively call to me for a return to the origins of marketing. The rise of consumer power, the brand as us, ideas for us to engage and play with as we please... all these suggest a critical need for agencies to embrace a new age of consumer knowledge and insight, and more forcefully start from understanding people more precisely and more deeply than ever before.

Certainly our clients in the C-suites agree.

> The most proactive CMOs are trying to understand individuals as well as markets. Customer intimacy is crucial – and CEOs know it. In our last CEO study, we learned CEOs regard getting closer to customers as one of three prerequisites for success in the 21st century. This sits squarely in the CMO's domain.
>
> ('From stretched to strengthened' – IBM Global CMO's Survey 2011)

Sharpening our thinking

What I still find fascinating about Stephen King's piece is that he uses his theoretical definition of a brand to quickly map out suggestions for how we might sharpen our thinking; how we organize ourselves, how we plan for business, how we use research, and of course how we use advertising.

And in this book also, we see authors take their belief and apply it to how we might sharpen up our understanding of 'what we need to do, therefore'.

In order to encourage this, in editing this book I decided it would be interesting to go back to the authors and ask them to add to their original 'I believe... and therefore' piece with what they actually *did* do therefore in their work, their career and even their life. This I have placed in front of the original thesis.

The result, I hope, is a very unique 'double whammy' of practitioners' perspectives – the original 'I believe' and the follow-up 'therefore'.

The practitioner's tale

The new 'therefore' pieces, taken together, illustrate an equally compelling story of what I would call *a new 21st-century strategic mindset*.

The last 10 years have seen the rise of the doers. In a world of fast change and ever-growing complexity there has been almost a call to embrace doing as a form of strategy – to learn via beta testing; to borrow concepts of MVP from tech companies; to start many small fires in order to fan the one that catches light; to drive forward by action; and reactions vs strategy or vision.

I was fascinated, if not surprised, that the delegates here betray in their new pieces the same instinct for, even fear of, the danger of too much thinking, of the abstract and theoretical, or of ivory tower thinking. Without exception they call upon themselves to *act* on their beliefs.

But I was also pleased to see that they all, without exception, also recognize the value of what the Diploma has given them: models of thinking, theories from which to start, *beliefs on which to act*.

The Diploma seems to develop in the delegates a new *mindset*, which I hope Stephen King would have applauded – a mindset of 'I think, therefore I do'.

And surely this 'think, do' mindset is right. To do without thinking is just tactics signifying nothing. Equally to think without doing swiftly and forcefully in this fiercely competitive, complex world, is death by analysis.

Both approaches are unprofessional. I believe, and so do the Diploma-schooled practitioners featured here, that the true professional has theory and practice as equal bedfellows.

In his opening, Stephen King references the business challenges the industry faces and notes:

> Usually when we discuss such difficult and controversial subjects we rush in and start to argue about techniques. So often we try and solve problems without working on the theory of the thing first.

Our 21st-century professionals would agree.

Notes

1 King, S (1971) What is a brand?, in Baskin, M and Lannon, J (eds) (2007)
A Master Class in Brand Planning: The timeless works of Stephen King,
John Wiley & Sons, Chichester.

I believe
the pendulum
has swung too far

NICK KENDALL

I have pushed the Diploma delegates very hard across these 10 years to think about what they believe.

So I guess it is only fair that I kick off their 'I believe' pieces with what I believe.

I grew up believing in brands

At its simplest, I believe in brands.

I have spent most of my career thus far sitting at the feet of Messrs Bartle, Bogle and Hegarty.

So baked, even beaten, into my thinking from an early age (I was 25 when I joined) was an unwavering belief in the power of brands and advertising's unique role in building them.

Every pitch I did over 27 years would first step back to define the client's business challenges, then step forward to define the vision for the brand that would solve them. Only then would the brand idea be introduced. A brand idea that is – not a script, not a one-off execution!

I remember we presented ourselves, in early agency credentials, as part of the *manufacturing* process. The BBH building was designed and pictured as a 'creative factory'; its role to build intangible value. We pitched ourselves at the front of the process, not the back, as integral to the product as the designer building innovation into an Audi.

John Bartle's favourite proof of the value of brands was the Coca-Cola/ Pepsi blind taste test (where famously Pepsi wins in the blind and Coca-Cola wins in the branded test, reversing the results completely). For John it was proof of the power of emotion in shaping how we perceive and read the world around us.

Our favourite brand diagram therefore was a simple rational/emotional yin yang with the brand's vision at the centre and its rational support and emotional benefits either side. Since those early days I have seen keys, onions, pyramids aplenty, but that simple BBH yin yang brand diagram stripped down and enshrined the simplest definition of a brand. It was enough to drive the rise and rise of Levis, Audi, Axe/Lynx etc – and enough for me.

My belief has grown, not wavered

As my experience and knowledge deepened, so has my respect for the value of brands.

I learned of brand's ability to sustain a premium, its ability to secure loyalty, to resist competition and reverse the power of distribution. In short, I learned the value of brands to business as well as to consumers. It is easy to forget that during my time I have seen brands become as much a part of balance sheets as any other asset.

And, as the world around me changed, I have seen the uses and benefits of brands multiply. Brands are marvellously adaptive tools. Intellectual Swiss Army knives with a built-in update ability.

For example, as the economy became global, I have seen brands give clarity, consistency and leadership across different countries and stakeholders as well as across different brand and consumer histories.

As markets have shifted to service and experience propositions I have seen brands being used to shape and engage company culture as well as consumer culture.

I have seen brands become platforms for innovation as single product brands became, by economic necessity, multi-category.

As the world has gone digital I have seen brands become networks and communities of interest offering peer-to-peer support and added-value services to its members.

I have even seen brands become the living conscience of companies in a connected world where transparency is a given and sustainable consumption is a must.

In short, I believe brands have utility not just as communication organizers but as alternative CEOs. Brands can supply vision – a compass to guide a business, a living expression of the contract between company and consumer, a tool to shape the experience of the whole business not just a blind taste test, all stakeholders not just consumers.

In particular, I believe in brand ideas

I believe not just in the power of brands but also the power of brand ideas.

Indeed, I should confess, I love them. I love ideas.

Not executions (though I love them too) but big, fat brand ideas; the bigger the better for me.

So though I am a planner by trade, when I am asked for my CV, I give 'my book' of those brand ideas I am most proud of having been part of creating. Why take Liberty's?, The Original Jean, The Cream of Manchester, Dedicated to Pleasure, Keep Walking, Dirt is Good.

But I do this not just because I love creativity but more importantly because I feel they are my ultimate proof of whether, as John Hegarty puts it, I have managed to turn 'intelligence into magic'. For me this has to be the ultimate job of the individual in the business and the ultimate role for, and value of, agencies.

If our first job is to help lead client to a clear brand vision I feel brand ideas have a special value beyond the articulation of brand on paper because of three critical qualities:

- *First, they are the epitome of distillation and reduction.* In a world of overchoice they precisely and swiftly picture the choice for the consumer. They are the haikus of brand management and I love haikus.

- *Second, brand ideas have a public tangibility* that any amount of brand diagrams and videos cannot capture. Brands on paper are abstract. Brand ideas out in the real world are concrete. If brands are conceptual glue, brand ideas are tangible superglue.

  They are by definition public and therefore accountable for what they promise. That is why the broader media so often hoists a company by its own brand idea. There is no place to hide, no way to fudge with a brand idea.

- *Third, brand ideas by definition are required to engage and be felt* in order to cut through. A brand idea might take months to develop (maybe too long?) but it takes only moments to enter the head and then live in the heart forever. And that is why I believe in the true leadership power of the brand idea to motivate, unify and inspire where charts and insight and brand keys have not. I have found people – internally or externally – tend to prefer to work with an idea, not an explanation, with an emotion not a rationalization.

It is these three qualities I believe that make brand ideas a unique business tool in our consumer empowered, overchoiced, lazy, even cynical world. I do believe that 'Yes You Can' still change a market with a great brand and even more importantly, a great brand idea.

I am less sure whether market forces agree with me

So far most of what I have said is uncontroversial.

So let's see if we can go a little further and create a little more debate.

Even as I/we all admire and proselytize the power of brands and brand ideas I believe market forces beyond our control are pulling us *away* from putting those beliefs into action.

Sometimes I fear we are in danger of becoming an example of the modern-day 'cookery shows as porn' inversion – apparently we spend more time watching them than actually cooking! Maybe we are beginning to spend more time talking about brands and brand ideas than actually building them.

Indeed, I would go further and argue that those forces are pulling us *into* a focus on the short term and the tactical vs the long and broad.

And, in so doing, these forces are pulling us from our core added value role as client partners – building brands and ideas for the long run.

The market forces at play are manifold

For me there are manifold forces, all acting together, all interacting to seduce us away from the long and the broad effects of what we do.

In the broader environment I see the rise of economic theories in books like Simenson's and Rosen's *Absolute Value* that focus on purchasing as a wholly rational process and brands as losing their purpose 'in a world where (nearly) perfect information exists'. I love that '(nearly)'!

I see the rise of business commentators such as James Surowiecki of *Wisdom of Crowds* fame claiming in his *New Yorker* column that the 'economic value of brands – traditionally assessed by the premium a company can charge – is waning'. And our beloved *Wired* magazine picturing brands as a kind of emotional con that allows companies to live off past performance.

In the business environment I see the rise of accountability and the need for proof driving us to focus on what we can measure most easily no matter how often we warn ourselves against doing it. As well as the rise of 'next quarteritis'!

In the media environment I see the rise of just-in-time targeting that allows us to focus on those in the marketplace now vs those in the future or on the periphery as onlookers.

I see the rise of interactivity that has inevitably drawn our focus onto the final part of the *consumer journey into purchase; the final click,* and the fulfilment of demand vs the creation of it.

I see the rise of promotional offers as a share of total budget. I recently read an article in *Harvard Business Review* by Teixeira that reported that in 2013 promotional budgets were 2.5 times bigger than advertising budgets, vs being evenly matched in 2000.

In the research environment I see the rise of research and data tools that focus on the intermediate or immediate effect of any idea – the definition of success around 'share growth in the next six weeks' for example or the use of dwell time and click through rates and 'likes' without any reference to their long-term value.

In the management environment I see the rise and rise of a focus on efficiency (particularly in Western, mature markets) in managing costs and resource across all aspects of business but including marketing again with the inevitable focus on tangible short-term measures.

I see the rise of pressures on the back of this drive with its focus on unit costs and norms leading to an atomistic approach (as Stephen King put it) vs holistic, and a focus on implementation and execution hours vs quality of input and long and broad advice.

I see the decline in the average tenure of brand managers and CMOs leading to stop and start management and discontinuities and the average length of agency/client relationship dropping in length from seven years and two months in 1984 to just two years and six months today.

These are just some of the market forces I see at play. I am sure you see others.

Together, I believe they almost build to a kind of *perfect storm of short-termism*. Each reinforcing and encouraging the other in a kind of viscious downward spiral into the managing of the *here* and *now* vs the *long* and *the broad*.

I believe the forces of the market undermine our belief in the long term

I believe these forces combine to create foreshortened horizons. Ask most people in today's brand management world – either client or agency side – and they will admit to a sense of 'constant running', even panic, and the dominance of the next deadline. The opportunities for perspective happen only occasionally in one-off away-days quickly to be swamped again on return into the real world of these market forces.

To be clear the forces do not mean to do what they are doing. Each of these forces is a necessary part of the world we live in in business today. Indeed many, particularly the rise of data and interactivity and the media distribution of content, are wonderful opportunities. They are not malevolent 'agencies'. We are simply the victims of the economic 'law of unintended consequences', variously ascribed to either Adam Smith or 'Murphy', depending on how serious we want to be about it.

To be equally clear I am not an 'either/or' kind of guy. I believe in '*and*'.

Any modern practitioner and professional, and any modern agency has to build the mindset, skills and capabilities to *combine* and *blend* these new forces into their thinking and ideas.

They offer us a new golden age of communication where we can create things people want *and* inspire people to want them, to manage the long *and* the short, the broad *and* the particular, the strategic *and* the tactical.

But the pendulum has swung too far

So I am not trying to go back. To put Pandora back in the box.

But I do believe the pendulum has swung too far.

When the CEO of the world's most famous agency, Kevin Roberts, stands up in front of a room of senior business leaders at the IOD and proclaims brands and big (brand) ideas are dead...

> Brands have run out of juice. Now the consumer is boss. There is nowhere for brands to hide... the big idea is dead. There are no more big ideas. Creative leaders should go for getting lots and lots of small ideas out there.

I guess I just worry.

And when young Diploma delegates follow their leaders and herald the end of strategy and the triumph of tactics, or that long is just a series of shorts, or that we should light lots of small fires and see what happens. I guess I just am not surprised.

Maybe we just love anything that proclaims the death of something, that headlines a paradigm shift. We love a good shock to the system, of course. But I fear the market forces are becoming us and our own views. They are becoming our beliefs.

I believe we need brands and brand ideas even more, not less

In a fast-moving world, in a fragmented world, in a short-fix world, there is, I believe, a clear and present danger that 'the centre cannot hold', that people become confused, that things do not add up, that nothing lasts and that therefore nothing should be built to last. We fall into a kind of existential brand anxiety. The promise of agile marketing becomes sound and fury, signifying nothing.

I do not know about you but in this world my answer is to look for things that can create coherence and clarity, that can create meaning, that can integrate a broken world.

I do not think I am alone – our audience needs them too.

And so I would argue that in *our* world brands and brand ideas are needed *more and more* to glue things back together – both conceptually and tangibly. We need ideas to fix it.

Indeed, I would argue for *bigger,* not smaller, ideas.

If you think of what a brand idea is ideally required to do in today's world it *needs* to be a be a big one.

It needs to be inspiring enough to create demand *and* agile enough to exploit it. It needs to be emotional, functional and *social.* It needs to engage inside and outside to create loyalty. It needs to spark communications across channels and innovation in product and service.

To achieve this it needs to be *baked-in* to the business idea and become more than an executional tool – a *cultural* tool.

In my book, in anyone's book, that is a big idea. Call it by any other name – idea as hardware for software to run on, idea as organizing principle, idea to live by – it needs to smell as sweet. It needs to do the heavy lifting business needs. It needs to be a bold, brave, beautiful, bountiful, *bigger* brand idea.

And therefore...

When Stephen Woodford asked me to create and run the Diploma I could not resist his charm. But also I must admit I could not resist grabbing my chance to keep the faith.

By focusing on brands and how to bring them alive, I do hope the Diploma helps in some small way to swing the pendulum back into equilibrium.

In truth the long vs short debate has to go much broader than the Diploma and we need to 'sharpen up' our practices across the board not just in the area of professional development.

If we believe in the long and broad we need to provide and publish more proofs of their value in the boardroom. Pieces like Peter Field's and Les Binet's IPA *The Long and the Short of It* need to be added to every year. I would love to see an equivalent piece on the value of communication across multiple stakeholders from consumers to staff to city analysts to management.

And not just around creative ideas but around the value of long-term branded media properties (another thing I totally believe in) and long-term conversations vs short-term.

We have to build new cases that illustrate how in the modern screen world we can glue together the consumer journey (after all it is only media selling that is fragmented) from famous one to many, to personal one to one.

Indeed I would go so far as to call for more long and broad cases in the IPA Effectiveness Awards.

Maybe we need to commission and create our own long and broad effectiveness cases.

I, for one, would prefer to learn about the value of Nike having one brand vision and one brand idea over nearly all my career and across multiple markets both sporting and geographic (even if they don't need to use the line anymore it is the same territory!) vs Reebok's multiple short-terms ideas or Adidas's idea changeover every four or five years. Or learn more about British Airways ROI on 'To Fly To Serve', both internally and externally, for example, in helping them reshape their holiday proposition *as well as* how it improved summer sales or click-through rates.

Most critically for me we certainly have to finally, once and for all, find a new form of remuneration that focuses reward on the long and the broad as much as the short.

And on the back of that, develop brand dashboards that balance and relate short- *and* long-term metrics as part of our everyday management of brand ideas.

But within these and other 'therefores' (and I would love to hear from you about other ideas you might have) I do believe training our future stars in the fundamentals of what is a brand in the 21st century? is something we *have* to do.

Not everyone can have the pleasure of learning from Messrs Bartle Bogle and Hegarty. But they can all study the shared texts, learnings and case histories of our business and of our great and good. And they can all be encouraged to think what they believe on the back of that.

They do not, of course, have to share my personal beliefs about the value of brands and brand ideas.

But I defy them not to! In the last 10 years Diploma delegates have offered me many original and fresh perspectives that I have found brand affirming even after my 27 years believing.

I hope, in turn, they can do the same for others.

On this 10th anniversary we have gone some way to starting a new brand belief movement. I would like the movement to grow. Both broadly by extending the Diploma around the world and around agency groups and inspiring many more future leaders.

But also in the long term by Diploma alumni inspiring others one by one, team by team, agency by agency.

And, of course, I also hope this book inspires you, dear reader, to think about what you believe is the value of brands and brand ideas and the industry and agencies that deliver them.

In doing so, I believe we can tip the balance back to our future.

PART ONE
What is a brand?

Introduction
I believe we must consider a brand's behaviour, not just what a brand is

MARK EARLS
Herdmeister, Herd Consultancy

" *It's... bigger on the inside.* (DR WHO)

The questions we ask reveal far more than you'd think: not just the answers we hope to uncover, but more fundamentally the ideas we have about the world and how things are.

Someone who asks how God could allow terrible things to happen to themselves, to their family or to innocent victims of a natural disaster half the world away reveals not only the assumption that there is a such a thing as a divinity, but also that said super-being has some kind of control over what happens in the world or, indeed, that he/she/it tends to keep good and evil in balance, rewarding the good and protecting them from bad stuff.

In other words, the kinds of questions we ask reveal an awful lot more than we imagine they do. They are – in the famous words uttered by all those entering Doctor Who's Tardis – 'bigger on the inside than on the outside'.

Over the years, all discussions of the idea of brands and branding have tended to start with the same simple four-word question: *what is a brand?*

What does this question tell us about the ideas and assumptions floating around in the background?

Well, first off, perhaps it presumes that there is such a kind of thing as a brand, that it's a thing like a poster, or a promotion or an advert. Second, that such a definition can be definitive, universal and long-lasting. Third, and perhaps most telling, that there's a need to provide a definition.

A different kind of question

What's fascinating about the excellent pieces that follow, is that none of them ask this kind of question at all. Which is curious, given that after 10 years of the Excellence Diploma we still start the programme with this question.

Instead, the striking thing about all of the different points of view which we've collected here, is that they focus more on what you might do in the modern world than in defining the concept precisely – whether that direction is informed by new insights from the behavioural and cognitive sciences (as, for example, John Willshire's 'Communities are the future of brand communications' does), new emerging ways of engaging with people beyond the narrow confines of advertising and marketing (Graeme Douglas' 'Brand new religion' or Tim Jones' excellent 'Gaming your brand'), or just by a pragmatist's wisdom and acceptance not to overthink things.

Unlike their predecessors, these new voices don't seem to need the security of a reductionist definition of this brand thing – a statement of initial conditions, if you like. They seem perfectly happy to accept that arguing the toss about what a brand is less interesting than getting on with the messy but exhilarating act of brand-building. As one essay (Nick Docherty's 'Brand is a word that has outlined its usefulness') puts it: 'how helpful are the concepts of brand and branding as they are currently used?'

Rather than be confused by all this theoretical definitional wheel spin, these practitioners are working through ways to get on and make a difference.

Each of the authors quickly tells us what they believe a brand to be, but use that definition to explore how that changes how a brand should engage.

These are informed and thoughtful practitioners (not dumb do-ers), but not would-be theorists. And that is a good thing for the industry, surely.

What lies beneath

All of which serves to reveal a bigger and more important shift than we're seeing elsewhere in marketing and advertising, for example it informs the work the IPA Social Works Group is trying to bring the same kind of rigour to understanding social media effectiveness as has been developed for mainstream advertising.

Put simply: we are in transit from a world of stable certainties to one of fluid multiplicities. From a largely unchanging landscape that merely needed detailed observation to describe exhaustively, to one that is rich, complex and ever-changing.

In media terms, this means we're not switching from a world of TV and print to one that is now and forever dominated by Twitter and Facebook (although I'm sure they'd secretly like us to believe that). No, the newer technologies are both additive *and* at the same time provisional – they will in turn be superseded themselves. 'Facetube', as my father-in-law calls it, is not the final word.

The works collected here describe really useful ways of thinking about brands and brand-building in this new, messier, constantly changing landscape.

The rise of 'WE' and other things

All of which is not to say that there aren't any consistent content themes that emerge from these excellent pieces of work.

Given my own efforts over the last decade,[1] I'm particularly gratified to see the widespread adoption of what I've called the HERD insight – the notion that we humans are fundamentally social creatures and that our behaviour is shaped by the behaviour of those around us (certainly much more than we'd imagine). This serves variously to recast the nature of a brand as a knowledge centre and editor ('The communis manifesto' by John Willshire), challenge the structure of the consumer–brand relationship (David Bonney and the rise of 'WE' brands) and delve into the nature of brand experiences and how to build them (Ian Edwards and open-source innovation and Graeme Douglas' essay 'Brand new religion').

Equally, there is an intriguing golden thread that runs through many of these papers about brand as a user-led concept. While none of the authors are crass enough to mention Jeremy Bullmore's famous metaphor of brands being built by consumers as birds build nests, the user-perspective lies at the heart of all of these papers. Which is refreshing to those of us bored and frustrated by company-led definitions of brands ('it's what we tell them it is') and all the more so, given how naturally it is expressed.

A new hope

So, for those Jeremiahs bewailing the end of advertising or some such, these kinds of essays, with their very practical and thought-through prescriptions, are a breath of fresh air.

Or, then again, maybe not: it's curious that such an apparently simple question, can lead to such practical and fresh directions for the future.

Notes

1 Earls, M and Bentley, A (2011) *I'll Have What She's Having: Mapping social behaviour*, MIT Press, US; and Earls, M (2009) *Herd: How to change mass behaviour by harnessing our true nature*, John Wiley & Sons.

I believe brand is a word that has outlived its usefulness
2005/06

NICK DOCHERTY
Global Planning Director, Wieden + Kennedy Amsterdam

I believe 'Brands' and 'branding' are words that have outlived their usefulness, deriving as they do from a time when they referred to static badges and didactic communications. I believe that their roots are now a cause for confusion, and that the terms 'morph' and 'shaping' do a more intuitive job of explaining the things that we all do in our roles as marketing professionals.

Editor's therefore, for your brand...

Your brand thinking: If the 'b' word was banned in your organization tomorrow, what language would you use to replace it?

Your brand engagement: If branding is 'shaping' can you list all the things, big and small, that currently shape your brand?

Your brand organization & capability: Is your brand shaped across all touchpoints and by *everyone* in your organization – or just by a narrow group of marketing specialists?

...and author's personal therefore

In retrospect, the Diploma's real value to me was in helping me first understand, and then challenge, the theoretical underpinnings of everything that we do as an industry. It made me read all the books that I never would have otherwise read, and then rip them up (Byron Sharp's peerless *How Brands Grow* aside, it turns out that marketing textbooks are mostly a colossal waste of paper). It allowed me to get the over-thinking out of the way and get on with the serious business of doing. Which shouldn't be confused for doing *without* thinking. That's something else entirely.

So, is what I believed *then* the same as what I believe *now*? Not really, and I would be colossally disappointed if that wasn't the case. What I do believe is that the very last thing marketing needs is yet another definitive right answer to the issues it faces. But what has endured for me is an attitude and approach that challenges assumptions and believes in the primacy of real-world practice over intellectual theory. That takes to heart the old military adage that no plan ever survives contact with the enemy, but acknowledges the need for a decently thought-through plan in the first place – and an ability to argue its merits with equally informed people.

Here's a brief overview of how my drive to do more, and over-think less, has shaped my life and career over the last decade. They are in the form of some general principles rather than rigid commandments.

Work: learning is doing

We humans are a pretty conservative bunch. In a world built on shifting sands we cling to what we know, treat received wisdom as fact, assume that the past is an effective guide to the future, and fear change – however loudly we lionize novelty. But once you understand this, the world opens up. Because whatever anybody says, whichever way a brief's been framed, however a problem is described, the only important thing to remember is that everything's up for grabs. Everything. And the only way to get clients or colleagues out of their comfort zones and into a more interesting frame of mind is to stop the endless talking and take everyone along for the ride. Setting out to do stuff together in a spirit of experimentation acknowledges that you don't necessarily have all the answers upfront, helps the outcome to be flexible, makes everyone feel invested and positions what we do as the epic journey of a lifetime rather than a disposable weekend break. Among other things, seeing 'doing' as learning helped me change the whole conversation around drink-driving in the UK; persuade the world's most international beer brand to broaden its horizons globally; and prove the effectiveness of both these approaches. It also made me understand that the doing is never done.

Career: just do it

Given this philosophy, it's probably no accident that I've ended up at Wieden + Kennedy. This is an agency best defined by the attitude of Nike, their founding client: 'Just Do It.' More than any other influence Wieden has probably had the most lasting impact on my career. It's taught me the enduring value of getting the culture right in any organization, it's given me the belief that anything's possible – however unlikely it may seem at first – and it's underlined the fundamental truth that it's better to seek forgiveness than ask permission. Just doing stuff puts a premium on entrepreneurship and has given me the confidence and the freedom to get on with things rather than leaving them in the hands of a committee. Through doing things simply because they felt like the smart thing to do, the interesting thing to do, or even just the crazy thing to do, I've worked with some amazing brands, been given global responsibility and won a Cannes Grand Prix for Heineken. And if that doesn't illustrate the power of just doing it, then I don't know what does.

Life: a little less conversation

Elvis Presley had it about right: a little less conversation, a little more action please. What's worked for my work and my career seems to have worked out pretty well for my life too. Most importantly, 'doing' has taken me from the avenues of London to the canals of Amsterdam, and in the process has given me a perspective on life that's more global than I ever anticipated. I wasn't sure at the time that it was the right thing to do, but I did it anyway. And it's proven to me that travel may broaden your horizons, but only by living and working in another country can you really change them.

So, in conclusion:

I believe that doing always beats over-thinking.

I believe brand is a word that has outlived its usefulness

In a recent trip to the Tate Modern I came across a glass of water placed on a transparent plastic shelf about eight feet from the floor. It was called *An Oak Tree*, by Michael Craig-Martin, and there was a piece of writing next to it. It was a Q&A with the artist which explains why this glass of water, in his view, actually has *become* an oak tree (Figure 1.1).

And there's more where that came from. The purpose of this example is not to kick off a laboured analogy between the development of 'art' and 'brands', but *An Oak Tree* did make me think. It struck me that the stakes in art, as in branding, have been raised. Art began with cave paintings, tribal artefacts, religious depictions, landscapes, then Mona Lisa's, Picasso's and finally an artist telling us that his glass of water's actually an oak tree. With brands it was slaves, cattle, soap, service brands and lately institutional, entertainment, personal and experiential brands. These days, pretty much anything can be a piece of art and pretty much anything can be a brand. Or can it? Is this a recent thing, or has it always been the case? If so, what are the implications for how we think about, interact and work with brands in the future? And how helpful are the concepts of 'brands' and 'branding' as they are currently used?

The more I read about brands the further away I get from any clear, universal definition of what one is. There are as many interpretations of a brand as there are articles and books on the subject – a short trawl of the major dictionaries will show that even the *OED* and *Collins* don't agree. And that is both astonishing and disturbing. Brands are commonly held as fundamental to what we do – we're judged on our success in building them, we frame our theories in their terms, we have conversations with our clients about them, we live and breathe them. But while we use their language as shorthand for something we presume we all understand, it would appear that we're all talking about completely different things.

I believe that the reason brands can seem so nebulous is that they're simply a way of describing how our brains interpret the world. Gary

FIGURE 1.1 *An Oak Tree*, 1973, Michael Craig-Martin

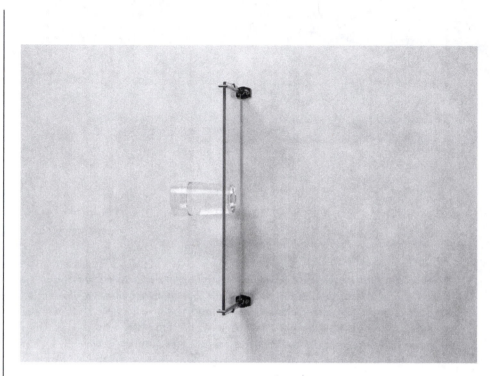

Q: To begin with, could you describe this work?
A: Yes, of course. What I've done is change a glass of water into a full-grown oak tree without altering the accidents of the glass of water.
Q: The accidents?
A: Yes. The colour, feel, weight, size ...
Q: Do you mean that the glass of water is a symbol of an oak tree?
A: No. It's not a symbol. I've changed the physical substance of the glass of water into that of an oak tree.
Q: It looks like a glass of water ...
A: Of course it does. I didn't change its appearance. But it's not a glass of water. It's an oak tree.
Q: Can you prove what you claim to have done?
A: Well, yes and no. I claim to have maintained the physical form of the glass of water and, as you can see, I have. However, as one normally looks for evidence of physical change in terms of altered form, no such proof exists.
Q: Haven't you simply called this glass of water an oak tree?
A: Absolutely not. It is not a glass of water any more. I have changed its actual substance. It would no longer be accurate to call it a glass of water. One could call it anything one wished but that would not alter the fact that it is an oak tree.
Q: Isn't this just a case of the emperor's new clothes?
A: No. With the emperor's new clothes people claimed to see something which wasn't there, because they felt they should. I would be very surprised if anyone told me they saw an oak tree.
Q: Was it difficult to effect the change?
A: No effort at all. But it took me years of work before I realized I could do it.
Q: When precisely did the glass of water become an oak tree?
A: When I put water in the glass.
Q: Does this happen every time you fill a glass with water?
A: No, of course not. Only when I intend to change it

into an oak tree.
Q: Then intention causes the change?
A: I would say it precipitates the change.
Q: You don't know how you do it?
A: It contradicts what I feel I know about cause and effect.
Q: It seems to me you're claiming to have worked a miracle. Isn't that the case?
A: I'm flattered that you think so.
Q: But aren't you the only person who can do something like this?
A: How could I be?
Q: Could you teach others to do it?
A: No. It's not something one can teach.
Q: Do you consider that changing the glass of water into an oak tree constitutes an artwork?
A: Yes.
Q: What precisely is the artwork? The glass of water?
A: There is no glass of water any more.
Q: The process of change?
A: There is no process involved in the change.
Q: The oak tree?
A: Yes, the oak tree.
Q: But the oak tree only exists in the mind.
A: No. The actual oak tree is physically present but in the form of the glass of water. As the glass of water was a particular glass of water, the oak tree is also particular. To conceive the category 'oak tree' or to picture a particular oak tree is not to understand and experience what appears to be a glass of water as an oak tree. Just as it is imperceivable, it is also inconceivable.
Q: Did the particular oak tree exist somewhere else before it took the form of the glass of water?
A: No. This particular oak tree did not exist previously. I should also point out that it does not and will not ever have any other form but that of a glass of water.
Q: How long will it continue to be an oak tree?
A: Until I change it.

Glass, water, shelf and printed text   5 7/8 × 18 1/8 × 5 1/2 inches   15 × 46 × 14 cm   © Michael Craig-Martin. Courtesy Gagosian Gallery

Duckworth[1] describes how the first brand any of us respond to is our Mum. We ascribe brand values to things as diverse as the local school, that row of flats opposite, the Monarchy, our new PlayStation 3 and 'Big Brother'. We all latch onto things that make sense of our surroundings, that make the complex simple. We see the world in terms of brands because our brains are pre-programmed to generalize, stereotype and then label frighteningly complex things, groups and entities. It's instructive to see what happens when our minds go wrong as an indication of how reliant the mind is on brands. In Oliver Sacks' *The Man who Mistook His Wife for a Hat*[2] the eponymous hero can only recognize the constituent elements of objects he is presented with, rather than that object in its entirety. He describes a glove as 'A continuous surface infolded on itself (with) five outpouchings', and as such is completely unable to navigate the world as normal people do. To co-opt Bullmore's 'scraps and straws'[3] analogy, this was a case of someone being able to see the twigs, but not being able to discern the nest that they made up. Brands are how we make sense of life, not simply a way of choosing between two different types of baked bean.

Because of this, I do not believe that brands only set up shop with the age of mass consumption as so many, including Peter Doyle,[4] have suggested. They did not simply 'appear' when society got to some kind of Keynsian critical economic mass. They are not just 'A badge of certainty in an uncertain world' as Feldwick[5] would have us believe. Brands live in people's heads rather than on the side of washing powder; they constantly and subtly change according to stimulus, internal and external. Duckworth[6] does not go far enough when he says 'brands enable us to make sense of the social world of consumption in which we participate' – what he should have said was 'brands enable us to make sense of the *world* in which we participate'. There are brands in communist countries such as Cuba, there just aren't labels – people still associate the best food with a particular restaurant, or associate a particular value to the local salsa band. For all of these reasons, I think that the very word 'brand' (with its roots in tangible and predominately economic signs and symbols) is inherently misleading – but more about that later.

While brands as a concept have not fundamentally changed since humans have existed (just that we only started talking about them relatively recently), I do believe that brand*ing* has, and that it has changed fundamentally. This is an important distinction to make. When Simon Clemmow[7] talks about the emergence of institutional and political brands (ie the Monarchy/New Labour), he isn't actually talking about genuinely new brands, he's referring to the application of new marketing techniques to existing brand entities. The Labour party of the 1950s was no less a brand than it is now, it's just that people's perceptions of it weren't quite as systematically manipulated. Indeed, the act of branding has changed immeasurably over the years. To take Dove as an instructive example. Dove used to be a bar of soap. Then it was a bar of cream. Then it was the feel of soft skin. Then achieving an ideal of beauty. And now it is a belief in the diversity of beauty, a point of view on life. It's the classic progression up Maslow's hierarchy of needs, and mirrors the ways in which a number of brands have been consciously manipulated over the years (Persil used to get your clothes clean and now believes that 'Dirt is good', Honda sold cheap cars but now represents the 'Power of Dreams').

I think that rather than the 'types' of brand that will develop – I don't see the need to distinguish between an 'entertainment' and a 'technology' brand – it is the nature of branding that will change most dramatically, because of how we all react to being told what to do or think. There is much of the Arms Race in the way that branding has evolved in the 20th century. But rather than subscribe to Alan Mitchell's[8] view of a zero-sum game between competing brands (his 'New! Improved!' syndrome), I see the zero-sum game as being between branding and the consumer. Most pieces that look at the future of branding try to second-guess the 'next big thing' – whether it's going to be Pine and Gilmour's[9] 'experiential brands' or whether it's going to be in the arena of branded economies, or times of day. But I see dangers in applying branding techniques to more and more areas of our lives because, where once brands were our natural way of navigating complexity, now a proliferation of brands deriving from 'over-branding' has begun to confuse rather than clarify. And this is largely because of the intrusive and didactic nature of the large majority of communications. Many people have cited Steven Spielberg's *Minority Report*[10] as a prescient example of where branding could be going in the future – a dystopian vision of consumers ambushed by personalized holographic communications in shopping malls – but I think that the future lies elsewhere, which is where Dove comes back in.

Travelling up an escalator in Oxford Street tube recently, I noticed that the tick boxes on every single Dove 'Manifesto' poster (which ask you to decide whether the woman depicted is, for example, 'Fat' or 'Fit') had been filled in by hand. They had got noticed and had persuaded someone into action. Even if that someone had been a bored teenager, I think it does illustrate what a powerful force branding can be when you give people options, when you try and involve them, when you start a conversation rather than just telling them what to think. It is the opposite of someone informing me that a glass of water is actually an oak tree – indeed, the kind of didactic approach to art pioneered by Marcel Duchamp[11] in the early 1900s, and continued by Craig-Martin today, has resonance with much that is wrong with many traditional attitudes to brands and branding. Even the word 'branding' itself is unhelpful because it implies a static, one-time-only, indelible act, and I don't believe that it's enough to bludgeon people into getting their attention – we need to nudge people in the way we want them to go, give them a choice in how they respond to our brands, treat them like adults and have a genuine (rather than forced) dialogue with them. Maintaining a clear point of view, and allowing that not every-one will agree with that point of view, is key. It is what Dove is starting to do now that good branding will most resemble in the future.

Finally, since I have a problem with the terms 'brand' and 'branding' as they are currently (mis)used, I would like to tentatively suggest clearer alternatives – while trying to avoid the pitfalls of other recent, jargoning, attempts (such as Kevin Robert's *Lovemarks*[12]). And this is where Tony Hart[13] comes in. It might be more helpful to think about the term 'morph' rather than 'brand', after the ever-changing clay creature of *Hartbeat* fame. Morph was a dynamic entity that evolved according to both an inner compulsion and external manipulation, but always maintained a readily identifiable character. This is far closer to how I think brands are built in our heads, how they alter and develop. Leading on from this I would change the term 'branding' to 'shaping'– to denote a subtler, more evolutionary way of manipulating the behaviour of brands, and to imply that branding is a collaborative approach in which the consumer has as fundamental a role to play in the process as marketers. If we could begin to think in terms of 'morphs' and 'morph shaping' instead of 'brands' and 'branding', then we might at least start to move towards a narrower, and more practically relevant, definition.

So, what do I believe? I believe that brands are simply a way of describing how people navigate the complexities of life. I believe that brands existed before branding was systematically practised. I believe that branding is the deliberate manipulation of a brand's behaviour. And I believe that 'brands' and 'branding' are words that have outlived their usefulness, deriving as they do from a time when they referred to static badges and didactic communications. I believe that their roots are now a cause for confusion, and that the terms 'morph' and 'shaping' do a more intuitive job of explaining the things that we all do in our roles as marketing professionals.

And the future? The future belongs to Tony Hart, rather Michael Craig-Martin.

Notes

1 Duckworth, G (1999) Brands and the role of advertising, in *Understanding Brands: By 10 people who do*, ed D Cowley, Kogan Page, London.

2 Sacks, O (1985) *The Man Who Mistook His Wife For A Hat*, Gerald Duckworth & Co, London.

3 Bullmore, J (Lecture, December 2001) *Posh Spice and Persil: The value of fame*, London [Online] www.wpp.com/wpp/marketing/branding/articles-poshspice/

4 Doyle, P and Stern, P (1998) *Marketing Management and Strategy*, Prentice Hall, Essex.

5 Feldwick, P (1996) Understanding brands: defining a brand, in *Understanding Brands: By 10 people who do*, ed D Cowley, Kogan Page, London.

6 Duckworth, G (1999) Brands and the role of advertising, in *Understanding Brands: By 10 people who do*, ed D Cowley, Kogan Page, London.

7 Clemmow, S (2003) *Campaign* Essay.

8 Mitchell, A (2002) *Right Side Up: Building brands in the age of the organized consumer*, HarperCollins, London.

9 Pine II, B J and Gilmour, J H (1999) *The Experience Economy: Work is theatre and every business a stage*, Harvard Business School Press, Harvard.

10 *Minority Report*, film directed by Steven Speilberg (2002) 20th Century Fox.

11 Duchamp, M (1917) 'Fountain'.

12 Roberts, K (2004) *Lovemarks: The future beyond brands*, Powerhouse Books, New York.

13 Hart, Tony (1978–1994) *Hartbeat*.

I believe in the Darwinian evolution of brands
2006/07

02

IAN EDWARDS
Managing Partner and Head of Strategy, Vizeum UK

I believe Brands originated as a means of *categorizing* – a way of distinguishing different products from one another, and then developed into *tools of tribalism* – a way of defining one group vs another. In the future, as new means of engagement allow people to interact and modify brands for themselves, I believe brands will increasingly become means of differentiating by *personal identity* – a way to define my individual difference against another's.

Editor's therefore, for your brand...

Your brand thinking: Should a brand publicly 'open-source' its DNA so that consumers can develop and critique it?

Your brand engagement: How can you truly personalize your brand or brand communications so that people can use it to develop their personal identity?

Your brand organization & capability: How do you develop a culture and a process that can cope with not only two or three target subsets but 20/50/100s?

...and author's personal therefore

My work: do a job you care about

The Diploma is pretty big on forcing you to think about what you believe in and encouraging you to put that into action. So it had an immediate impact on my career; I resigned halfway through and moved into a strategy role as I wanted to find a job that let me influence how communications was used in the broadest sense. I'm still doing that role today and enjoying it.

One of the biggest benefits of the Diploma is that it gives you a rounded view of the industry and helps you identify the areas you are most passionate about. For companies, this shouldn't be viewed negatively. The Diploma is raising the overall quality of the industry and getting people into the right jobs. I was a pretty terrible account man and didn't particularly enjoy it, but moving to strategy has kept me in the industry and motivated. Good thing.

My career: take time out and have a point of view

If there's one thing that the Diploma teaches you, it's to take a step back, look at the evidence and then develop your own point of view. Last year I actually did this exercise again to work out what I thought was really important in how communications worked today. In true Diploma spirit it was a mix of academia (I worked with a great neuroscientist – Dr Jack Lewis) and it even involved some TGI analysis (still the window into the soul of consumers for much of the industry). This resulted in the S C I E N C E of brand growth, which I think summarizes my approach to work at the moment. I won't go through it in detail, but the broad principles are as follows:

- **Surprise:** When someone is surprised it does some pretty amazing things to the brain. We should never be predictable with our communications and should tap into the power of surprise at every opportunity.
- **Consistency:** Perhaps slightly counter to surprise, it is vital to be consistent over time with the look and feel of campaigns to build brand associations.
- **Integration:** It turns out matching luggage really does matter across a campaign.
- **Ease:** Reach people in what the great man Daniel Kahneman calls 'moments of cognitive ease'. In order words, target people with your messaging when they are happy and they will be more easily persuaded.
- **New news:** Have something fresh and exciting to say.
- **Context:** You can't win all the time so focus on the right context to deliver your message.

- **Extend:** It's light consumers who are most influenced by advertising. Not the loyal core. Remember your target audience is a lot broader than you think as well. Who would have thought that 14 per cent of the consumer base for Stella Artois is made up of 45-year-old women!

My life: be surprising

I went to a talk organized by Contagious in 2012. Seymour Powell was speaking. He is an incredibly inspiring man and at one point he stopped, looked around the room and spoke directly to the assembled crowd of advertising folk and told them that they had the potential to do anything. He showed a picture of Galileo's helicopter and made the point that in the 1600s it was technology that held back what was possible and not ideas, but today the reverse is true. Whatever idea you have is almost certainly technically possible, it is just your imagination that holds you back.

The Diploma really encourages you to think big and push the boundaries of what's possible, and it's great to see some of the alumni going on to produce amazing, pioneering work. But is the wider industry doing this?

In the last couple of years, there have been some moments of brilliance and incredible work produced – a quick look through the 2014 winners at Cannes shows that. But the industry is also becoming increasingly cautious. Investment in TV this year is set to break the £4 billion mark for the first time – a significant landmark. I work at a media agency so I am never going to complain about this, but I do think it demonstrates lazy thinking and that the industry is going back to planning-by-numbers, rather than embracing technology and pushing what's possible.

I believe the industry needs to stop being so predictable, and Byron Sharpe makes this point brilliantly. In a rather open attack on modern marketing, he compares its efficiency to the medieval practice of bloodletting. Referring to a study of 143 UK TV campaigns, he points out that in a startling 84 per cent of cases, consumers were unable to correctly identify which brand the advertising was supposed to be promoting. Pro rata this up, and businesses could be wasting anywhere up to £8 billion every year on advertising that has no effect.

Bryon wouldn't necessarily pinpoint this answer, but I believe the way forward is to embrace technology, push the boundaries of what is possible and start doing the unexpected. Aim big and surprise consumers with what is possible. After all, £8 billion per year should be enough to do something that gets noticed and remembered.

I believe in the Darwinian evolution of brands

For the past 100 years, you could have been forgiven for thinking that the rules that govern the *dynamic* world of brands change about as quickly as natural selection. Despite constant product evolution and the ever-changing media landscape, brands have been much slower to change. In 19 out of 22 product categories, the company that owned the leading brand in 1925 was still there in 2001.[1]

However, if we look at brands over the last five years, one might say that natural selection has given way to a brand revolution. It could be said that the traditional rules finally seem to have changed. Last year, the top five most admired brands were Google, Apple, Skype, IKEA and Starbucks.[2] The digital media revolution has nurtured a new type of brand. Not one of these had been on the list in 1995, let alone 1925. Does this mean we are seeing a new brand revolution, which will ultimately mean the culling of the aristocratic brands of old? And are these new super brands something fundamentally different?

There could be a flaw with this view. The brands have changed, the media has changed, but the human mind has remained the same. Our biological evolution finished around 150,000 years ago. The underlying way we make decisions, store information, fulfil various physical and emotion needs[3] has not changed since this time – knowledge, beliefs and attitudes are (in my view) software operating on the same mainframe.

Stage 1: Categorization

Paul Feldwick points to Bass Red Triangle registering the first trade mark in 1876 as the moment brands sprung into existence. Brands obviously existed before this (eg on livestock, slaves, etc) and the concept of a branded logo obviously existed in terms of products (eg Guinness beer being brewed since 1759). However, 1876 represented some kind of tipping point from which the scale and volume of products that were branded grew exponentially.

The cultural context to 1876 was an increasingly mobile population and an increase in population densities. This basically meant that people were no longer living in small, trusted communities. In addition, new production techniques were enabling goods to be mass produced. *The Economist* suggests that brands emerged because they allowed people to make decisions quickly and safely. This is still true today – there are other less functional attributes involved, but brands essentially still allow consumers to make quick and reliable decisions much as they did in 1876.

Using a brand enables people to *categorize* a product based on its attributes and this taps into a key principle by which the human brain organizes information. Steven Pinker describes the human brain as the ultimate categorizer. He believes that the human mind categorizes everything and gives each category distinct properties: the more we know about something the more detailed the list of properties that can be ascribed to that category.[4,5]

These days, even though brands are more sophisticated, the fact that the brain is constantly trying to categorize the world is very important. Advertisers who realize that the brain stores information in categories and makes it easy for consumers to link all points of contact with a brand together, are ultimately going to form a more salient representation in the consumers' minds.

The 2006 Guinness campaign that runs across radio and TV taps into this idea and the creative in both channels builds on the same story of a man in the fridge. This allows consumers to quickly identify that the campaigns are linked and (hopefully) to take the same message (that canned Guinness is as good as draught) from both channels and put together in one Guinness-in-a-can category.

Stage 2: Tribalism

> Shopping is not merely the acquisition of things; it is the buying of identity.
>
> (John Clammer)

John Grant believes that a second type of brand started to emerge in the 1950s. During this period society was rapidly changing – the class system and religion were declining as rigid frameworks, and this meant that people were no longer defined by their 'birthright'. Mass media turned the idea of being born and having your destiny mapped out in front of you on its head – people began to believe they could create their own identity. All of a sudden people had to choose and create their identities. New communities formed and these were based on group ideals and aspirations. Brands became linked to 'image', and helped people identify group membership.

The need to identify with, and know your status within a social group is something that is fundamental to human nature. Mark Earls (1994) described humans as 'herd animals'. This is not true. Herd animals find safety in numbers, but for humans the reverse is true. During our evolution the biggest threat to human life was other humans. For this very reason there has been an evolutionary pressure to identify a 'friend', and a potential

FIGURE 2.1

Walters, D (2007) DSC_0262, Flickr, licensed under CC BY 2.0

'enemy', very quickly. Identifying what particular 'tribe'[6] someone is from and, as such, their likely reaction to you is critical and there are lots of mechanisms that have evolved to enable us to do this.[7]

We also do it through language – think of the conversation when you first meet someone – What do you do? Where are you from? We rapidly try and establish links with new acquaintances and find out their intentions. I also believe accents evolved to allow people to identify regions of origin very quickly, which historically is a very good indication of your 'tribe'.

In his paper 'What becomes an icon most', Douglas Holf points out that brands which become icons are more than simply delivering a promise. He believes that iconic brands beat the competition, not just by delivering innovative changes, but by forging a deep connection with culture. A brand becomes an icon when it offers a compelling myth, something that brings together a particular section of society and allows them to unite in a common cause. Holf goes too far by saying that myths are what create iconic brands; it is enough to say that iconic brands identify 'something' that unites their target audiences and allows them to feel connected with a group. Think of the culture of Mods and Rockers and the brands associated with each 'tribe'.

This has many implications for brands – if you can identify 'something' that unites your consumers and makes them feel a part of a bigger, unified group then that can be very powerful. Beer and sports companies often try and tap into the tribalism young men feel towards their teams, exploiting this emotion. Guinness has done this by building a strong association with rugby and sponsoring the Premier League. The fundamental idea is that something bigger than just Guinness ties this group of people together and Guinness can become the icon that links this group of consumers together.

Stage 3: Connectivism

The third stage of branding does not represent a change in the concept of what a 'brand' actually represents in the mind; it is about the fact that brands are now formed in a different way. Technology has connected more people than ever before and this means that information is transmitted faster by people themselves – we are no longer reliant on traditional media to find out about the world at large.

The chairman of Sony famously once said that the public do not know what is possible and that is why it is down to us to tell them what they want. This is no longer true – people have ways of finding out what is possible and what's more if they like it, they will let their tribe know and quickly.

Information spreads faster than ever before through networks of people (see Figure 2.2). This has changed the way we receive information. Think about the way major news stories break these days. Take the London bombings in 2005: the story was initially spread via mobiles and e-mail. The mass media was used to verify the story and pull the pieces together after the event.

This has had profound implications on brands. They no longer break via the mass media – how did you first know to type in **www.google.com** or **www.friendsreunited.com**? Someone (almost certainly) told you. These brands did not emerge through mainstream communications channels. The mass media was used to verify their existence through news stories, but people first found out through their network of connections.

FIGURE 2.2   The effect of additional connections on the speed with which a message spreads

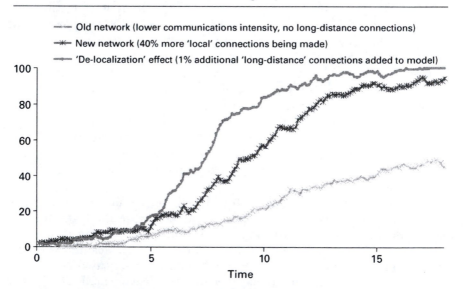

Future Foundation (2001) The New Web of Life, Future Foundation, London

The major implication for brands is to get people involved and talking and, to get people talking, you need to ensure that information has enough social currency for it to be worth the effort of passing it on across the network. For a brand such as Guinness, giving people a reason to talk about the brand to each other is central – building a kind of community that is connected by the brand will allow Guinness to maintain its position as the icon that links this 'tribe' together. One campaign aimed at achieving this was the Guinness Blog, which encouraged people to express their opinion about the brand within a virtual community.

Stage 4: Innovation

Our species is defined by its ability to innovate. Our hominid ancestors such as Neanderthal man and *Homo habilis* made stone tools – very beautiful stone tools in the case of Neanderthal man.[8] However, the really striking thing about this is that while these tools were technically advanced, they did not develop over time – no innovation! When modern humans appear in the archaeological record, technology shows huge degrees of innovation and not all for functional reasons. Humans change things for aesthetic, symbolic and, most astoundingly, religious reasons. We all have this need to modify[9] – for most people this is restricted to our hairstyles, houses and immediate surroundings, but other humans, such as Alexander Graham Bell, make changes that have had more profound implications.

Brands are beginning to tap into the need to innovate with the concept of 'Open Source'. The philosophy behind Open Source is simple – if you give people total access to your products (like a new piece of computer software) they will discover new ways of using it, and will improve on it, because thousands of pairs of eyes are much more likely to see something that one pair might miss. iPhone is a good example. Apple actively encourages consumers to write new code to make improvements to the product – one such example is the new application that will download an album cover to your iPhone, which was a customer's innovation.

Obviously all brands innovate, but in the past they have had to try and work out what their consumers want. By letting consumers make the changes they no longer need to guess.

Conclusion

So what do I believe? I believe that brands emerged as a way for people to recognize different products and make quick decisions – since then (some) brands have become linked to status and group membership. I also believe that the way brands are formed in the mind is changing rapidly and by allowing people to modify brands they will become increasingly linked with personal identity and as such take a more central role in peoples' lives.

I do not believe that what brands actually represent in the mind has changed beyond tribalism and categorization, but the way they are formed has, and will continue, to change. Because the new world of connectivity is very different to anything that has happened before, new brands are in a better position to grow because they know how to operate in this world. I do not believe that the new super brands such as Google represent anything fundamentally different; maybe the products are slightly different (search engines, online communities), but they still allow people to make quick decisions and navigate the world (even though it may now be a virtual world). The aristocrat brands of old are perfectly entitled to operate in this world, but they will need to learn new rules if they are to survive.

Notes

1 Pavitt, J (2002) *Brand New*, V&A Publications, London.
2 The Brand Channel 2005.
3 Maslow recognized that all people need to fulfil the same universal needs to reach a state of self-actualization.
4 Pinker, S (1996) *How the Mind Works*, WW Norton & Company, US.
5 Gary Duckworth makes the same point for brands and suggests that the first brand we create is that of our mothers. He believes that this process of breaking the world down into relevant brands is what allows us to make sense of the world around us.
6 In evolutionary terms 'tribe' would refer to the community in which you lived. I have used the term 'tribe' in modern society to denote being linked with a particular group of people.
7 For a detailed review of how different cognitive traits have evolved and are universal shared by all humans, see Mithen, S (1998)*The Prehistory of the Mind: A search for the origins of art, religion and science*, Phoenix, London.
8 The stone tool technology of Neanderthal man is referred to as Mousterian Culture and mostly consists of large hand axes. See Cuozzo, J (1998) *Buried Alive: The startling truth about Neanderthal man*, Master Books, Arkansas.
9 Jerry Fodor (1983) suggests that the ability to innovate is what distinguishes our species from all other species that have ever existed.

03

We believe the people should control the means of branding

2007/08

DAVID BONNEY

Founder, Atheist Shoes/The Meaningful Shoe Company

I believe A new era of 'WE' is dawning. An explosion of collective action, fused with an increasing desire to serve the common good, promises to make the world a better place. Most brands serve shareholder interest rather than the common good. But with more demanded of corporations, values become as important as value, and they seek to remain competitive by putting wider concerns at the heart of their strategies.

Editor's therefore, for your brand...

Your brand thinking: What is the 'force for good' your brand could celebrate and support?

Your brand engagement: Should all brands offer their audience a 'share' in their brand; could your shareholders be your most powerful evangelists?

Your brand organization & capability: How could your brand have consumer representation on your board, brand council or brand team?

...and author's personal therefore

In July 2008 (before we had President Obama, Kickstarter or a financial crisis), I wrote a paper considering the rapid growth in mass collaboration, collective consciousness and 'ikinomical' phenomena, asking what they might mean for the future of branding.

I wrote my Diploma essay as fiction, because the radical overhaul of branding I predicted felt unlikely. However, reading those predictions afresh, six years later, it's remarkable how closely they ape what's happened (at least in one small corner of the branding world).

You may be wondering if I took my prediction of a web-based tool, organizing 'collective investment', and founded Kickstarter? Well, nope, and I do feel a tinge of regret that I didn't have the foresight to become a crowd-funding billionaire. However, I did do something equally postmodern... harnessing the power of 'WE' to launch a brand called 'ATHEIST Shoes'.

This admittedly peculiar concept was born in Berlin.

I'd moved there to write my Diploma essay in 2008. With so many ideas and questions inspired by the course, it felt a good time to take a break from London and my foreseeable career as a planner. Berlin was in a special state of flux, drawing people from across the globe, all in search of a little purpose, mojo and time to think, or create. I was no different and, within days of arriving, I had a bike, a job playing piano in a comedy show and the fullest intention to stay.

It was in Berlin that I met Jule, a talented shoemaker. I asked her to teach me her trade and, the more I learned, the more I realized how terribly difficult it is to make shoes. This difficulty kept entrepreneurship and new thinking out of footwear – poor quality and lazy branding were rife – which excited us, because it left room to create a kick-ass shoe brand.

A brand built on the values of 'WE'

Following my essay, we knew it might be rewarding to launch a brand that resonated with a particular audience, defined by their common values.

Our first idea was silly... a Christian shoe, with water in the sole, to democratize the walking-on-water experience. But we weren't Christians, and much better we launched something we truly believed in... which wasn't much... hence 'Atheist Shoes'.

Atheists were passionate, bright, monied, funny, a sizeable long-tail niche. Best of all, they were increasingly active and easy to find online.

'WE' told us to do it

We made a prototype, still not convinced this was anything but a curious folly.

The design was beautifully Bauhaus in appearance and ridiculously comfortable, made from the finest leathers. On the sole was embossed

'ICH BIN ATHEIST' allowing wearers to out themselves to fellow heathens, just by popping their foot over their knee, or leaving footsteps in the snow... like 'Grindr for the godless'. It was part joke – the 'Life of Brian' of shoes – and part serious attempt to encourage openness about non-belief.

We posted pictures on Reddit, which had a pretty lively atheist community. And the result was astonishing – 650,000 page-views and 900 e-mails in 24 hours. The 'WE' wanted their ATHEIST shoes. So we quickly had to chart a path from prototype to business.

'WE' gave us the money to do it

Just as in my essay, we turned to 'collective investment'.

We'd already secured a little investment from sages of London's brand-land, such as Judie Lannon and my Diploma Mentor, Christ Forrest, whose contributions and support have been immense. But we needed more.

Kickstarter appealed because it bought us time to find the right manu-facturing partner – we could capture the Reddit interest immediately, in cash, yet customers wouldn't expect us to ship product for months. Kickstarter was also a good way to involve customers in our development, giving them the feeling of being co-founders and (hopefully) inspiring life-long advocacy.

We raised £60,000 on Kickstarter. Two months later, in June 2012, we had 1,200 pairs of shoes and launched **www.atheistberlin.com**.

'WE' does our marketing and finds our concept useful

Our customers are responsible for our growth. Our message and tonality has tickled some of the nicest people and turned them into passionate, heartfelt advocates. For many, it's the tongue-in-cheek provocation of the branding. For others, it's our tiny size relative to the behemoths of fashion. And, for everyone (eventually), it's the incomparable quality of the shoe.

All this 'word of foot' has helped us overcome understandable reluctance to buy shoes online. As has endorsement from celebrity fans, like Tim Minchin. And it's been delightfully easy to get free media coverage – for example, when we undertook a controlled experiment to demonstrate 'discrimination' by the US Postal Service against atheists. The story was carried, from our blog, to *Time* magazine, NPR and the *Daily Mail*.

Most gratifying, is that ATHEIST has been genuinely useful and moving to people. Some have used their shoes to tearfully 'out' themselves to reli-gious loved ones. Others to express themselves in the Bible Belt. Love affairs have ended, and begun, over the shoes. Proud photos of ICH BIN ATHEIST marks, in snow and sand, have been taken all over the world. And there are several legs tattooed with our black hole logo.

'WE' buys our shoes

I'm proud that we've managed to make such an unlikely concept as ATHEIST Shoes a reality. Since June 2012, we've sold 6,000 pairs, everywhere from Tokyo to Tennessee, Saudi Arabia to Stockholm. We've done it primarily with long-tail e-commerce, no wholesale – just two of our own shops in Berlin and San Francisco – and zero marketing spend.

It's been lonely at times – there aren't appropriate benchmarks for a business like ours, no identikit strategies to borrow, nothing to tell us how well we should be doing.

And production is *much* more difficult than I made out in my essay. Making a world-beating prototype is one thing. Getting producers to match your quality expectations, every time, is another.

But the downsides have been few and we've thoroughly enjoyed cresting on waves of 'WE'.

ATHEIST wouldn't have happened without the Diploma. It inspired and reinvigorated me. Connected me with the most intelligent and supportive people. And gave me the balls and urgency to do something entrepreneurial.

I'm also grateful for the present opportunity to gather my thoughts, reflect and write... it's timely, because we may soon launch a new brand, a sister for ATHEIST... and the spirit and curiosity of 2008 is a lovely place from which to begin that journey.

We believe
the people
should control
the means of
branding[1]

Here follows a fictional extract from a fictional book, *Commons People: In their own words, the stories of 10 individuals who laid the foundations for Capitalism 3.0*. Published in 2019, to coincide with the establishment of a 'Commons Sector' in the UK, it charts the factors that converged to allow government to redirect society towards working for the common good and the creation of 'FLOW'; the perfect, customizable, common-good brand.

Origins of FLOW – the perfect common-good brand

Verne Bose, founder of FLOW, tells the story behind the brand's creation; from the rising importance of common good in 2008, through collective investment and consumer-owned cause-brands in 2011, to his agency's founding of the 'customizable' common-good brand in 2013.

The power of WE: the internet facilitates remarkable collective achievements

> The individual must exist for his own sake. The pursuit of his own rational self-interest and happiness is the highest moral purpose of his life.
>
> (Ayn Rand, 1957)[2]

I was a child of the Century of the Self.[3] Since I could utter the word 'me', I was groomed for an individualist world. I would learn alone, be employed alone, record successes as mine alone. My status relative to others was my worth, my identity my means, and my happiness a distant actualization of 'self'.[4]

Yet, in 2008, something jolted profoundly within me, as I began to recognize the extraordinary power of 'WE', unleashing the pent-up potential of the world. Where once I'd viewed collective action as sweet, but impractical idealism, an affliction of one's early 20s, the tumbling costs of collaboration saw an explosion in 'Wikinomical'[5] phenomena, as distant people united online to pursue shared agendas, achieving great things as 'WE' they otherwise couldn't have.

If *Time* magazine's 'Person of the Year' in 2006 was 'You',[6] then (with a relaxation of the definition of a person) 2008's might have been 'WE':

- Barrack Obama had swept to the Presidency, his victory built on internet fundraising of small donations from multitudes who'd never before been involved in politics.

- A vaccine against HIV resulted from collaboration among thousands of scientists, sponsored by the Bill & Melinda Gates Foundation.

- The impeachment of GW Bush only happened after an online petition drew 1,276,405 signatures.

- For the first time in history, the entire world was collaborating around a single issue – Al Gore's 'Wecansolveit.org' brought millions together, to fundraise and force political action on global warming.

Collective action, no longer the preserve of idealism, was suddenly possible (and effective) on a massive scale. The authors of *Wikinomics* charted the advantages for business, envisaging 'deep changes in the modus operandi of corporations, based on new competitive principles of openness, peering, sharing and acting globally'.[7] For example, P&G used open-sourcing to strengthen their innovation stream.[8] But *Wikinomics* also made it easier to collaborate for 'the common good'; an opportunity that would become my obsession.

The goals of WE: a growing interest in the common good

> We've been living in this bubble where individualism was the highest value, amplified by phenomena such as 'cool', celebrity, self-help. But all the major trends reshaping our world are pushing towards a more collective view.[9]

Hand-in-hand with the rise of collective action was a growth in collective consciousness and a desire to redirect resources to serving the common good ('the greatest possible good for the greatest number of people'). As British society grew older and wealthier, wider concerns came to the fore. This shift was reflected in behaviour; how people shopped, their career choices. And something was clearly afoot when the Tories put 'society' back into their politics.

The change was out of necessity as much as anything:

- The imminence of environmental catastrophe: 'Climate change is the classic example of a common problem that individuals cannot solve by acting independently. No family can opt out of climate change or buy their own little patch of retro weather.'[10]
- Britain was sick of the classic example of a common substance-abusing,[11] after decades spent on a hedonic treadmill, in pursuit of wealth and status.[12] 'Well-being Economics' and 'Positive Psychology' taught us that authentic happiness and health are only possible in a society with high levels of community and trust, both lacking in the UK.[13]
- As much means as cause, the internet made it easier to pursue 'common-goodery' and spawned a 'Net Generation' who instinctively thought as 'WE' and had a firm sense of social justice.[14]

A think tank called Citizen Renaissance, founded in 2008, believed the convergence of these three factors constituted a 'perfect storm', the energy from which would facilitate a 'citizen renaissance' leading to happier, sustainable living.

But, if thinking as 'WE' was necessary, it was also fashionable. Scuppies (Socially-Conscious Upwardly Mobile Persons)[15] used wider concerns to keep up with the Joneses. And 'Feel-anthropy' was trendy, as Live8 and Red asked you to 'accessorize your compassion'.[16]

The psychology of 'WE-actualization': fulfilling the destiny of our brains

Some explained our declining ego-centrism as society en-masse approaching 'self-actualization'.[17]

But Lord Layard felt the term was inappropriate and, in a public letter to David Cameron at Christmas 2008, christened it the era of 'WE-actualization'. People wanted belonging, community, loss-of-self in service of common feeling, all of which had been linked with the highest states of happiness. Some of these phenomena were present in Maslow's conception of 'self-actualization', but Maslow was the daddy of selfdom and his highest state remained fundamentally about self-interest. Layard's new term underlined that an even higher state was possible, one very much about unity with others, and having no business being associated with 'self'.

The thirst for 'WE-actualization' made sense to evolutionary psychologists – our most advanced brain functions had evolved to assist common good; social emotions such as guilt,[18] functional mechanisms such as 'cheater detection',[19] the phenomena of trust, empathy, language... all adaptations to help man work for the good of his group. Biologically, collective action in the service of common good was humanity's cause

FIGURE 3.1   Brand adopts attractive 'me' mask in universe of 'me's

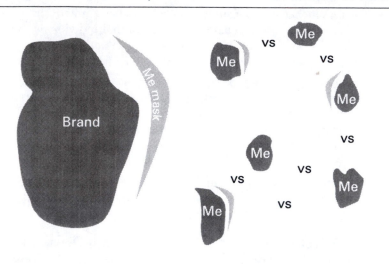

FIGURE 3.2   Brand adopts 'WE' face in universe of loosely-bound 'me's

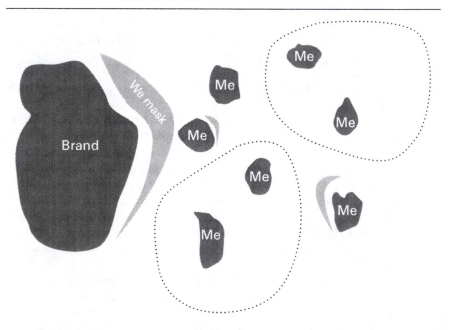

d'être and, although relatively lacking in the Western world, it had always flourished somewhere, from the Flavellas of Brazil, through the Amish communities of Pennsylvania, to the 'Honour system' wine bars of Berlin.

Our century of selfish motives, the 'business reflex of self-interest'[20] was a peculiar blip in our psychological development. In 2008, with the means of internet and desire to 'WE-actualize', humanity was returning to its natural inclination of working as we, for we. The remainder of this paper describes the impact this had on branding and consumerism, culminating in the story of how my colleagues and I created FLOW, the perfect common-good brand.

The 'WE-actualizing' consumer: voting for values

> The demand for things like ethics, corporate citizenship and social responsibility is a demand for agency in the sphere of values: a demand that organizations act 'for' me not only by providing products and services, but by acting with values I approve of.
>
> (Mitchell, 2002)[21]

In 2008, my mum started shopping in Lidl, because 'the same people make the branded stuff as make the Lidl stuff'.[22] After years of being wedded to particular brands, she dropped the lot in one, logical move. In fact, The National Consumer Association in Ireland stated in 2008 that Lidl was more than 50 per cent cheaper for a basket of 28 own-brand goods than Tesco. And consumers were responding – TNS revealed in August 2008 that both Aldi and Lidl were delivering double-digit growth in the UK, the stores growing 19.8 per cent and 12.3 per cent respectively in the 12 weeks to 10 August.

Mum bore little resemblance to the passive 20th-century 'consumer' brands wanted her to remain. Instead, she was a marketing-cynical,[23] price-premium questioning, we-actualizing, 'post-materialist'[24]... more interested in meaningful communion with the world than treadmill-like pursuit of status.

Mum now gave a toss about the wider values companies held.[25] Pessimistic about business ethics,[26] she expected brands to do better[27] and would pay price premiums to support that.[28]

Mum also boycotted unethical brands.[29] Such was indicative of a new impatience and chutzpah in the way she 'consumed'. New opportunities for online collaboration had a lot to do with it – she enjoyed forcing lower prices from sellers, having a say in production, functioning as media... even joining the 'boards' of companies. Mum was front-and-centre in a power shift towards consumers, a 'Right-Side-Upping' of marketing as it became more buyer-centric, intent on bringing about outcomes consumers (not sellers) wanted.[30] Every purchase was a vote, used to manipulate companies' resources to do more for the world. Consumer pressure like this (and increasing product parity) saw values-based selection between brands become important. Suddenly, values and value went hand-in-hand.

Government incentivizes 'WE-friendly' companies

In 2008, the UK government was already experiencing pressure to create conditions for the common good to flourish, by incentivizing companies to put 'wider issues' (sustainability, well-being) at the core of their strategies.

Ultimately, pressure from lobby groups such as 'Green Alliance', and economists and psychologists such as Layard and Oliver James,[31] would tell and, over a nine-year period, the government introduced radical measures to influence companies' relationships with the common good: tax incentives, replacement of GNP with the Well-being Index, and founding Capitalism 3.0 in 2019 by creating a 'commons sector' which, together with the 'corporate sector', would give society two engines to run on.

Social innovation: social values at the heart of everything companies do

> If business is to prosper, the environment in which it operates must prosper too.
> (Wilson, 2001)[32]

In 2008, one of our wiser clients realized it was necessary to do more for the common good. Consumers were evolving fast and everyone anticipated pressure from the government. So, the idea emerged that society and social values should be at the core of business – not for ethical reasons, but because it made good business sense.

Michael Willmott (2001) had reviewed a heap of research and concluded that: 'Good corporate citizenship, putting society at the heart of the company, is strongly related to commercial success. Companies gain strategic advantage by building brands with a citizenship component.'[33]

When Co-op Bank only invested in ethical funds, or when M&S made sustainability their 'Plan A', consumers responded favourably. 'Citizen Brands'[34] challenged the assumption that working for the common good was at odds with economic growth.[35] In fact, ultimately it might be corporate suicide *not* to behave as a citizen. The rules of business were changing – community, welfare and long-termism were increasingly important. Theorists raced to make sense of, and define, the new realities of capitalism. One was my good friend, Umair Haque, a *Harvard Business Review* blogger who summed it up in compellingly simple terms: 'There are now greater opportunities to profit by doing good than by doing evil. That's not a belief. It's an economic fact. Google didn't just launch Google Arms Trading. They launched Google Health.'

Haque believed 'evil' companies were doomed because they focused on extracting value, rather than creating it. Being evil destroyed potential for future value creation, while a 'good' company, such as Google, looked after the health of its community, ensuring everyone was better off in the long term.

Patrick Cescau, Chairman of Unilever, wanted his company to be 'good'. Cescau saw citizenship as opportunity for innovation and growth, coining

FIGURE 3.3   Brand allows 'WE' inside of it, in a universe of 'WE-actualizers'

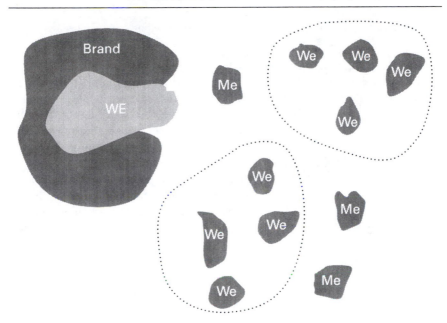

the term 'social innovation' – the development of new markets that could be good for the commons and profitable for corporations. He believed that if brand managers had deeper, less mercenary dialogue with consumers and found out what really mattered to them, there'd be competitive advantage.[36]

Cescau believed social innovation would be most meaningful in emerging markets (eg Unilever's Shakti initiative in India, turning women's self-help groups into door-to-door sales teams).[37]

It was a timely strategic evolution for Unilever, for they would be among the companies most seriously tested by values-conscious consumers. Consider the case of 'Lynx/Axe Ransom', resolved in March 2010. Sixteen-year-old Michael Davis from California launched a YouTube campaign to get Lynx/ Axe to apologize for objectifying adolescent males as sex-hungry morons. He and his friends, typical Net Generation kids, had grown up co-operating online and it seemed natural to ask millions of Lynx users to stop using the brand, until Unilever released an ad acknowledging that life for teenage boys wasn't easy, and making a £10 million donation for research into depression within their cohort. Two million YouTubers boycotted the brand and Unilever complied with the terms of the ransom. A remarkable illustration of the power shift from brands to consumers and the aggregation of consumer power to extract behaviour change from corporations.

Designing brands around common causes and values: The 'good' communications agency

We must stop believing in what we sell, and start selling what we believe in.
(Bill Bernbach)

It was around 2010, that this story became my story.

I'd been a typical advertising planner for six years, and if there's one thing I felt a good planner understood, it was the fears, hopes and values of consumers. For a while I'd had a gripe about the emotional shallowness of brand communications and was itching to build brands more meaningful and affecting to consumers.[38] I was also a member of 'Planning for Good' – after all, I was going through my own 'WE-actualization'.[39]

'Social innovation' was a marvellous opportunity for planners who wanted to bring more 'good' to their work. Off the back of a random brand-repositioning project, with a favourite client, I cobbled together a 'Brand Creation Agency'[40] with a couple of fellow IPA Excellence Diploma graduates. We offered clients the consumer empathy and creativity they needed to innovate in these new, scary times.

Calling ourselves 'Groundswell', we worked by identifying popular causes and developing brands to support them. We believed solving real problems created value for everyone.

We were principled, existing as much for fulfilment as financial success. We were motivated by the meaty upstream strategic challenges that brand creation (vs pure communication) offered. We were motivated by fairness – a frustration with the payment-by-retainer culture dominating advertising (we'd profit-share on brands we created). And our biggest motivation was the feeling of helping causes greater than ourselves.

Groundswell quickly won business, with existing brand owners, to develop new brands, designed around the UK's most poignant causes.

The Groundswell method

We began by identifying worthy causes – through intuition, social media analysis of sentences containing the words 'feel', 'wish', 'hate',[41] and by penetrating support networks organically developed around common goals (eg groups on '43things.com', a social networking site where people pool their support around common goals). We also engaged with health experts and academics to determine the values and behaviours most in the interests of our targets, whether they knew it or not.

Next, potential consumers would collaborate with us in refinement of brand concepts. This not only harnessed their feedback but, as predicted by the Hawthorne Effect,[42] earned us their advocacy. Part of the process was a fictional investment game, where we asked 'is this idea good enough that you would invest to see it happen?' If a critical amount of hypothetical funding was secured, we would launch the brand.

Trading ownership for advocacy

Consumers were upset when they realized they couldn't invest for real in our concepts. It occurred to us that, if they were allowed to invest, it might generate unrivalled levels of consumer advocacy (much as you can't stop a new father talking about his child). And not only advocacy – what better way to shore up consumer trust than having consumers part-own the brand?[43]

Some Groundswell clients saw the potential in this (actually just two brave clients – the legal complications of shareholder ownership were generally prohibitive). So we created two brands that were co-owned by companies and a multitude of their customers – fascinating 'missing links' between the consumer-owned brands we have since co-created, and the famous shareholder-owned brands of the 20th century:

- 'Grow Your Own' – Heinz consumer-co-owned urban farms, helping young urban families to experience community, responsibility and ownership.
- Cadbury spent years marketing the fleeting 'joy' of chocolate, but we got them to do something that might make their consumers lastingly happier. 'Futurelife' was designed to overcome a flaw in human psychology, our inability to accurately perceive the future.[44] 'Futurelife' was an online game, where people created avatars of themselves, but 25 years older, allowing them to witness the impact today's decisions will have on tomorrow's happiness, and to better estimate their future financial means.

More 'common goodery' was possible than shareholder ownership permitted

Groundswell was part of a revolution, helping corporations improve welfare and develop new markets at the same time.

But it was a small revolution. Few companies embraced social innovation. And our clients' raisons d'être remained shareholder value, meaning they could never be as genuinely interested in serving the common good as companies with multiple bottom-lines, founded to pursue objectives alongside profit.

We rarely heard much about these privately or co-operatively-owned companies, because they often chose not to grow, thus eschewing conventional business fame. But these 'small giants' were really good at achieving their non-economic targets – Patagonia battling environmental problems, Zingerman's Deli promoting the welfare of its Michigan community, or the employee-owned TCHO chocolate company, existing to be a place people wanted to work.[45]

There was also one famous example of a company founded to dedicate *all* profits to the common good – Newman's Own, whose 'Shameless exploitation for the common good' generated $250 million for charity.

Owning the means of branding: collective investment democratizes the brand

Trust thyself: every heart vibrates to that iron string.

(Ralph Waldo Emerson)

The year 2011 was the year Groundswell changed branding forever. The inspiration came from one of our online brand-development communities.

We'd brought together some depression sufferers, to discuss social innovation concepts in support of depression research. It was all going well until one guy lost his temper and wrote a moving post, entitled 'Why do we need this coffee company... can't we get together and fight depression by ourselves?'.

It was a great point. Why did we need clients to create common-good brands? We certainly didn't need their capital.

While, historically, the capital behind any venture came from the few, it could now come from the many; just look at Obama. But experts of the time, like the *Wikinomics* authors, hadn't recognized this new potential for a multitude to invest tiny amounts, collectively accumulating a powerful amount of capital to help some common cause. 'Micro-credit' companies such as Kiva were lauded,[46] but the Obama phenomenon was more like 'micro-investment'... although the term 'collective investment' would eventually stick.

Groundswell's hypothetical brand-investment tool held great potential as an orchestrator of 'collective investment' (you'll remember that people desperately wanted their investments in our concepts to be real). Given our recent experience with social innovation, we thought it would be interesting to invent entirely consumer-owned cause-brands. Would such brands, authentically existing to the total benefit of a good cause, be unbeatable propositions to values-hungry consumers?

It was the inevitable next step in consumer empowerment. The masses had already taken some control over pricing, production, media and brand values... could they now add 'brand-ownership' to their achievements?

Product would be an afterthought as we developed our brands. But we chose to work in FMCG, our domain of greatest experience. FMCG was 'low-innovation' – breakthroughs in technology were rare and superfluous incrementalism rife. With limited need to innovate, we could rely on existing producers. Product parity was widespread and, as Seth Godin said, this was an era of cheap production – it was 'easier than ever to ensure quality'.[47]

The failure rate of new FMCG launches was high, but we were confident our brands' values would earn us preference with consumers and retailers. In FMCG, values were the key differentiator between brands and we would have the strongest possible.

Among some weird and wonderful brands, we launched:

- A coffee brand supporting research into depression, the fastest growing illness in the world – 'Pull Yourself Together' was founded thanks to £1,370,000, raised across 260,000 investors worldwide. Waitrose agreed to distribute and, as a 'charity', we paid no tax.

- A natural chewing gum brand, promoting awareness of 'Papyrus', a charity for the prevention of youth suicide. Eighty-three thousand adolescents invested to raise £260,000, with some offering their labour for free. American Apparel and several nightclubs (mourning atmospheric cigarette smoke and its ability to hide bad breath) stocked the brand. E-commerce was also significant.

These consumer-founded brands existed purely to serve the common goals of their distributed founders. And the authenticity of their ethical stances resonated strongly with consumers.

It didn't all go swimmingly

We did have failures – a bottled water campaigning against street violence and a popcorn with quiet packaging, promoting decorum in cinemas. Our collective brands would be the first noble failures in trying to democratize brands for the common good.

FIGURE 3.4   Brand = 'WE'

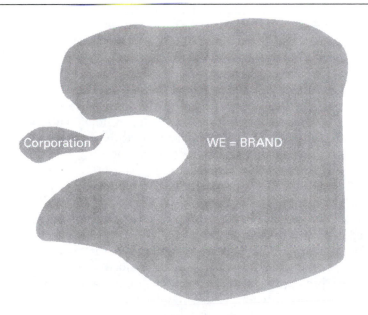

FLOW: Where would you like your profit to go?

Our biggest problem was that causes can be incredibly niche – one man's pony sanctuary is another's adult literacy.[48]

But, upon re-reading the classic marketing text, *Right Side Up*,[49] I realized, just as agent brands can aggregate consumer needs to increase buying power, we could aggregate consumer causes to increase branding power. It'd be easier to sustain one brand representing all causes, than to maintain separate brands for niche causes. Aggregating those causes would create vast economies of scale. And aggregating the deep emotions associated with each cause would build a massive bank of goodwill for this 'super-brand'.

We'd name the brand FLOW[50] and the trick was this – consumers could choose, at point of purchase, where the profit on their FLOW purchases went. Having already visited our website to select a cause they wished to support, they would use their FLOWcard when paying for goods, to ensure the premiums they paid went to their chosen cause. FLOW was a customizable brand, which could stand for anything you wanted... an unbeatable ESP (emotional selling proposition).[51] And, if 100,000 consumers assigned their premiums to one cause, and if FLOW managed to have a decent offering in every FMCG category, that would mean a hefty income for the cause.

Easier said than done. In 2013, we used our old friend, collective investment, to launch FLOW in three commodity categories. But it was on a visit to Venezuela to negotiate a coffee deal for 'Pull Yourself Together' that we realized how interested benefactors would be in helping us expand. Hugo Chavez had heard about FLOW and was excited about its potential as a 'socialist' competitor for Western interests. He offered us $120 million to grow the brand, which we politely turned down. However, the resulting PR led to others (Bill Gates, Arpad Busson) making similar offers, and it was these benefactors who helped FLOW grow so rapidly – things would have taken decades longer had we to wait for individual products to generate sufficient profit to facilitate expansion to new categories. Nonetheless, we were a sustainable charity and every one of our FLOW lines would eventually become self-sustaining.

We marketed FLOW through Cadbury's hugely popular 'FutureLife', showing consumers what they could achieve with 25 years spent on FLOW goods.[52] But we had scant need to deploy paid-for communications, as word-of-mouth worked wonders.

We wanted a FLOW presence in every FMCG category. And, if we couldn't ensure product quality working with unbranded producers, we'd work with branded producers, even taking over brands and their infrastructures. Innocent and Gü became FLOW brands in 2015.

The FLOW website became a buzzing community of 'WE-actualizers', making friends, campaigning for their causes. And, even though there was nothing stopping individuals arranging their FLOW profit to go to a personal beer or holiday fund, the vast majority chose to support the common good.

With FLOW instilling such a strong sense of community, we were once again facilitating deep, social emotions. Not just empathy, kinship and responsibility, but guilt... whenever you chose another brand over FLOW, you weren't just letting down some company, but your friends and the better part of humanity!

In 2017, after four years of trading, we released our first profits, a total payout of £314 million to good causes. We were in 32 FMCG categories in six countries, occupying position one or two in 21 of those categories. We also had a fashion label and, with the revised goal of being omnipotent, had begun negotiating partnerships with corporations in high-innovation categories, such as automotives and computing.

As important as financial success, FLOW customers in 2017 scored significantly higher on measures of authentic happiness.[53] Longitudinal studies (initiated in 2013) indicated that switching to FLOW increased feelings of community, trust and happiness. And 'FLOW-or-nothings' (loyalists who only purchase FLOW products) were significantly less likely to suffer from depression and reported fewer GP visits.

Owned by the people, for the sake of the people, FLOW, more than any brand, actually helps people to 'we-actualize'. And, personally, although FLOW hasn't made me wealthy, I feel extremely rich to have found a way to use consumerism, and my work, to make the world a happier place.[54]

Epilogue

Is this an unlikely story? Possibly. Is it impossible? No. Some concluding thoughts:

- In the future, the engines of society may be geared towards making the world a better place, not just wealthier. Personal growth may be as important as economic. And any system allowing people to aggregate their purchasing and brand affiliation, for the common good, will flourish.

- Brands should move beyond superficial image branding, to facilitate authentic social-emotional experiences, even personal growth.

- Brands will win by putting common good at the core of their business plans.

- Consumers will increasingly extract behaviour-change from brands that don't help common interest. Brands should consider the advantages of giving co-ownership to customers.

- Communications agencies should ask (a) whether their skills might be better (and more fulfillingly) employed, for the long term, in brand creation and brand ownership, and (b) whether they would rather be wedded to consumer clients, as agents of values; organizing consumers to ensure they get maximum return for the values they hold.

Notes

1 A word-play on the Marxist concept 'means of production', representing the shift in power from production to branding.

2 Rand, A (1957) *Atlas Shrugged*, Random House, London.

3 Curtis, A (2002) [Film] *The Century of the Self*, produced by BBC and RDF Media.

4 Maslow, A (1943) A Theory of Human Motivation, *Psychological Review*, 50, pp 370–96.

5 Tapscott, D and Williams, A (2008) *Wikinomics*, Atlantic Books, London.

6 Grossman, L (December 2006) You – Yes, You – Are Time's Person of the Year, Time magazine [Online] http://content.time.com/time/magazine/article/0,9171,1570810,00.html

7 Tapscott, D and Williams, A (2008) *Wikinomics*, Atlantic Books, London.

8 *ibid*.

9 Grant, J [Accessed 2008] Brand Tarot blog [Online] www.brandtarot.com/blog/?p=552

10 Cook, Robin (10 December 2004) Only Collective Action Can Overcome the Climate Crisis, *Guardian*.

11 James, O (January 2006) On the money, *The Observer* [Online] www.guardian.co.uk/lifeandstyle/2006/jan/01/healthandwellbeing.features

12 Substantiated by Layard, R (2006) *Happiness: Lessons from a new science*, Penguin, UK; and Seligman, M (2003) *Authentic Happiness: Using the new positive psychology*, Nicholas Brealey Publishing, UK.

13 Layard, R (2006) *Happiness: Lessons from a new science*, Penguin, UK.

14 Tapscott, D (1997) *Growing Up Digital: Rise of the net generation*, McGraw-Hill, New York. Research updated in *Wikinomics*.

15 Soames, G (May 2008) 'Scuppie Power', *The Sunday Times*.

16 (BLOG)RED [Accessed 2007] (RED) Force One [Online] http://blog.red.org/2006/10/red-force-one.html

17 Willmott M (2001) *Citizen Brands: Putting society at the heart of your business*, Wiley and Pringle, H; and Thompson M (1999) *Brand Spirit: How cause related marketing builds brands*, Wiley, Chichester.

18 Bonney, D (June 2008) Emotion – a familiar friend we barely know, *Admap*, **44**.

19 Barkow, J H, Cosmides L and Tooby, J (eds) (1992) *The Adapted Mind: Evolutionary psychology and the generation of culture*, Oxford University Press, New York.

20 Mitchell, A (2002) *Right Side Up: Building brands in the age of the organized consumer*, HarperCollins, UK.

21 *ibid*.

22 McCawley (July 2000) Shelving Own Label, *Marketing Week* [Online] www.marketingweek.co.uk/shelving-own-label/2015288.article

23 Levine, R, Locke, C, Searls, D and Weinberger, D (1999) *The Cluetrain Manifesto: The end of business as usual*, Basic Books, New York.

24 Middleton, C (2005) How important is ownership?, *Market Leader*, Issue 29, WARC.

25 Davis, C and Moy, C (June 2007) The dawn of the ethical brand, *Admap*, Issue 484: People aged 55–64 show the strongest commitment to ethical brands. Women are more likely to buy ethical brands than men.

26 Davis, C and Moy, C (June 2007) The dawn of the ethical brand, *Admap*, Issue 484.

27 Davis, C and Moy, C (June 2007) The dawn of the ethical brand, *Admap*, Issue 484.

28 Davis, C and Moy, C (June 2007) The dawn of the ethical brand, *Admap*, Issue 484: 43% of consumers thought brands with 'ethical' claims put pressure on others to become more accountable. And consumers would pay to see ethical brands grow. Almost 50% claimed that they would pay at least 5% more, almost a quarter 10% more.

29 The Ethical Consumerism Report (2007) *The Cooperative Bank*: '68% of US and European consumers have boycotted a food, drink or personal care product on ethical grounds, and UK companies lost US$2.7 billion of sales through consumer boycotts in 2003. Now, 70 per cent of UK consumers say they will deliberately avoid buying goods from organizations they think are unethical, and 85 per cent claim to be interested in ethical issues.'

30 Mitchell, A (2002) heralds the dawn of 'Right-Side Up' marketing in *Right Side Up: Building brands in the age of the organized consumer*, HarperCollins, UK.

31 James, O (2008) *Affluenza: How to be successful* and *stay sane*, Vermilion, London.

32 Andrew Wilson, Ashbridge Management College, cited in Willmott, M (2001) *Citizen Brands*, Wiley, London.

33 Willmott, M, formerly of the Future Foundation, author of *Citizen Brands* (2001).

34 Willmott's term for brands wise enough to put society at the core of everything they do.

35 Herman Daly in *Beyond Growth: Economics of sustainable development* (1997) Beacon Press, exposes the foolhardiness of any notion of 'sustainable growth', arguing that growth is actually unnecessary for the maintenance of a healthy and wealthy society. See also Bill McKibben, *Deep Economy: As if the world mattered* (2007) Oneworld Publications.

36 Cescau, P (May 2007) [Speech] *Beyond Corporate Responsibility: Social innovation and sustainable development as drivers of business growth*, INDEVOR Alumni Forum: Integrating CSR into Business Strategy, France [Online] http://oldwww.wbcsd.org/plugins/DocSearch/details.asp?MenuId=MTY1&ClickMenu=LeftMenu&doOpen=1&type=DocDet&ObjectId=MjQ3ODI

37 30,000 Shakti entrepreneurs now operate in 100,000 villages serving 100 million consumers. The revenues are close to $100 million a year, similar to what Unilever achieves through its mainstream distribution channels.

38 Bonney, D (December 2006) Sad-vertising, *Admap*, Issue 278.

39 [Blog] http://planningforgood.blogspot.com/

40 A number of 'communications agencies' have crossed the divide to become brand owners, by innovating new brand concepts themselves (eg Droga 5, Anomaly).

41 Harris, J and Kamvar, S (2007) [Blog] We Feel Fine [Online] www.wefeelfine.org/methodology.html

42 Marsden, P (March 2006) Measuring the Success of Word of Mouth, *MRS Annual Conference* [Online] www.research-live.com/news/ilive-from-research-2006/i-word-of-mouth-gets-people-talking-at-conference/3001764.article

43 Kelly, K (1995) *Out of Control: The new biology of machines, social systems and the economic world*, Basic Books, New York.

44 Gilbert, D (2006) *Stumbling on Happiness*, Vintage Books, New York.

45 See: [Accessed 2008] Heuristics, *TCHO* [Online] www.tcho.com/tcho_is/heuristics; and Burlingam, B (2005) *Small Giants*, Penguin.

46 Loans that change lives, *Kiva* [Online] www.kiva.org/ [Accessed 2008]

47 Godin, S (2005) *All Marketers are Liars*, Penguin, London.

48 *ibid*.

49 Mitchell, A (2002) *Right Side Up: Building brands in the age of the organized consumer*, HarperCollins, UK.

50 Csíkszentmihályi, M (2002) *Flow: The psychology of optimal experience*, Rider, London: FLOW is the highest state of happiness.

51 Hegarty, J (1999) [Speech] The Future of Advertising: The secret ingredient, *AICP Session*, New York.

52 Twenty-five years of expenditure on FLOW food products could amount to £38,000.

53 Segilman, M [Online] www.authentichappiness.sas.upenn.edu/: Martin Seligman has developed reliable and valid questionnaires for the measurement of happiness.

54 Godin, S (August 2008) Destroying Happiness [Online] http://sethgodin.typepad.com/seths_blog/2008/08/destroying-happ.html

I believe in gaming your brand
2009/10

TIM JONES
Director of Strategy, 72andsunny, New York

I believe Games provide the ideal template for building a modern brand. This piece is not about creating branded games as executions, but about using the principles of game to codify a brand and define its behaviour. By defining a brand in this way, you can create a truly interactive system with engagement and behaviour at its heart vs a proposition or message that can only ever be a one-way form of communication.

Editor's therefore, for your brand...

Your brand thinking: If 'interaction' is now key, what form of interaction is appropriate for your brand? Gaming, conversation, fandom or doctor/patient etc?

Your brand engagement: What game is your brand? What is winning? What are the rules for participation? Who are the stars of the game?

Your brand organization & capability: How can you structure for real time, 24/7 interaction?

...and author's personal therefore

Although I have benefited enormously from my dissertation, I cannot say that I have built a whole career around it. That's not because the thinking was wrong (which would be embarrassing), but because over time it has become less provocative, and therefore less useful in today's world.

I believe that there has been a genuine shift in the industry: interactivity and behaviour change is now central to most brands and their campaigns. We judge marketing by its ability to engage vs interrupt, and impact in terms of action vs attitude. Like most things in life, Mark Zuckerberg, Larry Page and Eric Schmitt are probably to blame/credit for how we view business today. The rise of digital as a core part of marketing means we now game our brands without even realizing it – we seek playful ways to tempt people into addictive behavioural patterns that ultimately create value for our clients and ourselves.

Real people have also naturally adopted a gamed approach to every day. We are drawn to data about ourselves, health, finance, even love making. We constantly look for ways to quantify our performance and self-coach improvement.

A few years on and 'Gamification' has become so ubiquitous it is almost not worth talking about. However, putting the shtick to one side, there are principles underlying the thinking that are still good and continue to influence me today.

I believe we spend too long banging on about propositions and not enough time on what we actually want people to do. I believe behaviour is more important than message and my favourite work reflects this.

AXE: living the brand benefit

In 2013, AXE launched its most ambitious campaign of all time – The AXE Apollo Space Academy, a global initiative to send 20 lucky guys into space, because girls love a hero.

The campaign marked an important shift for the brand: we weren't just going to tell guys that AXE made them more attractive to women, we were going to engage guys in a behaviour that would actually make them more attractive: we were offering them the chance to go to space – to leave a man and come back a hero. Participation was at the core of the campaign and scaled from mass/light touch social behaviours (canvassing for votes) to high engagement behaviours for those who progressed further (visiting Space Camp in Florida).

AXE Apollo was the brand's most successful launch for three years, tracking 13 per cent to 17 per cent higher (value) in key markets than the nearest competitors.

Virgin Media broadband: nudging to a sale

The Virgin Media 'Challenge Your Broadband' campaign was built around an understanding of the consumer journey and the behavioural nudges needed to move people from one stage to the next. Realizing that people needed to directly compare their broadband to Virgin Media in order to see the difference, we ditched telling people about our speeds and used superfast spokesperson Usain Bolt to prompt prospects to 'challenge their broadband' via an online speed checker. After completing the speed test, consumers were guided through a buying process by Bolt himself until they found the right package for them.

The campaign resulted in a +3 per cent increase in market share vs a significantly lower media spend.

Smirnoff Sours: ritual out

Smirnoff Sours is a uniquely sour-tasting drink designed to grow market share in bars. The product itself has such an intense flavour that you cannot help but react after drinking it; resistance is futile. Rather than tell people this, our campaign leveraged an existing social behaviour (#myfacewhen – capturing facial reactions to extreme moments) to create a new ritual around the product. In-bar activity prompted people to try the product and share their facial reactions over social media; paid media was used to amplify the results and propagate the behaviour.

The campaign is brand new, so no results yet, but we've got our fingers crossed.

My career: staying relevant

If the Diploma taught me anything, it was that new ideas get old fast. The challenge for anyone working in communications today is to stay relevant. This is easier at the beginning of one's career when you're the generation driving change, it's harder when you're a bit older and have to make an effort to be part of the next big thing.

A simple response to this inevitability is to stay close to where the heat is. Nick Kendall often remarked that he continues to run the Diploma in order to gain exposure to fresh ideas (kind of like a friendly intellectual vampire). Having also joined Nick on the marketers' side of the desk, I can see what he means. As I get a bit older my career has certainly benefited from staying close to the heat; joining younger consumers on nights out to understand their lives, making sure we have a thriving intern programme and staying close to the leading graduate schools had helped us keep our ideas, our work and our agency fresh.

My life: making it fun

Researching 'Gaming Brands' taught me that we are happier and more productive when we make everyday life fun. Whether we turn chores into games, or use Fuelband to make fitness competitive, life is better when you approach it with a playful attitude. I sometimes think I'm a bit immature for my age, and definitely for my work, but when these thoughts pop into my head I remember that as long as you're having fun then everything else will probably be ok.

I believe in gaming your brand

Why games?

Games don't need to exist. On the surface, they seem to serve no rational or evolutionary purpose, yet they have been part of our culture for as long as we have records, with the earliest games appearing as early as 9000 BC. Games are a part of what is means to be human.

Rather than dismissing games as a leisure activity, I believe that they not only provide a good model for how we play, learn and develop, but also that games provide a template for building brands suited to the modern world.

Level I: gaming life

Homo ludens: the playing man

> A game is a problem-solving activity, approached with a playful attitude.[1]

Humans are natural-born problem-solvers. We can't help it, it's the way we are wired. Solving problems triggers the release of dopamine, a neurotransmitter associated with reward.[2] Playing around is our way of learning about the world and it is constantly re-enforced by neurotransmitters that make the experience 'fun'. The positive emotions play invokes represent an adaptation that encourages us to try new things and learn with more flexibility. In fact, Melvin Konner, an anthropologist and neuroscientist, suggests that play may be the primary means nature has found to develop our brains,[3] a theory that has been bolstered by many developmental psychologists that have linked play to social, language and cognitive development in children.[4,5,6,7]

Play is an important learning mechanism, but it is also much more than that. In *Homo Ludens*, cultural theorist Johan Huizinga explores the role of play in human culture, and concludes that the two cannot be separated. Huizinga finds characteristics of play evident in cultural inventions such as education, law, politics, religious rites, art, poetry and philosophy.[8] We have to conclude that civilization is, in its earliest phases, played. It does not come from play like a babe detaching itself from the womb: it arises in and as play, and never leaves it.

It seems our natural predisposition to play is evident in all aspects of life: we create games to enhance our leisure time and turn our less enjoyable tasks into games to enhance those as well. We game life to make it more fun. The emotional reward that game playing can bring to behaviour can turn mere task completion into an enjoyable experience. It is this dynamic that prompts us to game aspects of everyday life by introducing game-like elements such as competition, scoring and winning.

Gaming life modifies behaviour

The emotional rewards gained from 'winning' games can act as powerful incentives to change behaviour. When I was young, my parents often turned chores into games. The 'clean your room in under 10 minutes' game or the 'get ready for bed' races between me and my brothers were more effective than just telling us what to do. Gaming life tasks can also work for adults; the internet-based game 'Chore Wars' allocates points and rewards to house-mates that complete household chores. Chore Wars provides the tools to game housework, creating a behaviour change system that incentivizes a task most of us would rather avoid.

Game-like systems can be used to change behaviour on a mass scale for commercial gain. Airline frequent-flyer programmes (FFPs) provide points, levels and rewards that allow consumers to game air travel; the challenge to the player is simple: level up by collecting as many air miles as possible. The FFP game is so compelling that it actively changes consumer behaviour. Over 80 per cent of FFP users have taken an unnecessary flight in order to gain extra air miles. What is more, the success of FFPs cannot be attributed to external rewards alone; in 2007, there were over 10 trillion unredeemed air miles globally, this represents each FFP member saving five times more miles per year than they redeem. For some, the points seem to be enough.

The important observation here is we 'game' everyday life to make it more emotionally rewarding, and that these emotional rewards can be harnessed to change behaviour.

Gaming life is working for brands

Brands and services have also begun to catch on to the possible value that can be realized by providing the tools needed to game everyday life tasks. Facebook, Amazon and LinkedIn have all taken the first steps towards allowing consumers to game their services. Friend counts, likes, reviews and ratings all give users parameters to play within.

Marketing initiatives have also started to behave like games. Nike+ has embraced this thinking with great success; it gives runners the tools to 'game' running. Objectives, challenges and rules are all applied to create a system that promotes 'on brand' behaviour. Fiat EcoDrive and Foursquare operate in similar ways.

Games provide a powerful system for behaviour change that can be harnessed by brands in profitable ways.

Level II: gaming brands

From broadcast brands to interactive brands

The need to build interactive brands that invite participation is something many marketers take for granted in the modern world, but our ability to build interactive brands is being held back by outdated thinking.

Media often dictates the message. The 'USP' was invented for, and belongs to, the broadcast media age when the need to deliver a message in a single shot drove the planning process.[9] However, the USP is still at the heart of brands today. Propositions are inherently broadcast, however we choose to distribute them. Interaction in this case often means 'how do we get people to interact with our brand message?' rather than 'how do we create a brand that is inherently interactive?' The media landscape has now evolved, and now so should our brand planning process; we need a new template that puts interaction at the heart of our brands. Games by definition are built on interactive principles; they demand you play rather than listen.

I believe that games provide a practical template for developing truly interactive brands.

From attitude change to behaviour change

Brands exist to change consumer behaviour in a way that benefits the interests of the client. The traditional role for communications has been to build brand awareness, consideration and preference, assuming that change in attitude will result in a corresponding effect on behaviour. However, the fundamental assumption that behaviour change follows attitude change is highly debatable.

Psychologists have challenged the idea that attitude leads behaviour. As humans, we are biased towards the easiest route to reducing the uncomfortable gaps that can exist between our attitudes and behaviours (cognitive dissonance). This often means we adjust our attitudes to reflect our behaviour rather than the other way around; this is why smokers are less inclined to believe cigarettes are bad for one's health. This direction of influence is contrary to what would be expected if attitude came first. This speaks to me on an intuitive level: how often do we attempt to justify current behaviours we know to be wrong vs actually changing them?

Marketing theory has also challenged this assumption from various angles. The behaviours of others, the context of a decision and behavioural 'nudges' are all arguably more influential than our own beliefs or attitudes. Further evidence from the IPA Databank shows that campaigns that set a behavioural objective are more effective than those that set awareness or attitudinal objectives.

I believe that games provide a practical template for brands that actively change behaviour.

A new template for brands

As long as traditional brand planning models put a statement at their core, they will be fundamentally unsuited to interactive brands with behaviour at their core. We need a new model.

Games provide an alternative template to traditional brand planning models that allow us to build rich, interactive brands that actively promote behaviour change. Games are characterized by:

- Win condition – which serves as a criteria for completing the game successfully.
- Objective – what the player has to achieve.
- Action – the behaviour the player has to exhibit to play the game.
- Obstacles – what the player has to overcome to achieve the objective.
- Rules – constraints that must be observed while playing the game.

Applying this structure to 'eye spy' helps us understand the model (Figure 4.1).

FIGURE 4.1   The structure of 'eye spy'

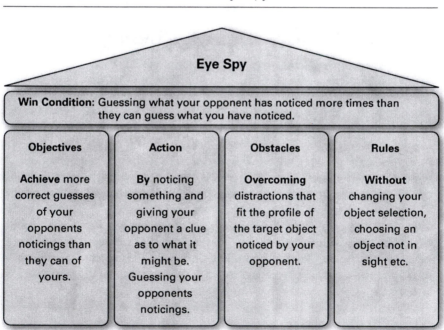

Structuring brands as games

The template of a game can easily be adapted to re-create a brand in a game-style, behaviour change system.

- Win condition – what behaviour does the brand help consumers 'game', how do they win?
- Objective – what are we actually asking people to do?
- Action – how does the player go about gaming that behaviour, what does the brand provide to make this possible?
- Obstacles – what obstacles will the player encounter, how does the brand help the player overcome them?
- Rules – what are the rules of the brand game, and how are they enforced?

Level III: gaming your brand

Gaming a familiar brand

To understand the power of planning brands as games, we will apply these principles to a familiar brand, AXE (Lynx in the UK). There are five steps.

Step 1: Choosing a behaviour

AXE has always had a very clear product benefit. Axe makes guys smell great, helping them feel more confident and attractive to girls. This benefit has been wrapped up into a brand idea, the 'AXE Effect'. As one would expect, the majority of AXE communication has dramatized the AXE Effect. Over time, many executions have worked to establish this brand idea.

For a brand to be credible in this space, the brand benefits must have an active role in gaming the behaviour. In this case, the behaviour we are looking at is 'pulling', ie getting the girl. It's easy to see that is a valid behaviour – guys already 'play' at pulling, whether it's counting notches on the bedpost, or playing 'pull a pig',[10] guys are already playing informal games around pulling girls.

Step 2: Understand consumers as gamers

Developing a brand that helps consumers game a behaviour requires a different approach to consumer understanding. Computer game designers have naturally already considered what gamers want from games. Game designer and theorist, Richard Bartle, has established four subgroups of gamers that are described by their gaming motivation.[11]

Gamer typologies

Killers are interested in doing things to people, ie in acting on other players. Killers get their kicks from imposing themselves on others, they especially like to win at the expense of other players.

Achievers are interested in doing things to the game, ie in acting on the world. They regard points gathering and rising in levels as their main goal; all other activity is in the pursuit of this aim.

FIGURE 4.2

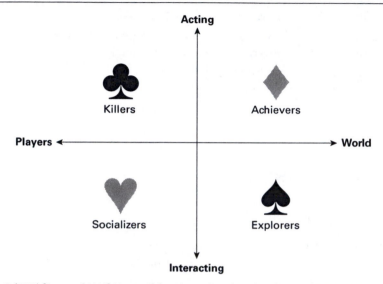

Bartle, R (1996) [Accessed 2010] Hearts, Clubs, Diamonds and Spades: Players Who Suit MUDs
[Online] **www.mud.co.uk/richard/hcds.htm**

Socializers are interested in interacting with other players. Socializers are interested in people, and what they have to say. The game is merely a back-drop, a common ground where things happen to players.

Explorers are interested in having the game surprise them, ie interacting with the world. They delight in having the game's internal mechanisms exposed to them; their fun comes from discovering new parts of the game, especially if they are the first to do so.

Most gamers are actually a mixture of these typologies, and most games are designed to appeal to all typologies to a certain extent. Understanding the balance of gamer motivation is key to understanding how consumers might game a chosen behaviour. Through an online survey we identified that AXE consumers score highly in the 'Achiever' and 'Killer' segments.

Step 3: Gaming a behaviour

Understanding that AXE guys are a mix between the 'achiever' typology and the 'killer' typology helps us define how pulling behaviour should be gamed. In this case, pulling is gamed though competition: guys like to keep score (Achievers) and ultimately compete against their mates (Killers).

Step 4: Setting a win condition

To construct the AXE brand as a game, we will define the brand idea as a 'win condition', ie, what consumers as players need to do to successfully game 'pulling'. Given we know that guys keep score, and are competitive among their friends, setting the win condition 'pulling more girls than your mates' is appropriate.

Step 5: Building the brand

Once a behaviour to be gamed has been chosen, and win condition set, the rest of the brand can be built. Understanding the context that your brand operates in informs the structure of this game.

'Pulling' can be broken down into three broad areas that guys must be proficient in. These stages are used to form the actions that the player must exhibit successfully to meet the brand's win condition:

- Training – is getting ready to play, both physically and mentally. For guys this means everything from grooming, to making sure they have the best chat-up lines up their sleeve.
- Playing – this is where the action happens, this is where guys are actively trying to get the girl, this is the chatting, the flirting etc.
- Scoring – this is the actual scoring bit, the success; the pull.

Campaigns as challenges

Defining the AXE brand as a game has implications for execution. Brand activity cannot be thought of in terms of message, but in terms of challenges that build towards the brand's win condition.

Training challenge: look your best

A range of product innovations would be a natural place for AXE to address a guy's preparation needs. This approach would see each AXE variant given a specific role in the preparation ritual. The resulting campaign brief would then revolve around establishing the challenge in the minds of the player, and the role of the product in answering that challenge.

Playing challenge: get in there

Content in itself can be a tool to aid guys in the 'playing' stage. The AXE brand could provide content that helps guys gain popularity among girls. This might take the form of humorous viral content, or even 'how to' style content that gives guys girl advice.

Scoring challenge: take her out

Promotional mechanics can also now be informed by the brand game and used to address the 'scoring stage'. Competition prizes could be items that further a guy's chances of success, ie gig tickets for two.

Gaming other brands

Since not all brands are as playful as AXE, one might question the applicability of gaming principles for the full range of brands out there.

Gaming social causes

Our predisposition to game life is not limited to light-hearted activities. The term 'serious game' was first coined in 1970 by Clark Abt,[12] who defined them as games that have real-life consequences.[13] Some organizations promoting the uses of serious games already exist;[14,15] examples of their work include:

- 'Against All Odds' – a UNCHR game that puts the player in the shoes of a refugee.[16]
- 'Windfall' – a strategy game about building wind farms to create clean energy profitably.[17]
- 'Akrasia' – a US Department of Health game that allows the player to explore the issues surrounding substance addiction.[18]

Serious games are not just the preserve of education; in her TEDspeech, Jane MacGonigal explores how gaming can be used to solve real-world problems with mass multiplayer games such as 'Superstruct'.[19] This game had a serious aim: the win condition was saving the human race. It was essentially a huge brainstorming tool that allowed thousands of players to suggest initiatives that could solve real-world problems. The game yielded many new suggestions for how these problems might be tackled.

Gaming financial service brands

Expressing a financial service brand as a game is easier than one might imagine; they are already set up with a lot of mechanics that lend themselves to gaming. Win conditions would depend on the specific client's business model, but could include:

- becoming debt free;
- being able to retire at 55; and
- doubling your investment returns.

As with the AXE brand example, the purpose of a gamed financial brand would be to develop a range of activities that help players meet these challenges.

Gaming a typical FMCG brand

Persil have done a great job in defining a brand benefit in a compelling way: it cleans so well, mums don't have to worry about their kids' clothes getting dirty. This benefit has been wrapped up in the creative idea 'Dirt is Good', which champions children getting messy as a natural part of learning, playing and generally enjoying life.[20] 'Messy play' is a great behaviour to game; the Persil win condition could be expressed as:

- kids take part in more messy play than clean play;
- kids play outdoors more than they play indoors; and
- kids are never clean for more than 24 hrs.

The Persil product works as an enabler for these win conditions, removing one of the barriers to messy play – the resultant dirty clothes. Defining Persil as game requires every piece of brand activity to build towards the win condition. Campaign challenges such as 'play in the park once a week' could lead to interesting ideas, from entertainment properties to utilities.

Boss level: gaming brand value

Gaming brand value

Gamed brands as ecosystems

A gamed brand presents an ecosystem, or network, that breaks down the brand win condition into easily tackled behaviours, each of which is in turn addressed by individual pieces of brand activity. The structures and properties of ecosystems, and the value they bring to business has been explored extensively by Marco Iansiti of Harvard Business School: 'There is a growing awareness that by structuring problems so that they can be viewed as networks of smaller problems, difficult tasks can be completed more efficiently.'[21]

The properties of a gamed brand structured in this way have direct implications for building brand value in both an equity and commercial sense.

Gamed brands drive customer acquisition

Level I established our natural predisposition to game everyday life; leveraging this instinct is at the heart of gaming brands. Brands that are gamed effectively use our innate reward mechanisms to incentivize behaviour. The emotional highs that gamed behaviour triggers can enhance positive experiences like 'pulling', or even provide an emotional dimension to life's least fun tasks, eg financial service brands. It is the enhancement of consumer experience that drives customer acquisition, and ultimately commercial value.

Gamed brands drive weight of purchase

Gamed brands are structured to reward involvement. The player's feeling of progression and achievement increases as they approach the brand win condition. A correctly gamed brand uses each piece of brand activity, including products, to bring the player closer to this win condition. Positioning brand activity in this way makes each piece inherently attractive to the player; brand activity becomes a stepping stone that takes the player closer to 'winning'. This structure naturally lends itself to cross-selling and up-selling, which drive weight of brand purchase.

Gamed brands drive loyalty

Gamed brands incentivize involvement, but they also punish disengagement. As a player progresses through the gamed brand towards the win condition, effort is expended and emotional value accumulated. Dropping out of the brand game becomes harder the longer it is played; this is driven by the cognitive bias of loss aversion.[22]

Bonus level: conclusions and implications

Conclusions

Gamed brands are fundamentally more suited to the needs of brand building than traditional approaches. The gaming brand's approach is rooted in human instinct, from the moment we are born we are driven to understand the world through play, and strive to manipulate it though gaming. Gaming provides a powerful model that helps us understand how brands interact with the world, but also provides a practical template for building rich and experiential brands. By structuring brands in a way that leverages our gaming instinct we can transform them from message transmission devices, to behaviour change systems that ultimately drive brand value.

Implications

Gaming brands represents a fundamental shift in brand planning, providing brands with interaction at their core. The brand 'win condition' is at the heart of this approach. Defining brands in this way focuses the marketing mix around developing brand activities that help consumers 'win' at a behaviour they either have to, or want to, do. This ultimately positions the brand and its products as a tool that helps consumers to 'win at life', making the brand both attractive, and indispensable.

Gaming brands also has interesting implications for consumer understanding. Developing research methodologies based on the likes of Bartle's gamer segmentation help us understand our consumers as active participants, rather than as passive respondents, and build brands accordingly.

Finally, gaming brands also has implications for brand measurement. Consumer funnels have been designed assuming a passive consumer, whose attitudes are at the mercy of the advertiser. A model based on behaviour, that reported on consumers as they progressed through a brand game would be more appropriate.

Game over.

Notes

1 Schell, J (2008) *The Art of Game Design: A book of lenses*, Morgan Kaufmann, Chicago.

2 Kang, M J, Hsu, M, Krajbich, I M, Loewenstein, G, McClure, S M, Wang, J, Tand Camerer, C F (2009) The wick in the candle of learning: epistemic curiosity activates reward circuitry and enhances memory, *Psychol Sci*, 20 (8), pp 963–73.

3 Konner, M (2010) *The Evolution of Childhood: Relationships, emotion, mind*, Harvard University Press, Harvard.

4 Ginsberg, K R (2007) The Importance of Play in Promoting Healthy Child Development and Maintaining Strong Parent-Child Bonds, *Pediatrics*, 119, 182–91.

5 Tamis-LeMonda, C S, Shannon, J D, Cabrera, N J and Lamb, M E (2004) Fathers and mothers at play with their 2- and 3-year-olds: contributions to language and cognitive development, *Child Dev*. 75, pp 1806–20.

6 Shonkoff, J P, Phillips, D A (eds) (2000) *From Neurons to Neighborhoods: The science of early childhood development*, National Academy Press, Washington, DC.

7 Tamis-LeMonda, C S, Shannon, J D, Cabrera, N J and Lamb, M E (2004) Fathers and mothers at play with their 2- and 3-year-olds: contributions to language and cognitive development, *Child Dev*. 75, pp 1806–20.

8 Shonkoff, J P, Phillips, D A (eds) (2000) *From Neurons to Neighborhoods: The science of early childhood development*, National Academy Press, Washington, DC.

9 Frost, J L (1998) Neuroscience, play and brain development. Paper presented at: IPA/USA Triennial National Conference; Longmont CO, 18–21 June.

10 [Online, Accessed 2010] www.urbandictionary.com/define.php?term=Pork%20the%20Pig&defid=3408160: A questionable game played by clubbers. Trying to pull the ugliest girl, or 'pig' in the club.

11 Adapted from graph by Bartle, R (1996) [Accessed 2010] Hearts, Clubs, Diamonds and Spades: Players who suit MUDs [Online] www.mud.co.uk/richard/hcds.htm

12 Bartle, R (1996) [Accessed 2010] Hearts, Clubs, Diamonds and Spades: Players Who Suit MUDs [Online] www.mud.co.uk/richard/hcds.htm

13 Abt, C (1970) *Serious Games*, The Viking Press, New York.

14 Zyda, M (2005) From visual simulation to virtual reality to games, *IEEE Computer*.

15 [Accessed 2010] Serious Games Initiative [Online] www.seriousgames.org: The Serious Games Initiative is focused on uses for games in exploring management and leadership challenges facing the public sector.

16 [Accessed 2010] Games for Change [Online] www.gamesforchange.org: Games for Change (G4C) is a non-profit which seeks to harness the extraordinary power of video games to address the most pressing issues of our day, including poverty, education, human rights, global conflict and climate change.

17 [Accessed 2010] Against all odds, Online game, [Online] www.playagainstallodds.ca/

18 [Accessed 2010] Persuasive games, *Windfall* [Online game] www.persuasivegames.com/games/game.aspx?game=windfall

19 [Accessed 2010] Games for Change, *Akrasia* [Online game] www.gamesforchange.org/play/akrasia/

20 McGonigal, J (February 2010) Gaming Can Make a Better World, *TED talks* [Online] www.ted.com/talks/jane_mcgonigal_gaming_can_make_a_better_world

21 [Accessed 2010] Dirt is good, *Persil* [Online] www.persil.com/dirtisgood.aspx

22 Iansiti, M (2004) *The Keystone Advantage: What the new dynamics of business ecosystems mean for strategy, innovation, and sustainability*, Harvard Business School.

23 Some studies suggest that losses are as much as twice as psychologically powerful as gains. Loss aversion was first convincingly demonstrated in Kahneman, D, Knetsch, J L and Thaler, R H (1991) The endowment effect, loss aversion, and status quo bias, *Journal of Economic Perspectives*.

I believe in a brand new religion

2006/07

05

GRAEME DOUGLAS

Group Chief Strategy Officer, Havas

I believe The future success of brands can be secured by understanding and adopting the modus operandi of arguably the most enduring and successful marketing exercise of all time: religion.

Editor's therefore, for your brand...

Your brand thinking: If brands are religions can we learn from different types of religions around the world? What is a Buddhist brand? What is your brand Tao?

Your brand engagement: Is your iconography truly iconic and inspiring? Are you spending enough time and money on making it famous?

Your brand organization & capability: How do you make your team religious zealots? Who are your disciples inside and outside the organization?

...and author's personal therefore

In the eight or so years since I completed the Diploma, my life has changed immeasurably; for better, for worse, forever. Having entered the start of the Diploma a decade ago as what used to be described as a comms planner at one of the big media-buying houses, I write today as a cross-discipline Chief Strategy Officer, having being a brand strategist, a head of digital, and a creative director in-between, and these unique diverse experiences I've had the fortune to be a part of inspire my thinking every single day.

However, there's still a nagging frustration, and one that I fear I have been complicit in promoting during the earlier days of my career. It's the continued, dogged and persistent assertion that we can model what we do, or worse, reduce it down to a predictable process or a theoretical framework. Throughout those years, those jobs, those briefs, those clients, those wins, those loses and those brands, one single thought can be held aloft above all others. No matter what anyone tries to tell you: there is no panacea.

There's no grand unifying theory of everything in our business. No magic formula. No golden ratio. Agency X's proprietary process is no greater than Agency Y's brand framework. Not only does the rate of change around us render any such processes irrelevant almost as soon as they're written, the nature of our business is one of discovery, breadth, diversity, and of course, creation: traits that stubbornly, eternally and beautifully refuse to be confined and constrained by order and predictability. We are a business of people. Individuals, not algorithms. Every brief, brand, problem, person, task and team is different and needs to be treated as such.

This isn't to say we shouldn't pay attention to marketing theory and the scholars that seek to learn from rigorously analysed data. It's just to say that we shouldn't seek answers where none can exist.

So, based on this, where does that leave me with a brand new religion? Well, of course, brands can learn from religion. As brands can learn from almost any area of life if you look hard enough. The tenets that I outlined in my original essay – community, leadership, semiotics, sacred text, ritual and myth – continue to be interesting and useful pillars when it comes to brand building. But the problem is, when you start applying frameworks you start applying boundaries, and it's in this restriction of free thinking that homogeneity is bred. To continue the religious theme, beware false gods.

The IPA Excellence Diploma was a hugely challenging and enormously rewarding project. But its greatest advantage wasn't to be in the theory, the frameworks or the models, it was in its promotion of challenging free thinking. Paradoxically, adding to the pantheon of brand theory during the course helped free me of the shackles of it.

There's an oft-cited idiom in the reception of a dear place where I used to work. In their reception resides 'Blenderman'. Blenderman carries a briefcase upon which the plea 'Walk in Stupid' is emblazoned. And that's exactly what the Diploma helped me to do.

I believe in
a brand new
religion

Introduction

> A religion is a unified system of beliefs and practices relative to sacred things,
> ... beliefs and practices which unite into one single moral community called a
> Church, all those who adhere to them.
>
> (Emile Durkheim, 1912)[1]

You awake on the Sabbath. You join the congregation, where the minister
evangelizes about the benefits of being a believer. All around you, like-minded

FIGURE 5.1

BOOTS
NINTENDO
WALKERS
VODAFONE
SMIRNOFF
NOKIA
AMERICAN EXPRESS VIRGIN
PIZZAHUT MCDONALD'S
ADIDAS BRITISH AIRWAYS
SAMSUNG
NIKE
SONY
BURGER KING
PEPSI
ABBEY NATIONAL
L'OREAL
DELL
BARCLAYS
TESCO
COCA COLA

Design by Lewis Coe

people are sharing the same experience, hypnotized by what they are witnessing; people from all walks of life, all races and ages, bound together by the common desire to be a part of the collective experience. Once the speaker has finished espousing the virtues of faith and belonging, the collection plate comes around. But you're a believer, and the experience was good, so you happily part with your hard-earned cash. Enlightened, you leave the Apple Genius Bar[2] with your new purchase.

And lo, it was good.

Brands in the modern world

We find ourselves today in a society saturated by products, brands and commercial messages, and as such there is increasing resistance to commercial messages ('people are tiring of ads in every form'[3]), compounded by the unprecedented power consumers now have to edit paid-for communications out of their lives. As Naomi Klein states in her polemic *No Logo* 'logos, by the force of ubiquity, have become the closest thing that we have to an international language'.[4] It is no longer enough for brands to simply guarantee quality; consumers are acutely aware that own-label products are manufactured by the same factories that supply branded goods, and it is unusual to find a genuinely substandard consumer product. To continue to justify their existence (and their price premium), brands have to work harder than ever to engage and excite the public.

But just how can brands work harder? Obviously they have to deliver against all of the promises that they made during the 'trademark' age of branding, but in isolation increasingly this isn't enough. In the face of anti-consumerism, mass consumer choice, and cheaper, unbranded rival brands we have to offer more than functional and one-dimensional emotional benefits. So what is the key?

I believe that it's about transcending the physical product, and adding genuine, life-affirming value to people. It's about helping address the issues that modern life throws at you, and about navigating the world in which we live. It's about making a statement, and showing others who you are. It's about being part of the community, conversing with others who share your outlook. It's about being indispensable to a consumer. But just how is this achievable?

The opportunity for brands

We are no longer restricted by pre-ordained, society-imposed rules that may have shackled generations before us. Gender, age, race and other such 'definers' are rapidly decreasing in relevance. The formulaic and rigid rules of yore no longer apply. We have increased levels of opportunity and, within Western society at least, we are presented with almost infinite choice and options.

While empowering the individual, the changes mean that we don't have a set path to follow. Life is what we want to make it. However, with empowerment comes uncertainty. Psychologically, certainty and stability are important to us,[5] and when we do not feel fulfilled in these areas, we will look out for constants – points of reliability, familiarity, focus and guidance – that can address these deficiencies.

Religion, of course, will continue to fulfil this role in the lives of many consumers. However, we live – in the UK at least – in an increasingly secular society and some sources suggest that many people no longer actively engage in religious organizations or embrace a faith system as part of their lives; especially younger generations. BMRB data from 2006 shows us that in the UK, only 25 per cent of people under 35 see 'faith as an important part of my life' (with an index versus the UK average of 82) compared to over 33 per cent for the over 35s (index 108).[6]

But can brands also sate these requirements?

In the eight years since John Grant described brands as 'a set of ideas people live by',[7] the technological and social changes that helped define the 'third age' of branding have developed at such a pace that today brands stand in a position of potential power and relevance that has never before been possible. I firmly believe that as our societal waypoints erode and become less relevant to large swathes of the population, brands have an opportunity to occupy the resulting gaps that appear, and in turn, operate at a 'higher order cognitive state'.[8]

We can now begin to glimpse brands' potential as something much larger and more powerful than many of the more prosaic and practical descriptions would have you believe. Brands as multi-dimensional 'living, breathing entities'[9] that help shape how you live your life, what you do, what people think about you and what type of person you are. This is getting closer to the area that religion has traditionally occupied.

Religion: a sociologist's perspective

I started this essay with a classic summary of religion from Emile Durkheim: 'A religion is a unified system of beliefs and practices relative to sacred things, ... beliefs and practices which unite into one single moral community called a Church, all those who adhere to them.'

Durkheim never stipulated precisely what he categorized as 'sacred things' – other sociologists have gone so far as to include nationality, political activists, and professional sports within this phrase – and as such, I believe one would find it very difficult to argue a case for brands being excluded from this definition.

Durkheim also described religion as a socially constructed reality: 'an expression of our collective consciousness, which is the fusion of all of our individual consciousnesses, which then creates a reality of its own'[10]; that religion is essentially an innate product of society, a product of human nature, our fundamental desire to be part of the herd and our metaphysical need to find meaning within the complexity of life. While societal structures and technology may have developed immeasurably since Durkheim's day, the human condition and our innate wants and needs have not (Maslow's hierarchy of needs remains, for the time being at least, intact).

We are, after all, herd animals;[11] we still yearn to be part of a community, we still require structure, familiarity and security in our lives[12] (perhaps more so than ever in the post-modern world in which we now live). We will always seek to sate these requirements, whether it be through religion, or via another vehicle that can meet the requisite criteria (as, I shall go on to argue, carefully nurtured brands can).

The modus operandi of religion... a blueprint for brands?

Religions, regardless of when and how they formed, all have universal commonalities that create 'the experience' for the adherent or devotee. As we begin to explore exactly what brands can learn from religion, we need to understand what these universalities are and what their role is within the overall religious framework.

The core elements are:

- Leadership.
- Sacred text (containing either God's word and/or a set of guidelines to live by).
- Semiotics (Iconography and Symbolism).
- Ritual.
- Myth.
- Community.

Leadership

The concept of leadership – be it guidance from an inspired mortal or the recorded word of a deity – is central to any entity that purports to be a religious organization. From the anthropological curios of South Pacific cargo cults (ranging from the worship of the enigmatic 'John Frum' through to the slightly more familiar Prince Philip), to the major Abrahamic religions (in their worship of one God), every faith system ever recorded has had one or more figures of perceived divine ordinance whose word forms the very ethos of the movement.

There are a multitude of positions of 'leadership' in an organized religion. There is almost always a god or god-like figure (or in the case of polytheistic

FIGURE 5.2   Richard Branson: The Virgin 'god'

With kind permission of Virgin Group Ltd

faiths, more than one god), but beneath this, there are often sacred prophets or apostles, who hold a semi-divine position, right through to living representatives of the religion who hold a position of authority.

The idea of a business person or company representative as a type of 'divine leader' has a long heritage in brands and marketing. The archetypal examples are of course Richard Branson (Figure 5.2) and the late Steve Jobs, of Virgin and Apple respectively. They are physical embodiments of their brands, their companies infused with their own personality and ethos. Inspiring, passionate, seemingly benevolent and often, amazing considering the personal wealth of both, with a whiff of the underdog about them, both with evangelism skills outstripping the vast majority of religious preachers.

It could also be argued, however, that the position of commercial 'god' need not be a person. If the aura around a brand is strong enough (or could be built to be so), it is entirely possible for the brand itself to assume this role. Think for a moment about Nike. Although many could claim Nike to be akin to a 'religion' (and indeed, they may be correct), could it also not be as accurately described as a god? If the role of a 'leader' in religion is to provide focus, guidance and inspiration, isn't this exactly what Nike offers amateur sportsman around the globe, through their passion for running, technology to aid the athlete, and events such as Run London?

The criteria for success here is that the brand has something to stand for, an issue that is both relevant and motivating, and one that the brand can credibly link with. If achievable and delivered effectively, the common issue can provide a strong focal point which, if realized across other areas of the business, could certainly assume a position of 'leadership'.

Sacred text

A sacred text is often central to the culture and philosophy of a religion. From the Torah in Judaism through to the Scientologist Dianetics, the axioms by which adherents live their lives are captured within a core set of writings that usually have their roots in the leader or ancient founders of the movement.

As well as the words and principles of the sacred text being revered by adherents, often physical manifestations of the text will also hold a sacrosanct position within the religion; for example, worn-out copies of the Qur'an will be respectfully burnt or buried by Muslims, rather than simply discarded or recycled as one may do with other books.

It is the role of the sacred text (and what it contains) that is important to us in this context. All religions must provide a set of guidelines by which an adherent will – to a greater or lesser extent – live their life. While many will veer away from the path from time to time, or choose to interpret the often ancient words within a modern or liberal context, the guidelines will still remain an important structural element of any religious organization.

As mentioned earlier, the concept of 'brands as a set of ideas to live by'[13] suggests that perhaps these ideas should be recorded somewhere, in a way perhaps that the great religious texts record their dictum. Unusual and odd as it may seem for brands to physically script how their users should lead their lives (something that would seem slightly incongruous with the world of the modern, liberated and empowered consumer), the concept of adopting a certain tone of voice, and conveying a set of values in their communication, is certainly something brands do on a regular basis. To go back to Virgin, their communications are usually quite explicit in conveying the essence of the brand, traits that reflect the public personality of their god, Branson. By, in effect, communicating 'The Word of Branson' (albeit indirectly) through their brand communication (at every level – PR, advertising, point-of-sale) one could argue that every piece of messaging that Virgin Enterprises runs is consistent with the idea of a sacred text.

Semiotics

Renowned semiotician Marcel Danesi defined two of the major 'meaning of signs' as the icon and the symbol.[14] An icon is essentially like the thing it represents, for example the murti (figures of gods usually in a human-like form) worshipped by Hindus. (It is worth noting that this type of worship does not apply across all religions, with the worship of icons receiving accusations of idolatry from many.)

Symbolism is defined as a sign that represents or alludes to something else, for example, the Christian Ichthys, the Taoist Taiji or the Jewish Star of David, all of which are immensely powerful immediate signifiers of historical events, ethics, culture and of course religiosity.

The roles of iconography and symbolism vary from religion to religion, and operate sometimes in very separate areas, and sometimes overlapping (the areas of semiotics are not mutually exclusive). From a sociological perspective, both serve important roles in the development, maintenance and identity of the group. Inwardly (for the direct benefit of the individual or the close-knit group) they can serve as a point of focus and reverence, ranging from day-to-day reminders of their faith, through to glittering celebrations of the culture and belief system to which they subscribe. Outwardly (appealing to others) they are identifiers, badges that immediately indicate the group to which they belong, allowing others to draw from their own experiences, opinions and cultural references to instantaneously form a set of opinions about that person without meeting them.[15]

Semiotics and branding are inextricably linked. As we covered earlier, the earliest brands were guarantees of quality and authenticity: a promise that you were buying what you thought you were buying, and the hallmark of a brand, or the 'logo' (to use marketing parlance) was a simple semiotic shortcut to making this promise. The oft-cited 'Bass Red Triangle' of the mid-19th century is an early and archetypal example of this – the first major recorded instance of creating a simple image to represent a physical product.

Ritual

Sociologists argue that rituals can aid in creating a firm sense of group identity, and that humans have used rituals to create social bonds and even to nourish interpersonal relationships, both of which are fundamentally important in the formation, maintenance and development of a religious community.

There are two major areas of 'ritual' and both serve equally important yet often very different roles within a community. Broadly speaking, there are 'functional' rituals (eg those which serve a tangible purpose within a group, usually transmitted through a group generation to generation, the roots of which can be traced to a functional task or requirement), and there are 'mystical' rituals (those which have their roots in myth or magic).

Functional rituals: The Sikh Langar (Figure 5.3) is a good example of a 'functional' ritual. It is a 'free kitchen' – a meal open to anyone with every member sitting as equals, designed to promote 'the ethics of sharing, community, inclusiveness and oneness of all humankind'. Introduced by Guru Nanak in the 15th century, the Langar was intended to dissolve parts of the divisive caste system of India prevalent across previous generations.

Mystical rituals: John Grant defines rituals as 'formatted sequences of human behaviour designed to produce a psychological, physical and (in old belief systems) magical or metaphysical result',[16] a statement that perfectly captures the essence of the 'mystical' ritual. An extreme example of this type of ritual in religion would be sacrifice among ancient Shamanistic religions, often undertaken to purge the community of a perceived bad spirit or other malevolent force.

Ritualistic behaviour, both functional and mystical, is prevalent in our daily interaction with brands. The perceived perfection achieved by pouring a pint of Guinness 'just so' (119.5 seconds of carefully crafted beer theatre involving six key steps[17]) is a classic example of functional ritual. Thanks

FIGURE 5.3   A modern Sikh Langar

Virk, K (2007) Lagar Preparation at Guru Ram Das, Flickr, Licensed under CC BY 2.0

to this ideal preparation technique being purported through advertising, word-of-mouth, and skilled bar people around the world, the consumer expects their pint to be poured in adherence to the ritual. Of course, a pint poured carefully but not in strict observance of the technique is likely to taste as good (as tested in my own research group with friends at the local pub), but this would still be unacceptable to the Guinness connoisseur (or devotee).

Brand rituals purporting to elicit a metaphysical outcome are also common, and some advertisers have taken this search for a magical result as a central focus for their brands. The leitmotif of Lynx's brand communication is the notion of superlative sexual attraction in a can ('Spray More, Get More') and is intended to lead to a ritualistic use of the brand, essentially: 'Use Lynx before you go out and you'll be a female magnet'. Although there is no scientific evidence to suggest that the ritual will have the desired effect, the belief that it will is sufficient enough to encode this faith into a behavioural effect.

Myth

The realm of myth is one that is intrinsically linked with religion (as it is with brands). Myths are memes; by their very nature vague, polysemous and propagated only as transient cultural exchanges. It is, however, within these ambiguities that much of the magic of religion exists, to both the follower and the external observer.

In fact, myths form the very backbone of religious development. After all, it is via language (myth) that 'culture is transmitted, thinking develops and learning occurs'.[18] The stories that are passed down from generation to generation form the cultural essence of a religion, units of cultural currency imbued with both the experience and beliefs of current devotees as well as previous generations.

Douglas Holt describes the commercial building of a brand myth in his paper 'What Becomes an Icon Most'[19] when he discusses the ascent of soft drink 'Mountain Dew' to iconic status in the US market. Holt proffers the following description of the role of commercial myth: 'simple stories that help people deal with tensions in their lives.'[20] The route to achieving this, he argues, is (among others) to build myths that 'target national contradictions', 'lead culture' and 'draw on cultural knowledge'.

Mountain Dew built a myth around the 'country ideal', that 'virile guys live to play dangerously, not to sweat it out in the office',[21] conveyed through all of their communication, running completely counter to the prevailing city culture of wealth accumulation and self-aggrandizing. As Holt puts it: 'Mountain Dew championed the wild man against the emasculation of corporate work ... by asserting physical toughness and derring-do over the flaccid cowboys of Wall Street.'[22] A simple myth, based upon a potent cultural insight, carried the brand to enormous success – enough to rival the cola behemoths of Coca-Cola and Pepsi.

Community

Whether it is a physical gathering accommodated by an actual structure such as a synagogue, mosque or church, or a virtual congregation bound together by their common beliefs, the concept of community is fundamental in fulfilling the social cohesion role of religion discussed earlier.

As well as fulfilling a cohesive function, the interaction that occurs is also an important aspect of building the culture of a religion: the theory of 'social interactionism' asserts that the core development of the group (culturally, intellectually, etc) is driven by peer-to-peer interaction; learners constructing their own knowledge and understanding through participation and engagement with others.

As well as being vital for the nourishment of the wider group, the religious community also has an extremely important function on an individual level. Individual experience is magnified when encountered as part of the group,[23] and paradoxically this can lead to a purer, more condensed experience when part of the collective than when witnessed alone. An example of this is the famous Ardh Kumbh festival, where up to 70 million Hindus descend upon Allahabad in India to bathe in the river Ganges, in an effort to purge themselves of sin.

In the world of brand communication, the word 'community' is likely to crop up in just about any conversation with anybody who is active in this field. In the networked world, consumers are free to build links with anyone else, with communities springing up around every subject, mindset or ethos imaginable.

Harley Davidson and Apple are probably the two classic exemplars of brands that have a defined sense of community around them, with both exuding a set of clear, unifying principles that binds their users (in short, the idea of 'freedom and rebellion' for Harley, and the idea of 'liberation of creativity' for Apple). The commonalities between all of them seem to be[24]: the brand uniquely differentiates its users from the population/their peers, and the brand has mechanisms for consumers to engage in a public experience.

Communities are also incredibly important to brands as they have the capability to offer that most powerful of communication channels: word-of-mouth advocacy. Proven to deliver business gains (the London School of Economics reported in 2005 that a 7 per cent increase in word-of-mouth advocacy around a company unlocks 1 per cent additional growth),[25] it is clear that in the modern, networked world, harnessing consumer advocacy is more important than ever.

Conclusion

I believe that:

- Humans have an innate set of needs and wants that have remained, and will remain, constant regardless of social and cultural changes.
- Brands today have an unparalleled opportunity to transcend the product/service and operate at a 'higher-order cognitive state'.
- Analysing the modus operandi of religion yields a blueprint that can provide a framework for the building of indispensable, enduring and profitable brands.

Final note: All reference to religion and religious practices are written from an agnostic perspective and all due care has been taken to ensure that they have been correctly interpreted and represented within this work.

Notes

1 Durkheim, Emile (1912) *The Elementary Forms of the Religious Life*, George Allen & Unwin, London.

2 [Accessed 2007] Apple Genius Bar, *Apple* [Online] www.apple.com/uk/retail/geniusbar/: Taking 'retailtainment' to the next level, these stores offer lectures, seminars, one-to-one consultations with an Apple 'genius'. Apple devotees can meet up, experiment with the latest equipment, and discuss technical issues with experts. Some also run in-store Apple Summer Camps, where children are not taught about technology or computers, but are encouraged to explore and develop their creativity (www.apple.com/uk/retail/camp).

3 (June, 2004) The harder hard sell, *The Economist* [Online] www.economist.com/node/2787854

4 Klein, N (2001) *No Logo*, Picador, US.

5 [Accessed 2007] Social Psychology Network [Online] www.socialpsychology.org: Various Needs Theorists argue that consistency and stability is a fundamental human desire.

6 BMRB TGI Survey (2006).

7 Grant, J (1999) *The New Marketing Manifesto: The 12 rules for building successful brands in the 21st century*, Texere Publishing.

8 Harris, S (2004) *The End of Faith: Religion, terror & the future of reason*, The Free Press.

9 Grant, J (1999) *The New Marketing Manifesto: The 12 rules for building successful brands in the 21st century*, Texere Publishing.

10 Durkheim, Emile (1912) *The Elementary Forms of the Religious Life*, George Allen & Unwin, London.

11 Earls, M (2007) *Herd: How to change mass behaviour by harnessing our true nature*, John Wiley & Sons.

12 Maslow, A (First published 1943) 'A Theory of Human Motivation', *Psychological Review*, 50, pp 370–96.

13 Grant, J (1999) *The New Marketing Manifesto: The 12 rules for building successful brands in the 21st century*, Texere Publishing.

14 Danesi, M (1993) *Messages and Meaning: An introduction to semiotics*, Canadian Scholar's Press, Toronto.

15 Jamieson , H (2007) *Visual Communication: More than meets the eye*, Intellect Books, Bristol.

16 Grant, J [Accessed 2007, Blog] Brand Tarot [Online] www.brandtarot.com

17 Murray, F (March 2007) How to pour the perfect Guinness, *Esquire* [Online] www.esquire.com/the-side/opinion/guinness031207

18 Pachler, N (2005) 'Theories of learning and ICT' in M Leask and N Pachler (eds), *Learning to Teach Using ICT in the Secondary School: A companion to school experience*, Routledge, Oxford.

19 Holt, B (March 2003) What becomes an icon most? *Harvard Business Review* [Online] http://hbr.org/2003/03/what-becomes-an-icon-most/ar/1

20 *ibid.*

21 *ibid.*

22 *ibid.*

23 Pine, J and Gilmore, J (1999) *The Experience Economy*, Harvard Business School Press, US.

24 Kalman, D M (2004) 'Brand Communities, Marketing and Media', *Terella Media* [Online] www.terrella.com/wp-content/uploads/2009/01/kalman-brand-community-marketing1.pdf

25 Marsden, Dr P (September 2005) Advocacy Drives Growth, *London School of Economics* [Online] www.lse.ac.uk/newsandmedia/news/archives/2005/word_ofmouth.aspx

I believe communities are the future of brand communications

2007/08

JOHN V WILLSHIRE
Founder, Smithery

06

I believe The brand communications that evolved in the mass-media era are becoming more ineffective at changing people's perceptions of companies and brands. The connections people make and communities they form nowadays are increasingly where they source their information; people are influenced most by people and communities. I believe the future of brand communications lies in finding a way to become part of communities, and communicate with them in a way that is shared, participatory and reciprocal. In this way, companies can affect people's perceptions of them, and make all of their brand communications more effective.

Editor's therefore, for your brand...

Your brand thinking:
What kind of community
is your brand? What holds
it together?

Your brand engagement:
What can you create for
your community that is
genuinely useful?

**Your brand organization
& capability:** Is your own
brand team truly a
community or just
a loose collective of
separate disciplines held
together by a paypacket?

...and author's personal therefore

Why making things people want beats making people want things

A lifetime ago, I spent four years at the University of Stirling, a small feisty institution tucked down behind the sofa of civilization on the edge of the Scottish Highlands.

I was an inadvertent economics student. I'd originally gone to study English, but it was all talking and no writing. I tried politics, but that was soupy and inert. I fell into economics like a drunk in a village with one pub.

Thankfully, I can see now that 'the dismal science' taught me a tremendous amount that wasn't immediately obvious at the time. It's as if Mr Miyagi had been obsessed with price elasticity and GDP, rather than roundhouse kicks and catching flies in chopsticks. 'Tax On, Tax Off...'

For instance, it gave me various shorthand models and methods to employ when thinking about people, either as individuals (micro economics) or groups (macro economics), and how they react to changing circumstances.

It showed me the value in identifying which data you didn't have, as much as prizing that which you did. And it taught me that drawing and mapping things out helps you understand what might be going on, which in turn helps you explain those things to others.

All this helped tremendously when I came to write my IPA Excellence Diploma Thesis. Entitled 'The Communis Manifesto', it took the Latin root word for both community and communication, and showed the disparity between what the two things had evolved to mean for the brand world. At the heart of it lay this provocation: 'I believe that the future of brand communications lies in finding a way to become part of communities, and communicate with them in a way that is shared, participatory and reciprocal.'

Where has this idea taken me in the last six years?

My work: tone of action

Looking closely at it now, the central tenets of the manifesto seem pretty robust, especially looking at the world of brands today:

- Create inner belief, making sure a passion burns through the business.
- Spread the word, letting employees communicate this passion.
- Build relationships, with people on the outside of the business.
- Create community spaces, where everyone can mix and mingle.
- Allow messages to travel, ceding control over 'the brand'.

All very solid pointers that can be seen today as a multi-billion dollar industry, from social media start-ups to management consultancies, from the making of content to the measuring of effectiveness. Today, social business is big business.

Thinking back to 2008 though, you might have read that list and thought 'yes, but where does the brand stuff come in?' Fewer people used Facebook in the whole world than lived in the UK. Twitter had less than a million users. Myspace had already entered a terminal death spiral.

Back then, 'brand' for most companies was 'what we say it is', or more realistically 'what that onion that Chad presented in the last global marketing meeting said it was'. Nowadays, companies are a lot more open to the idea that everyone who is part of the company contributes to brand.

Yet some outdated models still hang on. For instance, take 'tone of voice'. If the internet is 'a dialogic space supporting the interplay of billions of voices' (Wegerif), then why would you pick just one voice to talk with (and a pretty generic one at that)?

What I've found more useful in my work over the last few years is the idea of a 'tone of action'. I try and help companies see that *everything* they do, absolutely everything, is part of the brand picture. Seeing that, and acting on it, gives them the best possible chance of deciding how their brand is perceived in the world.

This approach, however, means stepping into places that traditional agencies don't, won't or can't go.

My career: Smithery

In 2011, I started my own business, Smithery. It's founded on the principle that 'Making things people want beats making people want things'. To do this properly, you need to look at the whole picture of companies, the macro view. As a result, I've found myself working with all sorts of different people and in different spaces with organizations.

So far, Smithery has encompassed media communications, organizational design, new product development, lecturing at business schools, lecturing at art schools, culture change, interior design, service design, intranet design, field trips, account planning, corporate social responsibility, human resources, rest and recuperation, hack days, game design, manufacturing, blacksmithing (no, really), 3D printing, direct mail, art direction, social sector design, business mentoring, a smattering of art and even some illustration.

This sounds almost wilfully diverse, but the truth is it's all connected because it all feeds into what a brand is today; the sum total of all actions. In order to fully understand and explain this approach, I realized I need to think about it as deeply as I had 'The Communis Manifesto'.

So I've started writing a new thesis called 'The Relativity Matrix' (Figure 6.1).

The layers of an organization move at different speeds; the people layers, from slow to fast, are culture, leadership, marketing, commerce, actions. Then the space layers (again, slow to fast) are surroundings, structure, infrastructure, services, materials.

FIGURE 6.1

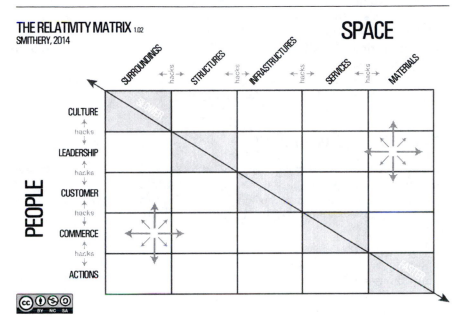

Put together, the two layers form a matrix which lets you see how everything that the people do in the spaces a company provides have relative effects on different parts of the business.

It then helps you make sure you're asking the right questions to change a company. For example, how do we change the day-to-day actions in a company by harnessing deeper cultural cues? What do our walls say about our relationship with the outside world? How do we supply the services for things we *might* make rather than the things we *do* make? What does local sourcing mean for us in different locations?

Working this broadly with so many different types of people only seems to broaden my own learning too. It's a much more interesting life too...

My life: meaning in production

So then, the life of a smith; what has 'The Communis Manifesto' meant for me personally? Clearly I'm doing new types of work, with a very different career path, but what does it mean for my life?

By starting afresh, and building a business slowly, carefully, and from the ground up, I think I've discovered a much happier route through life. You can work out the life you want to lead with your family, and design your work around that.

You can make the most of the technology, which means you can work anytime, anywhere, and free yourself from a daily routine that'll slowly kill you. You can bring together people you regard as heroes to work on projects then disband, like the *Avengers*, once the job is done.

Once you start to live in the long term, you begin realizing that the way to change things, for yourself and for clients, isn't to build another sort of business that burns brightly then sells to an advertising holding group after four years.

You can build a business you won't sell, create a job you'll never leave, and lead the sort of life you've always dreamed about.

What do I believe now...?

I have this idea about what 'Making things people want beats making people want things' means; rather than daubing fresh hieroglyphs on the tombs of brand gods people no longer worship, this new world is a place where we can explore making things fit for purpose if we work with people in the right way.

It's all about the people, and everything they do. That top-down, macro-economic view of the brand-as-community that I drew out six years ago in 'The Communis Manifesto' (Figure 6.2) is still one I truly believe in, but it's only now that I'm understanding and thriving in the complexity of it.

And I believe it because I see it every day. This stuff, it really, really matters, to all businesses and brands. But don't just take my word for it...

> What everybody wants to know about a brand is 'who are these people'? What motivates them? Why do they do the things that they do? What is their passion? What are their hatreds? Am I talking to real people, am I having a business conversation with real people, with a real voice, or is this some manufactured thing out of some system and process?
>
> I don't think we trust process. We don't trust communication that's been put together through focus groups and the rest of it. I want a human relationship, and that's what a brand is.
>
> If a brand isn't human, it isn't really worth shit.
>
> (Dan Wieden)

FIGURE 6.2

I believe communities are the future of brand communications

The words 'community' and 'communication' are both hugely important to the future of brands. Both stem from the Latin word 'communis', the root of many words we use today to describe people and the connections they make.

In its basic form, communis means 'common, public, shared by all or many'. While community is still used very much in this sense, communication has evolved into something very different. If we were to define communication properly, it would be as: 'a social and reciprocal act of participation, an act mediated by the use of symbols that have meaning among different individuals and groups.'[1]

However, in the context of brands and advertising, 'communication' in the 20th century evolved to mean little more than 'the sending of messages'.

This is not the result of manipulation by the owners of brands, but simply a result of how the communications landscape developed. Companies were schooled in creating and broadcasting homogenous, impersonal messages through a mass-media system.

Sending out identical brand messages to millions of people at once was a logical, efficient and effective course of action in a mass-media world.

People watched, read and listened passively and attentively. They did not expect the right to reply, never mind the ability to create and disseminate their own thoughts. But nowadays people *can* create, copy and distribute their own communications as far and as wide as any company, should they choose.

I believe that the future of brand communications lies in finding a way to make these communications shared, participatory and reciprocal. This involves companies becoming a credible part of the conversations; to do this, they first must understand why people form communities.

Why do communities form?

We have evolved as a social species and it has been the reason that we have done so well (Earls, 2007[2]); many, if not all, of our achievements would not have been possible without forming communities (Leadbeater, 2008[3]).

A community can be defined as: 'A group of people who form relationships over time, by interacting regularly around contexts which are of interest to all of them' (McKee, 2008[4]).

Drawing this out, there are three key elements:

- the people who form the community;
- the relationships they form to create and strengthen the community; and
- the context around which they form that community; the common shared interest.

If you imagine taking a crowd and gently pulling it apart, you will see the links between individuals in the crowd; these are the relationships we form with each other, around the contexts we are interested in.

We feel safe, we feel valued, and we work together to achieve what we cannot do alone. We also find that we affect each other profoundly when we talk to each other, share ideas and thoughts or give advice. In short, we benefit *from* being together, and we are influenced *by* being together (Figure 6.3).

FIGURE 6.3

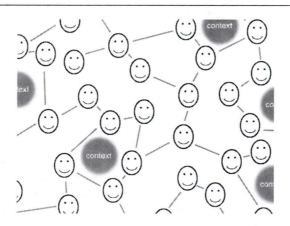

Coursing round this model are the conversations we have with each other and the communications we make. Each relationship we have, like it or not, affects the way we think (Earls, 2007[5]). Technology has fundamentally changed the way this works; it has taken the communication possibilities available to individuals to a hitherto unimaginable level, and it hasn't even finished evolving yet (Cerf, 2008[6]).

The network is linking us together in a completely different way; less encumbered by time, unrestricted by geography. But it still retains the same characteristics as smaller, pre-network communities.

The communities in each of these eras are distinctive because the communications available to people were so very different.

Changing communities

Before the industrial revolution communities were very self-contained. The *people* you could form a community with were restricted by both where you lived, and the social stratum you belonged to.

Being so close to your community, however, meant that *relationships* were very strong; all communication was face to face at places where people congregated, such as the market, the church or the local hostelry.

Word of mouth was hugely important, as it was the primary means of communicating information, particularly when the majority of the population was illiterate.

The *contexts* people formed communities around were also of local importance and central to how the community prospered (eg whose animals could graze upon the common and for how long).

Small communities were spread across the country with little in the way of communication to connect them; there was little chance to form communities around anything other than local concerns.

In this age 'brand communications', or how businesses and enterprises communicated their abilities and wares, were propagated by word of mouth.

Any local blacksmith, tavern landlord or shop owner realized that their participation in the local community was vital; as a business they thrived or died on their reputation in the local area. Their 'brands' were built through every interaction they had with the community.

This form of community and communication began to change with the industrial revolution, which revolutionized how products and services were created and sold.

Mass production meant identical goods could be rolled off a production line and shipped out to wholesalers and retailers, whereupon millions of 'consumers' across the country could buy the same product with the same guarantees of quality.

It wasn't just products that rolled off a production line, it was information too.

Creators of information invested huge amounts of money into the cost of production, for example journalists to report the news and printing presses to produce the newspapers (Benkler, 2006[7]).

More and more media forms were created and distributed like mass-produced goods: newspapers, radio, cinema, and television. People had access to national and international news, information and entertainment, a far cry from the information available to pre-industrial communities.

The mass media system dominated communications in the industrial era (Benkler, 2006[8]), and everyone across the country bought the same products and absorbed the same information... they became the same.

It was the age of homogeneity, and it made brand communications easy.

In order to capitalize on this, companies had to find something to fit within that system; every message to every potential customer had to be identical.

Brands solved this issue; at first companies created rudimentary, consistent stories about a product or service to appeal to as many people as they could (King, 1971[9]).

Brand communications were produced, copied and distributed across the country using the mass-media infrastructure.

It was very much one-way communication; people couldn't communicate back. But it didn't matter; they found these new god-like brands extremely reassuring; 'a badge or promise of certainty in an uncertain world' (Feldwick, 2002[10]).

In hindsight, it is no surprise that brand communications worked so well in this age. However a new era has arrived.

The network age

It seems passé today to speak of 'the internet revolution'. In some academic circles, it is positively naïve. But it should not be.

The change brought about by the networked information environment is deep. It is structural. It goes to the very foundations of how liberal markets and liberal democracies have coevolved for almost two centuries.

(Yochai Benkler, 2006[11])

We can now talk to anyone, anywhere, about anything we like; previous barriers to forming communities have been dismantled. The *people* who form communities can be anyone connected to the network;[12] many new communication tools available to us to create *relationships*, and the *contexts* we can gather around, can be anything we like, no matter how niche (Leadbeater, 2008[13]).

What's more, we can be connected to *many* communities at once; this composite identity making you entirely unique as an individual.

All of this has been made possible by the way technology has freed information from the mass-production model.

First, at home, most of us now have a machine capable of creating any number of communications. We can put together our own newspaper column in the form of blogs, produce new music, films and other audio-visual, and manipulate images and sounds that others have created. It is the democratization of creativity; the means of production are accessible to anyone with a £500 computer.

Second, with the advent of digital information formats, it costs nothing to copy information perfectly, instantly and as often as we wish. Think about how often you could copy a song from one tape cassette to another, then another, then another. Now compare that to how often you can with an MP3.

Finally, the network allows us to distribute whatever we have created or copied, as far and as wide as we like. Theoretically, we can pass the 'six degrees of separation' test perfectly; we e-mail *everyone* we know and tell them to forward a message to everyone they know, in the knowledge that the message will eventually get there.

With the means of production, duplication and distribution in the hands of the people, the people are not just passive 'consumers' any more.

The mass-information model has been weakened by technology; nowadays people can be involved in any stage of the information production process, even right from the very start.

With people creating and distributing their own information to communities, companies are in a difficult situation. They face an audience that not only has the means to form communities around any topic of interest they desire, but has the capability to produce communications around these topics and related brands and products.

Brands cannot afford to maintain a distant, faceless presence when people are having personal, instant, friendly conversations with each other and with the companies who already understand this. They have to change.

> The Earth has evolved a nervous system, and it's us.
>
> (Dan Dennett, 2008[14])

The 'wiring together' of communities in the network era is perhaps akin to the way the human brain works (Gordon, 2002[15]); the neurons are the people, the synapses connecting them are the relationships, and the brain area is the context.

This process is rapidly enabling society to evolve into a type of 'Hive Mind'; a collective consciousness where whatever one person knows, everyone else will soon know (if, of course, it is important enough). We've become a highly-connected, creative network of people, which matters for three reasons.

First, brand communications evolved around identifying a target audience and creating a communication that would appeal to as many of them as possible.

Targeting a group like '16-34 ABC1 men[16]' worked because every man within that audience was fed on a very similar diet of mass-media information, with identical cultural reference points. The goal was to create communications that would appeal to *enough* of a target audience to hit a set business goal.

However, society isn't as linear as it once was. The rise of niche communities means we can define ourselves by what we are interested in. The people we form communities with are a lot less homogenous than they used to be. Targeting by demographics is not subtle enough to connect to communities.

Second, the sheer volume and variance of the communications we now make is changing the nature of relationships; the barriers inhibiting word of mouth, such as location, speed and accessibility, are disappearing.

It's not just about the number of communications though; these relationships are not like the original 'face-to-face' conversations we had in previous eras.

They are a mixture of visual, audio, text or video, formal, informal, from friends, from strangers, long or short. And can be sent from anywhere you have network access.

Not everyone forms an equal number of relationships, just like Gladwell's connectors,[17] nor are they equal in the number of messages they send. But we are getting to a stage in the developed world that almost everyone is on the network, and almost everyone can find a community to join.

Finally, the network has freed us to come together around whichever contexts we wish, no matter how small and niche, or how few people gather around it. As we saw before, people can participate in many, many communities, so information can be passed through the entire network (Shirky, 2008[18]).

The mass-media age constrained this behaviour; anything too niche would be unprofitable for an information creator to get involved in producing, duplicating and distributing. 'We haven't had all the groups we've wanted, we've simply had all the groups we could afford' (Shirky, 2008[19]).

With the rise of niche contexts and the evolution of these other elements, companies must think differently about how they communicate.

Two levels of communication

Companies must operate at two different levels. First, there is the 'entity' level; the entity that is the brand speaks to the 'Hive Mind'. These are the traditional 'brand communications' crafted in bulk and aimed squarely at the majority of people.

If the 'Hive Mind' is already positively disposed to the company and the brand, it reacts favourably. If not, the communications are increasingly ignored.

Once, these same channels would then have been employed to *change* opinions about a company and its brands, but their power is waning. They are having less and less effect on people, because people are much more influenced by each other and by what they find out online.

In order to change opinions, companies must make greater efforts to engage at the '*community*' level. This is where communication, must become closer to the original 'communis' definition, and be 'a social and reciprocal act of participation'.

Think back again to the elements which form communities: people, relationships, context. To engage with communities, companies must:

- communicate with *people* as employees, not as the 'brand';
- encourage genuine, transparent *relationships* to form between employees and people outside the company;
- work *with* those people around *contexts* which are mutually beneficial.

Reaching out from within a company is increasingly becoming the only way to change perceptions of the company.

What follows is 'The Communis Manifesto', a set of five principles outlining how companies can allow and encourage their own community to communicate with others at the 'community level':

The Communis Manifesto

- create inner belief

- spread the word

- build relationships

- create community spaces

- allow messages to travel

Create inner belief

> If consumers know how a brand functions and how it 'thinks' and 'feels', then the new question that has to be answered is 'what does it "believe" in?'
>
> (Hamish Pringle and Marjory Thomson, 1999[20])

Any company is a community; groups of employees forming relationships around the context of what they do together.

However, where other communities are drawn together by an overwhelming desire to create, share and connect, companies are formed of people remunerated in exchange for their time and labour.

What we have seen over the last decade is the rise of companies who seek to combine the need to make a living with the same desires and beliefs that other communities have. These are 'passion brands' (Edwards and Day, 2007[21]).

Each 'passion brand' has a central belief in who they are and what they are trying to do. It transcends the traditional central brand team who use 'brand values' in 'entity' communications; it is something that resonates with every single employee in the organization. As an example, let's look at a successful network era business, Google.

Google is a great community to become a part of[22]; the work is 'challenging and interesting', the culture one of 'autonomy and empowerment', and everyone is on a mission 'to organize the world's information and make it universally accessible and useful'.[23]

People are trusted to interpret this together as a community, in whatever tasks they undertake.

Google has been highly successful in building a community of brilliant, dedicated people, united by a common desire to make things better for everyone.

FIGURE 6.4

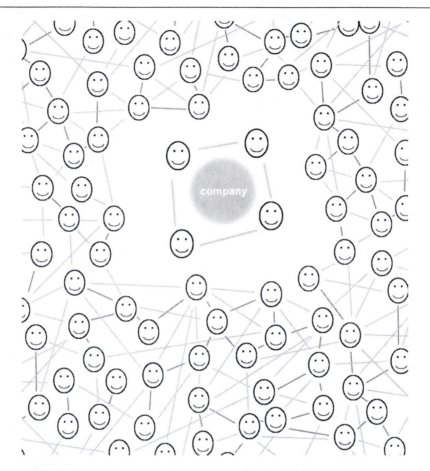

It is this form of infectious brand spirit that companies must capture at the centre of their community; the first audience for articulating and embedding brand beliefs must be a company's own people.

For companies created in the network era this sort of behaviour comes almost naturally. The challenge for industrial era firms[24] is to evolve their industrial business structures (Leadbeater, 2008[25]) into something that allows their employees to feel as warm as possible towards the brands they help create (Ind, 2007[26]).

Spread the word

Employees have always been one of the most powerful brand communications tools available to companies (de Chernatony and McDonald, 2003[27]), but nowadays it is more important than ever.

Every time people come into contact with employees, an impression is given about the company they represent, whether they are the dealers on a forecourt, an employee in a call centre, the blogger writing from inside a company or the designer speaking at a conference.

Recently, the biggest change is just how far employees are able to go in expressing themselves; they are just as willing and able to produce, duplicate and distribute communications as other people in the network age.

By letting employees take control of what they say, a company feels more like a community rather than a faceless entity.

This is what William Sledd did for Gap.[28] He was a store manager who started a video blog on YouTube offering fashion advice and opinion in short, six-minute shows. He put forward his honest views on fashion and the products Gap got right and wrong.

Additionally, because of the medium he used, people could comment back, interacting directly with someone inside the Gap community. So far there have been nearly 19 million views of his 58 shows.[29]

It is vitally important for companies to encourage employees who see the value in communicating with the wider world. They are the employees who:

- are passionate and enthusiastic;
- are community minded;
- are creative in their use of communications;
- have a multi-tasking mindset;
- have the ability to think outside the box;
- are already heavily involved in social networks; and
- already maintain ongoing relationships.

Whether it is the marketers who change the way they converse with customers, engineers who start contributing to open-source projects or product designers who co-create the next widget for a company with the wider community, employees must be allowed to build relationships however they see fit.

Build relationships

Why would people be interested in building relationships with employees from a company? Think about what people seek from establishing relationships: 'Social media users interact to find friendship, and friendship requires that you have something interesting to bring to the conversation' (Jimmy Maymann, 2008[30])

It is a form of 'permission marketing' (Godin, 1999[31]); if employees can provide something interesting, entertaining or useful in a community, they will be welcomed as a friend and given permission to continue talking to the community.

What a company can bring to a community that is of interest is a 'social object' (McLeod, 2007[32]); the thing that brings people together in conversation.

An example is the beta version of Last.FM.[33] When a new version of the software is being developed and before it is completely finished, Last.FM invites members of the 'beta group' to test it first.

They spot mistakes, make improvement suggestions and debate which fixes are the priorities, in order to make the product better. This builds trust between the loyal users and Last.FM; the users feel that they are contributing to something that they feel as passionate about as the employees themselves.

In order to let employees have conversations like these, be it about product testing, supporting causes, or even creating brand communications, companies need to give their employees five things:

- Trust – don't seek to control every employee communication.
- Access – encourage employees to use new communication tools.
- Time – make communication with communities part of everyone's job.
- Freedom – remove unnecessary bureaucratic or legal procedures.
- Transparency – don't expect people to be company mouthpieces.

The more that employees and people converse, then the more likely, willing and able they will be to form new communities around contexts related to the company and its brands.

And as employees connect with communities and relationships develop, a company will see an increase in advocacy by those people who communicate with employees.

Create community spaces

Once relationships develop between employees and people, companies can forge a real sense of community by creating places where everyone can gather around the contexts they care about. For instance, this could be a physical gathering, like 'the Innocent village fete' or perhaps online places where people can regularly interact, like Dell's 'Ideastorm'.[34]

Whether it is a celebration of a product and ethos that everyone believes in, or an online forum to improve customer service, these spaces offer a chance for employees and people to get together and have the conversations that lead to the formation of communities.

The communities then start to show their real worth; people and employees can *create*, *duplicate* and *distribute* a company's communications, or even its products, together. And what's more, the people from outside your company will be more likely to spread your messages further of their own accord.

Allow messages to travel

It is not simply the close community constructed by employees and people who are buying the products; there is a wider group of people who still need to be influenced who will not create and contribute as that core have done. 'The message that travels is the one that is created by the consumer, not the brand' (Steve Knox, P&G Tremor Unit[35]).

What companies must do is enable the core to connect with the wider audience to spread the warmth. It is the complete relinquishing of control of the communications about the company and brand: 'a social and reciprocal act of participation'.

Take this example of something created at the same time as the launch of Apple's MacBook Air. It's a direct remake of the TV ad which showed the MacBook Air being taken out of an envelope to emphasize how thin it was, and it's called MacBook Paper.[36]

It is not something that would have ever come out of the company itself, of course; a marketing department would have worried about the implications on product perception.

But someone who is clearly warm towards Apple has used the company's own images to create a *version* of the product message, which nearly 250,000 other people then watched.

Though these people did not participate themselves, they were reached not by the company, but by the person who took materials and inspiration from the company and created their own version, spreading their advocacy of the Apple brand.

FIGURE 6.5

Allowing messages to travel in this way is the final step in connecting to communities; let the people who are warm towards you spread this warmth however they choose.

In conclusion

The Communis Manifesto[37]

Entity communications are increasingly failing to change peoples' beliefs about a company, product or brand; it is people who have the biggest influence on people. It is only by creating warmth at a community level that broader communications will be welcomed, believed and acted upon.

A company's communications must be social and reciprocal acts of participation. In order to achieve this, companies should follow the principles laid out here, in 'The Communis Manifesto':

- Create inner belief among employees.
- Spread the word with every contact your employees make.
- Build relationships with the people who share your passions.
- Create community spaces to share and develop those passions.
- Allow messages to travel as far and as freely as people wish.

Notes

1 Giuntarelli, P, Nature in the City, *RomaNatura Regional Park Authority* [Online] www.fedenatur.org/docs/docs/334.pdf

2 Earls, M (2007) *Herd: How to change mass behaviour by harnessing our true nature*, p 31, John Wiley & Sons, Chichester.

3 Leadbeater, C (2008) *We-Think: Mass innovation, not mass production*, Profile Books, London, pp 93–95.

4 McKee, J [Accessed 2008, Online] The Community Guy (Blog) www.communityguy.com/

5 Earls, M (2007) *Herd: How to change mass behaviour by harnessing our true nature*, John Wiley & Sons, Chichester, p 31.

6 Cerf, V (August 2008) If you thought the internet was cool, wait until it goes space age, *The Observer* [Online] www.theguardian.com/commentisfree/2008/aug/17/internet.googlehttp://www.theguardian.com/commentisfree/2008/aug/17/internet.google

7 Benkler, Y (2006) *The Wealth of Networks, How social production transforms markets and freedom*, Yale University Press, US, p 30.

8 Benkler, Y (2006) *The Wealth of Networks; How social production transforms markets and freedom*, Yale University Press, US, p 30.

9 King, S (1971) 'What is a Brand', reprinted by *Campaign* in October 2007 [Online] www.campaignlive.co.uk/news/743160/

10 Feldwick, P (2002) *What is Brand Equity, Anyway?*, WARC.

11 Benkler, Y (2006) *The Wealth of Networks: How social production transforms markets and freedom*, Yale University Press, US, p 1.

12 Source: Ofcom 2008 Communications Market Report [Online] http://stakeholders.ofcom.org.uk/market-data-research/market-data/communications-market-reports/cmr08/

13 Leadbeater, C (2008) *We-Think: Mass innovation, not mass production*, Profile Books, London.

14 Dennett, D (2008) [Quote from TV series] *The Genius of Charles Darwin*, IWC Media.

15 Gordon, W (2002) Brands on the brain (Chapter 7) in *Brand New Brand Thinking: Brought to life by 11 experts who do*, ed M Baskin and M Earls, Kogan Page, London.

16 [Accessed 2008, Online] NRS Social Grade [Online] www.nrs.co.uk/

17 Gladwell, M (2000) *The Tipping Point: How little things can make a big difference*, Abacus, US, p 38.

18 Shirky, C (2008) The 'Small Worlds' theory (Chapter 9) in *Here Comes Everybody: How change happens when people come together*, Allen Lane, UK.

19 *ibid.*

20 Pringle, H and Thomson, M (1999) *Brand Spirit: How cause related marketing builds brands*, John Wiley & Sons, Chichester.

21 Edwards, H and Kay, D (2007) *Creating Passion Brands: How to build emotional brand connection with customers*, Kogan Page, London.

22 Murray, S (May 2008) Google: Success can be a game with many players, *Financial Times*.

23 [Accessed 2008] Company Mission, *Google* [Online] www.google.co.uk/about/company/

24 Fawkes, P (June 2008) How Long Can P&G Last?, *PSFK* [Online] www.psfk.com/2008/06/how-long-can-pg-last.html

25 Leadbeater, C (2008) *We-Think: Mass innovation, not mass production*, Profile Books, London, p 88.

26 Ind, N (2007) *Living the Brand: How to transform every member of your organization into a brand champion*, Kogan Page, London.

27 De Chernatony, L and McDonald, M (2003) Chapter 6 in *Creating Powerful Brands*, edn 3, Butterworth-Heinemann, Burlington, MA.

28 Meyers, M (August, 2007) Fashion guru revels in Web catwalk, *CNET News* [Online] http://news.cnet.com/Fashion-guru-revels-in-Web-catwalk/2100-1025_3-6201484.html

29 Source: William Sledd [Accessed 2008] YouTube channel [Online] www.youtube.com/profile?user=WilliamSledd

30 Maymann, J (2008) *The Social Metropolis*, Go Viral, p 12.

31 Godin, S (1999) *Permission Marketing: Turning strangers into friends and friends into customers*, Simon & Schuster, London.

32 McLeod, H (October, 2007) More thoughts on social objects, *Gaping Void* [Online] www.gapingvoid.com/Moveable_Type/archives/004265.html

33 [Accessed 2008] Last.FM Beta group [Online] www.last.fm/group/Last.fm+Beta

34 [Accessed 2008] IdeaStorm, Dell [Online] www.dellideastorm.com/

35 Ackerman, W (April 2008) WOM Lessons from P&G's Tremor Unit, *Social Media Playground* [Online] www.socialmediaplayground.com/industry-news/wom-lessons-from-pg%E2%80%99s-tremor-unit/2008/04/28/

36 MacBook Paper, (January 2008) *Apple* [Online] www.youtube.com/watch?v=i6yBo9NPkCQ

37 Levine, R, Locke, C, Searls, D and Weinberger, D (2000) *The Cluetrain Manifesto*, Perseus Books, US.

07

I believe brands should go supergnova
2013/14

JAMES BORRODELL BROWN
Senior Strategist, Zone

I believe Our new ability to instantly access the world's knowledge is a game-changer for society and brands. Knowledge is now our primary identity signal – what we choose to know personally is key to who we are. Brands, however, are busy **pumping** junk knowledge into the world. For a brand today to claim it stands for something, it must create new knowledge that can't just be looked up and give it away.

Editor's therefore, for your brand...

Your brand thinking: What can we learn from histories great knowledge-centres, eg the library in Alexandria, the British Museum, the Smithsonian?

Your brand engagement: What knowledge is your brand a true guru in? And how does it share its 'wisdom'?

Your brand organization & capability: How do you ensure your knowledge is not lost? Do you need a chief knowledge officer in charge of both knowledge of the consumer and for the consumer?

...and author's personal therefore

I'm writing this barely a fortnight after publishing my thesis, at the end of July 2014. The response has been bewildering.

I can sum it up with this example conversation.

The IPA, the judges, the trade press... our industry: 'We really love your piece. We think you're on to something.'

Me: Oh, thanks! What was memorable for you?

'We love the idea of tacit knowledge. That the most valuable stuff today is what you can't write down easily or just look up online. And about how tacit knowledge doesn't work at all when it's constrained by a piece of paper or a fixed-length TV spot.'

'Great! That's exactly why I created the paper as an interactive website, so I could include links and comments and such. So that anyone could quote it, steal it and remix it. And so that the industry and my colleagues could easily access the ideas at any time.'

'Right! We want to celebrate and distribute your piece. Please can you send us a 750-word version to be printed in *Marketing*, a 3,500-word version to go in our nice new book of the decade, and a big 7,000-word version to be printed in a *Campaign* supplement?'

The problem is worse than I thought

Not only are brands and agencies producing stuff that consumers don't want – what I call junk knowledge – but our entire industry is stockpiling its best thinking in the same, impractical way. We're set up to fail.

It's true that there is value in writing something that's going to be set in stone, especially when it has your name on it. These words are going into a book, and once they're printed I won't be able to change them. Just like the Diploma, it has made me stop and reflect much more than usual. What is it I really want to say?

But this isn't just another case of digital versus print. The problem is the process and our traditions. We're not organized for communicating the kind of tacit knowledge necessary for us to improve our work, and our supplies of best practice exist to preach, rather than to teach.

Surely this is an absurdity: the words I'm writing now won't be read by anyone for eight months! Today, consumers demand access to knowledge as soon as it's available. So I plan to publish this myself in the next few days.

Worse still, when I take a look at my day-to-day work, I find that most of my output (a brief, say, or a deck, or a report) is structured in the same kind of junk format.

Written down and printed out on a piece of A4, static, fixed in time, and delivered in a discrete package of words and pictures. These are unable to contain the kind of tacit knowledge I believe is critical for our industry's success.

So here's my plan.

A living, contemporary thesis

Communicating tacit knowledge is like training an apprentice. What would it mean to turn my website into a digital apprenticeship?

To start, it can't just hold a fixed and ageing 7,000-word essay. So by the time you read this, **http://gosupergnova.com** should be more like a magazine or resource hub.

Every day I see more examples that develop my argument, and have thoughts that extend the idea in interesting ways – now they will have a public home.

I also plan to start a podcast. It will be a series of short interviews and round-tables with colleagues, clients and others who agree and disagree with me.

Rather than organizing my ideas as an academic essay to be marked by a panel of judges, I'll arrange them as evolving themes that can be extended and remixed by others. Not just words. Photo galleries, quotes, videos, audio clips, animated gifs and conversation snippets.

This should make it more accessible and digestible, and help to structure questions and comments from others. I'll rope in some friends and colleagues to be guest editors.

Writing my original essay certainly helped clarify my thinking about brands and the work ahead for our sector. But I can't think of a worse format for publishing and distributing the tacit knowledge it contains.

Making tacit knowledge work

I've started using my new creative brief, the knowledge brief, with my clients. And my colleagues are testing it out too, giving me advice and questions for improvement.

How does this work for an always-on social strategy? Can we turn this into a workshop? How do we help our clients to figure out the secret tacit knowledge they didn't know they had? What processes should we put in place to restrict the amount of junk knowledge we're creating?

As we work all this out together, I'll be updating the documents and making them available.

My paper contained a new job description, for a senior knowledge planner. Truthfully, it was a description of the skills I wish I had! So I'm adding them to my personal development plan, and helping my colleagues to learn these skills too.

Education, semiotics, linguistics, anthropology – I want to understand these subjects well. I want to become expert at tools that get at what knowledge customers want, and how they show it off to others.

Now here's a tricky one: the actual output I create, all those static documents and reports and presentations with limited sell-by dates.

The number of times I've heard (or written myself) that 'this report will be a living document, which we'll return to and update regularly'. It never seems to match reality. Why is that? Figuring this out is vital, I think, to understanding how I can make tacit knowledge a fundamental part of my work.

Partly it's about technology and culture. Our company templates are in Word and PowerPoint, which don't lend themselves to nuance, creativity or revision. More than that, though, it's about the transactional, fixed-term relationships we have with our clients.

That's the biggest 'so what?' I can think of, that follows from my essay: we should charge our clients for the knowledge we give away, not the stuff we create.

I believe brands should go supergnova

I don't want you to read this essay. It's not meant to be read like this.

Because today, knowledge simply doesn't work very well for us when it's constrained by a piece of paper.

We explore and we look things up. We search, and browse, and follow our noses when things intrigue us. We demand multiple sources and perspectives. In a store, a third of us would choose to consult a smartphone rather than talk to a store employee.[1]

That's why this was originally created as a website. If you visit **http://gosupergnova.com**, you'll find an essay that's full of links, and has all these interactive comments and side notes, and audio clips, and YouTube videos, and a couple of animated gifs.

You can still read this version, of course. But you can also pop open your laptop or your phone. You're in control, which makes sense: today, we make our own decisions about how we want to consume knowledge.

> **gnostic** (adjective) /'nɒstɪk'/ – relating to knowledge, especially esoteric knowledge. Late 16th century (as a noun): via ecclesiastical Latin from Greek gnōstikos, from gnōstos 'known' (related to gignōskein 'know').

Most brands today are what I call agnostic brands.

They don't understand the knowledge space they are in, they don't keep up with knowledge that consumers expect of them, they don't contribute any new knowledge to the world, and they make false claims about what they know and believe in.

In short: they are weak brands, and they have little to offer consumers today outside of the functional, ie as an aide-mémoire and choice shortcut.

Some brands, however, have gone supergnova, and are finding ways to do the exact opposite. They understand what knowledge consumers want and expect of them, and are giving it away.

These brands are creating and providing new knowledge that consumers can't get any other way, which helps them to understand and signal their identities. This kind of knowledge is the new value-add, the new 'function-plus' that brands can help deliver, and to which customers can emotionally connect.[2]

> Knowledge is of two kinds. We know a subject ourselves, or we know where we can find information upon it. (Samuel Johnson, 1775)[3]

I believe the most significant recent development in society is our easy, instant ability to access knowledge. Led by the rise of personal, internet-connected devices, everyone knows where to find information upon any subject. And they can access it whenever and wherever they want.

With access to this ever-growing trove of information, we are approaching omniscience. We have what I call 'bottomless knowledge'.

Anecdotally, this absolutely rings true. Consider the pub arguments we used to have about what year a film came out, or whether it won an Oscar. Just look it up, stupid! Bottomless knowledge is a tap away. 'Hey Siri, what's the capital of Honduras?'

This has now reached the point that if you ask the world a knowledge question, it will roll its eyes and look at you with disdain. Try out **www.UseTheFuckingGoogle.com** on your lunch break.

Bottomless knowledge is a game-changer for society

Access to bottomless knowledge has happened so quickly, and its consequences are so deep and diverse, that I don't think we as a society (let alone the marketing/advertising industry) have really processed it all yet. It's fluid and happening around us right this moment.

It has deeply changed our understanding of privacy (eg Edward Snowden), copyright and intellectual property (eg the EFF), politics, activism and democracy (eg the Arab Spring or the Occupy Movement), trade and the economy (eg the rise of collaborative consumption) and more. It has profound effects on the nature of trust, lies, authority and expertise.

Knowledge is a moment away, and increasingly comes to us without asking (just try watching a hit TV show a week after everyone else). There is only so much time in a day. So the subjects we choose to know intimately have become key to who we are.

With such a superabundance of bottomless knowledge available, what do we choose to keep in memory, and say that we know personally?

Knowledge is now our primary identity signal

Today we experience a general pressure to be on top of knowledge, and to have perfect, up-to-date knowledge wherever possible. 'Oh, didn't you know?' is a cruel and embarrassing question to endure. The urge to check our e-mails, to check the score, and to know what's happening is addictive and strong.

That's because if we say something is important to us, then we are expected to know about it. You say you love West Ham football club, but you didn't know the final score from a couple of minutes ago? You didn't even know that the manager changed last week? Be real. You're no fan.

And since knowledge is now the most informative identity signal, other people are busy trying to understand what you know about. They'll find it by looking at what you say and do, and what others have said about you too.[4]

So it has become vital to keep a handle on what knowledge signals exist about you, and manage them appropriately.

How can brands add any value in a world where knowledge is bottomless and super-abundant? What kind of comms cuts through in this kind of culture? And how can brands help people to navigate more skilfully?

Tacit knowledge is the richest signal

There are many ways of categorizing knowledge. The most useful distinction is between explicit and tacit.[5]

Explicit knowledge is anything that has been articulated, written down or stored somewhere.

Classic examples include assembly instructions for a bookshelf, textbooks, manuals and newspapers. Modern-day examples are livestock tickers and sports scores, a photo album of a holiday, or a social media comment.

Explicit knowledge forms the vast majority of knowledge available to us at any time, and it has grown at an extraordinary rate. Ninety per cent of the world's explicit knowledge was created in just the last two years.[6]

Tacit knowledge is knowledge that can't be easily communicated or obtained. It is highly personal, and very difficult to capture.[7]

For example, I could read 100 books about karate, but that wouldn't make me a sensei. I can't speak Russian by rote-learning the grammar and the vocabulary. And I can look at plenty of photos of the deep jungle, but as long as I haven't spent a week in a tent surrounded by spiders, I can't say that I truly know it.

Acquiring tacit knowledge takes time, experience, and close contact with people who already have it. It might take days, years, or even a lifetime.

In a world where explicit knowledge is super-abundant, tacit knowledge has scarcity value and is a much richer identity signal. It's the stuff that you can't just Google and look up.

This distinction should seriously worry us.

Our industry is in the habit of creating explicit knowledge and paying to put it in front of people. But, like the invention of the photograph dealt an existential punch to the painted portrait,[8] so a world with access to bottomless knowledge, and its super-abundance, is throwing our traditional brand communications model into crisis.

Tacit knowledge is where we can help consumers to understand and signal their identities. But it cannot be transmitted via a one-off broadcast campaign.

Go supergnova

So here's how to actually do it. Three steps:

- Step 1. Prove you get it.

- Step 2. Cut down on your junk knowledge.

- Step 3. Create new knowledge and give it away.

Step 1. Prove you get it

To say that your business stands for something greater than your products – to even have a brand at all – now means proving you've got the knowledge.

Sometimes proving that you've got the knowledge is less about what you say, and more about what you leave out. Danish science writer Tor Nørretranders invented the term 'exformation' to describe the idea.[9]

Unlike information, exformation is the stuff you leave out. Sometimes just a few words carry an enormous amount of knowledge. This keeps communication succinct, but it also creates a personal connection. It's like having a private joke.

For brands, this means understanding the language and knowledge space of your consumers and then using communications that show that you get it.

For example, when Budweiser first began sponsoring the Premier League – the first US brand to do so – they ran ads openly admitting their lack of expertise in the beautiful game: 'You do the football, we'll do the beer.'

By claiming to have no expertise with football, and acknowledging that they could not possibly have acquired true tacit knowledge about football in their short time as sponsors, they actually proved they had the knowledge. Slick.

In February 2014 Budweiser announced they were ending their UK football deal, which has paved the way for bigger things. They are sponsoring the World Cup in 2014, 2018 and 2022.[10]

Step 2: Cut down on your junk knowledge

As marketers, it's easy to think that we also have an infinite number of bullets in our marketing guns. As the third IPA Datamine report put it: 'There are few hotter topics in marketing these days than how to make best use of all the communications channels available to us.'[11]

With an increased number of consumer touchpoints, well-orchestrated multi-channel campaigns do have better cut-through and effectiveness (on the whole) than single-channel ones. But it's misleading to conclude that we must therefore pick up the machine gun and hold down the trigger.

Indeed, I believe much of our communications to consumers is giving them what I call 'junk knowledge'. Just as it's possible to add sugar, caffeine and fizz to a glass of water, so the same can be done to knowledge.

Witness the meteoric rise of news magazines like *Buzzfeed* and *Upworthy*, that have found ways to sprinkle sugar on the light knowledge that they're giving away.

By turning articles into Top 10 lists, photo galleries, or animated gifs, and using competitively emotive headlines, they have created a copywriting arms race. '9 *Out Of 10 Americans Are Completely Wrong About This Mind-Blowing Fact*.' '*Baby Polar Bear's Feeder Dies*.' '*25 Really Engaging Images About The Minimum Wage (as part of our series sponsored by the AFL-CIO)*.' And so on.[12]

But it's a very short-term hit. You read it, and you're on to the next. It only works because they're publishing hundreds of articles a day.

Songwriter John Roderick puts it nicely. 'As a culture, we're satisfied with worse, because there's so much more of everything. Nowadays, with everything we do, we're just flipping through index cards.'[13]

This is a warning sign for our industry. Many of our techniques for achieving cut-through (ramp up the emotion, the weirdness, the number of channels used) are based around conceits, exaggerations, or outright lies.

We need to cut down on our junk knowledge and remember that we have limited ammo. We're focusing on recall, but a better, longer-term goal is to focus on creating and sharing quality knowledge.

Consider the runaway success of near-live fact-checking services like FactCheck.org, an independently-funded group that monitors the factual accuracy of what's said by US political players, Channel 4's Fact Check blog, or the UK-based independent FullFact.org.

If customers can debunk any of our claims at any time, doesn't that make us look a bit stupid and vain for trying to win them over with false claims?

Step 3: Create new knowledge and give it away

We know more than we can tell.

(Scientist and philospher Polányi Mihály, 1958[14])

Tacit knowledge is intimately personal and stuck in our heads. It's knowledge that we know we have, but struggle to describe – like catching a ball, or picking out a rug that pulls a room together.

Tacit knowledge should be a fascinating concept to the communications industry. We spend our working lives working out the best ways to convey indistinct information. No doubt some of the brands we work on have been building up tacit knowledge for generations.

But we hit a problem right away. A defining feature of tacit knowledge is that it cannot be comprehensively articulated. How can it be transmitted at all?

Craftsmen and women regularly deal with this problem, as veteran workers are required to pass on their skills. Factories often attempt to do this by trying to write it down, or filming a mechanical replication. But this always seems to lose its 'feel' – a simulation just isn't good enough.

Academics, philosophers, management consultants, teachers and HR specialists have spent considerable time working on this puzzle. Here follow five different techniques, with suggestions for applying it to our discipline.

A close interaction over time

Transmitting tacit knowledge requires the close involvement and cooperation of the two subjects involved, over an extended period of time.[15] For example, to truly say you know Berlin, New York or Tokyo, you really need to live there, or stay over with someone who does.

Airbnb have captured this brilliantly with their recent campaign aimed at Londoners who crave that knowledge. As an Airbnb customer, you get to stay in a real Berlin house, and meet a real Berliner. By being so close to the real thing for a whole weekend, they are saying, that tacit knowledge is going to filter into your brain by osmosis.

FMCG brands, despite typically being purchased and used without too much thinking, are actually well placed to use this technique. Think how many hours you spend with Colgate or Kellogg's every day, over many years.

Imagine a campaign about the knowledge that you can only get by sitting round the breakfast table, however briefly, with your family every morning. Those fools who get a snack bar on the run are missing out.

Build up a shared understanding

When a subject is so complex and thorny that talking about it seems impossible, teachers, diplomats, negotiators and lawyers begin by agreeing some basic terms of reference.[16]

I know I'm not meant to use Dove Real Beauty as an example in a marketing paper, but... I believe one of the unexplored reasons for its success is that it provided a new language for all of us in society to talk about feminism and the female body in culture.

In its own way, it articulated something that a huge number of us had felt, but weren't sure how to express. It gave us a way to signal our knowledge.

Rather than trying to find a quick bit of added reach in earned and shared media, we should be measuring our performance by the extent to which the language of our marketing becomes long-term vernacular.

Create an apprenticeship

Polányi speaks highly of apprenticeships and mentoring. 'By watching the master, and making efforts in the presence of his example, the apprentice picks up the rules of the art.'[17]

Whether they realized it or not, Nike Football have created an apprenticeship scheme for us to learn from the masters.

They show us what the dream is like, what the masters do, what their incredible life is like. It's the kind of tacit knowledge that we can never attain, but Nike Football gives us a glimpse.

In 2009, they created the Nike Football Academy – a real-life, pro-level training programme that helps unsigned under-20 players find a club, organized by Nike. Who else could get Mourinho, Rooney and Ronaldo to pop over and coach for a weekend?

Their online shop follows this model right the way through to purchase. Not sure what to buy? Well, have a look through a Barcelona player's kit-bag, or what the pro players use just for their boring, everyday training.

Design it from scratch

Sometimes there's a business opportunity that means having to educate consumers – here's something you didn't even realize you could know about. New knowledge can be captivating, and 'transforms the entire slate of the knower's mind'.[18]

We can learn from inventive broadcasters, who have helped set the bar in this area.

Classic FM, for example, has spent 22 years teaching a generation the tacit knowledge of classical music. Reading a book about classical music only gets you so far, and they have found success by framing it as a relaxing hobby.

Channel 4's brilliant Paralympics teaser campaign, 'Thanks For The Warm Up', accompanied their moving superheroes spot. They followed it up with a round-up show called 'The Last Leg', featuring chat and stand-up from a one-legged man. It regularly pulled in over a million viewers each night of the games, and is now in its fourth series.[19]

This witty, self-deprecating take on disabilities gives viewers the knowledge and confidence to talk about inclusiveness, resilience and sport in a new way. Channel 4's willingness to trail-blaze has improved our society, and has been rightly praised for its commitment to communicating this complex tacit knowledge.[20]

A new type of creative brief

Often all it takes is some new documentation to change the way an agency behaves. So here's a new way of thinking about the creative brief: the knowledge brief. (It's also available as a Word document or pdf template with a pre-filled example from **http://gosupergnova.com**). Try asking these questions.

- What knowledge does our audience want and why?
- How/where will they be signalling this knowledge?
- What explicit knowledge do they expect of us?
- With so much junk knowledge, how can we be expert?
- Who else is giving away knowledge? (our competitors)
- What tacit knowledge do we have, to give away?

A final thought

Brands help us to see, feel, know and signal our place in the world. This hasn't changed. But access to bottomless knowledge has changed the nature and content of these signals, and as brand managers we must adapt.

There's a small company in Worcester called BeerBods, who for a small subscription fee will send you 12 beers in the post every 12 weeks. It's not like the Wine Society, though.

Everyone drinks one beer a week – the same beer, often at exactly the same time on the same night – as the story behind the beer is revealed. It has quickly turned into a remarkable community of (mostly) blokes, chatting online about the beer and whatever else comes to mind.

The whole concept is based on a brilliant insight. These 30-year-old-ish guys are settling down, aren't going out to the pub with their mates as much, and are losing their knowledge about beer and the latest banter.

Wait. Actually, it's much more than that. They worry they are losing knowledge about being a man.

And this brand is helping them to get it back, and to grow it anew. It's guiding them to the kind of knowledge that's profoundly personal to their lives, and giving them ways to signal it.

Today that kind of brand behaviour has a deep power to it. That's what it means to go supergnova.

Notes

1 (April 2013) How mobile is transforming the shopping experience in stores, *Think with Google* and *M/A/R/C Research* [Online] www.thinkwithgoogle.com/research-studies/mobile-in-store.html

2 King, S (1971) *What is a Brand?* London: JWT [Online] www.campaignlive.co.uk/news/743160/

3 Boswell, J (1791) *The Life of Samuel Johnson*. Fittingly, all of the knowledge contained in his book is now available to the world for free, thanks to Project Gutenberg, the world's first and largest single collection of free ebooks.

4 For more on this read Buckley, P (2012) Exploiting the implicit, *IPA Excellence Diploma President's Prize*.

5 Saint-Onge, H (1996) Tacit knowledge the key to the strategic alignment of intellectual capital, *Strategy & Leadership*, **24** (2), pp 10–16.

6 Dragland, A (May 2013) Big Data, for better or worse: 90% of world's data generated over last two years, SINTEF [Online] www.sintef.no/home/Press-Room/Research-News/Big-Data

7 Polanyi, M (1958) *Personal Knowledge: Towards a post-critical philosophy*, University of Chicago Press, Chicago.

8 Smith, Z (November 2008) Two paths for the novel, *The New York Review of Books* [Online] www.nybooks.com/articles/archives/2008/nov/20/two-paths-for-the-novel/

9 Nørretranders, T (1991) *The User Illusion: Cutting consciousness down to size*, Viking.

10 (February 2014) Budweiser ends FA Cup sponsorship after three years, *BBC News* [Online] www.bbc.co.uk/news/business-26087337

11 Cox, K, Crowther, J, Turner, D and Hubbard, T (June 2013) *Datamine 3: New Models of Marketing Effectiveness*, IPA.

12 [Accessed 1 March 2014] upworthy.com

13 Hurley, M (January 2014) Primary source material, an interview with John Roderick, *CMD+Space* [Podcast] http://5by5.tv/cmdspace/77

14 Polanyi, M (1966) *The Tacit Dimension*, University of Chicago Press.

15 von Krogh, G, Ichijo, K and Nonaka, I (2000) *Enabling Knowledge Creation: How to unlock the mystery of tacit knowledge and release the power of innovation*, Oxford University Press.

16 Eraut, M (2000) Non-formal learning and tacit knowledge in professional work, *British Journal of Educational Psychology*, 70 (1), pp 113–36.

17 Polanyi, M (2002) (1958) *Personal Knowledge: Towards a post-critical philosophy*, Routledge, London.

18 Kierkegaard, S (1978) Søren Kierkegaard's Journals and Papers: Autobiographical, 1848–1855, Vol. 6, Indiana University Press.

19 Holmwood, L (September 2012) Now C4 head for Hills, *The Sun* [Online] www.thesun.co.uk/sol/homepage/showbiz/tv/4531225/Channel-4-bosses-want-to-sign-up-Aussie-Last-Leg-host-Adam-Hills-for-David-Letterman-style-show.html

20 Nunn, G (September 2012) Language, laughter and Paralympics, *The Guardian* [Online] www.theguardian.com/media/mind-your-language/2012/sep/06/language-laughter-paralympics

PART TWO
What is a brand idea?

Introduction:
I believe we must abandon 'either or' and embrace the power of 'both and'

DAVID WILDING
UK Planning Director, Twitter

One of the quickest and most helpful ways of assessing the quality of an idea can often be to imagine that you're seeing it executed by a competitor and asking yourself whether you'd honestly be bothered – or indeed whether you'd even notice.

Working on Sainsbury's for five years this inevitably came to be known as the 'Tesco test'.

When reading again the papers in this section, the first thing that struck me was how each passed a mini version of the Tesco test with flying colours. How I wish I'd thought of that argument, made that point, or put something in such a fresh and incisive way as the author had done.

Because – as you'll see when you tuck into the essays in this section – there are few things more refreshing than the brightest thinkers in our industry challenging conventional wisdom and holding previous thinking up to scrutiny.

Each of the papers on brand ideas that you're about to read got me sitting forward excitedly and had my mind racing in new directions.

Each inspired me to reach my own 'and therefore', simply by being so challenging, well-argued and provocative.

And each asks big questions about the role and importance of brand ideas.

But what's particularly interesting to me is that they pose as many questions as they answer. And indeed they often take opposing views on the same subject – reflecting the increasingly glorious complexity of modern brand ideas.

For example, to what extent do people genuinely engage with brands and brand ideas? And to what extent do they want to? And, therefore, should we be encouraging people to think more about marketing or recognizing that they're actively avoiding it altogether?

You'll read one view stating that people will do almost anything to avoid brand marketing (and therefore that active ideas are far less important than latent associations), and another arguing that in this 'era of marketing' people are not only embracing marketing, but increasingly competing with brands in their daily lives.

And the questions, and very smart (if apparently contradictory) perspectives, keep coming.

In an era of hyper-authenticity should brands be adopting more human behaviours as many argue? Or – if anybody can be human and there's no distinctiveness in it – should they in fact seek to be Superhuman and seek to deliver the extraordinary?

Should brands seek to be a force for good and come across as the good guy on your side? Or does endless positivity from brands paint them into a restrictive, undifferentiated corner? Is bad therefore more compelling than good and what can brands achieve by embracing their dark side?

Should brands be ceding control to their audiences and embracing the principles of trans-media planning, as laid out so thoughtfully in Faris Yakob's piece? Or are they in fact better served clinging on tightly to the reins and demonstrating extraordinary control?

As we hear more and more about the importance of storytelling for brands – should we be embracing this and creating brand myths and brand fiction or, given that the unconscious makes so many decisions for us, does the spectacular over-commitment demonstrated in the best brand's body language say much more than words ever could?

Is the role of any brand idea ultimately simply to grab people's attention and to get the brand noticed and remembered? Or are we all guilty of being far too fixated on short-term noise and under-valuing permanence?

The era of 'both and'

What I find so fascinating about these questions is that at various moments on various different brands I could easily have answered yes to every single one of them – despite their very different perspectives on how brand ideas work.

And that, for me, is my main takeout from these essays. We live in a connected world where everything is essentially additive, and everything is commented on, and where apparently contradictory perspectives can, do and should come together to create a positive friction.

For me the very best brand ideas happen when we abandon traditional and conventional 'either or' thinking and embrace the power of 'both and'.

Brand ideas are ever more important.

My own belief is that it has never been more important to work consistently around a strong brand idea, and for the people coming into contact with it to have a very strong sense of what business a brand is in – less in terms of its vertical category, but more in terms of the role it plays in people's lives and the things that it enables people to do.

And, as this is a fundamental reason why the brand exists, this business, once defined, should be adhered to consistently – or be 'time binding' as it is brilliantly put in the excellent 'What's the long idea?' essay in this section. And in a fragmented world this brand idea is more important than ever in uniting and linking an entire company or organization together.

But that's very different to saying that a brand's behaviour and communication should be restricted, predictable and templated. In fact, I'd argue that one of the main benefits of having a consistently defined 'long idea' is that this enables a brand idea to be flexed and shaped according to context – and in today's super-connected, super-fast communication landscape this brings with it significant advantages.

While perhaps not always to everybody's tastes, UK brands such as Paddy Power and Specsavers know exactly what business they're in (mischief and avoiding short-sighted mistakes respectively), and also know exactly how to flex this business consistency to lean into, or even to create, events that are talked about in wider culture.

So I guess that my own 'both and' – inspired by these essays – would be around consistency and context.

You will have your own of course, and may well find yourself fundamentally disagreeing either with me or with the views expressed in these essays.

But what you certainly won't feel is short-changed by the originality and application in these essays, or the imagination and quality of the writing.

I believe the children are our future

2006/07

08

FARIS YAKOB
Founder and Principal, Genius Steals

I believe The emergence of the internet has shifted the way people who grew up with it consume, manipulate and propagate ideas, and the way that brands express themselves must change in response to this new kind of 'idea consumer'.

Editor's therefore, for your brand...

Your brand thinking

Your brand engagement

Your brand organization & capability

Your brand thinking: What part of the future of your market is already with you?

Your brand engagement: Who are the 'change-makers' and leaders in your market and how do you engage with them?

Your brand organization & capability: Do you ever research the next generation of your users? Do you ever talk to your audience's children?

...and author's personal therefore

Time flies like an arrow. (Fruit flies like a banana.)

It's been almost a decade since I wrote my credo. The present we live in was just presenting itself. It's 2006, 40 per cent of people in the UK have broadband (remember dial-up?). No iPhone. YouTube has just launched. Twitter launches in July (I joined in December.) In September, Facebook opens up to users outside academic institutions. Sony and Fallon begin their hot streak with Balls. A little-known agency called Crispin Porter Bogusky had begun theirs. Droga founds Droga5 and pretends to tag Airforce One. In a participatory media environment everyone has a voice and there is ever greater emphasis on doing things in the world.

Work: for the new idea consumer

The key strength of the agency business model is the ability to partner.

Many hands make all work. No man is an island, and nothing, not even the words I'm writing now, come solely from one mind, one pair of hands. I have been privileged to be involved in pieces of work I'm proud of, and every piece is the effort of a much larger team than you would imagine, from the outside looking in.

Turning a television script into a film contest – yes, I still champion the creativity of people (formerly known as the audience) – featuring then king of Twitter Ashton Kutcher, launched with a tweet. Helping the McCann office win its first cyber lion at Cannes. Acting as pundit on morning television for the Super Bowl, an advertising phenomenon I had never experienced before. Trying my hand as creative director, creating a documentary series, born for and of the web, for BMW. Building various teams and departments: social, digital, content, software, hardware. Creating a 5.9-second film contest, the year before Vine launched. Consulting on and featuring in *The Greatest Movie Ever Sold* by Morgan Spurlock. The brand *accessions* tracking of my paper became the social media reporting industry. Co-author of *The Digital State: How the internet changes everything* (Kogan Page), a sequel to my thesis; nominated for marketing book of the year. Creating new processes for agencies; crafting new product stories for P&G in China; pitch consulting for an agency in London from a beach in Bali.

Career: creating new roles and agencies

An industry that developed in the age of passive idea consumption will need to undergo a similarly seismic shift in order to successfully connect brands to active idea consumers.

A decade is a long time in advertising.

Communication Strategist at Naked Communications; London, then Sydney, then NYC. Sometimes dubbed ninja, forever embarrassed. Armed with an accent and an armful of articulated beliefs. The world's biggest advertising market – half of all global advertising spend. Everything is larger, budgets are the biggest. So many more options, on every shelf of the super-market. So. Many. Ads.

Approached to be Chief Digital Officer of the world's largest advertising agency, McCann Erickson. They found my IPA diploma thesis intriguing. Championed an exploration of new ways of working, edging a venerable tanker. I learned about how the mega agencies operate, at what speed and scale. Named one of 10 modern-day Mad Men by Fast Company. Madness.

Chief Innovation Officer (they love their titles) of the MDC network, catching the swan song of the creative director of the decade. Founded an agency, Spies & Assassins, looking to communicate with Arduino & Code, alongside Art & Copy. Lucky enough to speak all over the world, about the future, about the ideas I began to develop for the Diploma. Judged awards, chaired the Integrated Clios Jury, worked with the London International Awards to create the *new* category – championing evolutionary ideas in advertising.

Sold my stake in Spies. Founded Genius Steals with my partner – a strategy and innovation practice. Went fully nomadic. We wander – exploring, taking on projects, partnering with brands, agencies and rebels; searching for the awesome, to help build futures for the industry, learning more about business as we continue to build our own.

Life: digital enabled

The future is already here – it's just not evenly distributed.[1]

So I went looking for it – Sydney, NYC. The biggest agencies, holding companies, cultures: SXSW; TEDx; meet ups; Clios; One Show; organizing Twestival; advising Social Media Week. I met other explorers searching for substance, for a satisfying intersection of the new media technologies, people and brands. Met a nice girl from Nashville. Last year I proposed, we travelled Asia, feeling ignorant about half the world's population. Wrote a series about the future of travel for Fast Company. Started an agency together and kept moving, rolling from project to project across the USA. As I write this, we're in London, just married, working on clients in LA and NYC, digitally enabled, for the next month or two. I've just signed my name at the bottom of a book contract, with this very same publisher, now I have to deliver my chapters. Then, who knows? The world is connected, the dream of tele-working, itinerancy almost, enabled by the digital present that was emerging in my paper all those years ago.

I believe the children are our future

> *The future is already here – it's just not evenly distributed.*[2]
>
> **(WILLIAM GIBSON)**

Introduction

In which we consider prospection

Prospection, the act of looking forward in time, is a quintessentially human endeavour. In fact, some consider it *the* quintessential human endeavour: 'The human being is the only animal that thinks about the future.'[3]

The brief is an expression of the industry's collective desire to steer its own path into the future: as Alan Kay said, 'the best way to predict the future is to invent it'. We can motivate ourselves by imagining less pleasant tomorrows, of eroding relevance and margins, and thus engage in prudent, prophylactic behaviour.

It is by exploring how ideas function, how ideas such as brands influence behaviour, and how this is changing in the face of a new kind of consumer, that we will be able to explain that the future of brands is, quite literally, in the hands of the kids.

I believe the children are our future

In which we examine the titular proposition and consider the pitfalls of prognostication

I believe a generation has risen since the emergence of the internet that is different in the way in which it consumes, manipulates and propagates ideas, and that the way that brands express themselves must change in response to this new kind of 'idea consumer'.

We will demonstrate how this shift in behaviour will affect the future of brands by addressing the following:

- The new active idea consumer.
- Why the shift to active consumption is a discontinuity, which has created a digital divide.
- What a medium is and how this has changed.
- What communication is.
- What ideas are and what makes them successful:
  - function
  - form
- What kind of ideas brands are.
- How the form of a successful idea is dictated by its context.
- What the new characteristics of successful ideas are.
- What this means for communication planning.
- What these ideas look like.
- Why this requires new success metrics.
- What the implications are for the structure of agencies.

The digital divide

In which we argue that the shift to active idea consumption is a discontinuity and meet the 'Massive Passives'

In 2001, a challenge issued to the US educational system introduced us to *Digital Immigrants* and *Natives*:

> Today's students have not just changed incrementally from those of the past, nor simply changed their slang, clothes, body adornments, or styles, as has happened between generations previously. A really big discontinuity has taken place. One might even call it a 'singularity' – an event which changes things so fundamentally that there is absolutely no going back. This so-called singularity is the arrival and rapid dissemination of digital technology in the last decades of the 20th century.
>
> (Pensky, 2001)[4]

Interactive communication technologies have fundamentally altered the way in which thinking patterns developed in the generation born since their widespread adoption. Rupert Murdoch popularized these terms in 2005: 'A new generation of media consumers has risen, demanding content when they want it, how they want it, and very much as they want it.'[5] In Murdoch's speech to the American Society of Newspaper Editors he said 'Like many of you in this room, I'm a digital immigrant... My two young daughters, on the other hand, will be digital natives. They'll never know a world without ubiquitous broadband internet access... We may never become digital natives, but we can and must begin to assimilate to their culture and way of thinking.'[6]

For the medium term, the communication industry must embrace the fact that there is bimodal consumer base. For some we need to consider the brave new 'world of platform-agnostic content [and the] fluid mobility of media experiences',[7] but the majority will continue to operate much as they always have. Having grown up with an essentially passive relationship with media, the shift to becoming an active consumer of ideas is neither likely nor desirable.

So when planning for mass market brands today, we need to keep the 'Massive Passives' (consumers who have grown up in a passive media culture and have a primarily passive relationship with it) in mind, but we shall leave them here as a remnant of the present and continue our journey into the future.

FIGURE 8.1   Bimodal consumers and the Generational Chasm

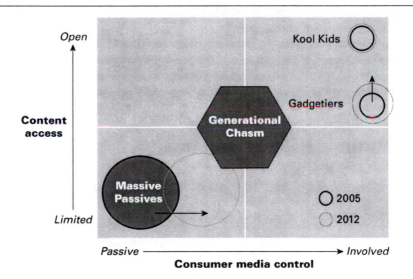

SOURCE: IBM Institute for Business Value

IBM Business Consulting Services (2006) The end of TV as we know it: A future industry perspective, *IBM Business Consulting Services* [Online] **www-935.ibm.com/services/us/imc/pdf/ge510-6248-end-of-tv-full.pdf**

The end of TV as we know it: A future industry perspective, shows the slight shift towards controlling their own media experience that the Massive Passives are projected to make by 2012. It is important to note that they will not reach levels of control over their own media experiences that the younger generation have already achieved by 2005.

The new media

In which we establish that a medium is a vector for ideas

As with a great deal of the key terminology of commercial communications, a medium is a poorly defined concept.

For our purposes, a medium can be considered a technology for storing or transmitting ideas – these are principally made up of language, text, sound and audio-visual imagery, although increasingly diverse iterations of these vectors are beginning to develop – ask yourself if a game or an event sits comfortably in these categories.

Hyperfragmentation was the first effect of digitization. It's important to consider, as it begins the journey towards consumers controlling their experience of ideas: fragmentation leads to choice and choice requires action.

With the emergence of interaction, new cultural behaviours began to develop that changed the way people dealt with ideas – media changed from passive to active. Once ordinary people were able to take control of the means of production and distribution, what had once been mass media became the media of the masses.

The important aspects to consider when looking at the media landscape are the behaviours it engenders, not the technologies themselves. We need to understand what communication is, what made ideas successful before, how this applies to brands, and then look at how this has changed.

Communication is persuasion

In which we suggest that all communication is persuasion

> Go ye into all the world, and preach the gospel to every creature
> (Mark 16:15, King James Bible)

Communication in its broadest sense can be defined as any means by which 'one mind may affect another'.[8]

Commercial communication can be described as the 'dispersion of persuasive symbols in order to manage mass opinion'.[9] However, this persuasion element is embedded in the notion of communication.

Humans have an inbuilt desire to spread their own ideas. There are compelling anthropological reasons for this. We pass on ideas in order 'to create people whose minds think like ours'[10] because this delivers an evolutionary advantage: there is safety in numbers.

All communication could therefore be understood as persuasion, rendering the idea of 'hidden persuaders'[11] either nonsensical or absolute. Every communication interaction is structured to optimize its persuasiveness – the form, language and structure of this essay is a specific attempt to make you, the reader, agree with the ideas that are being proposed – and that structure needs to be tailored to the audience: 'If you wish to persuade me, you must think my thoughts, feel my feelings and speak my words' (Cicero).

Ideas

In which we look at what ideas are and establish what success is

> And as imagination bodies forth
> The forms of things unknown, the poet's pen
> Turns them into shapes, and gives to airy nothing
> A local habitation and a name
>
> (Shakespeare, 2002[12])

Due to the objective of commercial communications – to influence mass behaviour, usually purchase behaviour, efficiently – the sort of successful ideas we need to understand are ones that establish themselves in the collective consciousness, propagate themselves and influence behaviour as they go.

The oldest, most successful idea in history provides a perfect example of how ideas worked in an oral culture. 'The Golden Rule' is a fundamental moral principle found in all major religions in almost the same form: 'Treat others as you would like to be treated.'[13]

Its prevalence is a clear indication of its hold on the collective and, as the foundation underlying religion, it is hard to envisage a more potent agent of behavioural change.

Like many of the ideas that have stuck for thousands of years, The Golden Rule is aphoristic. Proverbs are the oldest class of successful ideas, nuggets of wisdom that transcend centuries and cultures. The success of these ideas is driven by *function* and by *form*.

Choice paralysis

In which we see that the function of successful ideas is to save us from decisions

Choice is paralysing. We believe that we want the freedom to make our own decisions, but too many choices makes us anxious and leads to counter-intuitive behaviour.

A supermarket study involving choice of jams showed that although more shoppers were attracted by 24 varieties of jams on one stand, only 3 per cent of them bought any of the jams displayed. On the other hand,

30 per cent of the shoppers who stopped by the stand that offered only six varieties of jams bought some.[14]

Proverbs are successful ideas because they guide decisions. Whilst expressed simply, they contain complex ideas that function as heuristic devices for various situations.

At the supermarket, brands perform the same function.

The role of brands

In which we challenge the myth of simplicity

Things should be made as simple as possible – but no simpler.

(Albert Einstein, 1934[15])

There is an accepted notion that communication must be simple. This idea is reductive and misleading. Proverbs have simple forms, but contain complex ideas. Cervantes called them 'short sentences drawn from long experience',[16] a description that equally applies to a well-honed brand proposition.

A proverb is expressed simply, but contains ideas that build on what people already know (in the case of The Golden Rule, it relies on someone knowing how it feels to be treated themselves). By leveraging lower-level cognitive schemas, they express higher-level ones succinctly. When expressed abstractly, as in the proverb 'A bird in the hand is worth two in the bush', they function as generative metaphors, a term used to describe metaphors that generate 'new perceptions, explanations and inventions'.[17]

Similarly, brands are ideas that simplify choices, compress complexity and build on what consumers already know. They are compact and abstract, taking complex notions and packing them down; side-stepping into other territories to make them more tangible, they enable people to avoid making decisions from first principles, and they take on symbolic associations that allow us to employ them in the construction of our own identity.

Ideas made flesh

In which we analyse the form of ideas and determine how this has changed over time

We have established the underlying function that successful ideas, proverb or brand, share. However, the forms in which these ideas are communicated are very different. Aphorisms are specific expressions, ideally suited to propagation by word of mouth. They are dense generative metaphors, phrased in order to optimize storage in the mind and transmission – having a consistent and mellifluous form, they are Homer's 'winged words', flying from one person to another.

The form successful ideas take is delineated by the dominant communication technologies of the age.

Writing and the printing press enabled significantly more complex ideas to propagate across time and space.

The development of mass media heralded the Golden Age of brands and the forms that developed then are the forms we still recognize today – advertisements.

If a brand proposition is a proverb, an advertisement is a parable: it applies narrative or abstraction, or both, as devices to bring ideas to life in a memorable way.

It is not solely the medium itself that dictates the form ideas need to take; it is the *context* in which they operate.

The form is delineated by the relative scarcity of the vector – commercial broadcast time is limited and thus ideas are packaged into 30-second sound-bites on radio and television.

The arrival of the internet as a dominant communication technology thus effects not just how ideas are made flesh online, but also how all other channels will be used. The relative scarcity of media through which to communicate ideas has begun to vanish and we have an extraordinarily efficient way to store, access and transmit ideas. Rather than media, in the digital world attention is the scarce commodity.[18]

Traits of the emerging media landscape

In which we propose the new characteristics of successful ideas

The emerging media landscape, the context in which ideas exist, is qualitatively different from what has gone before because it is intrinsically active. Brought up online, the young naturally construct their own paths through media, branching hypertextually[19] from site to site. It follows, therefore, that the future of brands is participative. There are some key characteristics that will define the form of ideas, and thus brands:

- Convergent: every idea, story, brand and relationship will play itself out across the broadest range of channels, requiring a corresponding increase in the complexity and quantity of brand narratives.
- Recombinant: 'The remix is the very nature of the digital.'[20] Normalised via Ctrl C and Ctrl V, a generation has emerged that naturally treat ideas themselves as recombinant and as inputs to further remixing.

- Networked: media technologies are increasingly interconnected, allowing the effortless flow of content from person to person, or increasingly from many to many, replacing the sender/receiver mainstream media model of old.

Additionally, the internet has triggered a dismantling of the notion of authority that is also pertinent to the future of brands. The internet disrupts the notion of the expert, since all information is now accessible to all, and the increased transparency it has brought about has been accompanied by an erosion of trust in traditional authorities, such as government, corporations and traditional media, with a corresponding rise in trust in 'other people'.[21] Traditional singular authorities have been displaced by the authority of the collective.

In order to create ideas that leverage these new characteristics, we need a new model for communications planning in a converged culture.

Transmedia planning

In which we propose a new model for communications planning and use it as a live example of a successful idea

In October 2006, I wrote a post that outlined a new model for communication planning. The idea was built upon the transmedia narratives proposed in Convergence Culture, combined with Johnson's complexity arguments. A version of that initial post follows.

> Jenkins describes The Matrix as a transmedia narrative – a story that unfolds across different platforms.
>
> Rather than there being a film narrative that has spin-offs, key elements of The Matrix story are in the video game, animations and comic books. He argues that few consumers will be able to dedicate the time required to get the whole picture, which is why transmedia storytelling drives the formation of knowledge communities and triggers word of mouth.
>
> Since there are so many elements to the story, every member of the community is likely to have something to share, some social currency, so communities form and ideas are passed around the network. How might brands operate in this convergence culture?
>
> The model that has held the industry's collective imagination for the last few years is media-neutral planning. This is the belief that we should develop a single organizing thought that iterates itself across any touch point – a reaction against previous models of integration that were often the dilution of a television idea into channels that it wasn't suited to.

Media Neutral Planning looks like this:

FIGURE 8.2

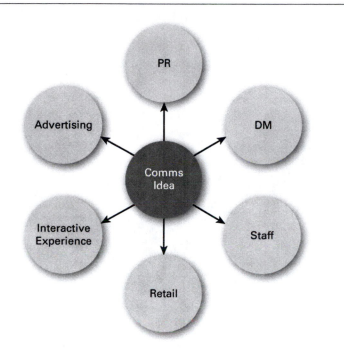

There is one idea being expressed in different channels. This is believed to be more effective as there are multiple encodings of the same idea, which reinforces impact on the consumer.

Now let's consider *transmedia planning*. In this model, there would be an evolving non-linear brand narrative. Different channels could be used to communicate different, self-contained elements of the brand narrative that build to create a larger brand world. Consumers then pull different parts of the story together themselves.

The beauty of this is that it is designed to generate brand communities, in the same way that The Matrix generates knowledge communities, as consumers come together to share elements of the brand. It generates endogenous word of mouth[22] by giving people something to talk about.

So transmedia planning looks like this:

FIGURE 8.3

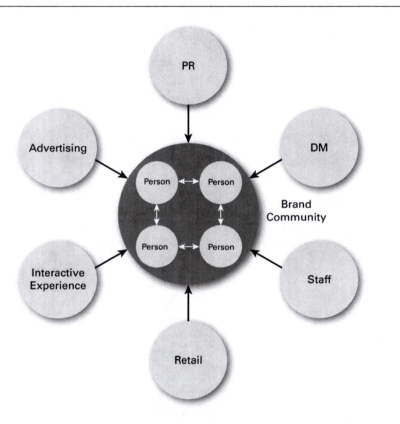

It gathered momentum and spread among a defined audience – the communication industry. The original post was voted Post of the Month[23] and was covered by dozens of blogs. The idea was presented at the APG 'Battle of Big Thinking', where it began to evolve into a separate strand called 'Propagation Planning',[24] based on the second half of the idea about tapping into consumers who are actively passing on brand messaging to each other.

The author of *Convergence Culture*, Henry Jenkins, Director of Comparative Media Studies at MIT, picked up the idea and posted about it on his blog,[25] where he further developed it:

> Will transmedia branding make a lasting contribution to contemporary marketing theory? It's too early to say. As an author, I am delighted to see some of my ideas are generating such discussion. As someone interested in marketing my own intellectual property, these discussions are themselves a kind of transmedia branding: after all, the more people talk about my book, the more people are likely to buy it. I don't have to control the conversation to benefit

from their interest in my product. The key is to produce something that both pulls people together and gives them something to do.[26]

Ideas from the future

Some examples that leverage active idea consumers

Seeking out collective authority is perhaps the most salient and discussed development in brand communication this year – it's called 'user generated content', and is currently being leveraged by brands including C4, Coca-Cola, Chevy, Sony Pictures and pretty much everyone else.

Whether it's Dove asking their consumer to make their next ad or Nokia seeding new handsets to bloggers,[27] this activity is an attempt to overcome the erosion of trust in conventional, singular authorities by reaching out to the collective and leveraging the media of the masses in the process. No longer a target audience; they are our 'partners in communication'.[28]

Sony Bravia: a future brand case study

In which we demonstrate how this new model has been put into practice

This thinking has already begun to be implemented within Naked, most recently on the campaign to launch the Sony Bravia television commercial, 'Paint'. Working with a team consisting of clients Fallon, Freud, Tonic and OMD we carefully planned, orchestrated and executed a campaign to turn the television commercial into a transmedia idea, leveraging the power of the collective and the recombinant.

Channels were loaded with different information, the process of making the film was opened up to interested parties and news of the director and the location of the shoot were leaked to the local media.

People were thus 'invited to participate', attending the shoot, capturing it, footage which then went onto Flickr and YouTube, two of the pre-eminent propagation platforms.

Consumer shots of the filming of the 'Paint' commercial were posted to photo-sharing site Flickr.

By building a transmedia narrative around the commercial, dripping developments online, a specific attempt was made to engage people in 'an open and transparent conversation with the brand'.[29] Bloggers responded well and built up anticipation for the ad, with numerous blogs picking up on the leaked material and using it as the basis for discussions.

FIGURE 8.4

FIGURE 8.5

The film was first released online and then on television, catering to the differing needs of youth and the Massive Passives. Online, the assets of the film were made available for remixing. The campaign was transmedia, recombinant and collective. Was it successful?

New metrics

In which we propose new behavioural diagnostic metrics to evaluate the success of new ideas

In order to determine the success of these new types of ideas, we need to create some new metrics to add into the traditional basket.

There are two classes of measures tracked in relation to communications: evaluative and diagnostic. Ultimately, all measure of success need to demonstrate a return on marketing investment. However, it has been recognized that 'advertising payoffs can seldom be demonstrated in the short term'.[30] The value of marketing is only accurately reflected when it is considered an 'investment in the long-term health of the brand'.[31]

Most measures tracked by agencies are diagnostics that are confused with evaluative measures. Since the total contribution marketing makes cannot be demonstrated in the short term, even with regression analysis to help untangle the solus effect on sales, advertisers began to analyse intermediate measures to understand what effect communication was having on the *mental* brand equity of consumers, as this can give 'indications as to the future profit trends'[32] and provide inputs into strategy, unpicking *how* communication shifts perceptions that lead to changes in purchasing behaviour. The confusion arises when objectives are confused with diagnostics – shifts in these 'magic numbers'[33] become stated objectives.

Cognitive measures tracked by survey all suffer the same flaws: they require consumers to tell us what they think and they analyse individuals and aggregate data to give an overall picture.

Image measures tend to correlate to *previous* rather than future behaviour. While they may give an indication of predisposition, they ignore what may be the most important drivers of purchase decisions: *collective* perceptions. Behavioural economics indicates key drivers of purchasing include *other people's behaviour* – people do things by copying others.[34] Earls has posited that 'the most important characteristic of mankind is that of a herd animal'.[35]

A single word-of-mouth interaction can overthrow the entirety of pre-existing brand effect on purchase intention.[36] Brands do not only influence consumers directly, but by introducing a persuasive influence into the network: the more virulent the idea, the greater the number of *transmissions*, which is a measure of *collective* brand salience.

In an age when half of all consumers actively avoid advertising,[37] another newly relevant measure is approaches to the brand, or 'accessions'.[38]

The emergence of web analytic tools enables agencies to measure both transmissions and accessions – not all occur online, but effects measured on the web aren't restricted to it. Google is a 'barometer of cultural interest'[39] and research has shown that online transmissions are a powerful influencer of brand perceptions and purchase behaviour.

Returning to the Bravia example, we can utilize a basket of metrics to determine its success. Blogpulse[40] and Google Trends (Figure 8.6) enable us to track transmissions and accessions.

FIGURE 8.6   Google Trends shows a similar surge in accessions over the campaign period

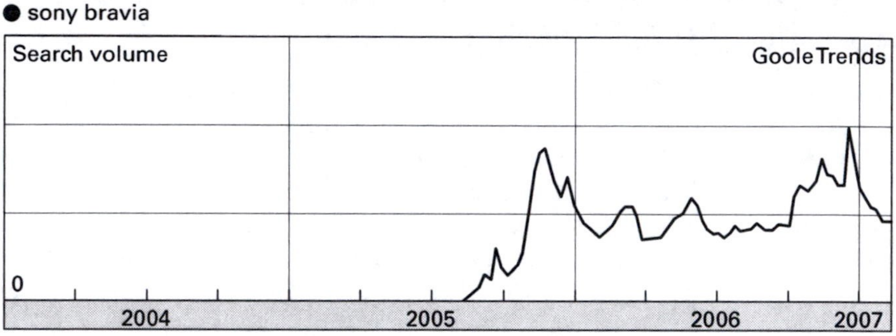

● sony bravia

In addition, there were:

- overwhelmingly favourable transmissions on OpinMind;[41]
- 168 separate uploads on YouTube;
- 19 remixes;
- hundreds of thousands of online views;
- 655,000 web mentions;[42] and
- 49,744 links to the Bravia-Advert site.

So the communication has driven a substantial number of positive transmissions and accessions; it was modulated and propagated by the collective – but did this translate into financial return?

'Strong sales of BRAVIA LCD TVs contributed to the TV business as a whole being profitable for the quarter.'[43] Sony's share price has risen by 40 per cent since the campaign began.[44] By measures of both effect and effectiveness, the campaign generated a positive return in short-term sales, collective brand salience, favourability and shareholder value.

The future of the industry

In which we propose a new model for an ideas agency

An industry that developed in the age of passive-idea consumption will need to undergo a similarly seismic shift in order to successfully connect brands to active idea consumers.

The agency of the future will need to be built around the value of ideas. While we have always dealt in ideas, 'we have allowed the emphasis, the value, and the fundamental business model of our industry today, to shift away from ideas and to focus predominantly on execution.'[45]

This is unfortunate, since the key strength of the agency business model is the ability to partner. By decoupling ideas from executions, agencies are able to execute any kind of solution, in theory, as long as they are able to envisage it.

The rate of change in communication technologies is going to *increase* over time and the only way for agencies to keep up is to outsource production to diverse specialists, just as production companies currently make films.

As it always has, technology will continue to drive changes in the way ideas are communicated. 'We tend to overestimate the effect of a technology in the short run and underestimate the effect in the long run.'[46]

Epilogue

As Gibson pointed out, 'the future is already here – it's just not evenly distributed'. A generation has grown up with digital media and thus has an intrinsically participatory relationship with ideas. It needs to be catered for differently than the Massive Passives, and transmedia planning is a new model for creating ideas in this context. By looking at how young people are consuming, remixing, producing and propagating ideas today, we can chart how brands will operate in the future and begin to change how we create ideas accordingly.

Notes

1 Gibson, W [accessed 2007, Online] http://en.wikiquote.org/wiki/William Gibson

2 *ibid.*

3 Gilbert, D (2007) *Stumbling on Happiness*, p4, Vintage Books, New York.

4 Pensky, M (2001) Digital natives, digital immigrants, *On the Horizon*, 9 (5), NBC University Press.

5 Gibson, O (March 2006) Internet means end for media barons, says Murdoch, *The Guardian* [Online] www.theguardian.com/media/2006/mar/14/newmedia.studentmediaawards

6 Murdoch, R (April 2005) Speech to the American Society of Newspaper Editors, Washington DC [Online] www.flickr.com/photos/lynetter/322112273/

7 (2006) The end of TV as we know it: A future industry perspective, IBM Business Consulting Services [Online] www-935.ibm.com/services/us/imc/pdf/ge510-6248-end-of-tv-full.pdf

8 Shannon, C E and Weaver, W (1949) *The Mathematical Theory of Communication*, University of Illinois.

9 Peters, J D (2001) *Speaking into the Air: A history of the idea of communication*, p11, University of Chicago Press.

10 Gilbert, D (2007) *Stumbling on Happiness*, p 215, Vintage Books, New York.

11 Packard, V (1957/2007) *The Hidden Persuaders*, Ig Publishing.

12 Shakespeare, W, *A Midsummer Night's Dream*.

13 This maxim is often attributed to Jesus Christ, but is in fact much older, recorded at least as far back as 500BC in the Analects of Confucius, *Chapter 15, Verse 23*.

14 Iyengar, S S (December 1999) Choice and its discontents, *HERMES* [Online] www4.gsb.columbia.edu/null?&exclusive=filemgr.download&file_id=3452

15 Paraphrase of a quote in Einstein, A (April 1934) On the method of theoretical physics, *Philosophy of Science*, **1** (2) p 165. See also: http://en.wikiquote.org/wiki/Albert_Einstein

16 Quoted in (September 1999) What is a proverb? [Online] http://cogweb.ucla.edu/Discourse/Proverbs/Definitions.html

17 Schon, D (1979) Generative metaphor: A perspective on problem-setting in social policy, in *Metaphor and Thought*, ed Ortony, A (1993), Cambridge University Press.

18 Goldhaber, M (December 1997) Attention shoppers!, *Wired*, Issue 5.12 [Online] www.wired.com/wired/archive/5.12/es_attention.html

19 Nelson, T H (first published 1980) *Literary Machines*, Mindful Press, California. See also: en.wikipedia.org/wiki/Hypertextuality

20 Gibson, W (July 2005) God's little toys, *Wired*, Issue 13.7 [Online] http://archive.wired.com/wired/archive/13.07/gibson.html

21 The Edelman Trust Barometer has shown consistent decline in traditional authority. The 2007 edition showed that 44 per cent of Europeans trusted conversations with friends and peers while 33 per cent trusted articles in newspapers. (February 2007) Edelman Trust Barometer 2007, Edelman [Online] www.slideshare.net/edelman.milan/edelman-trust-barometer-2007

22 Earls, M (2007) *Herd: How to change mass behaviour by harnessing our true nature*, John Wiley & Sons. Earls makes the distinction between endogenous word of mouth, which naturally occurs within the system, and exogenous word of mouth, which is when brands attempt to artificially cultivate buzz using agents, such as P&G's Tremor network.

23 Davies, R (November 2006) Post of the month: Faris wins [Online] http://russelldavies.typepad.com/planning/2006/11/faris_wins.html

24 Pollard, I (October 2006) Thoughts from Ivan Pollard [Online] http://theapg.typepad.com/battleofbigthinking/2006/10/thoughts_from_i.html

25 Jenkins, H (December 2006) How transmedia storytelling begat transmedia planning... (Part One) [Online] www.henryjenkins.org/2006/12/how_transmedia_storytelling_be.html

26 Jenkins, H (December 2006) How transmedia storytelling begat transmedia planning... (Part Two) [Online] http://henryjenkins.org/2006/12/how_transmedia_storytelling_be_1.html

27 (June 2006) Nokia sending phones to bloggers [Online] http://blog.experiencecurve.com/archives/nokia-sending-phones-to-bloggers

28 Pollard, I (October 2006) Propagation Planning, *APG Speech*.

29 David Patton, Sony quoted in Yakob, F (July 2006) Adticipation [Online] http://farisyakob.typepad.com/blog/2006/07/adticipation.html

30 McDonald, C (2003) Is your advertising working? A guide to evaluating campaign effectiveness, p 8, World Advertising Research Centre.

31 *ibid.*

32 (2003) Measuring brands and their performance, *Chartered Institute of Marketing* [Online] http://mktg.uni-svishtov.bg/ivm/resources/Measuring%20 Brands%20and%20their%20Performance.pdf

33 Shaw, R and Merrick, D (2006) *Marketing Payback: Is your marketing profitable?*, Pearson Education.

34 Shah, H and Dawney, E (2005) Behavioural economics, New Economics Foundation [Online] www.neweconomics.org/publications/entry/ behavioural-economics

35 Earls, M (2003) Advertising to the herd, *International Journal of Market Research*, **45**, Quarter 3.

36 Blades, F, Mason, C H J and Phillips, S (2005) MRS Conference Paper, *Decision Watch UK* [Online] www.meshplanning.com/content/wp-content/ uploads/2011/04/Decision-Watch-UK.pdf: 'Gary had been considering purchasing a Toyota Rav 4 and liked both the look and styling. The price was also within his budget. However, just before purchasing he saw a vague acquaintance of his driving one in the village and asked him how it was. Gary said "apparently he wasn't that happy so I went off the idea". The extraordinary power of WOM became obvious.'

37 (April 2005) Marketing Receptivity Study, *Yankelovich MONITOR think tank*: 54 per cent of consumers agreed that they try to resist being exposed to or even paying attention to marketing and advertising, 69 per cent said that they are interested in products that enable them to block, skip or opt out of being exposed to marketing and advertising.

38 [Accessed 2007, Online] http://dictionary.reference.com/search?q=accession

39 Smith, S (2004) What happened when Honda started asking questions?, IPA Effectiveness Awards, *IPA* [Online] www.ipa.co.uk/Framework/ ContentDisplay.aspx?id=4803

40 [Accessed 2007, Online] www.blogpulse.com is a tool for tracking the content of weblog posts. Each post that contains the specified brand or term is considered a transmission.

41 [Accessed 2007, Online] www.opinmind.com, a tool that measures mentions of the brand in proximity to positive or negative value statements and shows the results as a percentage split.

42 Tracked on Google 'Sony Bravia Paint'.

43 Q3 FY 2006, ending 31st December 2006. Results available here [Online] www.sony.net/SonyInfo/IR/financial/fr/viewer/06q3/

44 Share price rose from approx $37 at campaign launch to $53 (at time of writing, 2007). While share price responds to a number of influences, the Bravia campaign was the highest profile Sony communication campaign in that period. [Online] http://uk.finance.yahoo.com/q/bc?s=SNE&t=1y&l=on&z=m&q=l&c=

45 Goodson, S (March 2007) Change the Model, Change the World, Keynote Speech, *Future Marketing Summit* [Online] http://scottgoodson.typepad.com/ my_weblog/2007/03/future_marketin.html

46 Amara, R [Online] www.pcmag.com/encyclopedia/term/37701/amara-s-law

I believe in the power of the self-fulfilling prophecy

2005/06

DAVID YOUNG
Independent Marketing Consultant

09

I believe We have reached a turning point in our society where there is a kind of celestial alignment of prevailing cultural trends: the obsession with immediate fame; the fascination with conspiracy; the desire to decode and uncover unknown facts. Each of these combine in an almost alchemical way to produce the next evolution in Brand Theory. The climate has now been created to incubate and sustain faux-brands through their own self-fulfilled prophecies.

Editor's therefore, for your brand...

Your brand thinking: What do we really know about our consumer's inner needs and desires, and how much does your process start with creating it?

Your brand engagement: Could you reinvent, even reverse how you launch your new products? Could you inspire people to buy it before you invest in making it?

Your brand organization & capability: How does your team manage the most powerful media tool of all – word of mouth? Is it someone's responsibility or a happy byproduct?

...and author's personal therefore

In the immortal film *Back to the Future II*, the affable protagonist Marty McFly finds himself travelling back from the future (2015) to the past (1955), in order to put right something that went wrong so that he can safely return to a present (1985) which he knew and loved.

So, being asked to write a retrospective – in 2014 – about a sci-fi-esque thesis – written in 2006 – that was set in a future which is now in the past – in 2012 – feels like the same kind of dangerous meddling with the space–time continuum that can only end in DeLoreans being smashed up and wild exhortations of 'Great Scott, what's happened to the future?'

In 2006, I prided myself on being able to challenge conventional thinking – I confidently believed that I could bypass the whole of brand theory and conjure up a brand out of thin air. The central tenet of 'Faux Branding and Instant Fame' was that a brand could enter the conscious brains of susceptible consumers by faking a range of apparent events and promoting them so widely that people must have believed they were true – and that the brand consequently had stature. Basically, a brand could behave as if it was more significant than it actually was, as a way of gaining credibility. And when the strategy was exposed as a total fraud, people would have enjoyed the deception enough to feel positively predisposed towards the brand anyway, rather like the way in which we all love a good conspiracy theory, or the unexpected victory of the underdog.

The thesis was admittedly flawed, because it didn't allow for the fact that internet search engines allow people to check the veracity of any brands claims, and that word of mouth spreads like wildfire. It assumed that people would want to play along, but then didn't focus enough on how to sustain that initial awareness-building exercise. However, before sounding too harsh about the concept, it was essentially an exploratory account which tried to use creativity and humour to suggest ways in which a brand could avoid having to follow a sustained programme of marketing investment in order to achieve high levels of awareness.

As 2012 came and went somewhat predictably, POD devices weren't actually dotted up and down the supermarkets of the land offering tired consumers the opportunity to receive sensory stimulation and euphoria in exchange for their neurological preferences that would be seized on by neuro-marketing agencies.

However, I would venture to suggest that the world of the smartphone in 2014 is not all that different. Substitute 'Neuro-stimulation' for 'Cookies' and 'Euphoric POD Comas' for 'YouTube clips about cats doing crazy things', and we essentially have the same slightly concerning scenario. Consumers mindlessly consuming technology in bite-size chunks as a form of sedative to ease the pains of the daily grind, while software and phone companies study our online movements in order to tailor advertising that supposedly precisely matches our needs. That should raise alarm bells, as we claim to be a world obsessed with data protection and all the safety that affords, yet give away our preferences and propensities more freely and more comprehensively than we ever have before. If I had written about smartphones instead of POD devices back in 2005, perhaps my thinking wouldn't have been quite so wide of the mark. If nothing else, the paper hopefully helped to start the debate which rages today about the power of the crowd, and the democratizing of the brand creation process, which are certainly major tenets of modern-day brand theory.

While none of my creative outpourings may have come true (which was never the point, but always laid the ground for the potential creation of a full fictional novel along those lines – which is still a possibility), there is a fundamental aspect of that writing process which lives with me to this day.

The nature of the Excellence Diploma was such that we consumed the enormous corpus of brand theory that had been published up to that time. It gave us the navigation tools we needed in order to understand how brands affect our consciousness and our decision-making. It was only armed with that knowledge that I felt comfortable to mock that whole process by disregarding it and playfully inventing a new paradigm. It only worked because of the awareness I had built up about how brands do actually behave, and the way I felt confident enough to plant subversive references to that theory in a way which pretended to belittle it, ready to pre-empt and dismantle the conventional arguments about why it wouldn't work. I researched the workings of the brain in some detail (eg the Amygdala references) in order to display a level of knowledge that sounded fully credible.

If anything, that approach has guided my career and whole approach to life to date. Wherever there is a conventional problem, be it ways in which to try to buy a house I can't quite afford, or to overcome a seemingly tangled professional issue I can't quite understand, I've frequently found that challenging the conventional thought processes – by seeking to understand the usual approach and then pushing the boundaries as far as possible – has yielded huge rewards.

So, while I don't really believe in 'Faux Branding and Instant Fame', I do believe in the Excellence Diploma, for its rigorous approach to disseminating and applying brand theory, as well as its cheerful regard for the way in which brands affect our everyday challenges. While I personally don't wish to revisit 2006 in order to correct my predictions of the future that are now in the past (in the same way that Doc Brown wanted to destroy the time machine at the end of the *Back to the Future* film trilogy in recognition of how such meddling never helped anyone), it's that whole approach which gives me the appetite to explore conventional problems in an unconventional manner, and long may that continue.

I believe in the power of the self-fulfilling prophecy

...and the winner of this year's 'Celebrity Big Brother' is... Chantelle.

A tiny piece of our British cultural identity expired on the evening of Friday 27 January 2006. Davina McCall's announcement to 11 million members of the television-viewing public had been eagerly anticipated for 23 days. At precisely 9:48pm, she declared to the nation that a previously unknown office temp called Chantelle Houghton had won Channel 4's 'Celebrity Big Brother' programme, an announcement which immediately sent the social commentators into fits of hysteria. The next day's papers were deluged with various incredulous musings about the apparent malaise penetrating the core of our cultural consciousness.

Had the nation become so vapidly obsessed with the cult of celebrity that neither talent nor looks were any longer a prerequisite for reaching iconic status?

But perhaps we should start to question this strangely compelling instant fame after all? Having done nothing but appear on television, Chantelle has – for now, at least – become a household name. GlaxoSmithKline paid somewhere in the region of £80 million for a sustained global re-branding effort to achieve slightly less brand awareness than Chantelle has notched up by simply behaving in a rather insipid manner on national television.

Could it be, though, that this 'instafame' capitalizes on our prevailing cultural mindset to confer upon a brand (or a personality) a totally unique and immediate fast-tracking into the nation's cultural consciousness? Could it be that only then does it become subjected to the standard theories of declining brand salience, having already attained temporary awareness levels that would have ordinarily cost several tens of millions of pounds, and several carefully orchestrated launch campaigns to achieve?

But exactly how could an unknown brand or personality achieve this meteoric rise to fame? What qualities *does* it need to possess to capture the nation's collective imagination? Does it need to promise to reconcile some of the acute ideological tensions of the age?,[1] or could it perhaps bypass the received wisdom of branding theory and achieve pre-eminence in the nation's collective conscience through a series of ingenious tricks, scams, fabrications and spurious claims?

Everything which follows is mere fabrication.

2012 IPA Effectiveness Award Winner: Perfect Brand

The year 2012 was noteworthy for being the year in which the IPA elected to confer the unique and much-lauded title of Perfect Brand to a small UK-based manufacturing company, established in January 2007. The company's revolutionary and unparalleled branding and advertising practices had been deemed by the IPA to demonstrate every facet of perfect branding. The Company is called POD™, and here follows their remarkable story.

Background

The POD™

The POD is a free-standing, multi-media capsule designed to accommodate a single human being in a semi-recumbent position. The POD physically resembles a shiny chrysalis, and is constructed from titastic plasma (a titanium-plastic hybrid with pixel-imaging and sound-creation capabilities inside every plasma molecule – the POD's interior is a total-surround audio-visual screen). Its slick exterior contouring is broken only by a single unobtrusive digital LCD display to denote when the unit is in use. The POD's interior is equipped with advanced bluetooth-enabled neuro-sensors which measure and record electrical and chemical impulses from the amygdala system in the occupant's brain[2] (a technology patented in March 2008 by the then newly-merged corporation SonyAstraZeneca). The POD's on-board computer continuously processes each user's unique neurological response data in order to achieve real-time variations to the exact type of images, sounds and smells that they are exposed to during their 'podcoma'. (Podcoma has been the colloquial name affectionately used to describe the user experience by journalists and the general public since 2008.) The POD generates its own power from its exterior solar panelling and by harnessing the energy released from the binary fission of Xenon traces in any exhaled air trapped inside the POD.

The POD experience offers unrivalled and unique solace to each user, and the units are frequently found in the staffrooms of corporations, the communal areas of institutions and the public precincts of shopping centres right across the UK. The POD de-stresses, relaxes and recharges both body and mind. The POD also offers the public a place to pray, a place to think, a place to watch videos, to video-conference, to access the web and even to vote. The POD is a neurological life-support machine which offers a slice of serenity in an increasingly fast-paced world.

The POD is predicated on a unique business model. It is completely free to use, in exchange for the user's consent to view brief advertising messages, and to release their unique neurological-response data to POD's subsidiary neuro-marketing organization, Biocom (**www.biocom.org.uk**).

Setting the historical context: the zeitgeist of fin-de-siècle angst

The end of the second millennium was characterized by abnormally pronounced levels of collective human anxiety – much more so than the close of previous centuries. A plethora of historical records document the typical feelings of anxiety experienced by civilizations as they approach the dawn of a new century. They begin to question their core identity and the direction that they will forge out for themselves over the following years. The arrival of the third millennium heralded an even greater feeling of concern as the problems associated with the 'Millennium Bug' brought about previously unknown feelings of technical angst. The thought that our own technological creations – the true mark of our advancement as a species – could fail and perhaps even threaten to kill us, represented a huge undermining of our own confidence in who and what we had become... Indeed, this prevailing mindset gave rise to a literary and artistic climate of 'questioned authenticity'. We defined ourselves through our ever more prominent desires to doubt the veracity of even seemingly undeniable truths. Had Diana been assassinated on Prince Philip's orders? Did Neil Armstrong actually set foot on the Moon back in 1969? Were the atrocities of 9/11 somehow hauntingly predicted in the annals of the Bible? We even lived in a climate in which video and photographic evidence was no longer a trusted purveyor of the truth.

This climate was conducive to the incubation, and then hatching of the first successful, entirely spurious brand in the UK in 2007. Never before had a brand so adeptly prophesized and engineered its own superiority and salience, and – through entirely fabricated claims – managed to earn such a genuinely respected position within the nation's consciousness.

POD as spurious brand

Indeed, the POD was the first organized brand communication strategy entirely predicated on spurious claims, observations and pseudo-facts. The story began in January 2007, when Companies' House received an inauspicious application for POD Holdings to register as a limited company. Two weeks later POD Global published on its website its entirely fabricated first-year accounts for 2006, as well as several intriguing but entirely innocuous-sounding neurological patents filed through the UK Patent Office. Initial public reaction was almost non-existent, but after various carefully seeded e-mails, blogs, message forum observations and a handful of carefully targeted letters to publications such as the *New Scientist*, people began to believe that POD was at the forefront of understanding about the intricate workings of the human brain, and that it had begun to develop the ability to correlate visual imagery with neuro-specific data.

The buzz spread insidiously through the city and within academic journals. It wasn't long before it attracted legions of sci-fi and conspiracy theorists in its wake. People were desperate to experience first-hand the neuro-enhanced escapism alleged in the articles. The fact that some recent scientific discoveries concurred with the articles was an ingeniously timed marketing kick-start for the brand. Other claims, such as the neurological breakthroughs, were totally fabricated. Curiously, however, more money was ear-marked by the major pharmaceutical companies for conducting research into these exact same neurological studies – galvanized into action through fear that they would lose their competitive edge in the wake of the alleged developments being reported by a rival company. This increased investment elicited the rapid genuine discovery of those self-same spurious scientific claims, and thus became an incredibly useful self-fulfilling prophecy for both science at large and the POD brand itself.

Nobody knew what it was, but everyone wanted to find out about it. It promised to revolutionize the human condition, and as such became perceived as aspirational, cutting-edge and trendy. Jeremy Bullmore concluded in 2009 that:

> Since the brand didn't exist other than as buzz on the internet and in the mind, it couldn't be tainted by the usual theories associated with typical branding. There were no 'unaccountable number of brand stimuli' which usually helped to create potentially negative perceptions in the mind of the general public. The only perceptions could be positive, and the way this important formative period was managed was a true masterstroke of modern-day branding.

By late 2007 the marketing community had begun to sit up and take notice. And then came the second masterstroke. The company released a paper attesting to the effectiveness of its overall inception, and disseminated it among the marketing community on the pretence of furthering modern-day brand theory. On the one hand it was a cheap joke aimed at poking fun at an occasionally pompous industry that could be preoccupied with its own self-importance, but on the other it demonstrated an intelligent understanding of the power to leverage this zeitgeist of spurious celebrity, conspiracy theories and the powers of the self-fulfilling prophecy. Effectively, the brand concept was being incubated within the journals of advertising theory in order to shore up goodwill towards a brand that didn't even exist.

By falsely claiming its own brand salience, POD was beginning to get noticed in academic journals and starting to achieve just that. It was effectively the Chantelle Houghton of brands.

So it came to pass that, by late 2007, the POD had listed an entirely fabricated set of annual accounts, and awarded itself a completely fictitious accolade for perfect branding. The initial perceptions of the brand could only be positive, because of the fact that only intrigue and fascination had been spread about it. The public were predisposed to the brand before they actually experienced it, on the grounds that they enjoyed the innovative way in which it had been allowed to incubate in their consciousness before they had actually experienced it in reality. This achieved two important things: First, nationwide awareness on a non-existent marketing budget, and second, but more importantly, a huge wave of anticipation to experience the actual brand promise itself.

The more traditional brand theorists were initially dismissive of 'the Great POD fiasco', as it became known in January 2008 after it had finally emerged that all the stories about its development were fabricated. Although the public were initially impressed with the spurious brand's ability to leverage the current prevailing obsession with faux celebrity, conspiracy theories and examples of success against all the odds, detractors sought solace from the fact that all brands, no matter how salient at any one given moment in time, needed to invest in maintaining their salience. More importantly, they also needed to deliver a genuinely rewarding and differentiating product experience. POD responded ferociously – it was not about to haemorrhage the positive effects of this accumulated ocean of goodwill.

The management team appointed David Young as Brand Salience Director in March 2008. His first initiative was to write a letter to the marketing community called 'What's keeping this Great White moving?', reference to the need to maintain and build upon the current public goodwill towards turning the brand into a reality. In that paper, and still unable to unleash any real details about the actual product itself, Young decided instead to give an insight into the actual naming of the brand itself.

What's in a name? POD and linguistic branding

Not only was 'POD' an accurate lexical descriptor of the shape and self-sealing nature of the units that were about to go into physical production, but it also stood for an acronym which succinctly described the overall product experience itself: 'Privacy On Demand' – POD. POD was predicated on the notion that employees in busy corporations never quite knew how to spend their lunchtimes, and that the 2008 Gallup Poll had revealed that the national average time taken for lunch had slipped from 45 minutes to 40 minutes. This didn't quite equate to enough time to go to the local gym, and this is where the POD had identified its niche. It offered 20 minutes solace from the pressures of work by allowing the user to climb inside and personalize their POD experience by selecting their preferred sounds, sights and smells.

Keen to generate marketable buzz at every opportunity, Young then spuriously post-rationalized a theory that part of the success of POD was attributable to extensive semantic analysis at the point of the brand's inception. He researched various academic papers written by the late linguist Ferdinand de Saussure, and then initiated various threads of e-discussions and blogs in the academic community. In a blog on 21 May 2007, directed at the English Faculty at Oxford University, Young proposed that 'many words uttered in conversational speech had the latent potential to behave as cerebral micro-adverts in the minds of those people'. He advanced the suggestion that the most resonant word in the English Language was 'exterminate', on the grounds that it immediately and unequivocally painted a picture of the time-travelling Doctor and his crude robotic adversaries in the minds of over 98 per cent of the population. Young seized upon this unharnessed semantic power and referred to it as 'lingua-branding' in the various academic and intellectual debates that ensued. After his terminology had gained critical mass in academic circles, he wrote an article in *The Times* called 'Adam's Apple of Fortune', in which he taught the public about the powers of lingua-branding, and suggested that the strength of the POD brand owed its world-wide acclaim to the expedience of its linguistic parity to Apple's most significant and successful product of the century, the iPod.

Young argued that every time the word iPod was uttered in conversation it subconsciously engineered positive associations with his POD product. He contended that his brand was behaving in a 'linguistically parasitic fashion', nestling within the lexical descriptor for most famous brand of the century, 'iPod'. In so doing, POD was subconsciously appropriating some of the goodwill towards Apple's product and diverting it into its own. His brand had been the first to engage in such stealth lingua-parasitic branding.

POD and linguistic sponsorship

Young took POD one stage further. Rather than just capitalizing on the latent positive goodwill afforded by those iconic brands with lexical similarity to his own, he also wanted to engineer situations in which the brand name could be inadvertently uttered. In October 2008 Young appointed the world's first Lexical Sponsorship Director to join the marketing operations team at POD Global. The LSD would leverage the potential for sponsored utterances of the POD in a non-advertising context within theatrical or cinematic works. He hired Gerry Eisenberg, who had recently successfully revived Tom Stoppard's play *The Real Thing* in both London and New York, as a covert branding opportunity for the Coca-Cola Schweppes company. Recent qualitative research had demonstrated that even though the world's leading brand's end line had moved on from 'The Real Thing', there was still sufficient residual association with the old line to be spontaneously attributed to the brand upon first hearing. Studies showed that the subliminal associations with the brand end line and the theatrical work resulted in a 1 per cent uplift in sales in both London and New York throughout the duration of the show's run. Eisenberg himself said that: 'Consumers are now acutely wary of direct product placement and blatant advertising sponsorships, and they are often mistrusting of the clumsy links contrived between brand

and event. However, by covertly capitalizing on phrases and end lines only subconsciously associated with those products, we can deploy a kind of guerrilla advertising strategy that is unleashed within the fabric of language itself.'

For POD, Eisenhauer commissioned Alan Bennett to write a play called *Peas in a Pod*, which surmised the prevailing social concerns, namely the epidemic of commitment-phobia among 20- and 30-something adults in major conurbations across the country. The play resolved by proposing that a greater awareness of our spiritual essence would help to eclipse the obsessions with material advancement, work-related stresses and the emasculation of the male. It all subtly pointed towards respecting time and private space – a delicate allusion to the sensory and spiritual escapism offered by the POD itself. The sponsorship effort ensured that POD reached top-of-mind awareness, yet didn't register any of the typical negativity or cynicism so frequently associated with blatantly crude sponsorship events.

POD: Where the hype met reality

At the point that the POD actually went into physical production in September 2008, following 18 months of entirely fabricated publicity, it had achieved 50,000 forward orders from corporations across the country that were keen to demonstrate to their workforce that they were interested in investing in their welfare. Although many knew of the marketing scam and were positively predisposed to consideration of the brand owing to the ingenuity of the creation, the hard launch still had to be managed tactfully. Young leveraged the opportunity and playfully announced its arrival as 'The Second Coming of the Corporate Messiah', as an ironic statement about the fact that everyone was beginning to doubt its existence. It also leant a risqué air of pseudo-religious anticipation to the occasion, and somewhat heretically aligned the POD with the miracle-working capabilities of Jesus Christ. The ensuing hysterical fervour from the orthodox religious community ensured that the POD concept was extensively debated by a hugely influential sector of society. Before their musings were allowed to potentially taint the brand with suggestions of its sacrilegious nomenclature, or a potential furthering of an undesirable intrigue in the occult, Young deftly demonstrated to this sector of the community how the POD could be used to achieve religious solace and shared faith with networked conference communions and gospels, as just one of the POD programmes available from a whole religious menu of experiences. They were hugely appeased, and churches across the country began ordering PODs for their vestries, as well as mobile units for their religion-on-wheels service which was rolled out in 2009.

The hard launch date coincided with the publication of the latest NOP survey which decried the fact that the UK had the longest working hours in Europe for the 10th year running. Stress levels were at an all time high, and people slept on average for an hour less than only five years before. POD sponsored the provision of herbal sleeping tablets emblazoned with the word POD to various influential corporations across the land, as a way of leveraging the soporific qualities of the POD experience itself, and the appeal of a 20-minute, post-prandial slumber in the office environment.

POD as neuro-advertising effectiveness tool

So, the story thus far, is one of an unprecedented and carefully contrived meteoric ascent of a spurious brand into the nation's consciousness, through leveraging the prevailing obsessions with conspiracy theories and faux celebrity to achieve its own prophesized glory. It also speaks of how it sustains its relevance, like any good brand, by leveraging the manifold opportunities and possibilities created by the results of national surveys, technological discoveries and current affairs to continually reassert its relevance. Mark Earls invented a tool called a 'Brand Blog Salience Half-life (BSH)' which became a respected way of measuring the effect to which a marketing initiative had penetrated the social consciousness. He stated in 2008 that 'the almost ubiquitous presence of the blog and its associated blog search engines made it possible to chart the number of mentions relating to a specific branding stunt in the days immediately following its launch. The time it took for the number of daily blogs relating to that stunt to halve was subsequently known as its Blog Salience Half-life'. Young's marketing objectives were set against the requirement to initiate a new marketing stunt each time the Half-life had been reached for his previous stunt.

The POD itself is a freestanding media unit capable of offering the zenith of the Advertising Grail: A willing and attentive audience who are actually prepared to receive messages. POD, however, offered a unique portal into the neurological sensibilities of each of its individual users. During the experience of listening to music, seeing images and smelling different aromas, the levels of the chemical x3R10 in the Amygdala region of the brain were monitored by the POD's neuro-sensory interface. In fact, all sensory stimuli were monitored until those which correlated with the optimum sensory impact were found.

Many branding commentators asserted that the traditional loyalty card scheme was the strongest tool in the marketing arsenal, and this may explain why large percentages of ATL budgets were often appropriated by CRM teams for investing in loyalty initiatives in the early 1990s. However, the POD represented the flawless loyalty scheme, for rather than just arming the retailer with purchasing data, the POD provides neuro-statistical data which gives an indication about that person's unique cerebral wiring. For example, if being shown an image of an apple elicits a greater degree of neuro-stimulus and serotonin release than seeing an image of a banana, then the POD logs the data accordingly. The POD reconfigures the images and sounds it plays to the customer to elicit the most pleasurable and positive experience – all based on the unique set-up of that person's brain. This demonstrates how the POD itself possesses the core materials required to make it the most efficient advertising vehicle known to man.

The POD had effectively become a media space which offered unrivalled neurological data to prospective advertisers. This fundamentally altered its initially planned business model of the POD. Users gained 20 minutes free exposure to the semi-hypnotic euphoria delivered by the machine in exchange for the consent to release their neurological data, as well as the consent to view two minutes of advertising communication which would be specifically tailored to the neurological sense data gathered by the POD. Advertising awareness levels reached 100 per cent for the first time ever on the basis that the users were not only willing and focused on the communication, but they were guaranteed to be stimulated by the way in which the product was presented to them. Will Collin declared 'to the delight of FDs up and down the land advertising has at long last become a precisely quantifiable science'.

It was a basic tenet of branding theory that trusted brands were able to charge a price premium, and make certain predictions about their cash flow, on the basis of anticipated loyalties and increased propensity for repeat purchase. With the arrival of neurological data, the consumer could now be ranked in precise numbers relating to their neuro-affiliation to the brand. This was calculated by measuring the chemical activity in the Amygdala region of the brain during a show parade of competing products. With this, a new unit of brand loyalty was devised. Depending on levels of chemical activity a brand was scored accordingly. 'Grannie Smith 40mg/1' would demonstrate 20mg more activity than 'Pink Lady 20mg/1'. The time factor was also included to ensure that brands which had slower recognition times, but equally strong affiliations, were also captured: 'Coxes 40mg/2' meant that the same level of positive brain activity was recorded for Coxes apples, although it took twice as long for this chemical level to be reached as it did for Grannie Smith's. Rita Carter, in her 2009 book *Pushing All the Right Cerebral Buttons: Neuro-specific advertising of the future*, refers to this as the Neuro-Loyalty Index (NLI), and proposes that for the first time ever a brand was now able to accurately measure the level of predisposition to a product for every consumer for whom they hold this neurological data.

POD's social agenda

Having proved POD's ability to be a brand that was able to continually refresh its salience, as well as a powerful qualitative neuro-research tool and a unique media vehicle, Young sought to tackle ways in which to leverage the capabilities of the machine into a CSR programme that would positively affect the whole community. Following on from Steve Hilton's excellent essay 'The Social Value of Brands', in which he states that the most influential way in which a brand can contribute to society is not just by operating a programme of CSR, but by more proactively engaging in corporate social leadership, Hilton in fact chose to base his 2010 paper 'Paragon of Virtue' on the multivalent manner in which the POD's capabilities had been marshalled to effect a positive change in society:

> POD managed not only to engage in leading a programme of improving social interaction and promoting benevolence, but it elevated the significance of this broad social agenda into one of the very organizing principles of the product's function from the outset.

By leveraging the unique physical capabilities of the product itself, POD launched such initiatives as: 'Tax Confessional' (opportunity for individuals to anonymously shop colleagues or associates who they knew to be cheating the tax system); and the 'Remote Literacy Programme' (people were actively encouraged to give up half an hour of their time to make a POD call to under-privileged children and give real-time spelling tests, etc). The POD was able to forge connections across social demographics and geographical boundaries which hadn't been witnessed since the dawn of e-mail communication. Hilton concluded that 'POD demonstrated remarkable versatility as a unilateral education tool, a crime prevention unit at the same time as offering the zenith of leisure experiences – the exemplar of a Socially proactive brand.

Conclusion

The POD doesn't even exist, except as a figment of my imagination. Yet you have witnessed examples of its social leadership strategy, its lingua-parasitic branding tactics, and its neurological effectiveness data collection methods which transform the hazy realms of evaluation of advertising effectiveness.

POD has speculated its own way into your cerebral cognition, and by so doing has begun to shape a perception about a brand that doesn't even exist. It becomes easy to envisage its appearance, its touch and its impact on society. By working out how to leverage the powers of human perception, combined with a rough knowledge of basic branding theory, it is possible to cultivate a brand from thin air and ensure that its associations are continually reinforced in a positive way. Simply by announcing its existence, we have already become a little more receptive to the notion of it fulfilling that prophecy in actuality. Rather like the way Chantelle Houghton is now famous for simply behaving as if she was.

Notes

1 Holt, D (March 2003) What becomes an icon most?, *Harvard Business Review* [Online] http://hbr.org/2003/03/what-becomes-an-icon-most/ar/1: He proposes that for a brand to be recognized as a true icon it must somehow offer to reconcile these societal tensions.

2 Gazzaniga, Prof M (1996) *Conversations in the Cognitive Neurosciences*, MIT Press, USA. Gazzaniga discovered in 2007 that the Amygdala region of the brain released different chemicals according to the nature of the visual stimulus. SonyAstraZenneca collaborated with Gazzaniga and developed a patent for machinery able to measure, record and meaningfully interpret this neurological data in 2008.

I believe in the age of osmosis
2007/08

10

ALEX DUNSDON
Co-founder, The Bakery, and Investment Director,
SAATCHiNVEST

I believe We're entering an Age of Conversation where people have active dialogues with brands. This desire to 'engage' more is symptomatic of the industry's response to consumers not listening. We're hopeless optimists. The vast majority of brands simply aren't that important to people. In an era of time-famine, where people organize their lives around just-in-time information, this piece suggests the most effective brands will be those that demand the least of us. We need to shift our focus by losing our ideas obsession and helping people retrieve brand memories.

Editor's therefore, for your brand...

Your brand thinking: Should we be using a 'brand association map' more than a brand key? Do you even have one?

Your brand engagement: What are the top three triggers of behaviour/ purchase in your market? What do you do to maximize them?

Your brand organization & capability: Do you spend more time and resource talking about high engagement vs low brand osmosis?

...and author's personal therefore

My 'therefore' story is one from the overall Diploma course.

It's a story about learning from osmosis by reading, and reading, and reading until my own points of view crystallize.

And a story about a transformation from a bullish, but fundamentally scared ad exec, to someone with the courage to start his own business.

See, I did the course at a time when I was hungry and undernourished.

Lost in a sea of 'this is how it's always been sonny', where no one teaches you your craft in a meaningful way.

But all the reading and learning changed that. William Goldman summed it up for me in a book from the course, *Adventures in the Screen Trade*: 'Nobody knows anything... Not one person in the entire motion picture field knows for a certainty what's going to work. Every time it's a guess and, if you're lucky, an educated one.'

And I suddenly understood:

- *there really are no rules;*
- *that my own beliefs actually mattered;*
- *and it was ok to follow them;*
- *and it was amazingly liberating;*
- *and I kept questioning stuff – like a child again;*
- *it started with brands;*
- *then the process on how work got made;*
- *then the business models that nobody seemed to like;*
- *then my own time;*
- *and how I spend it.*

And my art changed.

My art became about finding the courage to stop doing what I don't believe in, and do more of what I do believe in (I had no option really – authenticity is a deeply held value of mine).

And... it took a while...

But eventually I found the courage to start my own business.

So now I run The Bakery London.[1] And run a technology venture fund.[2]

And it all started with a simple insight learned from the Diploma course – nobody knows anything.

I wouldn't be doing any of this without it.

I believe in the age of osmosis

Part one: the age of conversation

> It is a profoundly erroneous truism... that we should cultivate the habit of thinking of what we are doing. The precise opposite is the case. Civilisation advances by extending the number of important operations we can perform without thinking about them.[3]
>
> (A N Whitehead)

It is said that we are entering an age of conversation, a new world in which we are all eager participants; laptop in hand, blogging with brands and welcoming them into social media conversations with our mates. It is breathlessly hailed as the next big thing; a new way for brands to communicate; the future.

However, do consumers not have better things to do than talk to brands? This paper wonders whether, conversely, the most important role brands play is in helping us not to think, and whether some of the most effective brands will be those that demand the least of us.

Beware the source

One argument is that we should retain a healthy dose of scepticism towards these 'brave new world' proclamations because the sources tend to be comms planners in some guise, people who are very much immersed in the technology and blog far more than Joe Public. As Russell Davies notes, advocates get 'carried away with rhetoric and enthusiasm, [forgetting] that the likely scenario will be that everything will be a blurry munge like it was before, with this new element added in'.[4]

The point here is to question whether we are extrapolating genuine long-term trends or simply responding to the new. An extreme view would have it that the 'planning blogosphere' creates an insular world where such technology-based hypotheses become both self-confirming and self-perpetuating. Even an avid 'conversationalist' like Richard Huntingdon acknowledges this. He says 'we can overstate the importance of blogs simply because we (the planning community) use them much more than the majority of the public.'[5] Perhaps we should take a more holistic view by considering the internet as simply an additional touch point to the myriad already out there.

There is no certainty that conversations with brands will become a mass activity. The impression created is that everyone is at it, but Forrester's latest report on social media users tells a slightly different story. They show that only 17 per cent of people in the UK watch user-generated content and 10 per cent of people in the UK read blogs.[6] Moreover, there is evidence that the excitement with the new is reaching a peak. The latest blogosphere statistics show overall growth and rate of posts per day are all stalling, with the number of active blogs cresting at about 15 million while the number of inactive blogs continues to grow.[7]

Do people want to talk to brands?

Even assuming a widespread eagerness for interaction, it seems odd that people would choose to spend their time talking with brands rather than their family, friends, favourite band or football team.

Having said all that, it would be foolish not to accept that there are brands – the Nikes, Apples and Amazons of the world – that are having conversations with people. The issue here is the inevitability with which current thinking tends to project the behaviour of these few loved brands as the future of all brands. Do people really want an active relationship with a deodorant, sofa, or feminine hygiene brand?

It is therefore important for each brand to understand their relationship with consumers. The brands capable of having conversations will fall into the following broad categories:

- Brands that share a passion for an interest you have, like bands, football teams, media providers or hobbies (Radiohead, Chelsea, BBC, Nikon).
- Brands whose essence is fundamentally related to a cause you believe in (Innocent, Café Direct, Greenpeace).
- Brands that have an extreme point of view on life and make you feel like part of an exclusive club (Death cigarettes, *Vice* magazine).

Therefore, advising brands to embark on a platform of conversation when they do not have such pre-existing relationships is quite simply bad advice. In truth, this is symptomatic of any number of 'engagement' theories that typify our industry's response to consumers not listening. They all have a fundamental assumption at their heart – that people want to engage with what brands have to say.

Part two: brands fit around people's lives

Our biggest mistake as brand managers is believing that customers care a lot about our brand.[8]

(Patrick Barwise)

As a species, we are programmed not to think. It is estimated that at least 95 per cent of human activity is performed without thinking.[9] Breathing, moving your hands and brushing your teeth are just a few examples which highlight that to be human is to be unconscious.

Helping us to not think is therefore the raison d'etre of brands. They help us navigate our complicated lives by acting as heuristics, rules of thumb for quick decision making. Indeed, in a world where psychologists have demonstrated the paralyzing effect of too much choice,[10] and studies confirm the extent to which we are suffering from time famine,[11] the ability of brands to make choice habitual and automatic has never been more important.

We live in a world where, no matter where we are, we are only a simple text, click or phone call away from finding out anything we want. In a very real sense, it's a just-in-time information culture,[12] where the need to learn and retain information is replaced by an expectation that all the information we need is constantly accessible to us.

Accordingly, we are far choosier about the things we do take in. Nicholas Carr summed it up when he said: 'My mind now expects to take in information the way the net distributes it: in a swiftly moving stream of particles. Once I was a scuba diver in the sea of words. Now I zip along the surface like a guy on a Jet Ski.'[13] It is simply not realistic to expect people to spend time thinking about brands. We need a new way to communicate.

Part three: the age of osmosis

Osmosis – a gradual, often unconscious process of assimilation or absorption.[14]

The five commandments in the Age of Osmosis

We need an antidote to brands' increasingly desperate attempts to engage us.

We need to let go of the idea that people spend time thinking about brands and squarely assume they don't.

We need a much simpler communications model that fits around people's lives.

We need a model that works for the majority of brands people are indifferent towards, not just the minority that people adore.

We need to seek lessons from the past and, at times, be unapologetically backward looking.

Thinking holistically

In biology we learn that it's possible to speed up the process of osmosis. Therefore, if we take Heath's Low Attention Processing theory and embrace our capacity for passive learning,[15] we can propose a model where clients and agencies will shift their mindset from 'please remember' to 'help retrieve'. This means demanding less of people by making brand memories easier to absorb and, more than that, helping people retrieve them.

Our current system of advertising is geared around transmitting messages to people. We then use ideas to make these messages engaging to people.

However, brands are represented in the brain by a series of interlinked associations (called engrams). The memory evoked at any given time is dependent on the strength of these interlinking connections.[16] Therefore, instead of hardwiring these connections through the quick hit of active conscious engagement, we should focus instead on building these connections more iteratively, without expecting consumers to 'put something in to get something out'.

Current thinking is almost invariably based on the power of the internet. But there is a myriad of touch points out there that we have not even come close to using effectively yet. We encounter them everywhere we go – we carry them on our mobile phones and see them on buses, taxis, the underground and even in pub toilets.[17]

The upshot is that, in the Age of Osmosis, a long-tail media landscape will develop,[18] where a few media will reach a mass of people, but there will also be a morass of more niche touch points that are used along the consumer journey. Think of media as a set of signs that fit around people's lives, where the best brands help people retrieve the right memories at the right time.

Brands as clusters of associations

We need to make it easy to trigger brand memories and, to do this a brand should be seen as a cluster of associations. In essence, this means providing a raft of shortcuts which make it both easier for people to encode brand memories and to trigger them at point of decision making. Those that do this effectively will have a greater chance of being remembered where it matters most – the point of decision making.

Of course, utilizing associations is not a revolutionary thought, they are the very basis on which many successful brands from the past have been built,[19] but they may have more relevance than ever. At the turn of the century brands were forced to communicate associations to societies that were largely illiterate, relying on simple visual shortcuts in order to communicate to people. In a society where we're bombarded by 3.125 messages a minute,[20] would it not be better to borrow from these simpler communication techniques?

The brand to emulate: Coca-Cola

For illustrative purposes, Coca-Cola provides the clearest demonstration of how associations should be deployed in the Age of Osmosis.

Coca-Cola create associations

Coca-Cola has built a rich set of associations, from Christmas, authenticity, nostalgia to the hiss of a bottle opening.

Coca-Cola seed these associations simply in people's minds

They recently aired a series of five-minute TV spots which communicate a simple association (eg ice) without expecting consumers to actively engage or evaluate a complex message.

Coca-Cola then trigger these associations at the point of decision making

Their use of vending machines or digital posters outside supermarkets.

Encoding memories: putting associations at the heart of the process

Advertising people are obsessed with the idea of the idea. John Grant is one such ideas advocate; he puts them at the centre of the brand universe by actually defining brands as 'clusters of ideas'.[21] However, our ideas often expect too much of consumers. Instead we should reframe ideas as vehicles to communicate brand associations, putting associations to the top of the creative agenda.

Paul Feldwick recently questioned the very basis of our ideas – the 'message model'. He believes that relying on message transmission is not the important part in communications: 'What people [experience and respond to is] a wealth of material, visuals, music, dialogue, timing, colour, entertainment, emotions. We've got used to somehow sidelining all this as if any ad could somehow be summed up in a couple of words.'[22] The danger is that most of our thinking is going into the wrong bit. Instead of fixating on making our messages engaging through ideas we need to get this 'wealth of material' to the top of the agenda.

While ideas often rely on conscious evaluation associations demand little of consumers.

They are easy to encode

This is explained best by brain scientist John Medina who said that 'the brain pays attention to patterns. Remembering something we've seen before (like quicksand) is a useful evolutionary trait.'[23]

A brief exercise also helps to demonstrate the usefulness of associations.

1 Spend 10 seconds trying to remember these letters:
   BGITAELTEGDOHTE
   Most people can't do this. It's too complicated to take in.

2 Now spend 10 seconds trying to remember these:
   THE EAT DOG BIG LET
   Most people can do this. It is easier because you have a pattern to encode.
   This is an advantage that associations have in the era of time famine
   because they enable quick assessments of the brand message rather
   than expecting consumers to process information and evaluate it.

They aid hardwiring over time

An unfortunate by-product of the industry's ideas obsession is that we are always looking to the next one. We get bored quickly. However, Y&R's Adrian Holmes argues that 'we jettison campaigns at the very moment the public begin to get used to them.'[24] The importance of sticking with associations is backed up in psychology through a phenomenon called the 'exposure effect'. A number of studies have demonstrated how people express undue liking for things merely because they are familiar with them.[25] Therefore, associations require nurturing over long periods.

They allow us to target different mindsets

Associations create triggers at the point of decision making, the importance of which should not be underestimated. To use a retail example, it's an oft-quoted fact that people make 70 per cent of their purchase decisions in-store.[26]

However, Daniel Schacter has shown that all memories depend on the right triggers. He gives the example of someone being asked to remember a game of football. Asking them to recall 'that match they played on 7 December 1982' versus 'that match when that winger broke his leg'[27] makes a massive difference to their ability to draw on the right memory.

Any concept of brands having a USP has faded with the loyal monolithic consumer and instead, our repertoire behaviour reflects the fact that we are different people, with different moods and different triggers, at different times.[28] Therefore, the ultimate aim for brands is a rich world of associations to hit different people, in different mindsets at different times.

Changing the way we work

The four key steps:

Step 1: Identify territory

Brands can create as many associations as they can realistically support. To do this, brands will need to start by picking territories to translate into associations using the principle of word association. Benefits, propositions and messages overcomplicate the process; instead brands must pick the most relevant words that best represent the brand in people's heads. Brand tagging, developed by Noah Brier, is one tool we could use to get the truest instinctive reaction from consumers.[29]

Step 2: Create association

Examples of brand associations include icons, music, character, aspirational values, voiceover, celebrity, colour or shape. Celebrities are a very relevant example; it is no coincidence that their use in advertising has grown over the years as they deliver powerful shortcuts and provide multiple triggers (ie each time a consumer opens *Heat* magazine it should help trigger a brand memory).

We need to put association creation at the heart of the process. However, challenging the primacy of the idea is no small tweak; instead it's so fundamental to how all creatives think that we need a new structure to make it work.

New roles: Identity Creators + Creative Realisors

In this new structure 'Creative' is split into two parts – the 'Identity Creators' and the 'Creative Realisors'. A typical Identity Creation team would consist of a comms planner, creative and graphic designer. Their aim would be to develop associations with the triggering process 'front-of-mind', using the comms planner's knowledge of media opportunities and insight into the customer journey.

The Creative Realisors will be more like producers than 'ideas machines', with the emphasis firmly on assimilation skills. They'll be production-savvy and far more executional in their thinking, and their role will be the apotheosis of the 'it's-not-what-you-say-it's-how-you-say-it' school of thinking.

So is this advertising dystopia?

The fear is that putting 'associations first' would restrict creative freedom, and relies heavily on the much maligned concept of consistency. John Grant claimed 'only liars need to be consistent'.[30]

However, Y&R's Adrian Holmes theorized, as part of his 'inside-the-box' theory, that providing parameters 'has an extraordinarily liberating effect on the way people think'. He used a neat analogy of a tennis court to show how important these are to feed off. Without lines and a net we would not have a game.[31]

Moreover, as Paul Feldwick pointed out, 'somehow 30 seconds of entertaining nonsense leads to a situation where people pay 35% more for [PG Tips]'.[32] An exciting consequence of losing reliance on transmitting ideas to consumers is freedom from logical linear narratives, giving us the freedom to create lateral associations. The only criteria is that they communicate the territory required. They do not have to be logical – would associating a gorilla with chocolate get through any logical linear research, for instance? In the Age of Osmosis almost anything can become an association.

Step 3: Seed association

This is about using media away from the point of decision making to hardwire brand associations. Giep Franzen speculates that the brain is capable of holding a huge number of brands in the brain – perhaps 10,000.[33] Seeds allow us to hardwire as many associations as possible that can then be triggered later.

The emphasis will be on iteratively building associations over time. Key media trends include:

- *Frequency. Frequency. Frequency*: Without the big bang of conscious engagement, the emphasis will be on hardwiring these iteratively, but frequently.

- *Shorter time lengths will become popular*: At its most extreme, Blipverts will be used as an efficient means to seed associations. Tachistocope studies have shown the power of this; one demonstrated how 2,000 images were rotated too quickly for the brain to consciously perceive, but were later recognized with 90 per cent accuracy.[34]

- *Experiential marketing will boom*: Used properly as an enjoyable, non-intrusive part of people's leisure time, opening up opportunities for powerful and differentiating brand triggers.

Step 4: Trigger association

Seeded associations will be triggered to provide the most relevant just-in-time information to consumers. Examples of possibilities include:

Time-based triggers

Chris Kamara (a celebrity association seeded in Ladbroke's TV ad) could be used to trigger real-time bets on interactive shop windows. These can tailor messages to the second if needs be.[35]

Mobile phone retailers could trigger their brand when people's phones are up for renewal. There would be no words of 'persuasion' and no message evaluation, just a simple image, in the same style as their advert, to cue brand memory.

Audience-based triggers

Clothing retailers could seed associations that change according to the gender and age of each passer by using facial recognition technology.

Season-based triggers
Coca-Cola could change digital vending machines seasonally. Cold messages would be most relevant for summer, while Christmas associations could be employed in winter.

Location-based triggers
GPS systems on mobile phones will mean brands will have the ability to deliver communications when you are in the vicinity of the shop.

Mood-based triggers
Marmite could communicate love, strength and authenticity by using packaging more inventively. Packaging will prove a crucial media in the Age of Osmosis as brands will start to use different associations on different packs to trigger different need states.

Sense-based triggers
Martin Lindstrom's brand sense study has demonstrated the power of brands that use senses as triggers.[36]

Smell is the most subconscious of the senses and remarkably effective at evoking memory – people remember up to 50 per cent more of a movie when the smell of popcorn is wafted into the air. Companies such as Scentair can replicate certain smells at point of decision making to trigger brand associations.[37,38]

A recent analysis also found brands that use music that matches their brand identity are 96 per cent more likely to be recalled than those who do not.[39] Supermarket brands could play their sonic trigger on enhanced supermarket trolleys. The point is to keep the triggers non-intrusive – studies have shown how shoppers are programmed to keep moving not 'stop, look and listen'.[40]

Occasion-based triggers
Beer brands could prompt relevant drinking occasions very specifically around football grounds by using moving digital screens.

Experiential triggers
Carlsberg could build the ultimate pub. It would have the best freshly brewed Becks, served by beautiful waitresses and have great brands playing, providing the ultimate sensory pub experience. This would create an emotional marker to trigger every time they see or hear anything relating to that experience.

Part four: final considerations

Key implications

We will ask better questions

The brand name will simply be one of a number of stimuli we use. These won't necessarily be static and visual – we will test triggers like smell and refine the strongest associations.

We will test below the conscious threshold

Tachistocope Research is something we can explore – where key associations are rotated too quickly for the mind to consciously perceive would be one way to do this.[41] Doing this with key brand associations, and asking the brand evoked, would be a key measure of brand strength.

We will be better at testing instinctive emotion

We normally fall back on words and their meanings when testing emotional responses to brands, but these are blunt tools which force people to rationalize irrational responses. The emotiscape from Ipsos is one tool which could be used to overcome this.[42]

Pre-testing will be less reliant on comprehension

At the moment there is an emphasis on being understood in pre-testing.[43] Ads basically fail if they're not understood. We need to adapt our pre-testing models to be less reliant on comprehension and the rational take-out of messaging.

Conclusion

Brands will be judged on the strength of the associations they build in people's minds. The zenith will come when our awards system puts a premium on realization over ideas.

For smaller brands this will involve a heavily targeted approach and exploration of memetic associations (eg 118 runners, Budweiser's 'Wassup' campaign), while for non-purchase advertising the key will be to use triggers for maximum impact (eg Transport for London's anti-social behaviour campaign). For new news, news associations can be used as vehicles to carry the 'new' information. Brands that do frequent promotional campaigns can create associations to signpost offers (eg Asda 'Rollback' ads).

People are no longer listening, but is the industry's response to engage more the right one? Brands are just not that important to them. Instead we should stop trying to force our messages on people, and stop expecting them to remember all we say. Instead we should help them trigger the right brand memories at the right time.

Notes

1 The Bakery takes the risk out of doing new stuff. It's an Open Innovation marketplace connecting brands to the entrepreneurial ecosystem.

2 SaatchInvest invests in high-growth, early stage tech companies.

3 Whitehead, A N quoted in *Simply Better: Winning and keeping customers by delivering what matters most,* ed P Barwise and S Meehan (2004) Harvard Business Review Press, Harvard.

4 Davies, R (blog, May 2008) Asymmetric Politeness [Online] russelldavies.typepad.com/planning/thinking/index.html

5 Huntingdon, R (blog, 2007) We won't make that mistake again, *Adliterate* [Online] www.adliterate.com/2007/07/we-wont-make-that-mistake-again/

6 Bernoff, J (blog, May 2008) Data Chart of the Week, *Empowered* [Online] http://blogs.forrester.com/groundswell/2008/05/data-chart-of-t.html

7 (Blog, 2008) Expanding no more, *Valleywag* [Online] http://valleywag.com/tech/notag/expanding-no-more-255660.php

8 Barwise, P and Meehan, S, eds (2004) *Simply Better: Winning and keeping customers by delivering what matters most,* Harvard Business Review Press, Harvard.

9 According to neuroscientists, we are conscious of only about 5 per cent of our cognitive activity. See Szegedy-Maszak, M [Accessed 2008] Mysteries of the Mind: Your unconscious is making your everyday decisions, *US News and World Report* [Online] www.auburn.edu/~mitrege/ENGL2210/USNWR-mind.html

10 Schwartz, B (2004) *The Paradox of Choice: Why more is less,* HarperCollins Publishers, New York.

11 [Accessed 2008] [Online] www.doubletongued.org/index.php/dictionary/time_famine/

12 (January 2007) Ideas trends brand futures and intelligence, *The Future Laboratory* [Online] https://blogs.msdn.com/cfs.../Microsoft-and-futurelab-report.pdf

13 Carr, N (July 2008) Is Google making us stupid?, *The Atlantic* [Online] www.theatlantic.com/doc/200807/google

14 [Accessed 2008] [Online] www.thefreedictionary.com/osmosis

15 Heath, R and Feldwick, P (2008) Fifty years using the wrong model of advertising, *International Journal of Market Research*, 50; and Heath, R (2001) *The Hidden Power of Advertising: How low involvement processing influences the way we choose brands,* NTC Publications.

16 Franzen, G and Bouwman, M (2001) *The Mental World of Brands: Mind, memory and brand success,* NTC Publications. These rich complex associative networks are capable of holding as many as 10,000 brands in the brain.

The connections discussed are in constant flux – some die slowly while others become 'hardwired' through repetition.

17 [Digital Presentation, 2008] Digital Signage: The future is now, *Scala* [Online] www.youtube.com/watch?v=x_oTvZxtG94.

18 Anderson, C [Blog, accessed 2008] The Long Tail [Online] www.thelongtail.com

19 Heath, R (2001) *The Hidden Power of Advertising: How low involvement processing infuences the way we choose brands*. Heath is an advocate of associations. He talks here about some of the key ones over time.

20 This is calculated from the oft-quoted figure of being exposed to 3,000 messages a day. (June 2004) The Harder Hard Sell, *The Economist* [Online] www.economist.com/node/2787854

21 This obviously also provides a useful parallel to how this piece defines brands. See Grant, J (2006) *The Brand Innovation Manifesto: How to build brands, redefine markets and defy conventions*, John Wiley & Sons, Chichester.

22 Feldwick, P [Accessed 2008] Exploding the Message Myth, *Thinkbox* [Online] www.thinkbox.tv/server/show/nav.1015

23 Medina, J (2009) *Brain Rules: 12 principles for surviving and thriving at work, home and school*, Pear Press, Washington.

24 Holmes, A [July 2008], Presentation to creatives at M&C Saatchi.

25 [Accessed 2008] [Online] http://en.wikipedia.org/wiki/Exposure_effect

26 It has also been shown that 53 per cent of those are on impulse: Vollmer, C and Precourt, G (2008) *Always On: Advertising, marketing, and media in an era of consumer control*, McGraw Hill, US.

27 See also: Schacter, D L (1997) *Searching for Memory: The brain, the mind and the past*, Basic Books, New York.

28 Gordon, W (2002) Brands on the brain, in *Brand New Brand Thinking*, pp 103–121, ed Baskin, M and Earls, M, Kogan Page, UK. Wendy demonstrates how we are different people at different times. For more on the demise of the loyal consumer and how we are different people at different times see Miller, J and Muir, D (2004) *The Business of Brands*, pp 75–76, John Wiley & Sons, Chichester. See also De Chernatony, L and McDonald, M (2003) *Creating Powerful Brands*, pp 84–85, Butterworth-Heinemann, Oxford.

29 [Accessed 2008] [Online] www.brandtags.net/referrer.php?referrer=sethgodin

30 Grant, J (2006) *The Brand Innovation Manifesto: How to build brands, redefine markets and defy conventions*, John Wiley & Sons, Chichester.

31 Holmes, A [24 July 2008] Presentation: Thinking Inside the Box, M&C Saatchi: Adrian's presentation shows how great campaigns from Smirnoff, 'Inside the bottle' and Heineken's 'Water from Majorca' help illustrate.

32 Feldwick, P [Accessed 2008] Exploding the Message Myth, *Thinkbox* [Online] www.thinkbox.tv/server/show/nav.1015

33 Franzen , G and Bouwman, M (2001) *The Mental World of Brands: Mind, memory and brand success*, NTC Publications. These rich complex associative networks are capable of holding as many as 10,000 brands in the brain. The connections discussed are in constant flux – some die slowly while others become 'hardwired' through repetition.

34 Franzen, G and Bouwman, M (2001) *The Mental World of Brands: Mind, memory and brand success*, NTC Publications.

35 [Video, Accessed 2008][Online] http://www.youtube.com/watch?v=vJbb1v0Kkdo

36 Lindstrom, M (2005) *Brand Sense*, Free Press, New York: His 5-D BRAND sense study demonstrates its potential. For instance, it shows that a third of customers distinguish between cars simply by the sound of the door closing and more than half of people associated Nokia's ringtone with positive feelings.

37 Medina, J (2009) *Brain Rules: 12 principles for surviving and thriving at work, home and school*, Pear Press, Washington, US. See also: Hirsch, A R and Gay, S (1991) The Effect of Ambient Olfactory Stimuli on the Evaluation of a Common Consumer Product, *Chemical Senses*, **16** (5), p 535.

38 [Accessed 2008][Online] www.scentair.com/

39 Cesman, C (November 2006) Audio Branding in the Retail Environment, *BizCommunity* [Online] www.bizcommunity.com/Article/196/87/12649.html

40 (August 2007) Shopper Modality, *Nielsen* [Online] www.nl.nielsen.com/site/documents/ShopperModality_EUSept07.pdf

41 [Accessed 2008] [Online] www.thefreedictionary.com/tachistoscopes

42 (April 2005) Moods, Minds, and Motivations: Measuring emotions for advertising results, *Ipsos* [Online] www.ipsosasi.com/pdf/Global_Ideas_vol7.pdf

43 [Accessed 2008][Online] www.millwardbrown.com/solutions/slick-sheets/millwardbrown_link-for-digital.aspx

I believe it's what brands don't say that matters
2011/12

11

PETE BUCKLEY
Head of Strategy, MEC UK

I believe In recent years our understanding of how humans make decisions has improved considerably, but this has had little impact on most brand planning. Messages and persuasion are still central to the majority of briefs. This paper proposes a new way of looking at brand communication by broadening the perspective from explicit messages to implicit signals. Viewing brand communication through the lens of messaging can result in brands missing opportunities, and at worst contradicting themselves with their behaviour. Brands need to consider how they communicate implicitly and ensure that these signals reinforce their values in every way possible.

Editor's therefore, for your brand...

Your brand thinking:
When doing competitive analysis what are the implicit vs explicit messages of you vs your competitors?

Your brand engagement:
What do you do that can be truly defined as *spectacular*?

Your brand organization & capability:
If you list everything you do on your brand what could you sacrifice in order to focus resources on the truly extravagant?

...and author's personal therefore

A tale of neglected signals

We're in the boardroom of a major advertising agency. The client, an FMCG brand, is about to brief their cross-agency team on the big launch of the year – a new gourmet frankfurter brand. The rationale is solid; the data presented highlights a clear gap in the market to sell frankfurters to young affluent foodies as a snack.

The presentation reveals a plethora of further details about the new launch:

- where the product will be made (a factory in Greece which produces frankfurters for nine other brands);
- the packaging (bright, modern, slightly tacky);
- the brand name (it will be called Bingo Bosh);
- the ingredients and production method (as cost-efficient as possible);
- the price-point (in line with competitors);
- the sales targets (rapid growth is required within the first year); and
- the distribution (big supermarkets, supported by deep promotions, to deliver the growth targets).

Following the presentation both the agencies and client team enthusiastically start to consider how to build the brand and hit the ambitious growth targets.

Unfortunately, it's a case of so far so familiar.

While Bingo Bosh is a fictional brand the missed opportunities to exploit its signals are a reality for many brands and something I've experienced often since writing my essay.

Whether the agencies and client team working on Bingo Bosh recognize it or not, they're starting from a place of disadvantage. Many of the biggest opportunities for marketing to show its strength have been missed months before they were briefed. Signals which could have built on a solid brand story now threaten to undermine it: where it's made, its name, the packaging, the ingredients, the price-point, the mass distribution... all build to nothing. Messaging and spin alone are left to try to build the brand. Storytelling baked into the product is a distant dream; instead they're forced to take the slap-it-on-top approach to brand communications strategy. Focusing purely on the explicit messages and neglecting the implicit signals the brand will send.

Career and life: Why you should never use your company's PowerPoint template

The idea of transposing costly signalling from evolutionary biology into other fields was first proposed by Michael Spence in the early 1970s. Spence looked at how costly signalling works in the employment market (a piece of work which won him a Nobel Prize). His conclusion stated that impressive education on a CV is a costly signal which is worth much more than its intrinsic value.

Personally, the cost of doing the IPA Excellence Diploma (in effort and time especially) has created a strong signal which has clearly communicated more about me than any communication I created from years of efficiently doing my job day-to-day.

Like the brands I wrote about throughout the Diploma I've discovered that signalling can work as well for me personally as it could for them. And just like Bingo Bosh I've got some way to go to making sure all the signals I send are saying what I'd like (eg too many creased clothes, too much slouching).

Signalling theory teaches us that everything communicates, but it's those signals that are costly or perceived as unintentional which are most powerful.

Indeed, a recent academic study found that MIT students who abandoned the MIT PowerPoint template were seen to have better ideas than those who used the template; as they appeared as people who 'can afford to do what they want'. The same study showed that lecturers who dressed down and wore red sneakers were rated as more competent and intelligent than those who dressed more formally. As the study states, being perceived as autonomous can be a very powerful signal.

Whether you're a brand or an individual, we can all benefit from thinking about the signals we're sending and how we can exploit them more effectively. So next time you're putting together a presentation, stop a moment and think – what does this PowerPoint template really say about me?

I believe it's what brands don't say that matters

Introduction

> Ever since the arrival of television, brands, their owners and advisors have been
> obsessed with what brands say at the expense of what brands do.
>
> (Jeremy Bullmore, 2008[1])

In the late summer of 1904, the *New York Times* reported on a German
horse that could do 'almost everything but talk'. The subject of the article
was 'Clever Hans' a horse who could perform arithmetic and intellectual
tasks at the level of a nine-year-old child. His owner, Wilhelm von Osten,
would ask Clever Hans a question and then provide a number of answers;
at the correct answer Clever Hans would tap his right hoof. An investigation
by the Prussian Minister of Education confirmed that no tricks were involved.

Not everyone was convinced; a psychologist called Oskar Pfungst decided
to investigate. Pfungst discovered that the key to the horse's intelligence
lay in involuntary and unconscious cues displayed by the questioner when
they reached the correct answer. Without knowing it the questioner would
unconsciously lean forward slightly at the correct answer. Pfungst proved
this by showing if the questioner himself didn't know the answer Clever
Hans didn't either.[2]

Clever Hans may not have been such a clever horse, but he can teach brands
an important lesson – unintended, non-verbal, implicit communication is often
more powerful than the carefully composed message. While all brands communicate implicitly only some currently plan to exploit these less obvious
signals.

Simply put, implicit communication is a brand's body language: the non-
verbal signals a brand creates by its actions. This paper looks at how brands
can harness their implicit communications more effectively to drive business
advantage and stronger emotional connections.

We've known for a long time that unconscious feelings dominate human
decision making, but this knowledge has made few inroads into how we

FIGURE 11.1   Clever Hans and his owner Herr Wilhelm Von Osten

Das lesende und rechnende Pferd mit seinem Lehrer HERRN von OSTEN (Berlin)

approach brand planning.[3] While there have been theories around low involvement processing, it still remains conscious engagement, key messages, awareness and cut-through ruling the roost.[4]

This focus on messages means opportunities are often missed by brands. Explicit communications are easily controlled and planned and therefore dominate thinking.[5] But it is often signals from the brand's behaviour, or other people using/talking about the brand that can have the greatest effect.

These signals are often processed unconsciously by consumers and stored as feelings which greatly affect brand preference.[6] With the growing socialization of life and further personalization of media these implicit sources of communication are becoming ever more important.

I believe understanding and optimizing implicit communications offers great opportunities for brands, agencies and the discipline of marketing as a whole. Specifically, I believe greater attention on implicit communications will:

- allow a more holistic view of a brand and its communications;
- exploit the dominance of the unconscious in the decision-making process;
- provide a scientific rationale to what many in marketing already know but don't have the language to evidence;
- equip us with a new practical template for building brands in the future; and
- give marketers and their agencies a clear and indisputable reason to be present at the boardroom table.

We think we think more than we think

How we make decisions

> Unconscious prejudices which we form are often stronger than the conscious;
> and they are the more dangerous, because we cannot knowingly guard against
> them.
>
> (W B Carpenter, 1874[7])

Recent advances in neuroscience, behavioural economics and psychology
have led to it being accepted that our minds are dictated by emotional
unconscious thinking (instinct/gut feeling), often described as System 1
thinking – a type of thinking which is fast, automatic, effortless and rooted
in habit/heuristics.[8] We can and do engage rational conscious thinking
(System 2) but only when we have to.[9] The differences between the two
systems are summarized below:[10]

FIGURE 11.2   System 1 vs System 2

System 1	System 2
Unconscious	Conscious
Fast	Slow
Implicit	Explicit
Experiential	Analytical
Instinctive	Effortful
Emotional	Cognitive
Metaphoric	Propositional
Signals	Messages

Marketing, market research and advertising are still firmly rooted in System 2
thinking.[11] Advertising objectives continue to focus around the need to
communicate a message that is persuasive, has cut-through and delivers
recall – all objectives being directly targeted at System 2 rather than trying
to appeal to System 1.

The dominance of System 1 suggests that the models we have historically
used to understand how advertising works are wrong.[12] Understandably,
advertising approaches such as 'salesmanship in print' and 'message transmission' have been fundamentally challenged.[13]

Psychology and advertising research suggests that feelings and associations
are the most important behavioural drivers, and these are less influenced by
messaging and more by associations, heuristics and social copying.[14,15]

Research from the IPA Databank confirms this. Campaigns which contained little or no product message, but worked by appealing to emotions

or herd instincts, were shown to be twice as effective as conventional 'message' advertising.[16]

These emotional advertisements are explicit communication functioning in an implicit way. Implicit communication is processed unconsciously and creates associations and feelings about a brand which have a strong effect on brand preference and decisions.[17]

Implicit communication demands involvement

> In baiting a mousetrap with cheese, always leave room for the mouse. (Saki)

Implicit communication requires the receiver to be involved in the communication, as they need to 'join the dots' together themselves to create the meaning. This is similar to the philosophy of artist Marcel Duchamp who believed that creativity was 'not performed by the artist alone; the spectator brings the work in contact with the external world by deciphering and interpreting its inner qualifications and thus adds his contribution to the creative act'.[18]

The peacock, the gazelle and the horny toad: What brands can learn from the animal kingdom

Signalling theory and effective implicit communications

Much current marketing language is grounded in the old world of rational decision makers, filled with terms such as 'messaging' and 'proposition'. A brand's implicit communications can be better described as signalling (Figure 11.3).[19]

FIGURE 11.3   Messages vs Signals

Messages	Signals
Explicit	Implicit
What a brand says	Everything a brand does
Attention	Cost & intention
Added-on	Embedded
Persuasion	Feelings
Exact	Interpreted
Forced	Natural

Signalling is a concept from evolutionary biology which is often used in economics, but rarely mentioned in marketing.[20] At the core of signalling is the belief that businesses are constantly communicating through their actions, even when they are not intentionally communicating. Everything a brand does is a signal. Signals are automatically processed and stored as feelings, making them powerful in driving brand preference and choice.[21]

Looking at communications through the lens of signals considerably widens the perspective of brand planning. It makes every decision taken by the company a brand decision. Examining the difference between messaging and signals reveals how the concept of signals is a much better fit with our understanding of how people make decisions, using their feelings rather than their rational mind.

The strength of a signal can be determined by two factors: *Cost* – the more costly/harder it is to imitate the signal, the stronger the signal,[22] and *Intention* – signals perceived as unintentional are seen as more honest and therefore stronger than intended signals as they appear to have not been planned as communication.[23]

Cost – costly communications

In 1899 Thorstein Veblen introduced the theory of conspicuous consumption, in which he proposed that the leisured classes showed their superiority over the working classes through extravagant and non-functional expenditure.[24] Veblen determined that it was the 'waste' in these actions that communicated superiority and reputability.[25]

A century later, biologist Amotz Zahavi was looking at similar ideas. He wondered why peacocks have such extravagantly large and colourful tails when such displays are inefficient and evolution favours the efficient.[26] Zahavi wasn't the first person to think about this; back in 1860 Darwin had stated in a letter to a friend 'The sight of a feather in a peacock's tail, whenever I gaze at it, makes me sick.' He couldn't understand why evolution would allow such a terrible inefficiency.[27]

Zahavi discovered that the apparently wasteful peacock tail was actually a signal, the high cost of which ensured its reliability. He proposed the 'handicap principle': for signals to be reliable, they must be costly.[28] Animals had evolved costly signals to demonstrate their strength and status.[29] By displaying its ability to thrive even with such a handicap, the animal reliably signals its high quality (Table 11.1).

The vital component of meaningful signalling is that it is expensive and/or difficult to do. The cost does not need to be financially expensive, but it must be hard for competitors to imitate.

TABLE 11.1 Costly signalling in nature – 'In order to be effective, signals have to be reliable, in order to be reliable, signals have to be costly'

Gazelle Stotting	Toad Croaks	Super Territories	Bowerbirds	Hand Axes
Gazelles jump up and down when spotted by a wolf. The gazelle is signalling to the wolf that it has been seen; by jumping it wastes valuable time and energy thus sending a costly signal that it is able to outrun the wolf (it wouldn't waste the energy and time if it couldn't afford to).	A male toad mounts a female who is ready to lay. While on top the male croaks. The deeper the croak the stronger the toad. It is a costly signal as a deep croak is only possible if the toad holds the female very lightly. Weaker toads hold on too tight fearful of being knocked off meaning their croaks are high, signalling their weakness.	The size of an animal's territory can serve as a signal of their strength. A large territory proves the male's superiority and a better mate. The territory serves no purpose but to signal the strength of the male. Territories are costly as they take time and energy to maintain.	Bowerbirds build structures to attract females. The structures have no purpose beyond acting as a signal to females. The more elaborate and complicated the structure, the stronger the signal. The signal is costly as the bird must waste time and effort to create the structure.	Early man had a preference for highly symmetric, carefully crafted stone hand axes. These axes did not have a practical use but acted as a signal to a man's strength and ability. To make one, a man would need to have access to resources, fine motor skills and be able to sit and craft for hours and still survive.

Images: Yathin sk (2012) Springbok ponk, Wikipedia, licensed under CC BY-SA 3.0; Brown, T (2013) Calling from beside a pond outside of La Boca Village, Sancti Spiritus, Wikipedia, licensed under CC BY 2.0; Tambako the Jaguar (2013) Posing Wolf, Flickr, licensed under CC BY-ND 2.0; Picman2 (2014) Satin Bowerbird, Pixabay, licensed under CC0 1.0; Mercy (2009) Prehistoric man, Anthropos Museum, Brno, Czech Republic, Wikimedia, Licensed under CC BY-SA 3.0

TABLE 11.2 Costly signalling for brands

Waitrose Service	Honda Cog Ad	Bellagio Fountains	Goldman Lobby	Red Bull F1 Team
When you ask for the location of an item in Waitrose, the member of staff will always ask 'is there anything else I can do for you?'. The additional question doesn't cost Waitrose from a financial perspective but it does from an energy point of view. It takes effort to train staff that well. It acts as a clear signal of Waitrose quality. Importantly, no other supermarket does this.	There have been many examples of costly signalling through advertising. The Honda cog is selected as a good example as it is costly not only from a media and production perspective, but also from a skill perspective. The ad contained minimal CGI and took six months to create. Creativity is as much a costly signal as finance, as it is as hard if not harder to imitate.	The Bellagio hotel in Las Vegas spent $40 million on dancing fountains. A clear and reliable signal about the hotel itself, the fountains have generated vast amounts of social signals for the Bellagio. Appearing in 9 blockbuster films in the last 10 years and are taken home to millions of friends and families through photos and videos. Each time these are viewed, the association between the Bellagio and luxury is strengthened in a more reliable way than any message could ever appear.	Many banks have oversized lobbies containing art to signal their wealth. At the Goldman Sachs global headquarters in New York, the expansive lobby is home to a mural costing $10 million. Wasting so much expensive real estate and money is a clear signal of the bank's wealth and power.	Red Bull signals its association with adrenaline not by sponsoring but by owning an F1 team, which have won the last two F1 championships. The expense of F1 teams is well known, the Red Bull team is believed to have cost $400 million over three years. However, from a signal perspective, it demonstrates Red Bull's values more clearly than any message could and creates millions of social signals about the brand through F1 news reports and discussions.

Intention – signals perceived as unintended

Unintended, unconscious signals people create are more powerful than planned conscious communication precisely because they appear unplanned and therefore can be seen as more honest.[30] Joseph Stalin was aware of the power of *perceived* unintended communication. When meeting with his most senior generals in a marble floored room, Stalin would wear shoes with a velvet sole meaning his footsteps made no noise, while all the other generals clonked about in their heavy shoes.

Paul Watzlawick stated that 'every communication has content and a relationship aspect such that the later classifies the former and is therefore a meta-communication'.[31] In other words, the communication is what is said, but that communication is qualified and adapted by the tone and body language of the person communicating, and this is what he terms 'meta-communication'. Watzlawick found that it was the meta-communication and not the communication which dominated human communication.[32]

Well-known work by Albert Mehrabian has further evidenced this, demonstrating that non-verbal communication and tone of voice are more influential than words.[33] If words disagree with the non-verbal behaviour, people tend to believe the non-verbal behaviour.

The same is true with brands and people. Any action, or even non-action by a brand, contains implicit signals which are more likely to be taken as truth than the words that compose a message because they are perceived as unplanned and organic. They can be seen as proof points for the brand, therefore 'in marketing, meta-communication is what really matters'.[34]

This has large ramifications for brands, how they behave and how they communicate. Everything communicates and it is those actions which are perceived as not having been planned as communication that can have the strongest effect. Detail suddenly becomes much more important.

So apparent is the power of communication perceived as unintended, that organizations monitor it (eg the ASA) and people complain when communication is made to look unplanned when it is planned. In June 2012, the ASA banned a Nike Twitter campaign which had used the brand's sponsored stars to tweet about the latest Nike campaign without clearly labelling the tweet as an ad.[35] The action taken by the ASA clearly illustrates the importance society attaches to defining the difference between signals which are perceived as unplanned as opposed to those seen as planned.

What this means for brand communications

Signalling theory teaches us that for brands to use their implicit communications effectively they have to appear wasteful and/or be perceived as unintentional (eg not the primary purpose of the action). The chart below illustrates how signal strength is determined by these two factors (with examples added for understanding). The further away from the centre

FIGURE 11.4   Chart illustrating how signal strength is determined by cost and intention

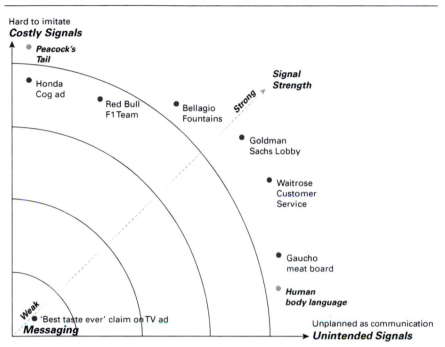

the brand behaviour is, the more powerful it is as a signal. As Figure 11.4 details, 'messaging' is perceived as explicitly intentional and easy to imitate and therefore a weak signal (sitting in the bottom left corner).

It is interesting to consider that brand behaviours on the outer edge of the chart not only create stronger signals, but are also seen as more honest and are more likely to generate social signals.

Figure 11.5 suggests that many brands have misunderstood what engagement means. The strongest signals are those which are perceived as unintended and costly as these signals are unquestioned. Being implicit, these signals require the consumer to join up the dots and it is this joining of the dots (whether unconscious or conscious) which can be seen as real engagement.

Many brands currently count encouraging people to upload their photo on Facebook for the chance to win a prize as engagement. The Figure 11.6 disputes this idea with this type of campaign sitting firmly in the bottom left – being easy to imitate and clearly intended as communication from the brand. Paul Adam recently wrote on his blog: 'marketers are building web apps. Ads that you can interact with. Ads... with multiple layers of interaction. Everyone building these "immersive" experiences... Almost every app built for a brand on Facebook has practically no usage... Heavy, "immersive" experiences are not how people engage and interact with brands. Pitched against strategies built around many, lightweight interactions

FIGURE 11.5   Chart illustrating that costly/unintended signals
have greater sociability

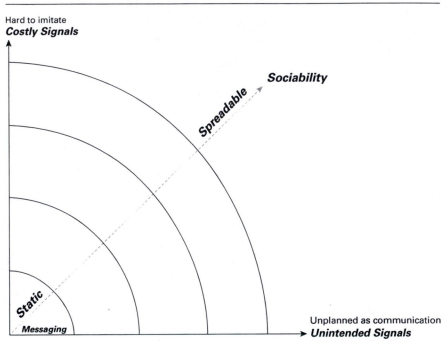

FIGURE 11.6   Chart illustrating that costly/unintended signals are
perceived as more natural

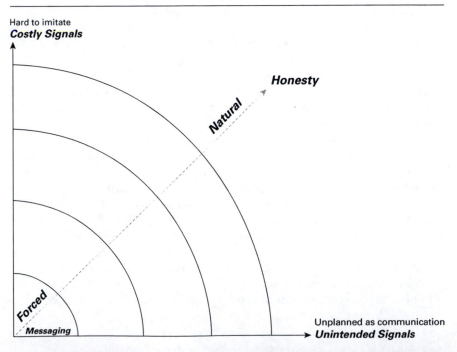

over time, heavyweight experiences will fail because they don't map to real life.'[36]

Signal brands

The best ads don't look like ads. (Amir Kassaei, CCO, DDB)[37]

Blurring the lines – Signal Brands

Brands which understand the importance of implicit communication ensure all their signals amplify the brand's values and have such belief in the brand that they are willing to create costly signals. These brands can be labelled Signal Brands.

Every action by these brands is designed to signal the brand's positioning as conspicuously as possible, they communicate directly with System 1 rather than relying on persuading System 2. This type of brand behaviour is only possible due to these brands changing the process by which brands are built.

Signal Brands blur the lines between product, marketing, social and culture. Traditionally, a product was developed then a marketing plan (potentially with a social element) would be added on top and forced on culture by targeting an audience.

The Signal Brand approach is different (Figure 11.7).

The product is created with the marketing and social elements built in: embedded into the product.[38,39] By its very design it tells the positioning story of the brand and encourages others to tell stories about it.

Signal Brands embed the product into culture; they do not force marketing campaigns on targets, they appeal to people and become part of their lives.

The diagram on next page visualizes the difference in approach of the traditional process vs Signal Brands.

Four principles of strong positive brand signals

There are four principles of creating strong positive brand signals:

1 Act extravagantly

2 Sacrifice more } Drive costly communication

3 Distinctive design

4 Concrete actions } Drive communication which is perceived as unintentional

FIGURE 11.7   The Signal Brand approach to brand planning

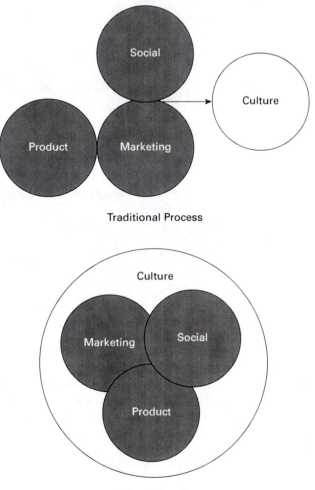

Traditional Process

Signal Brands

Principle 1: act extravagantly

> Brands should be spending less on communicating and more on conspicuous waste. (Professor Tim Ambler, London Business School[40])

Extravagance is the last thing many brands want, especially with the growing importance of procurement and the ongoing economic issues. But accountants aren't likely to think about the implicit communication of a brand and need marketing agencies to illustrate the benefits. Signalling theory gives such actions a much stronger rationale. Being extravagant and wasteful can improve the reliability of communication, making a brand's powerful implicit communication more effective.

Studies have shown that high levels of advertising spend communicates quality implicitly through the mere fact of spending (wasting) so much money.[41] Creativity can also be seen as a type of extravagance; in advertising the creativity is considered waste as it is beyond the functional communication purpose of the ad. The more wasteful you can be from a creative perspective the Better from a business perspective. Analysis of data from both the IPA Databank and the Gunn Report found that creatively awarded campaigns grew market share 11 times more efficiently than non-awarded campaigns.[42]

Extravagance can also be displayed by other brand behaviour. Many Nordstrom department stores in the United States have a pianist playing a grand piano on the ground floor, a clear signal about the brand. While relatively low cost, this can be seen as extravagant as no other department store chain has pianists.

As social media grows and media personalization increases, it is going to become necessary for all brands to find ways to act more extravagantly to create stronger positive associations about the brand.

Principle 2: sacrifice more

> Elegance is refusal. (Coco Chanel)

Costly signals can also be created by 'sacrificial' brand actions. Sacrifice may have negative connotations, but used well can be vital in strengthening a brand. Sacrificing sales or distribution in the name of the brand can send strong and effective signals about the brand, but the current economic climate can mean this principle is often overlooked.

Luxury brands are especially good at sending these types of signals. The champagne brand Krug increased its price from $19 to $100 over the period of 10 years to boost the brand profile and compete with Dom Pérignon (which had entered the market at a higher price point). The strong implicit communication created by the higher price point meant Krug lost 'bad customers' (negative social signals), gained many more attractive ones (positive social signals) and significantly grew market share.[43]

Consumer exclusion isn't just the realm of luxury brands; when GHD launched it was the only hair straightener on the market available solely through salons, instantly signalling the quality of the product.[44] Moleskine notepads grew distribution through bookstores and design shops, not stationery stores, helping to frame the brand as something separate from other notepads.

Many brands actively shy away from this type of sacrifice and weaken their brand by sending the wrong signals as a result.[45] Thornton's chocolates advertised in the window of Poundland may not be consciously remembered by a shopper, but the next time they are looking for a gift the Thornton's Continental selection box will feel that little bit less appealing.

Consumers make no distinction between purposeful 'brand communication' and any other encounter they have with the brand; all affect their feelings towards the brand and all will alter the saleability of the brand.[46] Faced with ever increasing choice the detail becomes increasingly important as people, consciously or not, look for reasons to reject brands.[47]

Principle 3: distinctive design

> Design is an opportunity to continue telling the story, not just to sum everything up. (Tate Linden)[48]

With the increasing importance of product placement and earned media, there is a need for brands to start seeing design as a central part of their marketing communications. A recent study by Millward Brown showed that distinctively designed brands have a 23 per cent higher average potential to grow than those that don't.[49]

An obvious example is the iPod white headphones. More interestingly, in 1916 Coca-Cola intentionally created a bottle (to quote the brief) 'a person could recognize even if they felt it in the dark, and so shaped that, even if broken, a person could tell at a glance what it was'.[50]

Distinctive design means a brand gets noticed (unconsciously or consciously) when it is encountered. There are many examples from fashion brands – the red heels of Louboutin shoes, the green and red stripes of Gucci, the oval metal plate on all Mulberry bags, all examples of distinctive design which allow the brand to conspicuously communicate implicitly.

In order to drive distinctive design, marketing needs to be involved much further up the production chain as it can affect the very nature of the product. The distinctive design of Beats by Dr Dre headphones means they are easily recognized when encountered, allowing the brand to grow through a strategy focused around product placement in music videos and celebrity use.

All brands must start to think about how visually appealing their product is for entertainment producers; supposedly Apple don't pay for product placement yet they appeared in 40 per cent of the films which topped the US box office last year.[51] The distinctive design of their products makes them an easy choice. Even with the new opportunity of digitally inserting a brand into a TV show, the producer still holds a veto and will undoubtedly fight against brands which don't look good.

Principle 4: concrete actions

> Some less friendly observers have said we will abandon our principles and reveal ourselves as shallow cynical exploiters. We must disappoint them... quite simply put, we walk our talk. (Gordon Roddick, Co-founder of the Body Shop)[52]

To appear 'unintended', marketing needs to be embedded into every part of the company, not just a bolt-on. Every encounter needs to visibly reflect the brand's values. Communication which is perceived as unintended can be seen as any action by the brand which does not have communication as its primary function. As transparency becomes more important brands must ensure that every encounter reflects the brand's values, and that those values are clearly demonstrated through clearly visible actions.

At Cannes 2012, Nike & R/GA won the Titanium Grand Prix for Nike Fuel. Speaking about the new product Stefan Olander (Nike VP Digital Sport) said 'the products and services are becoming the marketing. Nike+ Running started off as a marketing idea. It is not marketing anymore. This is now how we run our business.'[53]

The marketing and product merging has meant the Nike brand values are concreted into the brand's behaviour. It's important to remember that the real value of this innovation is more what it implicitly communicates about the brand than actual consumer participation. For example, Nike+ has a membership of 2 million globally (vs 46 million joggers in the United States alone), a relatively low penetration, but the real value is its effect on Nike's running credentials and brand salience.[54]

Concrete actions include ensuring every last detail aligns with the brand positioning.[55] At a Gaucho restaurant the waiter brings a selection of raw steaks for inspection and talks through the differences, illustrating the expertise of the staff and the quality of the meat. This drives social signals reaffirming the right associations with the Gaucho brand. Nearly every consumer review of Gaucho mentions this concrete piece of theatre.

The majority of brands miss these opportunities or never develop them. They presume that as the primary function of these actions is other than brand communication then they have no real brand effect. This results in substantial sums of money, which could have reinforced brand values, being at best under-utilized and at worst counter-productive.[56]

Significant implications for how we work

Implications for marketing

> It becomes increasingly clear that real marketing cannot be thought of as a department activity. It is a matter of harnessing all the company's resources.
>
> (Stephen King[57])

Many brands will find it difficult to adhere to the principles discussed, principally because marketing in their business will not enjoy the stature or reach needed to influence product development or act in an extravagant or sacrificial way.

In order for companies to build strong brand signals it will require them to rethink what marketing is and how it fits into the corporate structure. Often the brand is still viewed as the province of the marketing department and the basis for advertising and communication.[58] This is not a new issue; Stephen King highlighted the need to move on from what he termed 'marketing department marketing' back in 1985.[59]

If brands are to exploit their implicit communications effectively there is a need to realign marketing in the corporate structure. All departments need to become 'brand ambassadors' and all decisions need to go through a brand filter. Marketing needs to be involved at the start of product development. The process of passing a product to marketing to be sold does not fit with this thinking. Approaches such as semiotics need to be used by marketing to ensure any product developed communicates the right signals about the brand.[60]

Without these changes managing brand signals becomes a game of roulette as different departments make disparate decisions often resulting in opportunities to build the brand being wasted.

Conclusion

All brands communicate explicitly and implicitly. Currently, planning 'explicit communication' dominates thinking as it is easy to control and the clear remit of the marketing department.

A brand's implicit communication embodies everything a brand does, meaning responsibility is split across departments, making it harder to manage and exploit.

But difficulty should not mean prevention. The strongest brands in the future will be those that ensure every decision and action reinforces the brand's positioning.

As Clever Hans taught us, it's not what brands say but the signals they create which matter most.

Notes

1 Bullmore, J (April 2008) On the Campaign Couch... with JB, *Campaign* [Online] www.campaignlive.co.uk/news/805228/

2 Mlodinow, L (2012) *Subliminal: How your unconscious mind rules your behaviour*, Pantheon Books, US.

3 Scott, W D (1903) *The Psychology of Advertising in Theory and Practice*, in which Scott states 'our minds are constantly subjected to influences of which we have no knowledge'. A little more recently (1974) in the IPA classic *Testing to Destruction* Alan Hedges states that advertising and purchasing decisions most often work at very low levels of consciousness.

4 Heath, R (2001) *The Hidden Power Of Advertising: How low involvement processing influences the way we choose brands*, NTC Publications.

5 Bullmore, J (2000) Why every brand encounter counts: seductive, anarchic or catastrophic, *Market Leader*, Issue 9.

6 Goode, A (2007) The Implicit And Explicit Role Of Ad Memory In Ad Persuasion: Rethinking the hidden persuaders, *International Journal Of Market Research*, **49** (1).

7 Wilson, T D (2002) *Strangers to Ourselves: Discovering the adaptive unconscious*, Harvard University Press, US.

8 Kahneman, D (2011) *Thinking Fast and Slow*, Farrar, Straus and Giroux, US.

9 Wood, O, Samson, A and Harrison, P (September 2011) Behaving Economically With The Truth: How Behavioural Economics can help market research to better understand, identify and predict behaviour. *ESOMAR: Congress*, Amsterdam.

10 Wood, O (March 2012) How Emotional Tugs Trump Rational Pushes: The time has come to abandon a 100-year-old advertising model, *Journal of Advertising Research*.

11 Kahneman, D (Speech, 2012) You must recognise that most of the time you are not talking to System 2. You're talking to System 1. System 1 runs the show. That's the one you want to move [Online] www.telegraph.co.uk/finance/businessclub/management-advice/9307587/Think-Tank-Target-consumers-unconscious-and-reap-the-rewards.html?mobile=basic

12 Yakob, F (2012) Choose The Future, *Admap*, Shortlisted, Admap Prize 2012.

13 Feldwick, P and Heath, R (2008) Fifty years using the wrong model of advertising, *International Journal of Market Research*, **50** (1).

14 Yakob, F (2012) Choose The Future, *Admap*, Shortlisted, Admap Prize 2012.

15 Franzen, G and Bouwman, M (2001) *The Mental World of Brands: Mind, memory and brand success*, NTC Publications.

16 Binet, L and Carter, S (June 2010) Mythbuster: Off message, *Admap*.

17 Goode, A (2007) The Implicit and Explicit Role of Ad Memory In Ad Persuasion: Rethinking the hidden persuaders, *International Journal Of Market Research*, **49** (1).

18 Duchamp, M (April 1957) [Lecture] Session on the Creative Act, Convention of the American Federation of Arts, Houston, Texas.

19 Sutherland, R (2012) Communication: Accountability is not enough, *Market Leader*, Quarter 1.

20 *ibid.*

21 Goode, A (2007) The Implicit And Explicit Role Of Ad Memory In Ad Persuasion: Rethinking the hidden persuaders, *International Journal Of Market Research*, **49** (1).

22 Smith, J M and Harper, D (2003) *Animal Signals (Oxford Series in Ecology and Evolution)*, Oxford University Press, Oxford.

23 Pentland, A (2008) *Honest Signals: How they shape our world*, Bradford Books.

24 Veblen, T (2009) *The Theory of the Leisure Class*, Oxford University Press, Oxford.

25 Though Veblen is famous for the theory of conspicuous consumption, his own term was 'the law of conspicuous waste'. Veblen, T (2009) *The Theory of the Leisure Class*, Oxford University Press, Oxford.

26 Donath, J (2008) Signals, Truth and Design [Currently unpublished] Source: http://smg.media.mit.edu/papers/Donath/SignalsTruthDesign/SignalsCuesAndMeaning.pdf

27 Simons, M A (September 2011) The why instead of what of consumer behaviour: An evolutionary-based new model, *ESOMAR: Congress*, Amsterdam.

28 Zahavi, A and Zahavi, A (1999) *The Handicap Principle: A missing piece of Darwin's puzzle*, Oxford University Press, Oxford.

29 Donath, J (2008) Signals, Truth & Design [Currently unpublished] Source: http://smg.media.mit.edu/papers/Donath/SignalsTruthDesign/SignalsCuesAndMeaning.pdf

30 Pentland, A (2008) *Honest Signals: How they shape our world*, Bradford Books.

31 Waltzwick, P, Bavelas, J B and Jackson, D D (1967) *Pragmatics of Human Communication*, W W Norton & Co, New York.

32 *ibid*.

33 Mehrabian, A (1972) *Silent Messages: Implicit communication of emotions and attitudes*, Wadsworth Publishing Company.

34 Binet, L and Carter, S (June 2010) Mythbuster: Off message, *Admap*.

35 (June 2012) Nike's Twitter football advertising campaign banned, *BBC News* [Online] www.bbc.co.uk/news/technology-18517668

36 Adam, P (March 2013) The Future of Advertising: Many, lightweight interactions over time [Online] www.thinkoutsidein.com/blog/2012/03/many-lightweight-interactions-over-time

37 Kassaei, A (2012) DDB presentation, *Cannes*.

38 Bogusky, A and Winsor, J (2008) *Baked In: Creating products and businesses that market themselves*, B2 Books, Agate Publishing, Chicago.

39 Research by New York University Stern School of Business has shown that products with social embedded are more effective than those with it added on. Aral, S and Walker, D (June 2011) Vision Statement: Forget Viral Marketing – Make the Product Itself Viral, *Harvard Business Review*.

40 Ambler, T and Hollier, E A (Dec 2004) The waste in advertising is the part that works, *Journal of Advertising Research*, **44** (4).

41 Davis, E, Kay, J and Star, J (1991) Is Advertising Rational?, *Business Strategy Review*, No 2.

42 Field, P (2010) Creativity and Effectiveness in *Advertising Works 19*, ed David Golding, World Advertising Research Centre for Institute of Practitioners in Advertising.

43 Kapferer, J N and Bastien, V (2008) *The Luxury Strategy: Break the rules of marketing to build luxury brands*, Kogan Page, London.

44 (March 2008) King Tong: the man who brought GHD straighteners to Britain, *Times* [Online] www.thetimes.co.uk/tto/life/fashion/article1755310.ece

45 Ritson, M (July 2010) Marketing lessons continue to flow from Apple, *Brand Strategy Insider* [Online] www.brandingstrategyinsider.com/2010/07/marketing-lessons-continue-to-flow-from-apple.html

46 King, S (2007) *A Master Class in Brand Planning: The timeless works of Stephen King*, ed J Lannon and M Baskin, John Wiley & Sons, Chichester.

47 Bullmore, J (2000) Why every brand encounter counts: seductive, anarchic or catastrophic, *Market Leader*, Issue 9.

48 [Online] http://quotesondesign.com/tate-linden/

49 Fearn, H (2010) *Growing a Strong Brand: Defining your meaningful point of difference*, Millward Brown: Point of view.

50 Dean, N L (2010) *The Man Behind the Bottle*: The origin and history of the classic contour Coca-Cola bottle as told by the son of its creator, Xlibris Corporation, USA.

51 Burrows, P and Fixmer, A (May 2012) Apple, the Other Cult in Hollywood, *Bloomberg Business Week* [Online] www.businessweek.com/articles/2012-05-10/apple-the-other-cult-in-hollywood

52 (May 1993) [Interview] *The Times*.

53 Nudd, T (June 2012) R/GA Adds Titanium Grand Prix to Its Cyber for Nike+ FuelBand. Accelerometer is both product development and marketing, *Adweek* [Online] www.adweek.com/news/advertising-branding/rga-adds-titanium-grand-prix-its-cyber-nike-fuelband-141381

54 Weigel, M (October 2011) The Enduring Power of Stuff That Isn't Useful and Why 'Utility' Will Not Overthrow Magic [Online] http://mweigel.typepad.com/canalside-view/2011/10/the-enduring-power-of-stuff-that-isnt-useful-and-why-utility-will-not-overthrow-meaning.html

55 Gleeson, R (February 2012) 404, the story of a page not found, *TED* [Online] www.ted.com/talks/renny_gleeson_404_the_story_of_a_page_not_found.html Renny Gleeson (W+K Global Director of Interactive Strategy) recently showed in a TED talk that even a well-designed 404 error message on the web can improve feelings about a brand.

56 Bullmore, J (2000) Why every brand encounter counts: seductive, anarchic or catastrophic, *Market Leader*, Issue 9.

57 King, S (2007) Has Marketing Failed, Or Was It Never Really Tried?, in *A Master Class in Brand Planning: The timeless works of Stephen King*, ed J Lannon and M Baskin, John Wiley & Sons, Chichester.

58 Clifton, R (April 2009) Brand ownership should be everyone's responsibility, *Admap*, Issue 504.

59 King, S. Has Marketing Failed, Or Was It Never Really Tried?, in *A Master Class in Brand Planning: The timeless works of Stephen King*, ed J Lannon and M Baskin, John Wiley & Sons, Chichester.

60 Budha, K (February 2012) Semiotics: A sign of the times, *Admap*.

I believe brands must be superhuman
2013/14

12

EMILY FAIRHEAD-KEEN
Business Director, MEC

I believe Man has entered The Age of Marketing, where everyone and everything communicates with a marketing filter, mimicking brands. As brands seek to be human, the solution I offer is for brands to be Superhuman, delivering extraordinary fiction, performance and control.

Editor's therefore, for your brand...

Your brand thinking:
If everything is now 'marketing', how can we recover authenticity of communication?

Your brand engagement:
What are you doing that is truly superhuman, that your consumers think 'how did you do that' vs 'I could do that'?

Your brand organization & capability:
If your brand is to be superhuman what special powers in your team do you need to recruit to make it fly?

...and author's personal therefore

I have just completed this year's IPA Diploma and my plans to deliver super-human are currently hatchlings. They exist in their infancy as excited and ambitious tadpoles, waiting to grow legs, full of potential to be mighty frogs:

- My work: Nurturing and educating the tadpoles of the industry to be superhuman.
- My career: Delivering superhuman projects as a super producer, while broadening the definition of 'super'.
- My life: Championing a super creative world for my own tadpole.

My work: developing Superhuman talent

To get to extraordinary work, we have to not just be like the Hollywood masters and West End legends, but steal talent from them. We must access the best creative skills in the world, going on milk rounds to the London International School of Performing Arts and overseas to the American Film Institute.

We must also up-skill our existing tadpoles in the art of extraordinary performance and extraordinary fiction. To do this I plan to set up a formal programme of structured learning, a superhuman academy incorporating the following ideals.

Learning from superhuman centres of excellence

I want to borrow from Superhuman centres of excellence, copying modules from RADA and Central St Martin's.

Design must be a key focus. Creative cannot be left to the ad agency alone as design agencies compete against ad agencies and as Marketing Age Man now sees the world through rose-tinted spectacles (or rather a Hudson, Sutro or Nashville Instagram filter). We cannot rely on freelancers or creatives only to deliver visually mind-blowing ideas to either Marketing Age Man or client; visually they've both come to expect better and more.

Flying with supermen

I plan to set up a superhuman apprenticeship scheme – where agency talent copy and absorb superhumanly powers in a feat of power mimicry from the best superhumans from outside the industry. I want to parachute in existing agency talent into superhumans' studios, send them on drone missions to extraordinary performers' workshops, warehouses and places of wonder to learn and return as myth makers, choreographers, directors and ultimately as superhuman talent.

Learning from superhuman veterans

Too long has the advertising industry seen the over 50s disappear from the picture. In jest we speculate they elevate to secret global lairs, seek solace in cottages in Tunbridge Wells or simply circulate the after dinner speech scene, but we must learn from these superhuman veterans and we need to bring them back in as super teachers.

Young tadpoles must learn from these older extraordinary performers, who once delivered us the Milk Tray Man and knew the value of the industry, those who set us apart and made us distinct and different. Extraordinary showmen who wore braces and red socks as supermen, putting on their own Lagerfeld style individual performance of eccentricity.

For every Rory Sutherland, we need another 10.

My career: super producer

Super producer delivering super projects

Just as brands must exist in impressive physical superhero spaces like *The Guardian*'s King's Cross lair, agencies are beginning to invest in impressive new theatres, and once again physically house media and creative agencies under one roof.[1,2] As the coffee house was to the Enlightenment, these new lairs have the potential to be a 'hotbed of innovation and experiment-ation',[3] or what Ralph-Christian Ohr terms 'serendipitous collisions' of creativity.[4]

We must take advantage of the opportunity this physical proximity presents us with and go beyond simply sharing an office. Ad and media agencies must truly work together on shared clients, mobilizing superhuman talent, housed in new super spaces, on super projects as extraordinary as the Sydney fireworks display and as big as the Olympic spectacle. Stamina work which hurts, which takes months and years, not weeks, and delivered by super producer integrated teams capable of planning, choreographing, creating and orchestrating whole super events with the clout of a Weinstein and the confidence of a Jay-Z.

Benchmarking our work against a more competitive set

Extraordinary work must be judged beyond the industry lions and instead against the real lions. We have to ask ourselves, to quote John Hegarty, 'would we award it at the Sundance, would we give it an Oscar?'[5]

We must do this by changing the playing field essentially by restructuring our awards, casting the net wider than the industry. Entries must be assessed in the same league as non-industry extraordinary work, on the quality of the narrative, the extraordinariness of the performance, and the level of conversation around the work, the box office bums on seats performance (of sales) and the box office polls measuring consumers enjoyment levels. All worked into a Rotten Tomatoes-type percentage score in an effort to win.

My life: celebrating a super creative world

In my 39th week of pregnancy, a walking one-and-a-half, I want my child to grow up in a world away from one where we risk losing the ability to myth-make, resulting in dreadful soppy realism and small fires. Where children are warned of pernicious fairy tales by Dawkins,[6] where the tremendous natural talent children have as creative individuals is squandered with education systems Michael Rosen describes as learning 'without understanding... motivated by test scores, learning lists of facts'.[7]

Instead, I want to create a magical world where creativity is considered as important as literacy, one which Ken Robinson yearns for. Where the gift of imagination is celebrated, where the arts are not at the bottom in the hierarchy of subjects, where we embrace the raw and extraordinary capacity children have for innovation,[8] where the crowd queuing at King's Cross to push the luggage cart through the wall to Platform 9¾ and board the train to Hogwarts don't believe it's there; but they revel in the pleasure of let's pretend.[9]

I want to create a world of miracles, one which celebrates gorillas playing the drums, and talking guinea pigs.

To steal from Picasso, via Ken Robinson: 'All children are born artists; the problem is to remain an artist as we grow up.'[10] I want to ensure my child remains an artist.

I believe brands must be superhuman

The age of marketing

> Men want, say, rain. They begin by performing a rain dance, which often does not work. This is the Age of Magic. Then, baulked of success, they do the next best thing and fall to their knees and pray. This is the Age of Religion. When prayers do not work, they set about investigating the precise causes of the natural world, and on the basis of their new understanding attempt to alter things for the better. This is the Age of Science.[11]

I believe that civilization has entered a fourth cultural phase, the 'age of marketing'. By this I mean whereas once marketing was a skill reserved for professionals, and stages reserved for brands, now everyone is a marketer and everything communicates verbally and visually in marketing terms on the same stages as brands.

This has occurred because people are more aware of how they are seen by others as a consequence of technology beaming identities around the globe to millions. This has effectively given rise to the foundation of a new understanding and hyper-conscious state of self-awareness. Becoming a marketer in an effort to win in this world is the fourth cultural phase equivalent of the rain dance.

I shall explore in more detail:

- why this has come about;
- what people have become; and
- what culture has become.

Then ultimately what this all means for brands.

Why this has come about

New cultural phases appear to coincide with humanity's increase in self-awareness and a new type of consciousness of both their nature and limitations. Just as with the early civilizations of the Historic Age[12,13] and of the Axial Age where people became more 'conscious of their nature, their situation and their limitations with unprecedented clarity',[14] people are now looking at the world and themselves quite a lot more and in quite a different way.

Technology is hosting, and arguably creating, a hyper-conscious state of self. Once confined to the living room, on the bookshelf was where people were judged, by how interesting they were, where they'd travelled, what they'd read. Now the living room is 'on screen' to millions of people who can see and judge what they stand for, what they think about the world.

What people have become

In the same way people looked to magic, prayed for rain, looked to God for answers or used science to try and understand the world they lived in, people have become marketers to understand how the modern world works, and indeed win in it. They now tailor their identities in a way they never could, changing themselves with a filter, baking fiction into their timelines. On Twitter they sell 'current', 'witty' and 'smart'. On Facebook they hang their lives in photographs and in taglines. On LinkedIn they become the person everyone wants to employ. They create brand names, logos, photos, language, all giving off their own social semiotic code.[15] They hire third parties to manage reputation and mini teams of public relations entrepreneurs to brand their identities online.[16]

As marketing experts, these marketing age consumers understand the game brands play and are willing participants in the fiction. Comfortable with this permeable fourth wall, they are willing to adopt Kayfabe, the suspension of disbelief.[17] In the same way people get reality TV isn't real, but still enjoy the entertainment, the same is true in marketing. As Ogilvy quite rightly says, 'the consumer is not a moron. She is your wife. Don't insult her intelligence.'[18]

Living in a marketing society,[19] in this marketing age, we see the duality of marketing man:[20] the marketing age consumer willingly suspends reality, plays the game brands play, while at the same time being sophisticated in his critique of them. Marketing age man analyses the annual UK Christmas campaigns, and Super Bowl ads are dissected at length across the world.[21] Of the 20.9 million Super Bowl related tweets sent during the game in February 2013, 30 per cent were about the ads.[22]

What culture has become

Whereas once the marketing world borrowed from culture, now culture is borrowing from brand. Everything now copies how brands communicate and usurps the physical and virtual spaces where they do so. We are effectively seeing the commercial colonization of culture[23] in reverse.

Culture speaks to people now in marketing terms. Journalists bounce around marketing patter, describe naming your child as *branding* it, in the weekend papers. Marketing terms have become a generation's diction, not just reserved for marketing specialists.

Culture presents to people visually, with marketing signals. Editing tools once the sacred possession of the production houses, now come as standard on phones.

Politicians are chief marketers. No one more so than Obama, his marketing victories were well documented in real press, not just trade.[24] Politicians aren't simply asking people to vote any more, but asking people to share and indulge in their social currency in the same way Oreos does.

Even the physical spaces brands have traditionally occupied are under threat from non-traditional brand marketing.

From Mormonism:

FIGURE 12.1

To Jesus:

FIGURE 12.2

... All now occupying the same spaces we sell dog food in this marketing age.

This new marketing age has presented brands with two critical challenges

First, brands no longer compete for the precious real estate of the consumers' mind[25] against other brands in category, or indeed cross category, but with everything (and everyone). Everything and everyone is communicating *as* marketers, *in* the 'swim lanes'[26] and *on* the same stages. Unless brands find a way to cut through, they risk becoming invisible.

Second, everyone has become a marketing expert, interested in it, and analyst of it. We are now living in the midst of an 'I can do that too' generation of marketers. Everyone got better at the brand game, the bar was raised and expectations grew. Critiquing now comes from the streets, not just from the boardroom.

One solution the industry has offered is for brands to be more like people

Because people and brands are on the same stages, one industry mode prevails around a central thought: brands must be more human[27] 'in order to connect with consumers and build trust'. Thinking centres on getting closer to people in this 'human era',[28] brands relinquishing control, brands being more 'flawsome',[29] real[30] and transparent.[31]

Brands beg for love and attention: 'like me', 'engage with me', 'please play with me', effectively trying to form synchronized swimming feats with the consumer as buddies and best friends and getting 'close enough for contact to happen, like Michelangelo's God assuming the form of a man to better touch Adam's extended finger'.[32]

This 'human' Clark Kent trend has permeated brand communication and we see a kinder, gentler, more sensitive ad product with an inbuilt sense of vulnerability. 'Boy next door' rather than 'Super' in tone. For example, NatWest's 'Helpful Banking' executions[33] and the Milk Tray Man who was effectively emasculated when he became a more 'human', 'lighter in love' version, or what Julie Burchill termed in her article 'This Lady Still Loves Them...', published by *The Guardian* (London) 23 September 2003, 'castration-by-cuddles'.

I believe the solution lies in a fundamental shift away from current thinking

Go pricke thy face, and ouer-red thy feare
Thou Lilly-liuer'd Boy.
   (Shakespeare, *Macbeth*: Act V Scene 3)

While this doctrine can work for some brands and some categories, for example new brands like Jack Wills and Patagonia who build new brand myths by using transparency as a way to enhance their story, and where brands actually have sexy underwear worth seeing underneath, it isn't the ultimate solution.

Instead, I believe the solution to the challenges brands face, competing with everything (and everyone) and in the face of sophisticated marketing age critique, is a shift away from this rather lily-livered behaviour.

The solution lies in a superhuman belief system

I believe brands have got to be truly extraordinary and superhuman to beat Jesus and Mormonism, *The Lady of Shalott* and Joe Bloggs in his bedroom, and be truly super to cut through and impress these marketing age consumers (Figure 12.3).

By 'superhuman' I mean one who can deliver the extraordinary through:

- Extraordinary fiction: has a compelling fantastical, mythical story and is opaque and mysterious.
- Extraordinary performance: is from another world and brings the spectacular from his world to Earth.
- Extraordinary control: is in fierce control, living on his terms, exercising military jurisdiction.

FIGURE 12.3

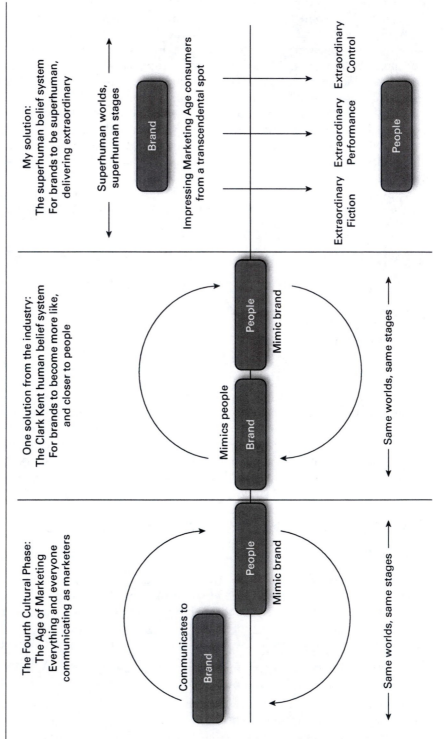

The Fourth Cultural Phase:
The Age of Marketing
Everything and everyone
communicating as marketers

One solution from the industry:
The Clark Kent human belief system
For brands to become more like,
and closer to people

My solution:
The superhuman belief system
For brands to be superhuman,
delivering extraordinary

Brand

Communicates to

People

Mimic brand

Same worlds, same stages

Mimics people

Brand

People

Mimic brand

Same worlds, same stages

Superhuman worlds,
superhuman stages

Brand

Impressing Marketing Age consumers
from a transcendental spot

Extraordinary
Fiction

Extraordinary
Performance

Extraordinary
Control

People

I recommend three shifts away from current human thinking. I will explain why superhuman is right, exploring the audience, brand, cultural and business reasons (Figure 12.4).

FIGURE 12.4

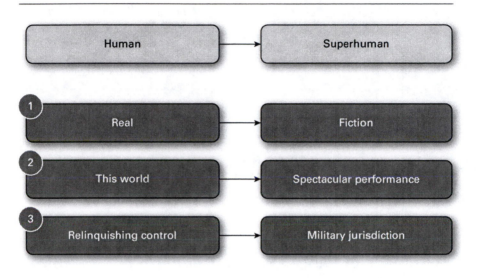

The first shift: from real to fiction

A deep cultural need for fiction and a cultural need for escapist fiction in complex times

A desire for fiction, stories, fictional heroes, a 'social need for extraordinary action'[34] and indeed myth is as old as civilization itself. People have always put fictional superhumans on pedestals, be it gods, goddesses[35] or subsequently superheroes as immortals.[36] Humanity looks for 'taboos', ways of 'insulating certain people from harmful social contact',[37] for fictional 'beings' with 'mystical charges ... operating like an electrical current'.[38]

Escapist fantasy particularly thrives in times of social complexity: Superman was born[39] in the midst of the Great Depression, on the cusp of World War II.[40] In the 19th century people looked to fairies and Gothic revival as an escapist solution to the rapid industrialization which had left them confused.[41] We are now seeing the revival of the Superhero in popular culture.[42]

People want fictional escapism in this overly transparent, information heavy 'world of information glut and gluttony',[43] 'traumatized by war footage and disaster clips',[44] where the internet has revealed everything. Emotional baggage from a brand can lead to what Corey Mull terms 'consumer cognitive overload (a condition where consumers have absorbed so much information that they're incapable of mentally sorting it all and making an optimal decision)'.[45]

FIGURE 12.5   Superhero Search Terms – Query trends

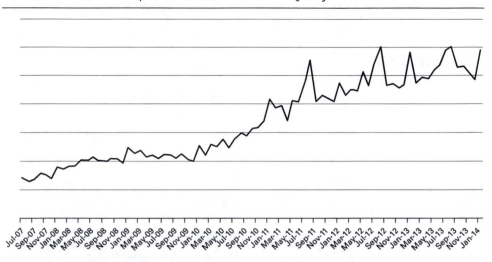

[Accessed 2014, Online] **www.google.co.uk/trends**

Whereas John Grant argues that in the absence of the formal and traditional societal structures, brands are simple ideas we look to, to help us navigate a complex world,[46,47] I believe that the marketing age consumer wants brands to provide simple escapist fiction in these complex times.

Real can feel 'faux real' to a marketing age sophisticate

I believe that brands are not real and the marketing age consumer gets this. In trying to be real, admitting their flaws, it can feel false because it is in perfection that they are authentic. Quite literally a brand's history lies in the stamp of approval, a promise of better.[48] On a deeper level, they've always offered utopian possibilities:[49] More sex (Lynx), the acceptance of any body shape (Dove), happiness (Coca-Cola). A brand isn't real but feeds upon reality: 'Publicity is effective precisely because it feeds upon the real... Publicity begins by working on a natural appetite for pleasure.'[50]

Marketing age consumers want fictional brand heroes and worlds, Milk Tray Men and Marlboro Men who come from the sky and occupy transcendental spots.[51] They buy into 'Mytho-Symbolic worlds' brands create, like McDonald's, 'a wondrous, magical place, where everyone is welcome, safe, happy... It does not matter that sometimes when we go there it feels more like a cafeteria food fight.'[52]

A business case for fiction

People don't pay for the real, they pay for the fiction, and this is one of the ways a brand can implement a price premium.[53] Take Field Notes stationery, able to charge significantly more than a standard Ryman's notebook because it bakes fiction into its brand.

We see this repeatedly with blind taste testing where own-label brands repeatedly beat named brands and where consumers buy into and pay for the myth, but often prefer the base product when myth isn't in the mix.

The second shift: from this world to spectacular performance

An appetite for extraordinary performance in culture

Given the 'pervasive impact of entertainment in our economy today'[54], and the 'number of entertainment options [which have] exploded to encompass many new experiences',[55] culture, from fashion to music, is delivering unforgettable performances in an effort to woo more demanding audiences. For example, in fashion, Chanel is just one of many, taking its shows to the extreme.[56]

FIGURE 12.6

© Chanel/Photo Olivier Saillant

An appetite for spectacular performance in advertising

We see this with the Super Bowl, where more than two thirds of viewers pay attention to the event commercials and 50 per cent tune in just for them.[57] We see this with the UK Christmas annual advertising fest. On TGI people profess to love the cinema ads[58] and we see spectacular creative performance in Cadbury's 'Gorilla' and the Red Bull famous 'Jump' accumulating views years after the event.

FIGURE 12.7

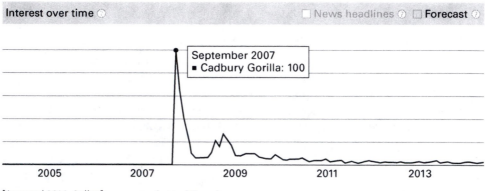

| Interest over time ⓘ | News headlines ⓘ ☐ Forecast ⓘ |

September 2007
∎ Cadbury Gorilla: 100

2005   2007   2009   2011   2013

[Accessed 2014, Online] **www.google.co.uk/trends**

A business case for spectacular advertising product

As we have seen with the Cadbury' 'Gorilla', spectacular advertising product can 'generate £5.22 million incremental sales, deliver a 5 per cent margin improvement, bring to life a more profitable model, re-energise the company, delight the investment community and maybe even contribute to shareholder value'.[59]

We also know from past research papers that highly creative advertising can drive market share and profitability: 'The link between creativity and effectiveness', published in 2011, concluded that creatively awarded campaigns are more efficient than non-awarded ones in terms of the level of market share growth they drive.[60,61]

The third shift: from relinquishing control to military jurisdiction

Successful brands are ruled with an iron fist

In order to deliver extraordinary fiction and performance, brands need to be ruled with military jurisdiction.

The world's most valuable brands adhere to strict processes, guidelines, rules and procedures in order to ensure perfection goes out the door every time. Sometimes they are ruled by one iron fist. For example, Apple, with its dictator style puppeteers from Jobs to Cook.

FIGURE 12.8

Category	Brand	Brand value 2013 $M	Brand contribution	Brand value % change 2013 vs 2012	Rank change
1 Technology	Apple	185,071	4	1%	0
2 Technology	Google	113,669	3	5%	1
3 Technology	IBM	112,536	3	–3%	–1
4 Fast Food	McDonald's	90,256	4	–5%	0
5 Soft Drinks	Coca-Cola	78,415	5	6%	1

Reproduced with kind permission from the BrandZ™ Top 100 Most Valuable Global Brands 2014 report

On top of this, we know that relinquishing control can humiliate brands. With the advent of social media the errors businesses make receive far more attention now than they might have in the past. We also know that relinquishing control can be very rational. Asking what a person wants their bank to look like, or what the next Starbucks product should be, are very rational lines of communication and I believe this is dangerous when there is a business case for the emotional rather than the rational in communication.[62]

In summary, there are many audience, brand, cultural and indeed business reasons why superhuman is right for brands in this marketing age, and why there are dangers in the human doctrine.

The practical application of a superhuman: a superhuman creed

I believe the practical solution lies in a superhuman creed with a three-panelled framework.

I shall explore how brands must implement this in the marketing age.

Extraordinary fiction

No idea too bizarre, no twist too fanciful, no storytelling technique too experimental.[63]

Brands have to tell fantastical stories which are as addictive as cocaine,[64] as unforgettable as the classics and as entertaining as the childhood stories we all remember. A brand's story has to be unforgettable, not just memorable.

Explicit and expected fiction

They must do this by treating each communication as if it is a new episode in the story, with a clear narrative for the audience to follow, explicitly in

FIGURE 12.9

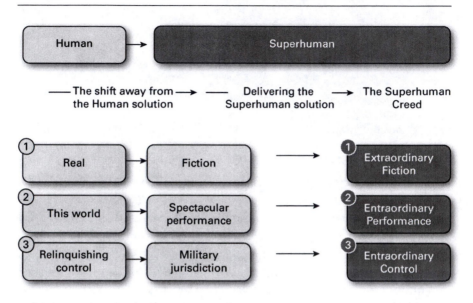

execution. For example, the Nescafé couple of the nineties or the current Compare The Meerkat narrative. Each execution, the audience looks forward to, discussing it like the latest episode of a soap opera.

Brands must look to own spaces and media where they can narrate the fiction, each campaign a new chapter in the drama, on the same stage each time. In the same way that Jack Daniels repeatedly buys the same London Underground hoardings, telling its story in the same expected places, week in, week out.

Brands must repeat their origin story again and again. Innocent is a super example of this, where it reminds consumers of its narrative in interesting and entertaining ways from its website to its YouTube vignettes, all repeating the same tale, now as familiar as Goldilocks and the Three Bears.

Playful fiction

> It is more fun to talk with someone who doesn't use long, difficult words but rather short, easy words like 'What about lunch?'[65]

Brands must be fun and funny and have fun. They must learn from the childhood tales, the simplicity and stickiness of the Hungry Caterpillar and Winnie-the-Pooh. Stories must be told with a sense of childish playfulness, executed with a simple playful energy, appealing to the consumer's inner child.

Brands must use their magic powers and play to the irrational in people. Just as round tea bags and smoothies with bobble hats excite people for no logical reason,[66] they must dial up the nonsensical and the ridiculous[67] and make guinea pigs talk,[68] bounce balls down hills in San Francisco,[69] get babies to roller skate,[70] teach ponies to sing[71] and make gorillas play the drums.[72] Championing the stuff humans can't do and offering entertaining escapism in this overly transparent society.

Bigger fiction

Brands must subvert other people's big myths and make bold claims. In doing so they emotionally put themselves on pedestals, as the protagonist in the story, elevated from people. This signals their powers of temporal duplication and timelessness, which marketing age consumers can't exercise. For example, with Coca-Cola owning Santa.

By doing this they are demonstrating they can do things the marketing age consumer can't, impressing them with their ability to pull Santa's strings, turn Jesus red, paint countries and stimulate mating behaviours, albeit all with the knowledge that consumers get the game but play along anyway.

Extraordinary performance

> Your advertisements should establish in the reader's mind an image she will never forget.[73]

In the same way the cycle of Superhero movies moved away from the real world approach in 2010 to 'expansive, fantastical' movies such as Cameron's *Avatar*,[74] brands have got to stop sucking on 'the lollipop of mediocrity'[75] and deliver mentally unforgettable performances, not just be mentally available.[76]

Blockbuster advertising performance

Brands must do this by constructing awe-inspiring event performances like the Red Bull space jump and advertising event performances like the annual John Lewis Christmas treat. People are everywhere; a brand's arrival should be special and built up, like Superman appearing in the sky. The performance must be appointment-to-view with a campaign built around the ad itself, as with the trailers for the Super Bowl ads.[77,78] The ad must be supported with *ad product* merchandise consumers want to buy, just as they buy Spiderman pyjamas for their children.

In the same way 'audiences respond to big name actors, special effects and in-your-face advertising'[79] for movies, brands have got to not spread money out in a series of smaller, safer bets, but invest in event creative like the studios are investing in event blockbusters, making the big bets. This means pooling monies into a handful of high-production, headline star super hits, not a series of low-cost mediocre creative. Harvard Business School Professor Anita Elberse's book *Blockbusters* shows that this strategy has also worked for book publishers, music labels, TV networks, and video game companies.[80]

Extraordinary control

I believe that in order to deliver extraordinary fiction and performance, brands have to exercise extraordinary levels of control over the brand, its plot and its communication. They must do this either with an individual or a team and deliver it with military organization and process.

Explicit brand rules

Brands must take back control showing marketing age man who is boss in how people interact with them. They must set the consumer explicit rules, making them play the game on their terms.

For example, Polpo on the London restaurant scene forbids bookings and the Bourke Street Bakery, a tiny corner bakery in Sydney (a phenomenal success),[81] is a place which has strict rules. It commands people pay in cash only and if a product runs out, 'there are no more buns, mere mortals'.

Pseudo democratization

We see this with rigidly controlled brands, for example Coca-Cola asking people to name their can and Walkers to choose their favourite crisp flavour. These are brands that don't really truly relinquish control, but successfully implement strictly controlled, tightly managed processes where people are kept at arm's length, merely acting out a pre-directed script, with readymade choices and template visuals. This can be entertaining for this marketing age consumer and adds to the escapist entertainment, as long as the strings are held tight.

Brand as teacher on stage

Brands should be standing up and explicitly expressing their authority as superior superhuman, teaching the marketing age consumer a thing or two, like *The Guardian* which puts on its masterclasses, performances which signal its superiority to its readers: a teacher, and one who exerts control.

In order to deliver superhuman, the industry must practice superhuman

Don't bunt, aim out of the park. Aim for the company of immortals.[82]

Like brands, the ad industry is also under threat in this marketing age. Once admen were distinctive, unique and different in the work we produced, in our eccentricity, now we are under threat from the belief that everything and everyone can and will do our job.

Whereas once we were confident in our value ('"Ring the bell," I said, and walked out... Too many masters, too many objectives, too little money')[83] the proliferation of agencies has now made us Yes Men, where we accept mediocrity, bland middle ground, and turn out turgid pieces of work.

Instead we must remember, 'like Hollywood and Disney, Madison Avenue is in the myth making business',[84] and Superheroes need courageous Superhero artists and powerful controlling directors to construct these extraordinary fictional performers.

We must practice what I have preached to brands and adhere to the Superhero Creed. I illustrate below two examples of how we must implement this.

Exert extraordinary control

In the same way brands indulge in pseudo democratization; this should be true of the creative process where agencies use 'pseudo beta' in that only the best prototypes see the light of day before they are ready. The best agencies in the world rarely, if ever, send work down the catwalk which isn't perfect, isn't outstanding, isn't the best.[85]

The most successful agencies out there now, the BBH's, the Drogas, the AKQAs and the R/GAs, they exercise control at the right points with the military jurisdiction of a Mark Rylance or Lloyd Webber. Agencies have to follow these superhuman agencies and truly deliver on being clients' most trusted business partner by bravely saying No to JFDI[86] prescriptive briefs, staying true to our own rules, in a battle for extraordinary work.

Hire superhuman performers

If we are to compete effectively against everything and everyone in this Marketing Age, and be unforgettable, we have to not just be like the Hollywood masters and West End legends, but steal talent from them. As artists, we must hire superhero artists to up our game, 'the job of the artist is always to deepen the mystery'.[87] We must hire supreme myth makers, story tellers, screenwriters, movie men, literally taking talent from other entertainment professions from Lady Gaga's wardrobe team to the Sydney Fireworks choreographers and designers, to write our myths and direct the extraordinary performances.

Conclusion

If brands are to compete against everyone and everything in this marketing age, communicating to marketing age man, they cannot afford to lower themselves to Earth as mortals and fellow humans, but instead must rise high above as supermen, delivering extraordinary fiction and performance, exercised with an extraordinary level of control.

Jesus and Mormonism must be left intimidated, and mortal marketing age man left awestruck, necks crooked, goose pimples pricked, at the sight of superhuman brands swooshing across the night sky. Just as Lois Lane looks up to Superman:

> Wondering why you are... all the wonderful things you are. You can fly. You belong in the sky.[88]

Notes

1 Baxter, M (March 2014) Ogilvy Rediscovers Harmony on the Southbank [Online] www.ft.com

2 Ridley, L (June 2014) Omnicom plots new London HQ with offer on South Bank mega-office, *Campaign*.

3 (December 2003) Coffee fuelled the information exchanges of the 17th and 18th centuries: The internet in a cup, *The Economist*.

4 Ohr, C-R (May 2003) Innovation and Serendipity, *Integrative Innovation* [Online] http://integrative-innovation.net/

5 Hegarty, J (2004) speaking at Cannes Lions.

6 Johnston, I (June 2014) Richard Dawkins on fairy tales: 'I think it's rather pernicious to inculcate into a child a view of the world which includes supernaturalism', *The Independent*.

7 Rosen, M (April 2014) Dear Mr Gove: Michael Rosen's letter from a curious parent, *The Guardian*.

8 Robinson, K (2006) How Schools are Killing Creativity, *TED* [Online] www.ted.com/talks/ken_robinson_says_schools_kill_creativity

9 Warner, M (June 2014) Richard Dawkins is wrong to dismiss the power of fairytales, *The Observer*.

10 Robinson, K (2006) How Schools are Killing Creativity, *TED* [Online] www.ted.com/talks/ken_robinson_says_schools_kill_creativity

11 Frazer, R (1890) Introduction, in *The Golden Bough*, Oxford University Press.

12 Armstrong, K (2005) *A Short History of Myth*, Canongate.

13 *ibid*.

14 *ibid*.

15 Hall, S (2012) *This Means This, This Means That: A user guide to semiotics*, 2nd edn, Laurence King.

16 For example: Flavours.me (owned by business card company Moo allows anyone to make a branded web presence using personal content from around the internet).

17 Bain, D (Autumn 2013) IPA Deep Dive. See [Online] http://en.wikipedia.org/wiki/Kayfabe

18 Ogilvy, D (1963) *Confessions of an Advertising Man*, Atheneum.

19 James, O (2007) *Affluenza*, Vermillion.

20 Duality of man: The intuitive and psychological confusing nature of mankind to be twofold. The state of being in two qualities and relates to dualism, denoting a state of two parts.

21 From CBS to the *Daily Mail* to *The Guardian* to *The Sun*.

22 Indvik, L (February 2013) Ads made up 30% of the tweets, in *Mashable* [Online] http:mashable.com, 2014.

23 Jhally, Prof S (blog, 2014) Advertising at the Edge of the Apocalypse [Online] www.sutjhally.com/articles/advertisingattheed/

24 Scherer, M (November 2012) Inside the secret world of the Ibama data crunchers who helped Obama win, *Time Magazine.*

25 Trout, J and Rise, A (2001) *Positioning: The battle for your mind,* McGraw-Hill Professional, US.

26 Comstock, B (January 2013) The Market Maker, *Google Think Insights* [Online] www.thinkwithgoogle.com/articles/market-maker.html

27 Parekh, R (September 2012) The newest marketing buzzword? Human, *Adage.*

28 Chahal, M (February 2014) How to be a 'Human Era' brand, *Marketing Week.*

29 (April 2012) Flawsome: Why brands that behave more humanly, including showing their flaws, will be awesome, *Trendwatching* [Online] http://trendwatching.com/trends/flawsome/

30 Hutchinson, A (February 2014) The importance of creating human connections with your brand in the social media space, *Social Media Today* [Online] www.socialmediatoday.com

31 Kolster, C (December 2013) A transparent marketing means changing the way brands advertise, *The Guardian.*

32 Morrison, G (2012) *Supergods: Our world in the age of the superhero,* Vintage, London.

33 Whitehead, J (June 2010) RBS and NatWest push 'Most Helpful Bank' promise in ads, *Marketing Week.*

34 Ndalianis, A (2009) Comic Book Superheroes: An Introduction, in *The Contemporary Comic Book Superhero,* (ed) A Ndalianis, Routledge.

35 Graves, R (1948) *The White Goddess,* Faber and Faber.

36 Frazer J G (1890) *The Golden Bough,* Oxford University Press.

37 *ibid.*

38 *ibid.*

39 Ndalianis, A (2009) Comic Book Superheroes: An introduction, in *The Contemporary Comic Book Superhero,* ed A Ndalianis, Routledge.

40 *ibid.*

41 Booker, C (2004) The Age of Loki: The dismantling of the Self, in *The Seven Basic Plots: Why we tell stories, Chapter 34,* Continuum.

42 Ndalianis, A (2009) Comic Book Superheroes: An introduction, in *The Contemporary Comic Book Superhero,* ed A Ndalianis, Routledge.

43 Gleich, J (2012) *The Information: A history, a theory, a flood,* Fourth Estate.

44 Morrison, G (2012) *Supergods: Our world in the age of the superhero,* Vintage.

45 Mull, C (September 2012) No Brands Aren't People and Consumers Don't Want Them to Be, in *Adage.*

46 Grant, G (2000) *The New Marketing Manifesto: The 12 rules for building successful brands in the 21st century,* Texere Publishing.

47 Erasmus, religion and the economy blog (March 2014) in *The Economist* [Online] www.economist.com/blogs/erasmus argues: 'much of the rich, northern hemisphere, commercial products and images are now the defining "archetypes" – displacing the old reference points of religion'.

48 Feldwick, P (2002) *What is Brand Equity, Anyway?*, World Advertising Research Centre (Warc).

49 Ndalianis, A (2009) Comic Book Superheroes: An introduction, in *The Contemporary Comic Book Superhero*, ed A Ndalianis, Routledge.

50 Berger, J (1972) *Ways of Seeing*, BBC/Penguin Books.

51 Randazzo, S (March 2006) Subaru: the emotional myths behind a brand's growth in emotion in advertising ii, *Journal of Advertising Research*, **46** (1).

52 *ibid.*

53 Bain, D (Autumn 2003) Deep Dive 1 [Seminar] IPA. He argues that marketing is a business tactic to get people to pay a price premium.

54 Wolf, M J (2003) *The Entertainment Economy: How mega-media forces are transforming our lives*, Three Rivers Press.

55 Pine II, J B and Gilmore, J H (1999) *The Experience Economy: Work is theatre and every business a stage*, Harvard Business School Press, US.

56 The Guardian fashion blog (March 2014) talks about Chanel's latest 'Warholian fashion extravaganza' in a staged supermarket.

57 Siltanen, R (January 2014) Yes, a Super Bowl ad really is worth $4m, *Forbes*

58 TGI data (2013).

59 Barreyat-Baron, M and Barrie, R (2008) Cadbury – How a drumming gorilla beat a path back to profitable growth: A real-time effectiveness case study, IPA.

60 The link between creativity and effectiveness fused together the Gunn Report database of creatively awarded campaigns with the IPA Effectiveness database (2011), www.warc.com

61 Weaver, K and Dyson, P (2006) Advertising's greatest hits: Profitability and brand value, www.warc.com

62 Field, P and Binet, L (2013) The long and short of it, *IPA*.

63 Morrison, G (2012) *Supergods: Our world in the age of the superhero*, Vintage, London.

64 William Casebeer of the US Defense Advanced Research Projects Agency (DARPA), a neurobiologist, argued that certain narratives can be as addictive as cocaine, cited in Russell Davies Typad (December 2012).

65 Milne, A A and Shepard, H A (1926) *Winnie-the-Pooh*, Methuen.

66 Binet, L and Carter, S (March 2014) Mythbuster: Marketing always needs to make sense, *Admap*. They rightly argue that it is actually 'sensible not to make sense' in marketing as people are drawn to things which make no sense at all: round tea bags, alphabet letters stamped on bread.

67 *ibid.*

68 In reference to the 2007 TV commercial for Egg.

69 In reference to the Sony Bravia 'Balls' TV commercial.

70 In reference to the Evian 'Babies' TV commercial.

71 In reference to the Three 'Pony Dance' TV commercial.

72 In reference to the Cadbury 'Gorilla' TV commercial.

73 Ogilvy, D (1963) *Confessions of an Advertising Man*, Southbank Publishing.

74 Morrison, G (2012) *Supergods: Our world in the age of the superhero*, Vintage.

75 IPA Deep Dive 3 [Seminar] (January 2014) AKQA's ECD Nick Turner.

76 Sharp, B (2010) *How Brands Grow: What marketers don't know*, Oxford University Press, Australia & New Zealand.

77 Walker, T (January 2014) Superstars, Super Budgets, Super Bowl, *Independent on Sunday* referencing Anita Elberse.

78 Cadbury 'Gorilla' and Honda 'Live' ads both ran campaigns around the advertising itself.

79 Stevenson, C (January 19) The secret to Hollywood's future?, *Independent on Sunday.*

80 Elberse, A (2014) *Blockbusters: Why big hits – and big risks – are the future of the entertainment business*, Faber & Faber. A recently published book on how the entertainment industry is obsessed with producing big blockbusters. Elberse decided to quantify the best entertainment business strategies, building complex models that controlled all kinds of factors.

81 Bourkestreetbakery.com.au, now publishing a cookbook and they have opened several other stores in Sydney.

82 Ogilvy, D (1963) *Confessions of an Advertising Man*, Southbank Publishing.

83 *ibid.*

84 Randazzo, S (March 2006) Subaru: The emotional myths behind a brand's growth in emotion in advertising ii, *Journal of Advertising Research*, 46 (1).

85 IPA Deep Dive 3 [Seminar] (January 2014) AKQA's ECD Nick Turner claims never to send anything out which isn't perfect.

86 JFDI – Industry slang for clients asking agencies to implement 'Just Fucking Do It' briefs.

87 Bacon, F [Online] www.egs.edu/library/francis-bacon-artist/quotes/

88 Lois Lane to Superman [Online] http//:www.imdb.com

I believe that brands should embrace the dark side
2009/10

13

SIMON ROBERTSON
Head of Communications Strategy, Anomaly London

I believe Positivity is negativity. It makes us produce samey, anodyne and irrelevant brands. By embracing bias and division, and building them into the fabric of our branding, we will create brands that stand out; that seem more real; that resonate more strongly; that fit to the tone of our developing landscape. It's only human to love a baddie.

Editor's therefore, for your brand...

Your brand thinking: Is differentiation or relevance the most important thing for your brand? Do you know? Does your team agree?

Your brand engagement: On a scale of 1 to 10, where 10 is truly different, how much of your work across the last five years scores a 10, what would your team score the work, what would your consumers?

Your brand organization & capability: What is your team's 'courage' quotient – its appetite for difference? When you look at yourselves does your team arguably only represent 'the moral middle classes'?

...and author's personal therefore

Returning to the heady days of 2010, my initial instinct was to begin with a retraction: to confess the adolescent posturing of a younger man in desperate need of attention, whose cynical position was a mere cover for a heartfelt desire to be loved, to bring to life the importance of differentiation, honesty and truth.

And then I thought about it for a bit, and concluded: to hell with that.

How honest was this dark side thing?

Some of the following essay is true. Dark side marketing was largely a rhetorical cover for much more positive concerns about the cultural and psychological impact of the internet, the position of honesty and truth in insight development and the vital importance of radical differentiation.

In my work, I've spent much more time trying to get brands to look and behave in unexpected ways – like making whisky communications that talk like Nike or Apple, mass-produced paint ads that look like something from the pages of *Love* magazine, and a high-end perfume brand based on Edwardian illustrated newspapers – than I have going dark.

Even my one shot at the dark side in action, as part of the team that developed the Refuge 'Don't Cover It Up' campaign, put these tactics at the service of a positive cause – using a shocking creative premise and harnessing the power of rumour in social media to transform the perception of domestic violence among young women for a wafer-thin budget.

Furthermore, many of those case studies used in my piece have – to the joy of my acquaintances – been disproved by time. Ryanair decided that a sado-masochistic online experience may not have the legs it once did; Karl Rove went into public meltdown on Fox News as his strategy melted in the glare of a new, sunnily diverse electoral coalition in the United States. Even the Double Down Burger is, sadly, no longer available.

Speak no evil, do some evil

And yet, my experience leads me to believe that dark side-style thinking is required more than ever in the process of building brands; if not as a strand of content, then certainly as a mode of behaviour.

Because behaviours that are often considered positive do not, in my experience, create positive results.

In a world dominated by global brands, proliferating platforms and ever-more-populous inter-agency groups, our work increasingly finds itself in the position of bowing to the whims of the tech, the global marketing forum, the group. Huge energies are focused on collaboration, on consultation, on *making it work*.

But here's the thing. Difference does not come from agreement. Brilliance does not arise from consultation. Making it work impedes make it wondrous.

An infinite number of inter-agency/cross-disciplinary/globally representative groups working in a collaborative fashion on an infinite number of decks for an infinite amount of time will not produce *Hamlet*. They won't even produce the Hamlet ads.

Reading back on 'dark side' now, the following quote sticks with me more than any other: 'Sometimes, a culture *"grows so alienated and banal that only a dose of the diabolical can stir it up"*.'[1]

We become alienated from consumers when we put platforms and tech above genuine insight and the thrill of original thinking; we consign ourselves to banality when we prioritize process and logistics over the awe and fear of a brilliant idea. I joined this industry for neither, and given the choice available, I'll sign up for a dose of the diabolical every single time.

Join the dark side, or die

The only elements of creative industries that survive radical technological change are those that cannot be reduced to an algorithm. Those that are unique.

Someday in the future – and it isn't too far away – we'll have to prove that we can do something that a self-optimizing, re-targeted 'skippable' cannot, in a world where people will choose the vast majority of branded interactions they have. I don't believe a capacity to work well as an inter-agency group will cut it. In my experience, major corporations have pleasant, sensible and effective people to spare. What they need is provocateurs who will inspire great, transformative communication.

Survival demands that we display different characteristics from other industries. And as a working model, I'm in favour of one that all the ladies love: The Dark Triad, referenced in my essay.

Adopting the Dark Triad

The Dark Triad is a set of characteristics cited in the kind of shaky psychological-anthropological research planners adore, and supposedly at the heart of the attraction we feel to characters like James Bond. They are as follows:

- Narcissism: manifesting as overweening self-confidence and grandiosity.
- Machiavellianism: the desire to manipulate others.
- Psychopathy: resulting in risk taking without fear of consequence.

It's your mate always beating you to the girls/boys at the school disco. It's also what it takes to create and execute great ideas.

It takes the callous disregard of a sub-clinical psychopath to take a risk on doing something different; the manipulative genius of a Machiavelli to create something that profoundly connects and affects millions; the grand narcissism of a modern teenager to believe in and protect an idea in the face of the urge to compromise and dilute.

Comfortingly, I find that none of these traits, done right, preclude a lack of decency, good manners or kindness to animals. In my personal life I've discovered that being a cynic is not the only way to build a relationship with a wonderful partner. Although it can help.

And in my career I've been lucky enough to work with some of the most powerfully creative, terrifyingly dedicated, legendarily effective people in the industry. All give off the Dark Triad in waves of brimstone. Almost without exception they are also likable, caring human beings.

But it's their dark side that will keep us all in jobs. More of us need that streak of the diabolical. It's what separates us from the accountants, the dotcommers, the management consultants – you know, the real bad guys. In the words of the immortal Capt Malcolm 'Mal' Reynolds from the film *Serenity*: 'A year from now, ten? They'll swing back to the belief that they can make people... better. And I do not hold to that. So no more running. I aim to misbehave.'

I believe that brands should embrace the dark side

The sun also shines on the wicked. (SENECA)

Part 1. Smile or die: how positivity is killing brands

In the world of advertising, the sun always shines. It's populated by the citizens of Getty Images. They are essentially benign. They like to hear good news. To be inspired. To dream. So that's what brands give them. And it always works.

It's a good time to be there. Digital culture is bringing these people together, unlocking what's inside them. As a result, they're making a better world: more communal, more transparent, more democratic, more creative, smarter. They're going to force brands to make the world a better place.

I kind of wish I lived there. Don't you?

Meanwhile, on planet Earth...

Humans are messy. We are as capable of idiocy as we are of brilliance, as ugly as we are beautiful, and as driven by negative emotions as positive. As digital media operate as 'extensions of man'[2], they will amplify and accelerate both the light and the darkness about our culture. In many ways, this may seem to be an exercise in stating the bleeding obvious. Looking at the version of life reflected in the advertising industry, I'm not so sure.

I believe that our inclination to positivity is painting us into a corner. I believe that it is making our brands increasingly homogenized and timid, and increasingly out of step with the way that digital culture is changing us. I believe that, by embracing the dark side – by accepting that human beings experience rage, fear and division as intensely as love, joy and unity, and by

building those elements into branding – we can develop genuinely differentiating and resonant brands that are appropriate to our developing culture.

What brands could be, what brands must be

A brand *can* be a citizen.[3] It can put 'the common good at the heart of its
business model.'[4] But a brand *must* be differentiated. It 'must be unique... it
must have no adequate direct substitutes – because it is in this, after all, that
value lies... it is through this uniqueness that the brand can offer sustained
profit margins'.[5] A brand can seek to endear itself to consumers. A brand
can speak to 'fundamental human truths about creativity, heroism, family,
happiness and unity[6].' But a brand *must* be resonant and authentic. It must
'invoke strong emotional responses and motivate commitment and action'.[7]
If we fail to do these things, we have failed to build successful brands,
regardless of whether we have made the world slightly more cheery with
someone else's money.

Figure 13.1 illustrates the mood of the nation over the past three years.
Consider the events of 2009, and ponder where our brands intersect with the
perceivable reality. At what point do the brands descriptors above genuinely
'resolve acute tensions people feel between their own lives and societies
prevailing ideology[8]'? At what point are they relevant to people's needs and
desires? Only in so far as all of our approaches seem to believe that what
people really need at the moment is a damn good cuddle. 'To create powerful

FIGURE 13.1   Some people are never satisfied

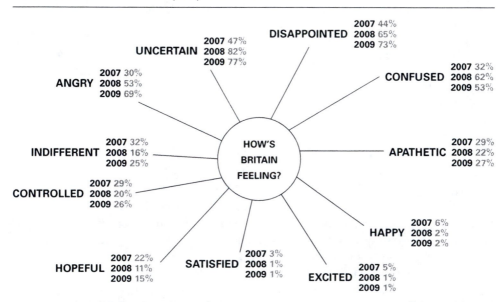

(Survey, 2010) Moody Britain, McCann Erickson [Online] http://www.brandrepublic.com/research/1028634/
Moody-Britain-2010-Putting-pieces-back-together/

myths, managers must get close to culture'[9]: over the past two years, the world was rocked by the most extreme and traumatic socio-economic events for more than a generation. Our industry response? Nostalgia. And nostalgia. And nostalgia. This is the collective corner into which our fear of acknowledging the less palatable sides of human nature pushes us, as compressed and identical as sardines.

The wind tunnel is us

Positivity is not a strategy, nor is it a creative approach. 'It is a cognitive stance.'[10] And it leads to what Jim Carroll has called 'wind-tunnel marketing',[11] a process which eradicates 'the edges, the uncomfortable, the unpalatable'.[12] While we can blame 'the same research, with the same consumers via the same research companies on essentially the same products',[13] I believe one of the most powerful elements of the wind tunnel is within our own culture and in our own heads, in our tendency to always emphasize the positive and in our discomfort in presenting the consumer (or client) with 'something different or challenging or hard to stomach'.[14]

The real world has never been a place where 'good' is inherently compelling, and it is developing to make 'good' less interesting every day, as digital culture makes consumers increasingly divided, subjective and confrontational. Our planets are drifting ever further apart.

Part 2. Here be monsters: how digital culture is making dark-side marketing more appropriate

We have to work the dark side, if you will... that's the world these folks operate in.

(Dick Cheney)

There is no such thing as an achievable Utopia[15]

The consensus on digital culture is that it is more than just good. It is credited with almost supernatural potential, based on an almost supernatural view of human nature. As John Gray puts it: 'In this fantasy, mankind in the future will be different not only from any other animal but also from anything it has ever been'[16]: collectively good, just, wise, smart and charitable. Bringing people together through digital media will improve literacy, civil society, creativity, and particularly marketing.

Five minutes involvement in an online debate will teach you that this isn't the whole story of digital culture. It is no surprise that one of the earliest cultural laws of digital discourse – Godwin's Law[17] – referred to the debasement of civil discourse on digital platforms. Digital media is 'our central nervous system... technologically extended to involve us in the whole of mankind and to incorporate the whole of mankind in us',[18] and our central nervous system is, charitably put, a quirky place.

Externalizing internal biases

In his book *True Enough*, Farhad Manjoo illustrates how the increasingly atomised and specialized nature of media in a post-digital environment plays into our inherent biases. A digitally filtered environment allows us to lead a life based on selective exposure, 'reading or watching or listening to ideas that confirm what you already feel, deep down, must be true'.[19] Inevitably, this leads to an increasingly subjective culture in which selective perception[20] is strengthened.

Conversely, digital connectivity also allows us to connect rapidly with people who see the things the same way as us, producing a social reality that entrenches our beliefs and produces a radicalizing effect. As Sunstein comments, 'when like-minded people deliberate, they typically end up adopting a more extreme position in line with their pre-deliberation inclinations.'[21] Digital media is all about allowing like-minded people to deliberate, and as we spend increasing time in the digital landscape, increasing amounts of what we see and hear, buy and do are shaped by it. We are increasingly encouraging each other to create lives built on subjectivity, displays of allegiance and mutual reinforcement. On an ongoing, low-level basis, digital culture invites us to become militants on subjects from political affiliation to crisp-flavour preference.

'O brave new world
That has such people in't!'[22]

Digital media allows us to believe what we want, form gangs and be nasty to each other. 'Online culture increasingly resembles a slum in disturbing ways... People are meaner is slums; mobs rule and vigilantism is commonplace.'[23]

Conditions of radicalization and mutual reinforcement are not the best for producing reasoned enquiry or objective truth.

Digital culture's combination of low-entry thresholds, sophisticated audio-visual technology, group polarization and the potential for social cascading make it almost uniquely suited to the creation and transmission of falsehood and rumour. As Nick Davies puts it: 'Google simply presents what everyone else is saying, without a scruple as to its importance or truth.'[24]

The internet is an anarchic marketplace of ideas that is rigged by our own, often subconscious, biases. The success of ideas is more likely to be down to whether they 'relieve "a primary emotional urge" and offer an explanation of why people feel the way they do', or whether they 'trigger strong emotions, such as fear and disgust'[25] than to whether they are provably true.

Releasing our 'inner troll'

This combination of bias, group polarization and subjective truth, combined with the 'drive by anonymity' and lack of consequence in digital culture, is a heady brew for human beings. At a low level, it produces the circumstances of de-individuation and de-humanization that Philip Zimbardo has proposed are key to the 'Lucifer Effect': the 'dynamic set of psychological processes... that can induce good people to do evil'.[26] More and more people are 'introduced to their inner troll': encouraged to be slightly less tolerant, less reasoned, less truthful than before.

The culture of sadism online... has gone mainstream[27]

Obviously, these changes aren't restricted to a discrete 'digital world'; they infuse our culture daily. 'A story can go from local to global in a heartbeat'[28] as digital events become the content of news stories on an increasingly frequent basis. Reaction on social networks is now used to judge political performance and discussed on the news. Subjective falsehood and rumour on the internet increasingly become accepted truth as they are 'locked in'[29] to a mass-media system. The nature of digital culture is increasingly the nature of our culture as a whole.

This, then, is our developing culture as we see it from the dark side. It is increasingly biased, divided, extreme and open to falsehood. Anger and parody are our cultural tonalities; mutually reinforcing and radicalizing gangs are our social units and friction between these units our cultural discourse; rumour is our medium, bias and disgust its accelerants. This is the cultural framework within which brands increasingly operate, and a policy of accentuating the positive is not going to stop brands appearing disconnected and irrelevant. Inevitably, they will appear more so.

Part 3. Sympathy for the devil: the attractions of the dark side

> You need people like me so you can point your fuckin' fingers and say,
> 'That's the bad guy'. (Tony Montana, *Scarface*)

We tend to believe that the best way to 'provide pleasure, interest and a sense of belonging' is to 'make [consumers] happier, even if only for a little while'.[30] This is not the case. Everybody, for want of a better phrase, loves a good baddy. It's what caused Alfred Hitchcock to coin the maxim 'the better the villain, the more successful the picture'. It's what makes the 'dark triad' of narcissism, thrill-seeking and deceitfulness 'a successful evolutionary strategy' that results in a higher number of sexual partners universally across all cultures according to researchers at New Mexico and Bradley universities. It's why the old *Star Wars* was awesome and *The Phantom Menace* sucked.

Flirting with the dark side, whether through the two archetypal variations – 'The Villain', who utilizes it, or 'The Monster', who embodies it – or in our real lives, thrills and satisfies us in a number of ways, filling a number of important functions.

The dark side simplifies

A key function of dark characters, like virtuous ones, is to personify and simplify complex issues. They become emotional focal points, allowing us to define, restrict and manage elements of the world. In this sense, dark characters are a simplifying force, 'an easy recognised package of information',[31] containing our fears, anxieties and frustrations. As with heroes (and brands), this symbolic function is key.

The dark side is differentiated

Unlike heroes, villains are more flexible and do not have to represent an Everyman or an ideal. Consequently, dark characters are considerably more individual than heroes, who are bound by the constraints of both morality and likeability. They can represent a fuller spectrum of human experience. After all, a villain who behaves kindly is enhanced, while a hero who performs an act of cowardice or rage is necessarily diminished. They are more recognizable and, perversely, often more empathetic characters than heroes.

The dark side is aspirational

Dark characters are a dream of freedom. All the way back to Lucifer himself, they represent freedom from authority and from the conformist moral pressures of society. 'The very heart of the notion of the villain is a refusal to submit to the social contract.'[32] They allow us to experience a life without boundaries.

The dark side provides release

Having the capacity to live vicariously through villains or monsters is a necessary release. They 'have a cathartic function, in the sense that they give our tamed, repressed impulses a brief holiday of Bacchanalian revelry. And after these virtual trips to our own hearts of darkness, we can better return to our everyday social world of compromise, accommodation, and compliance.'[33]

Part 4. 'Evil, be thou my good'[34]: dark-side branding in action

I am determined to prove a villain. (Richard of York, *Richard III*)

If the most successful brands 'compete for culture share',[35] we need to realize what all other fields of culture – music, film, theatre, literature – have gleefully accepted for years: sometimes, a culture 'grows so alienated and banal that only a dose of the diabolical can stir it up.'[36] The devil has all of the best tunes, apparently. Here is how we learn to play them.

Seven deadly sins: helping your brand to embrace the dark side

1 *Do be evil*
   The first rule of the dark side is to admit that there *is* a dark side. Make anger as much a part of your marketing vocabulary as love, put villain on the same par as hero. Look at the categories your brands operate in and see their dark potential; the internal tensions between groups and the frustrations and hidden shames that characterize your consumer's relationship with your brands or your competitors. Calibrate the angle to which happy-clappy brands have diverged from the reality of the interactions between brands, category and the consumers. Celebrate nature red in tooth and claw; identify the potential for skulduggery.

2 *Find the bias*
   Our bias is, increasingly, forming the information we process and how we process it. Understanding the biases within groups is at the heart of dark side branding: it allows you to understand how consumers form and define themselves (positively and negatively) and what messages they are likely to accept, screen and seek out. An understanding of the complex dynamics of bias within and between groups forms the heart of dark side positioning, messaging and communications plans.

3 *Be the villain, be the monster*
   Within the majority of categories, there will be a space for a dark side brand personality, and it is unlikely to have been occupied. This does not necessarily mean pronouncing a love of evil from the rooftops, any more than heroic archetypes are always explicit, it means *utilizing* the negative elements of the category to your ends. For example, a villainous building society would, during the economic crisis, have worked to reflect, stoke and channel populist rage towards the banks to its own ends.

4 *Pander*
   At heart, most people don't want their biases to be challenged. They want them to be affirmed, recognized, amplified, rationalized. Dark side brands will do this voraciously, espousing a worldview that makes anger, resentment, self-pity or frustration of the target consumer epic and justified. They will complain about the target consumer's complaints, share their sense of victimhood, bully who

they bully, hate who they hate. For years, this has been the modus operandi of successful politicians and media owners: the success of the *Daily Mail*, for instance, is based on 'Paul Dacre's ability to know instinctively, immediately and entirely what his readers want to be told about the world – the facts, the values, the moral panics.'[37]

5 *Divide and conquer*
Our culture is increasingly about Us and Them. Forget about universal appeal: 'not all great stories are for everyone.'[38] However, the people your stories *aren't* for can still be useful. You have two target audiences. One is your consumer. The other is 'the other side' against which they define themselves. Pick an enemy, chosen specifically for their conflict with, and visibility to, your target audience. Communicate to them alongside your chosen audience; parody them; direct your audience's antipathy towards them; infuriate them so that your audience can see it. As with the brilliant Marmite campaign, make your product the *point* of the dispute. The classic example of this is, of course, Apple vs PC, but most categories will contain internal tensions and disputes. Use the other side as a wall against which you bounce your brand.

6 *Unleash the power of rumour*
Make your brand one that is inherently rumour-producing. Plant half-truths and suggestions among your audience and the media. Lose the product in a bar and have someone else find it. Treat truth as a parlour game. Raise ill-defined concerns about developments in the economy, in the market, in culture. Behave oddly. Remember that disgust is an accelerant and employ it without scruple, whether aimed at the other side or to ignite the masochistic tendency within your own consumers. Make sure those rumours are gathered and channelled to major media outlets. All that is required is to know the bias sufficiently so that your rumours manifest as powerful 'dread rumours' or 'wish rumours'[39] and are sufficiently extreme to gain currency.

7 *Learn from evil*
Dark side brands avoid the easy answer of the palatable cultural phenomenon, the thing that 'everybody likes'. They research the things that disgust them and they take more interest in the people who parody and rail against products than those who like them. They research porn, the US right-wing, conspiracy theories, public hysteria and cult leaders, because these examples are likely to be richer, more differentiated, and ahead of the cultural curve in a way that the virtuous often aren't.

Dark side brands in action

As with all good marketing, the question of embracing the dark side is not a binary one; brands do not have to be all villain or all hero. Dark side branding is about acknowledging and embracing the potential for the dark side within your brand by identifying those areas where the consumer benefit is best expressed by being villainous, understanding the biases within consumers groups that facilitate message processing, or simply by knowing who your consumers want you to beat up.

Marmite created a brand around its own divisiveness; Apple picked up on its consumers' contempt for Microsoft and places it at the heart of its advertising; Pot Noodle realized that its product is the 'slag of all snacks' and flaunts it. All of these campaigns stand out because they feel *different*. They feel truer, smarter, more fundamentally honest, more interesting. This is what embracing the dark side does for us.

The villainous CEO: Michael O'Leary, RyanAir

Michael O'Leary does not want to be your friend. He thinks the idea that the customer is always right is nonsense[40] and does not want to have a conversation with you. Michael O'Leary wants to charge you to go to the toilet on an airplane. His company has a 'deserved reputation for nastiness' and has 'become a byword for appalling customer service'.[41]

Isn't he wonderful?

O'Leary has taught Europe 'how to be treated like shite in 15 countries... and still quite like it',[42] and he has done it by an absolute and vocal commitment to the values and personality of Ryanair. Ryanair makes air travel cheap, and does it with a ruthless, 'jeering rudeness towards anyone or anything that gets in its way'.[43] Including the customer.

This approach to 'dialogue' arguably helps enhance the consumer experience. 'Customer experience is not about delivering Disney-esque moments or trying to make people happy at all costs. Good customer experience management is about consistently delivering on brand promises that resonate with customers.'[44] Customers are absolutely clear about what they're in for with Ryanair, and may even gain some satisfaction from it: 'The Ryanair travel experience reinforces the trade-off you make for the very low fares and therefore dramatises the value that it provides.'[45]

The monstrous product: the KFC Double Down sandwich

The KFC Double Down burger is a product so absurdly provocative that even KFC's advertising seemed to acknowledge the general feeling that it 'seemed so egregious as to defy human comprehension'.[46] It launched on 1 April, with the strapline: 'It's Real!'

It immediately became the subject of furious conflict, a conflict that began in user-generated content and blogs and penetrated into the mass media.

On one side were those who saw the product as a 'troubling symbol of corporate irresponsibility' or, more colourfully, 'an edible Hieronymus Bosch painting wrapped in a paper straitjacket'. The US Physicians Committee for Responsible Medicine wrote to KFC requesting that the product not be advertised within 500 yards of schools.[47] At least two commentators expressed the sentiment that 'this is why the terrorists hate' the USA. Tracked buzz around the product was twice as negative as that around the Big Mac.[48]

On the other side were those who embraced the 'death-wish appeal'[49] of the Double Down, to whom 'hippy-punching as a meal choice'[50] appealed. For them, the overall culture context of 'the nanny state and the continued pussifying of food'[51] made the Double Down irresistible.

The fact is, *both* sides found the Double Down irresistible and the inter-action between the two groups made the product a sensation. In 'the mother of all viral campaigns',[52] thousands of pieces of user-generated content appeared in YouTube and Flickr, and the product garnered huge amounts of free PR across newsprint and TV.

By embodying all of the contradictions and divisions around food and corporate behaviour in the US, the Double Down became much more than a product: it was a Monster. It was communicated as a source of self-conscious disgust. And it sold 10 million units in less than six weeks.

Part 5. The road to hell is paved with good intentions

When I'm good, I'm very good. When I'm bad, I'm better. (Mae West)

But how do we make it happen? Embracing the dark side doesn't need financial investment, nor does it need new agency structures. It requires intellectual rigour, honesty and courage.

In order to develop these insights and approaches, we need to attempt to discover what is actually good and bad about the product, about our brand, about *people*. That requires getting our hands dirty with the arguments and squabbles people are having around our category, looking into unpalatable behaviour and trying to work out what of value we can take from it. It requires broadening out the remit of conversations we have with consumers, allowing them to complain and reveal themselves, widening Heath and Feldwick's approach that 'Research interpretations must be based... on how they behave... whether they smile, laugh or chat animatedly'[53] into expressions of annoyance, disgust or prejudice.

More than anything, it requires us to have the courage to refrain from being of the 'moral middle classes'[54] and bringing a complacent sense of 'good' to our analysis. It requires us to have the rigor to try to make something compelling and exciting out of something we might disagree with. It requires us to have the honesty to accept that a brand might frustrate and enrage some people, might shock and dismay others, and be the better brand for it.

Courage, rigor, honesty. These may seem oddly heroic principles, but as the author George R R Martin put it: 'the villain is just the hero of the other side.'

Notes

1 Eagleton,T (2011) *On Evil*, Yale University Press.

2 McLuhan, M (2001) *Understanding Media*, Routledge.

3 Willmott, M (2001) *Citizen Brands: Putting society at the heart of your business*, John Wiley & Sons.

4 Bonney, D (2009) We believe the people should control the means of branding, IPA Excellence Diloma essay [Online] www.ipa.co.uk/Document/We-believe-the-people-should-control-the-means-of-branding-by-David-Bonney

5 Handley, L (May 2010) Meet the teachers, *Marketing Week*.

6 Cordiner, R (2009) Brand story, IPA Excellence Diploma essay [Online] www.ipa.co.uk/document/brand-story-by-richard-cordiner.

7 Cato, M (May 2010) In brands we trust, *Campaign*.

8 Holt, B (March 2003) What becomes an icon most?, *Harvard Business Review* [Online] http://hbr.org/2003/03/what-becomes-an-icon-most/ar/1

9 *ibid*.

10 Erenreich, B (2009) *Smile or Die: How positive thinking fooled America and the world*, Granta.

11 Carroll, J (May 2010) Wind tunnel politics, *BBH Labs* [Online] http://bbh-labs.com/wind-tunnel-politics.

12 *ibid*.

13 Wigley, C (May 2010) Wind tunnel marketing, the sequel, *BBH Labs* [Online] http://bbh-labs.com/wind-tunnel-marketing-the-sequel-on-the-need-for-divergent-insight

14 Carroll, J (May 2010) Wind tunnel politics, *BBH Labs* [Online] http://bbh-labs.com/wind-tunnel-politics.

15 Lévy, P (1999) *Collective Intelligence: Mankind's emerging world in cyberspace*, Helix Books.

16 Gray, J (2007) *Straw Dogs: Thoughts on humans and other animals*, Farrar, Straus and Giroux.

17 See: [Online] http://en.wikipedia.org/wiki/Godwin's_law

18 McLuhan, M (2001) *Understanding Media*, Routledge.

19 Manjoo, F (2008)*True Enough:, Learning to live in a post-fact society*, John Wiley & Sons.

20 Hastorf, A H and Cantril, H (1954) They saw a game: a case study, *The Journal of Abnormal and Social Psychology*, **49** (1), pp129–34.

21 Sunstein, C R (2009) *On rumors: How falsehoods spread, why we believe them, what can be done*, Farrar, Straus and Giroux.

22 Shakespeare, *The Tempest*.

23 Lanier, J (2010) *You Are Not a Gadget: A manifesto*, Allen Lane.

24 Davies, N (2009) *Flat Earth News: An award-winning reporter exposes falsehood, distortion and propaganda in the global media*, Vintage.

25 Sunstein, C and Vermeule, A (2009) Symposium on conspiracy theories, conspiracy theories: causes and cures, *The Journal of Political Philosophy*, **17** (2), pp 202–27.

26 Zimbardo, P (2007) *The Lucifer Effect: How good people turn evil*, Rider, Reading.

27 Lanier, J (2011) *You Are Not a Gadget: A manifesto*, Vintage.

28 Shirkey, C (2008) *Here comes everybody: The power of organizing without organizations*, Penguin Books, US.

29 Lanier, J (2011) *You Are Not a Gadget: A manifesto*, Vintage.

30 Cato, M (May 2010) In brands we trust, *Campaign*.

31 Mitchell, A (2002) *Right Side Up: Building brands in the age of organized consumer*, HarperCollinsBusiness.

32 Alsford, M (2006) *Heroes and Villains*, Darton, Longman and Todd.

33 Asma, S (October 2009) Monsters and Wild Things, *Oxford University Press blog* [Online] http://blog.oup.com/2009/10/wild-things

34 Milton, *Paradise Lost*.

35 Holt, B (March 2003) What becomes an icon most?, *Harvard Business Review* [Online] http://hbr.org/2003/03/what-becomes-an-icon-most/ar/1

36 Eagleton, T (2011) *On Evil*, Yale University Press.

37 Davies, N (2009) *Flat Earth News: An award-winning reporter exposes falsehood, distortion and propaganda in the global media*, Vintage Books.

38 Godin, S (2009) *All Marketers Are Liars*, Portfolio.

39 Sunstein, C R (2009) *On rumors: How falsehoods spread, why we believe them, what can be done*, Farrar, Straus and Giroux.

40 Lyall, S (July 2009) No Apologies from the Boss of a No-Frills Airline, *New York Times* [Online] www.nytimes.com/2009/08/01/world/europe/01oleary.html?_r=1

41 (August 2007) Snarling all the way to the bank, *The Economist*.

42 Kilduff, P (2008) *Ruinair: How to Be Treated Like Shite in 15 Countries... and still Quite Like It*, Gill & Macmillan.

43 (August 2007) Snarling all the way to the bank, *The Economist*.

44 Temkin, B (August 2009) Ryanair's Terrible Customer Experience May Be Just Right, *Customer Experience Matters* [Online] http://experiencematters.wordpress.com/2009/08/03/ryanairs-terrible-customer-experience-may-be-just-right

45 Smith, S (December 2009) Ryanair – a branded customer experience? *Customer Think* [Online] www.customerthink.com/blog/ryanair_a_branded_customer_experience

46 Gold, S (September 2009) The KFC Double Down: This is why terrorists hate our freedom, *The Faster Times* [Online] http://thefastertimes.com/meat/2009/09/25/this-is-why-the-terrorists-hate-our-freedom/

47 Levin, S (April 2010) Nutritionists Ask KFC to Keep New Double Down Sandwich Away from Children, *Physicians Committee* [Online] http://pcrm.org/media/news/nutritionists-ask-kfc-to-keep-new-double-down

48 Hoyland, C (April 2010) Will Negative Buzz Mean More Sales for KFC Double Down? *QSR Web* [Online] www.qsrweb.com/news/will-negative-buzz-mean-more-sales-for-kfc-double-down/

49 Levin, S (April 2010) Nutritionists ask KFC to keep new Double Down sandwich away from children, *Physicians Committee* [Online] http://pcrm.org/media/news/nutritionists-ask-kfc-to-keep-new-double-down

50 Yglesias, M (April 2010) The Double Down, *Think Progress* [Online] http://yglesias.thinkprogress.org/2010/04/the-double-down

51 *ibid.*

52 Silverthorne, S (August 2009) KFC's 'Double Down's Sandwich: the mother of all viral campaigns?, *CBS News Money Watch* [Online] www.cbsnews.com/news/kfcs-double-down-sandwich-the-mother-of-all-viral-campaigns

53 Heath, R and Feldwick, P (2007) 50 years of using the wrong advertising model, *International Journal of Market Research*, **50** (1).

54 Eagleton, T (2011) *On Evil*, Yale University Press.

Hey, what's the long idea? I believe it's time the big idea had a counterpart

2009/10

14

SARAH MORNING

Strategy Director, adam&eveDDB

I believe I believe that our industry had grown up with a severe and dangerous bias in the way that it used communications technologies; that it has come to favour conquests of space over considerations of permanence. As a result, we fail to look at digital through a ritual perspective and ignore its potential as a much needed time-binding channel.

Editor's therefore, for your brand...

Your brand thinking:
Does your company or brand have a long view? What is your vision of you and your world in 10 years' time?

Your brand engagement:
What rituals around your brand could exist or be encouraged?

Your brand organization & capability: What are your team's biases? How do you inject other perspectives, either cultural or temporal?

...and author's personal therefore

I will subvert our industry's cultural biases

In 2010, I came to share a belief held by Professors Harold Innis and James Carey that the advertising industry had developed a dangerous bias in the way it used communications technologies; that it had come to favour conquests of space over considerations of permanence and was unable to see the possibilities of communications as acts of ritual as well as transmission. Today, although I am still determined that their ideas around permanence and ritual become a part of our industry's everyday lexicon, my thinking on this topic has evolved even further.

According to Oscar Wilde 'it is what you read when you don't have to that determines what you will be when you can't help it'. When I reached the end of the weighty (but inspiring) reading list from the IPA Excellence Diploma one of the first things I read was a comic, *Red Son* by Mark Miller. I read it partly for light relief after months of journals, but mostly because it has an ingeniously insane premise at its heart: what if Superman's rocket had been slightly delayed leaving Krypton? The Earth would have rotated a little further before his ship had landed and the man of steel would have been raised not on a homestead in Kansas but on a collective farm in the Soviet Union. The great American icon, reimagined as a Soviet hero. A Superman with a very different set of ideals and values to those we're used to, and a very different way of seeing the world (albeit still through X-ray vision).

What struck me, however, was that Innis and Carey had been doing a pretty similar thing to Miller, reimagining a great American icon (in this case advertising) through a very different cultural lens. And indeed, when I looked back at the thesis I had written I realized that Innis' critique of modern media had been firmly levied at the West; that he saw the modern-day bias towards space-binding media as being driven by the United States and the Western world. Likewise Carey believed that we had come to find ourselves 'glued to a transmission view of communication because this view is congenial with the underlying well-springs of American culture' and its 'obsessive individualism'.[1] Indeed he drew heavily from the language and ideas of collectivist cultures to frame his counter-balancing ritual view of communications.

Of course, both Innis and Carey formed many of their ideas during the height of the Cold War, when it could be argued that there was a trend for academics to adopt such stances against US thinking. However, I then read Richard Nisbett's *The Geography of Thought*. Subtitled 'How Asians and Westerners think differently – and why', Nisbett's book is not a comic but a psychological exploration of the differences in the way that people in interdependent cultures think compared to those in independent cultures. Now, whether or not you accept that such sweeping generalizations can be made, the idea of there being different ways of seeing the world, regardless of who does or doesn't possess them, is fundamentally intriguing. Indeed, the more I read of Nisbett's work, the more I came to believe that the big revolutionary ideas I'd come across while studying for the Excellence Diploma were in fact challenges to the dominance of Western models of thinking. Carey and Innis weren't the only ones trying to counter-balance Western-centric models of communication; Earls' MRS paper on herd behaviour was a direct challenge to the 'obsessive individualism'[2] preventing our industry from recognizing more interdependent consumer behaviours (indeed he references Nisbett in *Herd*[3]); Gordon and Valentine's re-thinking of the 21st-century consumer, a challenge to the Western assumption of independent personal attributes versus the Eastern view of 'the person as connected, fluid and conditional'[4]; and Robert Heath's theory of Low-Attention Processing, a challenge to the Western tendency to consciously attend to focal objects rather than environments and contextual relationships. (Indeed it is perhaps possible to argue that Heath's theory is only low-attention because we're culturally trained not to recognize that we're attending to contexts and environments, and that if advertising's rocket had in fact landed far away from Madison Avenue in an interdependent culture more consciously aware of its attention to contexts and environments, then maybe we wouldn't have spent '50 years using the wrong model'.[5])

Travelling in China and Japan made me reflect further about just how much our models and ways of thinking rise from the 'well-springs' of Western – and particularly US – cultural beliefs about the world. As such, after a load of travel guides and Manga titles, the next book I read was a punchy critique of the dangers that such thinking can have on markets and society, Barbara Ehrenreich's *Bright-Sided: How positive thinking is undermining America*. That got me thinking about how narrow our emotional vocabulary is, given that we're an industry supposedly built on emotions.[6] Thanks to our roots on Madison Avenue I think we share the same Disneyfied cultural obsession with optimism and positivity that the United States itself does; a situation only intensified in today's digital age by another US institution, Facebook. If our emotional vocabulary was limited to a few feel-good emotions before the digital age, then Facebook managed to shrink that even further with the 'like'. It became clear to me that cultural biases had made our industry's ability to articulate – and therefore, crucially, understand – emotion, pretty inadequate. I ended up writing a bit of a rant about it (for which I was lucky enough to pick up a Silver award at the 2014 Admap Prize essay competition and an agreement from my other half that my comic subscriptions now be considered a vital household expenditure).

So, do I still believe that our industry has a fundamental bias in the way that it thinks about space versus time? Do I still believe that we need to adopt a ritual perspective of communications to counterbalance our default transmission perspective? Absolutely. And thanks to Mark Miller's *Red Son*, I believe it more so than ever; in fact I now believe our obsession with space and speed to be just one of many cultural biases in our theoretical thinking that we must acknowledge and subvert as brands and technology go global.

Next up on my list of things I don't have to read is Alan Moore's *Swamp Thing*. Where that'll take me, is anybody's guess.

Hey what's the long idea? I believe it's time the big idea had a counterpart

In 1997 the Long Now Foundation, an organization dedicated to promoting long-term thinking, unveiled a prototype of a clock that would chime once every 10,000 years. Today it stands in the Science Museum, a lasting icon to long-term thinking from a group wanting to provide a 'counterpoint to today's faster/cheaper mindset'.[7] This paper is born from a similar desire; to help reset notions of time, because I believe our industry struggles to think long term in regards to both our ideas and our history; the former, a direct result of the latter.

A long view of our past

Television and radio have already been classified as old media and if I were to declare the printing press a recent innovation I would no doubt be met with derision. So, before I do exactly that and suggest that Gutenberg's invention is a recent bit of kit, some context is required. In 1948, Harold Innis undertook a sweeping survey of over 4,000 years of communications technologies;[8] from the stone, clay and papyrus of Egypt and Babylonia, to the oral traditions of ancient Greece and parchment of medieval Europe, up to the newspapers and emergent technologies of 20th-century United States. Against such a backdrop 500 years of print seems a recent development after all.

I believe we are coming to new technologies with assumptions drawn from the age of print, and that if we continue as we are, looking at the future through the lens of what is our recent past alone, we'll only ever have a limited understanding of what is happening. Take, for example, the rise of participatory audiences which has thrown the advertising industry into disarray; a long view shows that it is in fact the passive audience that is the anomaly. Before the introduction of the novel and private reading, Elizabethan audiences heckled and interrupted actors; and further back Homer's audiences shaped and changed the stories they heard. Participatory audiences are nothing new. They were in existence for thousands of years before the printing press led to their demise.

Four millennia of communications, two types of media

Innis charted 4,000 years of communication history to prove a theory; he believed that the fortunes of great empires were dictated by the media they favoured. Empires are concerned with two objectives; their duration over time and their extension in space, and different communication channels tend to bias either one. Innis thus divided media into two categories; *time-binding* media which are durable, carrying stories through many generations but reaching limited audiences (eg the Egyptian pyramids, parchment manuscripts, Homer's oral epics); and *space-binding* media which reach large numbers over large distances but do not last long (eg paper, newspapers, radio, television). He believed that a bias towards either category affected the nature of knowledge and power structures in a society; spatially-biased eras favoured centralized, militaristic organizations, whereas time-biased eras favoured decentralized, tribal and more orally-natured societies. As cultures became more time-binding, Innis found they became less space-binding and vice versa; they developed biases that led to their demise when communication technologies of an opposing category appeared. Survival relied on striking a balance between the demands of both time and space – something he felt the modern West was catastrophically failing to do.

The printing press fuelled a spatial bias in communications

The history of the West, to Innis, was 'the history of a bias of communication founded on print' where time had 'been cut into pieces the length of a day's newspaper' and 'the problem of duration or monopoly over time neglected, indeed obliterated'.[9] Print was a destroyer of time-binding media and the birth of advertising only heightened this. In 1836, the first newspaper included paid advertising in its pages, precipitating the emergence of modern agencies. But Innis saw newspapers' increasing 'dependence *on advertising*' as 'instrumental in telescoping time into a one-day world'. In his eyes an 'advertising-driven media' obsessed by 'present-mindedness' was fuelling the 'continuous, systematic, ruthless destruction of elements of permanence'.[10] Something our industry is even guiltier of today.

Advertising has a severe spatial bias

James Carey suggested that communications can be understood from both a *transmission* and *ritual* perspective. In a transmission view, communication is concerned with spatial dominance. In a ritual view 'communication is directed not toward the extension of messages in space but toward the maintenance of society in time; not the act of imparting information but the represent-ation of shared beliefs.'[11] Carey thought this perspective had been lost. Society was, he argued, 'glued' to an 'obsessive' view of *communication* 'as a process and technology that spreads, transmits and disseminates knowledge, ideas and information farther and faster with the goal of controlling space and people'.[12] In an age dominated by global branding it is hard to refute Carey's position; our spatial fixation is more acute than ever. Our goals are expansionist. Reach is our key media measure. With its focus on 30-second TV spots and dispos-able print runs, advertising has relegated time-binding media (eg packaging, promotional giveaways) to the periphery in favour of space-binding media.

Spatial thinking is embedded in our communications models. In *Empire and Communications* Innis noted how light, easily transported media such as paper fuelled a 'militaristic' model of imperialism 'concerned with the conquest of space'.[13] Tellingly we have adopted the same model to inform what we do. 'The similarities between planning advertising strategy and planning military strategy are,' the APG note, 'remarkable'.[14] We even have the same output; campaigns. We talk of 360-degree thinking, a term from the world of navigation. And at the heart of everything we do sits the Big Idea, a spatial sizing. What is worrying, however, is not that the transmission model is ingrained in our thinking, but that an awareness of temporal concerns has been lost as a result. Neither big, nor degrees have any meaning when applied to time. Space doesn't just 'infect our thinking'[15] it creates a bias in our language that prevents us thinking about ideas in the dimension of time. Worse still, some terminology undermines the ritual premise of 'promoting tradition and continuity'[16] altogether; our industry is built on interruption, the very breaking of the continuity of time.

Carey considered a ritual view of communications by contrast to be built on 'terms such as sharing participation, association, fellowship'.[17] These are a pretty good set of descriptors for Web 2.0 which begs the question, are we looking at digital from the right perspective?

We treat digital solely as a transmission medium

No doubt seduced by its name (how could something entitled the *worldwide web* not end up with a spatial bias?) we look at digital from a transmis-sion perspective. Staying true to our obsession with speed and space we conceptualized the emergent technology as a super-highway. Later it became cyberspace, a land to be colonized. Viral communications suffer a similar bias. In medicine a virus can spread in two ways; pandemically with a rapid spread over a wide geographic area, affecting a large number of people before disappearing, or endemically where it has a constant presence within a certain geographic area or population. Coca-Cola's secret formula is an endemic viral. Designed as a publicity stunt in 1920, the campaign created an urban legend that has continued to pass through generations. Despite digital's ability to remix culture in a way that facilitates the kind of mutation that has kept the Coca-Cola myth alive for generations in oral culture, industry talk of endemic virals is extremely rare. It is digital pandemics, how fast and far they spread, that remain our sole focus.

The electronic age developed under print mindsets. The same is now happening with digital. We have adopted metaphors from the printing press and the literate world to describe it; web-pages, book-marking, desktops, folders and scrolling. Advertising agencies are now even declaring themselves to be publishers. We've shackled digital in print-based thinking and the only way to free it is, I believe, to look further into our past.

Understanding digital through a different historical lens

Some academics, most notably John Miles Foley and Walter J Ong, believe we need to re-set our time frames, and recognize that emerging digital cultures mark a return to ways of thinking that were central to human societies before the advent of the printing press; that digital culture is fundamentally closer to an oral culture than it is to one created by print. Lars Ole Sauerberg has proposed the idea of a 'Gutenberg parenthesis'[18] (Figure 14.1), in which the 500 years of the printing press are an interruption in the broader arc of human communications. During this period composition was championed with originality, autonomy, individuality and stability becoming the defining

FIGURE 14.1   The Gutenberg parenthesis

PRE-PARENTHETICAL	GUTENBERG PARENTHESIS	POST-PARENTHETICAL
Re-creative	Original	Sampling
Collective	Individual	Remixing
Contextual	Autonomous	Borrowing
Unstable	Stable	Appropriating
Traditional	Canonical	Recontextualizing
Performance	**Composition**	

SOURCE: Thomas Pettitt
Pettitt, T (April 2007) Before the Gutenberg Parenthesis: Elizabethan-American Compatibilities, Media in Transition 5: Creativity, Ownership and Collaboration in the Digital Age, Plenary 1: Folk Cultures and Digital Cultures, International Conference, MIT [Online]
http://web.mit.edu/comm-forum/mit5/papers/pettitt_plenary_gutenberg.pdf

properties of texts and stories. By contrast, in the pre-Gutenberg world performance was the focus with stories consequently considered as re-creative, contextual, collective and unstable entities. Sauerberg believes that our current transition into a digital world dominated by sampling, remixing and borrowing, marks a return to a pre-Gutenberg understanding of texts and a closing of this cultural parenthesis; a shift the antithesis of that experienced in the Shakespearean era when we transitioned into it and away from a world of oral performance.

If Sauerberg is right, our declaring this the Age of Conversation[19] hardly seems to do justice to what is happening with digital. This is about more than mere conversations. This is a return to an oral-based media culture and a shift which raises doubts as to the primacy of our transmission perspective. Oral culture was time-binding, spreading ideas in ways that were 'persistent and difficult to destroy' (like Coke's secret formula). Indeed it was the restoration of an oral culture that Innis called for in order to redress the West's severe spatial bias. I believe that digital could prove to be this temporal counter-weight – although admittedly we're a long way from realizing its balancing potential. For, if time had been cut into pieces the length of a day's newspaper in 1952,[20] today it has been sliced even smaller into pieces the length of a minute's tweet. We now think in real-time, 'always-on', elevating the present. If digital does have time-binding properties we're certainly not currently seeing them.

It's time we changed our perspective

Innis's and Carey's warnings are being echoed by luminaries of the digital world. As founders of the Long Now Foundation, Kevin Kelly, Chris Anderson and Stewart Brand all believe that our concepts of time are dangerously out of kilter. 'Civilization is revving itself into a pathologically short attention span',[21] Brand warns in the foundation's manifesto. They believe that 'some sort of balancing corrective to the short-sightedness is needed'.[22] Digital anthropologist Jonathan Harris has also warned against our obsession with the 'nowism' of the web.[23] In 1952, few on Madison Avenue had heard of, let alone listened to Harold Innis; today, however, his warnings are echoing back from those at the forefront of digital, and I believe we need to listen.

According to Millward Brown 'trust remains the greatest guarantor of long-term brand success'.[24] Yet it is in decline. Figure 14.2 shows how brand trust has decreased by 50 per cent in under a decade.[25] Our myopic notions of time are in no small way responsible. Trust, we know anecdotally is built over time, not space. It is a future-facing promise built upon past experience; a feeling arising from 'our history with a brand and how that brand has treated us over time'.[26] Little wonder that an industry glued to a transmission view of communications, 'telescoping time'[27] into a one-minute world, is concurrently witnessing the erosion of a value built over time. 'Our existing models of communication,' Carey warned 'are less an analysis than a contribution to the chaos of modern culture'.[28] If ever we needed a counterbalancing ritual view of communications based on *Long Ideas* it is now.

FIGURE 14.2   The decline of brand trust

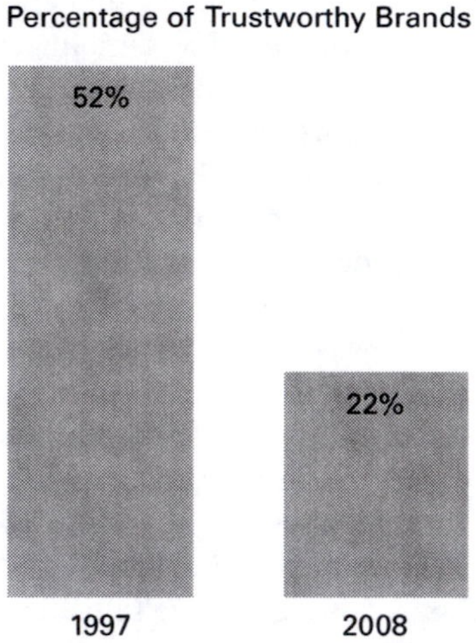

Percentage of Trustworthy Brands

SOURCE: Young & Rubicam BrandAsset Valuator: [Online, Accessed 2010] **http://www.yr.com/BAV**

Embracing a ritual view

Like digital, orality is a medium of the instantaneous present; sound exists only as it is going out of existence. Although oral societies live in the present their culture is one of continuity; a ritualized world where past and future are omnipresent. If the oral nature of digital gives it the potential to be time-binding we need to learn to look at it from the correct cultural perspective; from a ritual viewpoint, not just our default transmission approach. When Carey undertook this task for newspapers he argued that in a ritual view reading them was akin to 'attending a mass' where news is not information, but drama. Newspapers, he contended, do not simply describe the world, but portray an arena of dramatic action that 'invites our participation on the basis of our assuming, often vicariously, social roles within it'.[29] Likewise digital, it can be argued, is no longer just an instrument of the information revolution but a medium of dramatic focus and action; a post-parenthetical world of performance, where dramatic action and collective participation are once again becoming dominant social behaviours.

Some are already modelling brands as actions. In an argument echoing Carey's ritual view of communication as ceremony and prayer, Adam Stagliano and Damian O'Malley believe that we should be 'conceiving brands as actions, not artefacts; as enactments, not espousals'.[30] That we have found it seductive to think instead in terms of inner essences and personalities, they argue, 'says a good deal about our embedded biases'[31] – biases that in all likelihood stem from a parenthetical worldview. Walter J Ong has noted the inward turn of narrative that characterized post-Gutenberg literature. By the 18th century 'the oral narrator's protagonist, distinguished typically for his external exploits has been replaced by the interior consciousness of the typographic protagonist'.[32] Digital culture is marking the closure of Sauerberg's parenthesis, and Stagliano and O'Malley are voicing a model of brands that reflects the shift from a world of composition back into one of performance, where 'every business [is] a stage'.[33]

From campaigns to customs

Emerging from this 'enacted world of brands' is an alternative understanding of digital; where interaction becomes a way to create continuity with past and future, a sense of tradition. John Grant famously deemed brands 'surrogate traditions', but few unpicked the full implications of this weighty phrase. At first glance tradition, a word that implies repetition and stasis, sits awkwardly with our Gutenberg notions of creativity being synonymous with originality. Examining the fields of ritual in more detail, however, makes it clear that an industry built on creative invention has ample reason for interest.

Eric Hobsbawm introduced the idea of 'invented traditions'; customs which, although appearing ancient, are actually recent in origin. He defined them as 'a set of practices governed by tacitly accepted rules of a ritual or symbolic nature which implies continuity with the past'.[34] The Olympics, Wimbledon and Christmas are all examples, and many brands have found success through association with such invented rituals. Digital interaction, however, offers brands an opportunity to invent their own. Facebook for example, established itself by inventing a social custom; the poke, which morphed into the now ubiquitous 'like'.

Cultural anthropologist Catherine M Bell identified three types of ritual.[35] Brands are already enacting these behaviours in digital.

Calendrical rituals

Google is built upon the calendrical ritual of the Google Doodle. Throughout the year its logo becomes a decorative altar to days of note at which users share in the partaking of a piece of knowledge. Likewise, Orange transformed a sporadic pastime into a ritual by inventing Orange Wednesday, a mass-like weekly mobile ritual. WWF's Earth Hour has also established itself as an annual ritual thanks to its spread through blogs and social networks.

Festivals and games

Many long-running folk customs are little more than social games – the Olney Pancake Race or Gloucestershire's Cheese Rolling, for example. Levi-Strauss described ritual as being 'played, like a favoured instance of a game'[36] and games are becoming an important part of the digital world of brands; the quirky customs of a Global Village Fete. They traditionally belong to the

Figure 14.3   Calendrical rituals: The Google Doodle

world of sales promotion, by nature a short-term, tactically-led discipline. In digital, however, games now assume a very different role because of their socialized context; they act as rituals, collective customs that build continuity for a brand. Alex Bogusky even suggested that 'brands are games'.[37]

Rites of passage

Johnson & Johnson's BabyCentre imbues the process of pregnancy and infancy with ritual meaning. Different stages of pregnancy and child development have different rites. Women feel part of a shared ceremonial process as they progress. P&G's long-running Tampax community plays a similar role. As Bell notes, we are witnessing the invention of female 'rites for an age that has given women no other adequate form of ritual acknowledgement'.[38] The phenomenal success of sites such as BabyCentre and Mumsnet indicates that digital is at the forefront of this.

From interruption to anticipation

We equate the word 'ongoing' with a continuous stream of activity. That permanency in digital necessitates a constant, non-stop flow of content. A ritual view demonstrates, however, that although traditions and customs create permanence they are often also scarce. That's part of their value – Olympic medals are prized more than most because they can only be won every four years. So, alongside our default model of interruption we must now add a counter-balancing model of anticipation, where rituals connect us as much to the future as they do to the past. How different, for example, Volvo's brilliant Life on Board campaign would have been if they'd arranged for interviewees to meet again 5 or 10 years later, spawning an ongoing, future-facing myth. If Big Ideas thrive on interruption Long Ideas thrive, by contrast, on anticipation.

Restoring a ritual approach to communications

There is much to be gained by opening up to the idea that new media function on archaic behaviours – particularly if we adopt a ritual lexicon alongside our transmission-based nomenclature in digital. I agree with Bell that ritual terminology is 'overdue for an extended critical rethinking',[39] bringing with it as it does centuries of complicated baggage; but in a time when we are overrun with spurious portmanteaus and perplexing neologisms we should hold on to the battered terminology of ritual studies. How differently, for example, we might think about destination sites if we saw them as ritual sites; or how we might use a Facebook stage instead of a Facebook page. A simple change in terminology is enough to remind us that as marketers we're not the architects of beautiful pixel temples. We're the architects of ceremonies; we build what goes on at those sites. There is much in the vocabulary of ritual studies that needs refining (it carries too much religious weighting in our consciousness at present), but it does at least force us to take a different view of what we do – and as C S Lewis said, 'The abuse of an old word, if explained, may give less trouble than the invention of a new.'

A renewed plea for time

The printing press shaped our thinking for over half-a-millennium. It created the notion of individualism and elevated rationalism at the expense of the emotions, both ideas that our industry has done much to question. Now we must challenge the bias of space and speed that it also created by restoring a counterbalancing ritual view of communications. There will be those who resist. Nicholas Carr lamented on his blog that with digital we are 'turning our backs on the Enlightenment' and 'picking ritual over ideas and knowledge'.[40] But such talk is needlessly bellicose. As Carey always made clear, a transmission approach does not preclude the existence of a ritual approach and vice versa; the two can and should co-exist. So, although this paper ends with an echo of Innis's plea, it is by no means intended as an apologia for time alone. Like empires, successful brands require a balance between both spatial and temporal concerns. If we are 'to stand up to the current obsession with the short-term',[41] then we need to restore a ritual view of communications alongside our default transmission view; create brand campaigns *and* customs; Big Ideas *and* Long Ideas; and think in terms of interruption *and* anticipation.

When, in 2008, Kevin Kelly described the web as 'already less than five thousand days old'[42] he was, in his choice of unit, reminding us that for all it has achieved digital is still a medium in its infancy. Against a backdrop of 4,000 years of communication technologies and the ticking of a 10,000 year clock, I believe we should take heart that although we have a severe bias in our thinking, it's not too late for us to correct it and broaden the way we think about digital as a communications medium.

Notes

1 Carey, J (1992) *Communication As Culture: Essays on media and society*, Routledge, New York.

2 *ibid*.

3 Earls, M (2009) *Herd*, John Wiley & Sons.

4 Nisbett, R (2011) *The Geography Of Thought: How Asians and Westerners think differently and why*, Nicholas Brealey Publishing.

5 Heath, R and Feldwick, P (2007) *50 Years Using The Wrong Model Of TV Advertising*, University of Bath.

6 Binet, L and Feldwick, P (2007) *Marketing In The Era Of Accountability*, World Advertising Research Centre.

7 Brand, S [accessed June 2010] *The Long Now Foundation*, About Long Now [Online] http://longnow.org/about/

8 Innis, H A (2007) *Empire And Communications*, Dundurn Press, Toronto.

9 *ibid*.

10 *ibid*.

11 Carey, J W (1992) *Communication As Culture: Essays on media and society*, Routledge, New York.

12 *ibid*.

13 Innis, H A (2007) *Empire And Communications*, Dundurn Press, Toronto.

14 O'Grady, P and Park, B (2008) What can planners learn from military strategists?, The Account Planning Group.

15 Carey, J W (1992) *Communication As Culture: Essays on media and society*, Routledge, New York.

16 *ibid*.

17 *ibid*.

18 Pettitt, T (2009) *Before the Gutenberg Parenthesis: Elizabethan-American compatibilities*, Media in Transition Lecture Series.

19 Heaton, G and McLellan, D (2008) *The Age of Conversation*, Lulu.com

20 Innis, H A (2007) *Empire And Communications*, Dundurn Press, Toronto.

21 Brand, S [accessed June 2010] About long now, The Long Now Foundation [Online] http://longnow.org/about/

22 *ibid*.

23 Harris, J (2010) [accessed April 2010] Pratt Institute's Department of Digital Arts Lecture Series [Online] www.psfk.com/2010/04/insights-on-storytelling-nowism-indirection-and-humanizing-technology-from-jonathan-harris.html#!biiO9V

24 (2009) *BrandZ Top 100 Valuable Global Brands*, Millward Brown [Online] www.millwardbrown.com/docs/default-source/global-brandz-downloads/global/2009_BrandZ_Top100_Report.pdf

25 Gerzema, J and Lebar, E (2008) *The Brand Bubble: The looming crisis in brand value and how to avoid it*, John Wiley & Sons.

26 (February 2010) *Beyond Trust: Engaging consumers in the post-recession world*, Millward Brown.

27 Innis, H A (2007) *Empire and Communications*, Dundurn Press, Toronto.

28 Carey, J W (1992) *Communication As Culture: Essays on media and society*, Routledge, New York.

29 *ibid.*

30 Basking, M and Earls, M (eds) The Account Planning Group (2002) *Brand New Brand Thinking: Brought to life by 11 experts that do*, Kogan Page, London.

31 *ibid.*

32 Ong, W (2002) *Orality and Literacy: The technologizing of the word*, Routledge, New York.

33 Pine II, B J and Gilmore, J H (1999) *The Experience Economy: Work is theatre and every business a stage*, Harvard Business School Press.

34 Hobsbawm, E and Ranger, T (1992) *The Invention of Tradition*, Cambridge University Press.

35 Bell, C (2010) *Ritual: Perspectives and dimensions*, Oxford University Press.

36 Levi-Strauss, C (1966) *The Savage Mind*, Oxford University Press.

37 Bogusky, A (2010) Keynote speech, Mirren New Business Conference [Online] www.youtube.com/watch?v=pDSHi_3UJy4

38 Bell, C (2010) *Ritual: Perspectives and dimensions*, Oxford University Press.

39 *ibid.*

40 Carr, N (2008) Tom Lord on ritual, knowledge and the web, [Online] www.roughtype.com/archives/2008/11/tom_lord_on_rit.php

41 Steel, J (2008) Planning at 40: Solving the wrong problems, [Online] http://vimeo.com/1351826

42 Kelly, K (2008) Kevin Kelly on the next 5000 days of the web, [Online] www.ted.com/talks/kevin_kelly_on_the_next_5_000_days_of_the_web.html

PART THREE
How should we organize to deliver?

Introduction:
I believe we
need to ADAPT

IAN PRIEST

Founding Partner, VCCP, Group COO, CSM and IPA President,
2013–15

As an industry we spend a lot of time thinking about what we do. Rightly so. And we are good at it.

Indeed, there are few other business sectors where as much effort goes into providing practitioners with an intellectual underpinning and rigour that they can use to inform their work.

But it's equally important to think just as rigorously about how we organize ourselves. In an era of massive change, we cannot carry on as before. Without the right structures and mechanisms, we are unprepared for the challenges ahead.

If that is the case, then what we do will be less successful, and as partners to our clients, we will be less valuable.

All this has huge implications for creative agencies. Structure, therefore, is critical. So change we must.

But it would be wrong to see this as a threat. I regard it as an opportunity to do what we do even better, and to become more valued partners with our clients.

What I find so fascinating about the IPA Excellence Diploma essays in this section is the way they challenge us to think hard about organizational change. I don't believe there is any one answer, or one correct organizational model: different agencies will organize themselves in different ways.

But it's only by looking at the options, and the theory behind those options, that we can progress.

They are also important because they represent the thinking of a younger cohort.

This matters because much of the drive for change is going to come from the bottom up. We don't live in a top-down, hierarchical world any more. These are the next generation of ad industry leaders, and it's right that they're embracing change.

Sam d'Amato, for example – and his prescient essay 'Brands need to adopt an outside-in brand management approach' was written in 2006 – foresaw the rise of the empowered consumer. He posits that agencies should look to become recruitment consultancies for brands – enlisting consumers to participate in everything from research to NPD.

Also from 2006, Tom Roach, in his essay 'Evolution in the head' advances the theory of communications as consumer-controlled cultural memes. But that has implications for the role – and therefore the organizing principles – of agencies.

It's this need for change that I have put at the heart of my IPA Presidency, and which is the basis of my ADAPT agenda. The acronym is deliberate: Darwinian theory shows that the species that thrive are the ones that adapt best and fastest.

But if we are to do this, then change needs to be systemic. That's why the ADAPT agenda has five strands: alliances; diversification; agility; performance and talent. Change in one aspect of our organizational structure forces change on the others. If, for example, we produce different kinds of work in shorter time frames, or if we develop proprietary technology that benefits our clients, then the way we are paid should change.

I set out this agenda because of my passionate conviction that agencies must excel in what I call commercial creativity. I define this as creativity that achieves outstanding commercial results, and creates real long-term value for clients.

I also believe we can't change on our own. Clients recognize this too, and it's been heartening to see the way individual clients, as well as ISBA and The Marketing Society, have participated in key parts of the programme.

To me, it starts with the creation of a strong alliance between client and agency. Long-term relationships, ones that transcend individuals, are essential. But they also cultivate a climate in which the best work is done. You don't have to look hard around our industry to see that, where those long-term relationships exist, clients achieve commercial success.

Ross Farquhar's 'It's time for a new system for leading beliefs' essay, written in 2011, proposes a cross-industry body to promote best practice in marketing excellence, bringing together the best thinking from clients, agencies, academics and the research community. It's an example of how alliances can underpin our future.

One result of the alliances strand has been to create best-practice guides to help clients and agencies get their relationships off to the best possible start. Then, working with psychologists, we've created a Relationship Charter, which shows both sides how they can nurture and feed each other.

Strong alliances thus create the foundation from which agencies can do their best work. Increasingly they need to diversify their output – branded content, working with technology or gamification – and be agile in the way they produce it. This means working fast, with new partners, and often in real- or near real-time.

It may also mean working in completely different ways. In his 2014 essay 'Confronting complexity', Gethin James says that the complexity and inter-connectedness of today's world changes the rules for brands. Rather than agencies producing a 'failsafe' idea, brand strategy involves plotting a series of 'safe-fail' options, which calls for a series of small brand 'bets' that can be adjusted in near real-time based on feedback loops.

We looked at these areas in the diversification and agility strands. To turn diversification into action we are encouraging clients and agencies to devote – as with Coca-Cola's 70:20:10 model – approximately 10 per cent of budget and 25 per cent of time to new ideas and forms of communication. These also mean adopting a more three-to-five-year horizon, and a briefing process that prizes openness and a wider definition of creativity.

From the agility strand we are developing workshops to show agencies how to develop and implement real-time marketing, work with media in an agile fashion, and examine real-time measurement.

All of this undoubtedly impacts structure and payment for agencies.

But certainly, if we create long-term added value, then there is a case to be made for paying agencies by outcome, or for taking risk. Judging by the client reaction to the P or performance strand of the ADAPT agenda, they are moving in this direction too. Already we have worked with ISBA's Procurement Group to develop a Performance Charter that marries business and relationship principles to aid commercial creativity.

Matthew Philip's essay – 'From vanity to value' – is all about creating more long-term shareholder value for clients by approaching communication tasks with an investor mindset.

In his 2009 essay 'Data is our future' Matt Sadler puts data at the heart of the future agency, challenging us to marry maths and magic to produce data-driven creativity. That too demands change in the agency model, not least in the way we recruit and retain talent. What sort of creatives do we need? How do we compete to hire the best tech-led creatives? And how do we recruit or train data-savvy talent?

It is precisely these issues that led to the final strand of my ADAPT agenda – T for talent. Without the appropriate talent, all the other changes we make to agencies could count for little. That's why we have looked outside our own industry – and not just to the tech giants – to see what we can learn from others about recruiting, retaining and nurturing the next generation.

Other than believing we have to adapt the way we organize ourselves, I have no specific prescription for change. Each of us must find our own way – but it helps enormously to have something to stimulate our thinking. These essays do just that.

Happy reading.

I believe that the future of brands depends on confronting complexity
2013/14

15

GETHIN JAMES
Head of Planning, Lowe Profero

I believe Diversity in our thinking will open up our minds to the value of the novel interconnection of new ideas and bring a fresh proactivity to the planning process. I believe that the world has always been complex, but we convinced ourselves it was only complicated. This has had a profound impact on the way we think about brands: from our bias for analysis rather than action, to our preference for simplification. The paper proposes a way for brands to confront the complexity through probing, sense-making and system building.

Editor's therefore, for your brand...

Your brand thinking:
How do you understand the interconnections in your market and brand? What is your brand eco-system?

Your brand engagement:
Is everything you create connected to everything else you create?

Your brand organization & capability: How do you avoid 'silos' in your total team? Does everyone know what everyone else is doing?

...and author's personal therefore

Look back at your belief and write about what you did, therefore.

Look back? I've only just finished writing it. And, to be honest, I'm not sure I have even finished developing it yet; let alone put sufficient distance between me and it to have gained the clarity of hindsight. I am, as planners are wont to do, still cogitating on it.

Here though lies the first clue about what I have, or precisely have not, done *therefore*. Despite believing that 'the world can only be grasped by action, not by contemplation', here I am cogitating. Despite believing that we are better thinking about what we do as searching rather than planning, here I am still calling myself a planner. Habit loops can be difficult to break.

This should not be taken as a reneging on my belief. I don't believe that the world is complex. The world is complex. It is, to paraphrase Philip K Dick, 'that which, when you stop believing in it, doesn't go away'.

We can observe the effects of interdependence, feedback loops and non-linearity around us and there is a growing body of research from the likes of Albert-László Barabási, Duncan Watts and Steven Strogatz.

Despite the evidence, there will always be those who deny the existence of complexity in the world. There will always be a market for simplicity and oversimplification. The pithy sound-bite so often triumphs over an established body of evidence.

But that's ok. Until everybody believes in confronting complexity, there will be a competitive advantage for those that do. Differences in performance cannot come from beliefs we all hold in common, they can only come from minority views that better equip their holders to deal with the world around them.

In many ways this has been the gift of doing the Diploma: being forced to articulate an original and applicable belief has forced each of us to find our own point of departure from the industry consensus.

This is where the work really begins, not in forming the belief, but in acting on it. Instead of looking back to reflect on what I have done as a result, I will look forward to what I need to do therefore to make the most of my own minority view.

At first, acknowledging the complexity inherent in the world can seem daunting. It can seem like an awful lot of hard work to understand what's going on. It comes without any of the comforts of certainty or of following the 'sense – analyse – respond' consensus.

But, as they say, the first step to recovery is admitting you have a problem. And in this case, acknowledging the limits of analysis can be liberating. How many ideas are currently holed up inside corporations, being subjected to test after test to see if they are strong enough to put out into the world? A question we can never really know the answer to until we actually put them out into the world.

My first therefore is to stop cogitating so much. As a planner I have failed if strategizing becomes a displacement activity for actually doing something. Doing something is preferable to doing nothing. We will learn more, and more quickly, by 'poking the world with a stick' to see what happens.

Crucially doing something is not the same as doing anything. When we act we can act strategically. That is, we can act in ways that magnify and amplify our effort.

The person who focuses on creating the conditions for positive feedback loops to flourish will always make more of an impact than the person who sees the world as a series of linear inputs and outputs.

In my essay I outlined an approach to creating cumulative advantage and benefiting from positive feedback loops for brands: anchor the brand to existing habit loops, make using the brand easier to copy and develop internal capabilities, especially learning capabilities.

In many ways these principles are as applicable to my career as they are to brands, and so my second therefore is to do just that. To focus; ask myself what habits am I creating? What behaviours am I spreading? And what am I learning to do?

Most pertinently, I will therefore build on Grant McCracken's observation that 'brands need to be about becoming, not about being'. I won't fret about whether my belief in confronting complexity is consistent with being a planner as long as I am becoming someone capable of confronting complexity.

So I will allow myself one further cogitation. My essay ended with implications for brands, brand communications and brand communications agencies; it's worth reflecting on the implications of complexity on the lives we live.

It's tempting to believe in the just world hypothesis: that is that people essentially get what they deserve, that success is based on merit and therefore failure must also be deserved. But cumulative advantage disabuses us of that myth.

My final therefore is to recognize successes and failures as the lucky or unlucky products of cumulative advantage that they so often are.

I believe that the future of brands depends on confronting complexity

In the UK, we spend £16 billion on advertising each year.[1] And, despite this huge expense, most markets 'are in a long-run equilibrium where the relative position of the players is only temporarily disturbed by their respective marketing activities'.[2] No matter how hard any one brand tries to make a break from the status-quo, there are hidden forces pulling them back in line.

This occurs due to two simple and related reasons: people are more likely to buy what they have already bought and people are more likely to buy what others are buying. The consequence of which is that people behave in ways that reinforce any inequalities between brands, creating a cumulative advantage where the rich-get-richer and the poor get left behind.

If cumulative advantage did not exist and 'we were to imagine history being somehow "rerun" many times... explanations in which intrinsic attributes were the only things that mattered would predict that the same outcome would pertain every time'.[3]

But when cumulative advantage is present, we end up in a strange world where: 'even tiny random fluctuations tend to get bigger over time, generating potentially enormous differences in the long run'. The upshot being that 'even identical universes, starting out with the same set of people and objects and tastes, would nevertheless generate different cultural or market-place winners'.[4]

How can this be? How can a brand's intrinsic attributes not be the ultimate source of performance? As an industry, our language betrays a belief in the value of the things a brand has: 'We talk of brand essences (unchanging), brand values (abiding), brand architecture (surely built to last).'[5] Brands are supposed to succeed because of the properties they have built in.

This is the first clue that brands operate in a world that is more complex than we treat it. Ignoring the self-reinforcing effects of cumulative advantage can put a brand at a serious disadvantage.

How deep does the hole go?

In 1969, sociologist Morris Zelditch asked: 'Can you really study an army in a laboratory?'[6] At the time, the conclusion was that you couldn't. Half-a-century later, and researchers have realized they don't have to. Now, they can observe everything they need from the 'digital breadcrumbs' each of us leaves behind. 'For the first time we can precisely map the behaviour of large numbers of people as they go about their normal lives.' [7]

The more we look at how people really behave in society, rather than how they say they behave or how they behave in isolation, the more we realize that it is the interactions between people that really matter. 'What makes the social world complex isn't individual complexity but the way people go together, in often surprising ways, to create patterns.'[8]

Complex systems are characterized by:

- interconnectedness;
- feedback (both reinforcing and balancing);
- a memory of the past that impacts on the present;
- self-organization and spontaneous order;
- emergence of behaviours that are more than the sum of their parts;
- non-linearity such that small changes can produce disproportionately larger results;
- tipping points and thresholds;
- ambiguity surrounding cause and effect: 'A' causes 'B' and 'B' causes 'A'; and
- predictable looking back, unpredictable looking forward.[9]

And the more people study mass human behaviour, the more they come across the characteristics of complexity.

Our attention is bursty

Our activity isn't distributed evenly through time. We work, live and play in short bursts of activity followed by long gaps of nothing.[10]

We interact in flocks

The same forces that govern flocks of birds, schools of fish and swarms of insects also apply to groups of people. Out of separation (don't tread on any toes), alignment (follow those around you) and cohesion (stick together) emerge a wide variety of complex and unpredictable behaviours.[11]

We organize around hubs

Cumulative advantage is at play once more in the networks we create. The most well-connected people tend to become even better connected. The most linked webpages tend to become even more linked. The result is a few very well-connected hubs coexisting with many poorly-connected nodes.[12]

And separate into cliques and communities

Alongside a tendency for connecting with the better connected, people also have a tendency towards associating with people who more closely resemble them. This homophily causes networks to separate like oil and water into clusters of like-minded people.

Networks act as amplifiers

These clusters of like-minded people 'help confirm and thus amplify people's antecedent views'.[13] This illustrates a wider emergent property of networks: 'Social networks tend to magnify whatever they are seeded with.'[14]

Our chances of picking up on something circulating through the network increase as more of our connections also pick up on it. But this 'doesn't generate any new information, it only amplifies the consequences that a little bit of information can have, whether it is real information or not'.[15]

Allowing rumours to find a life of their own

Rumours start 'when a group of early movers... say or do something and other people follow their signal'.[16] As a rumour is passed on, it gets modified. Some form of 'evidence' may be added or it may be reformulated and re-expressed. Others may challenge its credibility through argument or new information. As the rumour evolves, the 'fittest' forms of the rumour spread the furthest and longest.

Bringing it back to brands

> Brands will need to find a place in this swirling, memetic media system where all sorts of information freely flows: word of mouth; fashion; trends; imitation; flattery; truths; half-truths; rumour; panic; entertainment; news; deals; alerts; brands; friendships; passions; tastes; memories; – pretty much everything that makes up our personal and professional lives. (Clifton, 2009[17])

It is clear that this is a system where 'the whole becomes not merely more, but very different from the sum of its parts'.[18] 'Nonlinear complex dynamics

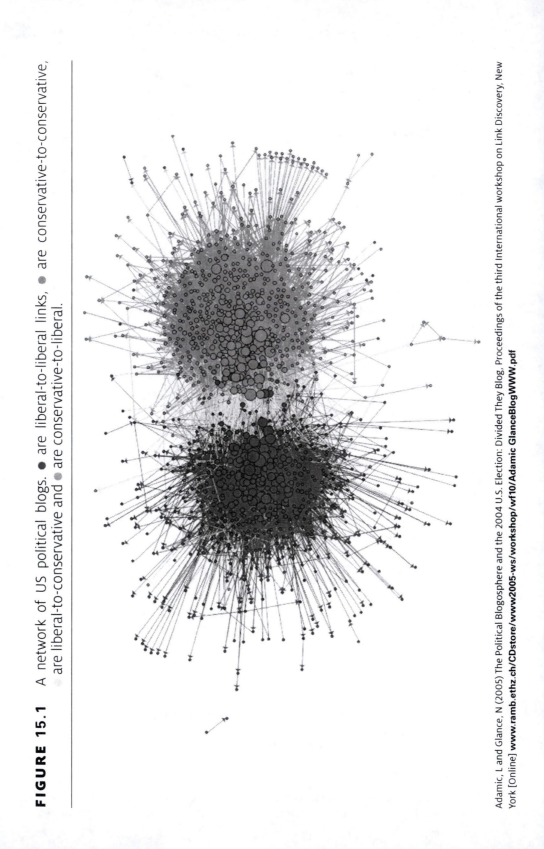

FIGURE 15.1 A network of US political blogs. ● are liberal-to-liberal links, ● are conservative-to-conservative, ● are liberal-to-conservative and ● are conservative-to-liberal.

Adamic, L and Glance, N (2005) The Political Blogosphere and the 2004 U.S. Election: Divided They Blog, Proceedings of the third International workshop on Link Discovery, New York [Online] **www.ramb.ethz.ch/CDstore/www2005-ws/workshop/wf10/Adamic GlanceBlogWWW.pdf** are around us: unpredictable variability, tipping points, sudden changes in behaviour, hysteresis—all are frequent symptoms of a non-linear world.'[19] This isn't how we usually think about the world brands occupy.

Implications for how we approach brands

The Cynefin (pronounced kuh-nev-in) framework[20] (Table 15.1) usefully illustrates the difference between complicated and complex worlds. It also sets out the difference in how we should respond to each.

TABLE 15.1   The Cynefin framework

Domain	Nature	Response
Simple	**Known knowns** The relationship between cause and effect is obvious	Sense **Categorise** Respond ↓ *Apply best practice*
Complicated	**Known unknowns** The relationship between cause and effect requires expert diagnosis	Sense **Analyse** Respond ↓ *Apply good practice*
Complex	**Unknown unknowns** The relationship between cause and effect is only knowable in hindsight	**Probe** Sense Respond ↓ *Sense emergent practice*
Chaotic	**Unknowable unknowns** There is no relationship between cause and effect	**Act** Sense Respond ↓ *Discover novel practice*

Adapted from Snowden, D and Boone, M (November 2008) A leader's framework for decision making, *Harvard Business Review* [Online] **http://hbr.org/2007/11/a-leaders-framework-for-decision-making/**

Our history with sense–analyse–respond

The classic planning cycle[21] follows the sense ('where are we?'), analyse ('why are we here?' and 'where could we be?') and respond ('how could we get there?') approach. We assume that a direct link can be found between our planned actions and desired effects. Research is commissioned. Agency expertise is applied, because we believe the right analysis will uncover the way forward.

If, for some reason, we don't succeed, our failure must be due to improper analysis. And so we call for yet more research and better experts to turn things around.

But if we are actually operating in a complex environment, then forecasting 'where we could be' is futile. The relationship between cause and effect can only be knowable in hindsight. And more analysis won't help anybody. No amount of prior analysis can provide certainty that doing 'A' will indeed lead to the occurrence of 'B'.

The pitfalls of sense–analyse–respond

'When you make the complicated simple, you make it better. But when you make the complex simple, you make it wrong.'[22] If we treat a complex system like it's a complicated system, then even the best possible analysis is likely to lead us astray.

Michael Raynor calls this the strategy paradox: 'organisations that embody what would seem to the best practices in strategy planning... can also be the most vulnerable to planning errors.'[23] Raynor argues that the main cause of strategic failure is not a bad strategy, but a plausible strategy that turns out to be wrong.

In a complex world, planning only provides the illusion of certainty and control when, in fact, neither exists. And this can be especially dangerous when it blinds us to other possibilities.

The alternative: probe–sense–respond

If we are to dismantle the traditional planning process, what should we replace it with? If we can't make predictions about the future, how else do we increase our odds of success?

Returning to the Cynefin framework, we must start by recognizing that 'the world can only be grasped by action, not by contemplation' (Diane Arbus).

Searching beats planning

A planner thinks he already knows the answer... a searcher admits he doesn't know the answer in advance.[24]

We need to openly acknowledge that there are limits to what can be planned and predicted. Searching acknowledges that we don't know what we don't know. It keeps us open to alternatives and primed for the unexpected. Searching is optimistic that there is a way forward, but pessimistic about the map we are holding.

Proaction beats reaction

Traditionally, research provides the fuel for the planning process. But, in a complex world, market research cannot be predictive, it can only be descriptive. As searchers, we will be less interested in describing how the world is and more interested in finding ways to change it.

We are not reacting to the world, but 'poking the world with a stick'[25] to see what happens. We can't do this by taking measurements first. We must proactively engage the world and track everything that happens as a result.

Diversity beats simplicity

The purpose of probing the world is to learn something about it. We learn the most by exploring widely rather than deeply. 'The only way to get a good idea is to get lots of them, even to let them proliferate independently and compete for primacy.'[26] Track everything and move on from anything that doesn't seem valuable.

Simplicity is fragile: it succeeds if it happens to be focusing on the right thing at the right time, but it also leaves the brand open to catastrophic failures. In contrast, diversity is robust: it can withstand rapid changes in tastes and behaviours. All bets are hedged.

Launching a brand into a complex world

'Most marketing funds are spent on tit-for-tat rivalry rather than pioneering marketmaking.'[27] This is understandable given the high risks involved.

However, pioneers enjoy both sales dominance and sales resilience in the face of competitive challenges. Other brands may enter later with a better product and a lower price, but they will be destined to play catch-up.

How do we approach the challenge of pioneering a new category if analysis cannot be relied upon to show the way? How should we now probe our way forward? 'Most brilliant entrepreneurs don't begin with brilliant ideas–they discover them.'[28]

The key here is to make small bets. Big bets and big ideas need to be fail-safe. So much is invested in them at the outset that they must not be allowed to fail. The focus is on matching the size of investment to the assumed size of the expected gain.

In contrast, small bets can be safe-fail.[29] They limit the initial investment so that both success and failure can be entertained. The focus is on how much the organization can afford to lose in pursuit of ideas of indeterminable value.

Generating options

This small-bets approach is necessarily resource light, but is also ideas intensive. It demands a quantity and diversity of ideas that most organizations are not geared up to deliver.

In his book *Where Good Ideas Come From*, Steven Johnson found that: 'the trick to having good ideas is not to sit around in glorious isolation and try to think big thoughts. The trick is to get more parts on the table... We are often better served by connecting ideas.'[30]

This works best if we can find a way to make long-distance connections between distant and divergent ideas. To do so, we will need to consciously replace our natural homophilia with a hetrophilia. We will need to cultivate diversity in both our personal and professional networks.

Prototype

On their own, ideas are ethereal; if they are to engage with the world they need to be given form: they need to be made concrete. In the spirit of safe-fail, we are looking for the shortest, most efficient and least costly method for making ideas concrete. A prototype is just that: an idea made just tangible enough to provoke a response from the world.

Test in culture

Prototypes don't have to be product prototypes. Brands and communications can be prototyped as well. All they need is to be given a form that allows for testing in culture rather than testing in a research facility. Brands and communications are cultural products, for which we are trying to 'find a place in this swirling, memetic media system'.[31] Since we cannot take a bucketful out of the river or put an army into a laboratory, we have to put something out into the world to get a read.

Feed a hit, starve a flop

'With conventional planning, it is considered appropriate to fund the entire project as the expectation is that one can predict a positive outcome.'[32] In a complex world, we need to maintain a flexibility in funding projects. We need to be able to withhold funding from initiatives that don't show promise so that we may double down on those that do. Ultimately, we are trying to create a feedback loop of our own, one that amplifies successes and dampens failures.

Rinse and repeat

Once we know what is taking hold in the world, we have learned something about the world as it stands. At this point, we want to be able to learn from early successes and increase our odds of doing more that works. We need to turn prototypes into templates for future hits.

We don't want rigid templates that trade diversity for consistency. We want generative templates that produce a diversity of new ideas from a prototypical example.

Think about how TV formats are originated and evolve. The success of MTV's 'The Real World' spawned the reality TV genre and everything from 'Project Runway', 'Total Wipeout', 'Ice Road Truckers', 'TOWIE' to 'Big Brother'.[33] Similarly, HBO has repeatedly mined the margins of society to create 'Oz', 'The Sopranos', 'Deadwood', 'Big Love' and 'Six Feet Under'.[34]

Portfolio management

The role of brand strategy is less about plotting a path into the future. It is more about creating a portfolio of options that will serve the brand well whatever the future may hold.

Therefore, the success of a brand team and their agencies should not be judged by the success or failure of any one idea. If we were to imagine re-running history, there are no guarantees that winners wouldn't become losers and vice-versa. Instead, the ultimate measure of success should be the fertility and resilience of the portfolio as a whole, offset against any investments made into the portfolio.

Growing a brand in a complex world

Given that the market share of most brands is stable over long time periods, it is safe to assume that 'if you find a position that works today, something quite substantial must change for it to stop working tomorrow'.[35]

Conversely, something substantial must also change for the brand to start performing more positively. Cumulative advantages build slowly and decay slowly. And whatever the brand does from one moment to the next has the long arm of history to contend with.

This explains why 'the relative position of the players is only temporarily disturbed by their respective marketing activities'.[36] Focusing on increasing sales in the short term does little to change the underlying mechanics of the marketplace in the long run.

I believe brands can achieve that year-on-year improvement if they make their short-term focus the accumulation of cumulative advantage. That is the only way for short-term gains to be compounded over the long term.

Anchor the brand to existing habit loops

We are more likely to buy what we have already bought because we form a habit loop around the brand.

A habit loop consists of a cue that triggers a routine that ends in a reward. The reward then reinforces the link between the cue and the routine in memory.[37] A habit loop is a reinforcing feedback loop: A causes B causes C, which in turn increases the propensity for A to cause B (and therefore C).

Brands that are triggered by more cues, or by cues that occur more frequently, are at an advantage. The more often the brand is cued, the more often it is used. The more it is used, the more often the loop is reinforced, further embedding the brand's advantage.

When P&G first created Febreze, they launched it as 'a revolutionary way to destroy odours'. They tried 'to create a whole new habit with Febreze', hoping that bad smells would trigger daily usage. Unfortunately, 'people couldn't detect most of the bad smells in their lives... even the strongest odours fade with constant exposure'.[38] Without people noticing bad smells, the brand was rarely cued, limiting its potential.

To turn the brand around, they anchored it to a different cue. Rather than anchoring the brand to bad smells, they anchored it to the end of the cleaning ritual. They 'piggyback[ed] on habit loops that were already in place', reframing Febreze as an 'air freshener used once things are already clean'.[39]

Make using the brand easier to copy

We are more likely to buy what others are buying, but not because existing users actively recruit new users to the brand. The action is not users influencing non-users, but non-users imitating users. And for imitation of a behaviour to occur, that behaviour must be visible enough to copy.

Making brand usage easier to copy is another point of leverage for brands looking to accumulate cumulative advantage. For example, most photos and videos taken each day are shot and shared without much visibility of the brand used.

When Canon decided to paint the outside of their pro-lenses white as protection from overheating when shooting under strong sunlight, they created a very visible behaviour that is easily noticed and imitated. This has driven the brands ubiquity at sporting events.[40]

GoPro has a visual distinctiveness that boosts copying. But the brand team also raise the visibility of the brand in other ways. They search the web for footage shot on a GoPro, polish it and provide a platform where it is viewed by millions of people. A single video created from found GoPro footage, of a firefighter rescuing a cat from a burning building, was watched 18 million times on YouTube.

FIGURE 15.2

Ann64 (2007) Formula One Photographers, Wikipedia, licensed under CC BY-SA 2.0

Develop internal capabilities, especially learning capabilities

There is a third source of cumulative advantage that is easy to overlook. It doesn't exist outside the brand but inside the brand teams (and their agencies). Specifically, it exists in the combined experience and capabilities that those teams have accumulated.

Anything these teams have learned to do particularly well, particularly quickly or particularly cheaply, can be a powerful source of cumulative advantage.[40] For example, Red Bull have an 'accumulated body of production and distribution expertise' built up over 20 years filming action sports,[41] including over a decade working with Felix Baumgartner. Other brands could have conceived of Stratos, but no other brand had the capability to pull it off. Not without going on the same long journey that Red Bull has already travelled. And even then, they would be destined to play catch-up.

Some brands go further still and develop a meta-capability: they learn how to learn more effectively. Pixar has evolved from the manufacturer of computer hardware via the creation of animated shorts and TV commercials into the feature film producer we know today. Pixar has been driven by 'prolonged and determined efforts to counter the natural human reactions to success by aspiring to proactively (and honestly) seek out and solve new problems constantly'.[42]

They not only put prototypes out into the world (their feature films often start life as digital shorts), they treat the entire organization as a prototype. Nothing is set in stone, everything is a hypothesis under study.

This is the mindset brands need to cultivate if they are to compete in a complex world. 'Brands need to be about becoming, not being.'[43] 'We cannot afford to think of strategy as something fixed, a problem that is solved and settled. Strategy... has to be embraced as something open, not something closed. It is a system that evolves, moves and changes.'[44]

Conclusion

I used to believe that the world was complicated and that our job was to make it simple. I now believe that the world brands and people operate in is complex, not complicated. It is highly interconnected and there are feedback loops everywhere.

I believe that these loops simultaneously prevent brands from gaining on larger competitors, whilst making the environment they operate in highly unpredictable.

I believe brands can succeed, but only if they confront this complexity head-on. I believe that brands must build their own capabilities and systems to search, probe, experiment, test and respond to the world.

Notes

1 Deloitte & Advertising Association (January 2013) *Advertising Pays: How advertising fuels the UK economy*, Deloitte & Advertising Association [Online] www.adassoc.org.uk/pdfs/AdvAss_Advertising_Pays_Report.pdf

2 Dekimpe, M and Hanssens, D (1995) Empirical generalizations about market evolution and stationarity, *Marketing Science*, 14 (3), US.

3 Watts, D J (2011) *Everything is Obvious: How common sense fails*, Atlantic Books.

4 *ibid.*

5 Earls, M (2002) *Welcome to the Creative Age: Bananas, business and the death of marketing*, John Wiley & Sons.

6 Zelditch, M (1969) Can you really study an army in the laboratory?, in *Complex Organizations* [2nd edition] ed A Etzioni, Holt Rinehart & Winston.

7 Pentland, A (2008) *Honest Signals: How they shape our world*, MIT Press.

8 Buchanan, M (2007) *The Social Atom: Why the rich get richer, cheats get caught and your neighbor usually looks like you*, Cyan Books and Marshall Cavendish, US.

9 Ladyman, J, Lambert, J and Wiesner, K (2011) What is a complex system? [Online] http://philsci-archive.pitt.edu/9044/4/LLWultimate.pdf

10 Barabasi, A-L (2002) *Linked: How everything is connected to everything else and what it means for business, science and everyday life*, Perseus Books, US.

11 Simkins, J (January 2014) The complexity of emergent systems, TEDx Event [Online] www.youtube.com/watch?v=htmntSoCasg

12 Barabasi, A-L (2002) *Linked: How everything is connected to everything else and what it means for business, science and everyday life*, Perseus Books, US.

13 Sunstein, C R (2008) *Why Groups Go to Extremes*, American Enterprise Institute Press.

14 Christakis, N and Fowler, J (2010) *Connected: The amazing power of social networks and how they shape our lives*, HarperPress.

15 Buchanan, M (2007) *The Social Atom: Why the rich get richer, cheats get caught and your neighbor usually looks like you*, Cyan Books and Marshall Cavendish, US.

16 Sunstein, Prof C R (2009) *On Rumours: How falsehoods spread, why we believe them, what can be done*, Farrar Straus Giroux.

17 Clifton, R (2009) *Brands and Branding*, Profile Books.

18 Anderson, P W (1972) More is different, *Science*, New Series, **177** (4047).

19 Boccaletti, G (2012) Scale Analysis, in *This Will Make You Smarter*, ed J Brockman, Doubleday.

20 Snowden, D and Boone, M (November 2008) A leader's framework for decision making, *Harvard Business Review* [Online] http://hbr.org/2007/11/a-leaders-framework-for-decision-making/

21 King, S (1977) Improving advertising decisions, in (2012) *A Master Class in Brand Planning: The timeless works of Stephen King*, ed J Lannon and M Baskin, John Wiley & Sons.

22 Gray, D (November 2009) Complicated vs complex, *Communication* Nation [Online] http://communicationnation.blogspot.co.uk/2009/11/complicated-vs-complex.html

23 Raynor, M E (2007) *The Strategy Paradox: Why committing to success leads to failure (and what to do about it)*, Doubleday.

24 Easterly, W (2006) Planners vs Searchers in Foreign Aid, *Asian Development Review*, **23** (2).

25 Cadell, B (2012) quotes in *Culturematic*, Grant McCracken, Harvard Business Press.

26 McCracken, G (2012) *Culturematic*, Harvard Business Press.

27 Goddard, J and Eccles, T (2012) *Uncommon Sense, Common Nonsense: Why some organisations consistently outperform others*, Profile Books.

28 Sims, P (2012) *Little Bets: How breakthrough ideas emerge from small discoveries*, Random House Business Books.

29 Snowden, D and Boone, M (November 2008) A leader's framework for decision making, *Harvard Business Review* [Online] http://hbr.org/2007/11/a-leaders-framework-for-decision-making/

30 Johnson, S (2011) *Where Good Ideas Come From: The seven patterns of innovation*, Penguin Books.

31 Clifton, R (2009) *Brands and Branding*, Profile Books.

32 McGrath, R G and MacMillan, I (July 1995) Discovery-driven planning, *Harvard Business Review* [Online] http://hbr.org/1995/07/discovery-driven-planning/ar/1

33 McCracken, G (2012) *Culturematic*, Harvard Business Press, Boston, Mass.

34 *ibid*.

35 Warren, K (2012) Strategy Dynamics Essentials, Strategy Dynamics, Princes Risborough.

36 Dekimpe, M and Hanssens, D (1995) Empirical generalizations about market evolution and stationarity, *Marketing Science*, **14** (3), US.

37 Pagel, M (2012) *Wired for Culture: The natural history of human cooperation*, Allen Lane.

38 *ibid.*

39 *ibid.*

40 Warren, K (2012) Strategy Dynamics Essentials, Strategy Dynamics, Princes Risborough.

41 Montgomery, C A (2012) *The Strategist: Be the leader your business needs*, HarperCollins.

42 Sims, P (2012) *Little Bets: How breakthrough ideas emerge from small discoveries*, Random House Business Books.

43 McCracken, G (2012) *Culturematic*, Harvard Business Press.

44 Montgomery, C A (2012) *The Strategist: Be the leader your business needs*, HarperCollins.

Data is our future: Welcome to the age of infomagination
2007/08

16

MATT SADLER
*Planning Director, Karmarama and
Co-Founder, Two Fingers Brewing Co*

I believe Data is alive with creativity and that marketing is destined to take place at the crossroads of information and imagination.

Editor's therefore, for your brand...

Your brand thinking:
What data is critical in your market or brand? What data could give you a competitive advantage?

Your brand engagement:
How is data used and communicated to inspire everything you are doing? Is it the same as 10 years ago?

Your brand organization & capability:
How is your data collected, managed and communicated? What three things could you do to improve it and its impact on your decisions?

...and author's personal therefore

The IPA Excellence Diploma changed my life.

It's been over seven years since I started the IPA Excellence Diploma and over five since my paper was published. A lot's changed since then. But then, in many ways, a lot hasn't.

Allow me to explain...

My work: just as much passion, but not as many portmanteaus

Up till a few weeks ago, it'd been a while since I'd read the paper that you're about to flick through. But, while a few of the examples may be a little dated, overall I was pleasantly surprised to find how relevant and timely it still feels.

Ok, ok, I would say that. I wrote it, after all. But, it's certainly true that in the years since writing it, the quantities and types of data haven't just kept on multiplying, they've mutated into a new and even more terrifying beast: *big data*. And, if data was a wolf, *big data* is King Kong. A previously unimaginable giant, we humans approach with awe and confusion, as we both hope to control it and fear it'll smash us to pieces.

In the face of all this information, I still believe imagination is more important than ever. And that the artists in our industry don't need to fear science, but learn to use it in the right way. After all, the IPA's number crunching has proven the link between creativity and effectiveness[1] – doubtless helping to give many clients the confidence to be braver than ever. And, if you've found that it hasn't, maybe you're not using the data in the right way.

In the years since the Diploma, I've evolved my paper into a talk I've given several times at IPA, on how to use the right numbers, alongside words, pictures and ideas, to tell inspiring stories that can galvanize teams and transform brands and businesses. As ever, it's not just the information, but the imagination you bring to it that counts. And ultimately, when you're presenting, the best data visualization is you.

Of course, if I could give a pointer or two to my younger self, there are a few things I'd change about my paper. For starters, now I've worked in the industry for a few more years, I've become sick of its self-important jargon and meaningless buzzwords. So, while I hope you enjoy the spirit of my essay, I can only apologize for my own, humble contributions to advertising's already dubious vocabulary. It was just a phase I was going through.

My career: proud to be a professional juggler

These days, I juggle two jobs. And in many ways, it's the fault of the men and women to the left and right of me right in this book.

My first job is (still) in advertising, working as Planning Director at Karmarama. Karmarama itself is a marvellous blend of imagination and information, spiced with mischief, where creative hotshots and data analysts come together under one roof – in order to help brands win. So I guess it's unsurprising that I've felt at home here.

My second title on LinkedIn, which I squeeze around the day job, is Co-Founder of Two Fingers Brewing Co – the only beer brand that gives back to the men that drink it, by giving all profits to prostate cancer charities. Our first beer, Aurelio, has won an International Beer Award for Best Craft Beer Innovation, been described as 'the best excuse to drink beer yet' by Jay Rayner and is now stocked across the UK by Tesco, Morrisons and Ocado, not to mention a growing number of bars and restaurants. And, in the not too distant future, we hope to start selling worldwide.

I won't go into the full story behind our beer here, but will say that I don't believe it would've happened without the guys who set up and ran the Diploma, who schooled me in originality and industry, or the smart, ambitious and annoyingly talented people who did the Diploma before, after and alongside me – many of whom have launched their own things and, quite frankly, made me jealous.

My life: any excuse for adventure

I'll let you into a little secret. I didn't set out to do the IPA Excellence Diploma. I was only vaguely aware of it and someone suggested I give it a go. As a lifelong *Karate Kid* fan, I've always believed in the value of training, however, so I checked it out and got stuck in.

A second little secret is that I didn't set out to write a paper about data being our future. I set out to write about the future of data. It looked big, interesting and criminally neglected as an area – so I thought it might help me write something original. It was only when I started writing that I realized just how profound the impact of data would be, so I believed there was a chance to show people that what they thought would be the dullest subject could actually be the most exciting – and swapped a few words around in the title.

A third little secret is that I didn't set out to launch 'a beer for mankind'. A chance meeting in an edit suite, where someone had brought in some homebrew, set off an idea in my head and things just snowballed, thanks to an amazing team of guys who share my belief that we should use our talents to make a difference for the world as well as for our clients.

I guess my point is that life will always be chaotic, random and unpredictable, but that the Diploma has given me the skills and the confidence to embrace the unknown, stand up for what I believe in and take the exciting choices, rather than the easy ones.

It's also taught me to quote the hell out of people a lot smarter than me. So, in the words of the US writer and social activist Helen Keller, my belief *now* is that 'life is either a daring adventure or nothing at all'.[2]

Data is our future: Welcome to the age of infomagination

Who's afraid of the data wolf?

To a lot of people, data is scary stuff. Talk to your Mum about it and visions of Big Brother come tumbling out. Mention it to your clients and they'll tell you they're drowning in the stuff. Tell your colleagues you're writing an essay on data and the fear they might get asked to read it is palpable. It's a fear you might be experiencing right now. Is reading this paper going to be like locking yourself in a lift with a maths teacher?

Fear not, however, because over the course of this essay I'm going to be setting the record straight. I believe that data is an unstoppable force in the future of marketing (not to mention life as we know it) and that the only way for us to succeed is to embrace, rather than fear it. The future belongs to those who can learn to love, nurture and play with the information around us. Don't worry, the data of the future does not wear tweed and speak in monotone. It does not want you to sit down, be quiet and behave. Quite the opposite in fact.

This paper begins with a quick survey of the sea of data that surrounds us. Next I'll be showing you how consumers' uneasy relationship with personal information is actually set to give more and more power to the people. Then I'll demonstrate how brands with data expertise are revolutionizing marketing, but how most clients need to develop new capabilities and new partnerships to succeed. Finally, I'll be proving that our data-driven future is alive with creativity and possibility. Along the way, you'll see how data's cold, secretive and dull past is being replaced by a warm, open and inspiring future – where success is determined by a potent blend of information and imagination. This is our future. This is the 'age of infomagination'.

Data, data, everywhere

Once upon a time, a mechanically captured memory was a rare and precious thing – limited to a formal photograph or the crackly recording of a voice. Now, it's all but impossible to avoid leaving a recording behind as you go about your day. We barely notice it, but each of us passes an average of 3,254 pieces of personal information into databases every single week.[3]

And that's only the beginning. While we humans connect and interact constantly, the objects around us are doing the same. Around 600 billion RFID (Radio Frequency IDentification) chips are already embedded in everything from buildings to ham.[4,5] Furthermore, almost every piece of data also comes loaded with 'metadata': data that describes the data. An image might come tagged with its time, date and location, for example.[6]

As these ripples of data gather, they soon become a tidal wave. Technorati now tracks over 70 million blogs, with 120,000 more created every day.[7] Companies hold an estimated 60,000 petabytes (about 63 million gigabytes) of data worldwide – a figure that's set to double within two years.[8] Tesco alone gathers over 5 billion pieces of shopper information per week.[9]

Such unprecedented amounts of information have fundamentally changed the world we live in – not to mention the rules of marketing. The implications for how people feel and how brands and agencies must adapt are massive.

Consumers and data: from concern to control

Information consternation

To anyone who's picked up a newspaper recently, it's clear that 'data' has become synonymous with 'danger'. Whether it's fear over identity theft, concern over ID cards or repeated losses of sensitive information,[10] the warning signs are everywhere.

Quid pro quo

With all this bad PR, it's no surprise that people are extremely wary about the information that's held on them. Studies show that when requests for personal information are sweetened by the promise of 'better service', however, the picture changes dramatically.[11]

After all, we might not like to think about the data that's held on us, but we're grateful to Amazon for recommending us the right books and to Tesco for sending us vouchers for the food we like. Personalization is just too powerful a driver to resist – and Kevin Kelly, founder of *Wired* magazine, believes this makes information sharing inevitable: 'total personalisation will require total transparency... to share is to gain.'[12]

Our data, our selves

With the benefits of supplying personal information too strong to give up, but concern over how our information is used deepening, the result is a growing movement that seeks to give people control of the data they create. Organizations like dataportability.org are working hard to create a 'free, open, re-mixable web where your identity, contacts, relationships, personal details and media are free to follow you wherever you go'.[13] The result will be to make our data more complete and connected – and to put us in charge of it.

Consumers: the new data analysts

In the throws of the digital revolution, data is fast becoming democratized – and brands certainly aren't the only ones collecting, analysing and comparing information.

The evidence is everywhere. From the comparison websites which deliver data on a whole range of markets right into consumers' hands, to the apps that let us analyse everything from our sleep cycles, to our diet, to our musical tastes.

With consumers set to take ever greater interest in their own data, brands need to start giving them access to their information, together with the tools to explore. In the battle for better service, knowledge is power.

Summary: data power to the people

Tomorrow's most successful companies will be those that use data to their customer's advantage, as opposed to their own – while those that don't, risk it being used against them.

In the age of infomagination, the limits of how a brand uses data are defined only by its creativity. I'll be exploring a few possibilities here later, but first let's take a look at how brands and agencies are adjusting to the information revolution.

Brands and data: understanding and overload

Analysis breeds advantage

Jack Welch of General Electric once said that 'There are only two sources of competitive advantage: the ability to learn more about our customers faster than the competition and the ability to turn that learning into action faster than the competition.'[14]

In the past, learning about your customers meant sitting behind a two-way mirror in a research facility somewhere. While qualitative can yield great insights, however, it's a fact of life that people often 'don't say what they mean or mean what they say'.[15] To really understand people you need to find out what they actually do. This is where data comes into its own – giving us unprecedented power to discover who's doing what, where and when they're doing it and what they're saying about it. As a result, it's no surprise that the companies leading the data revolution are changing entire industries through the use of high-speed analytics.

Google is on a mission to organize the world's information – and the more data it sucks up, the smarter it gets.[16] Whether it's digitizing the world's book and newspaper archives,[17] or launching its Chrome browser, which reports on surfing habits,[18] it's always on the hunt for more. The upshot is that Google knows what people want and how to give it to them; a sure-fire recipe for the world's most powerful brand.[19]

The social music website Last.fm monitors every track its users listen to, in order to recommend similar artists – notching up 20 million fans, plus providing insights on listening trends.[20]

And, of course, Tesco has quietly revolutionized the marketing world with Clubcard, using hourly sales data on over 12 million shoppers to guide its key business decisions and deliver personalized service through incredibly tailored offers.[21,22] Despite printing 4 million Clubcard mailings at a time, normally only two people get the exact same set of vouchers.[23]

The principle is the same throughout – better data leads to better customer understanding, leads to better service. Companies like these, who have invested heavily in analytics, show us that the future is already here. The rest of us are running along behind.

Most marketers aren't waving, but drowning

For most organizations, information is a messy and overwhelming affair.[24] In our rapidly changing times, marketers must be more rigorous than ever to justify investment. Yet, they are caught in a paradox. While they need to react quicker than ever to the data they have available, the sheer abundance of information can easily trigger analysis paralysis.

Clients need partners to help them surf the data wave

The changing information landscape dramatically changes the type of people, processes, and capabilities brands need to succeed. Now, alongside creativity and technology, data proficiency and speed are the keys to competitive advantage.[25]

For this reason, clients will increasingly look for partners with superior data-crunching skills.[26] Something that opens the door to management consultants, or even Dunnhumby, getting a bigger piece of the marketing pie.[27]

To compete, comms networks will need to develop their information capabilities. In recent years there's been a big rise in partnerships with entertainment, media and content developers. In the future, networks will also look to make technical partnerships that bring crucial competencies to the table.

And even if specialists are covering the sharp end of data, it doesn't mean that the rest of the communications industry won't have to learn to play the game. Data literacy and competence must become de rigueur if we're to speak the same language as our clients and optimize the planning and execution of our campaigns.

How are agencies feeling about the data revolution?

I surveyed 122 people in a mixture of creative, media, direct, digital and PR agencies.[28] While they agreed that reliance on data was increasing (rating it an average 4.1 out of 5), there was little sense that their employers were committed to training them to use it (with employer commitment rated an average of 2.5 out of 5).

When asked what they disliked about data, respondents lamented that it was 'boring', 'cold' and 'limits creativity'. Pretty much the opposite of what we're aiming for in our work. I disagree fundamentally that this should be so, but I understand where the concerns come from. Advertising has had an uneasy relationship with science ever since Bill Bernbach declared 'I don't want academicians. I don't want scientists. I don't want people who do the right things. I want people who do inspiring things.'[29]

Fortunately, while Bill was right on a lot of things, he was wrong to imply the two are mutually exclusive. As well as giving us the skills we need to succeed, recruiting the right kind of 'academics' will make the future a much *more* inspiring place. We need people who are part scientist, part artist, all creative. 'Data Punks', armed with a potent combination of brains *and* balls, who can fuse information with imagination and lead us into the Age of Infomagination. Now let's get a taste of what we've got in store.

Use your infomagination

We've got the information, so let's utilize it

Making useful tools out of the world's data is an area of rich creative potential. Whilst some of us are wandering, lost in the data woods, the smart ones are wondering what they can build with all these trees...

Mashups make 1 + 1 = 3

When you hear the word 'mashup', data probably isn't the first thing that comes to mind. Mashups started in the music world, when producers like 2 Many DJs took two unrelated tracks and 'mashed' them into something new. Mashup a bit of Nirvana with a little Destiny's Child and the result 'Smells Like Teen Booty'.[30]

Operating on a similar principle is the trend for 'data mashups' – where information from multiple sources is combined to create new and distinct services not provided individually. Let's explore a few that are out there already.

I Am Near and Wikinear take location data from your mobile phone and mash it up with location data on pubs or Wikipedia pages to show you the ones near you.[31] This kind of thing seems begging to be developed by brands.

The government also got into the mashup game with its website **showusabetterway.co.uk,** which held a public contest to generate innovative uses for the masses of data it collects.[32] For instance, if you mashup travel data with crime statistics you can tell people the quickest and safest way to get home. This makes me wonder what companies could do with the data they have available, if only they mixed it together properly – or found the right partners to mash it up with.

On that note, my final example is more than just a data mashup – it's a brand mashup. Just stick a Nike+ sensor in your shoe and a receiver into your iPod and you can capture, analyse and compare data about your running ability. As a result, Nike and Apple have created the world's largest running club, connected and powered by their brands.[33] In the future, I believe brands will increasingly foster partnerships like this, combining complementary resources for the mutual benefit of themselves and con- sumers. Agencies can play a role here too, by encouraging 'data dating' among their clients.

Re-mix your thinking

Using data for your customers' advantage, rather than your own, is a new way of thinking that challenges old beliefs and practises. Once, corporate information was something to be kept secret – 'Data Protection' was the watchword. The data of the future does not want to be hidden away, however. Mashups teach us that tomorrow's data is open, socially connected and likes sharing. 'Data liberation' is the theme from now on.

Data is a wondrously multifaceted beast – not just useful, but also fascinating and beautiful. And in our business, 'fascinating and beautiful' can be a great way to engage an audience.

Data is the new video

No lights or cameras were used to make Radiohead's video for 'House of Cards' (**www.youtube.com/watch?v=8nTFjVm9sTQ**). Just data, collected by laser scanning systems. For brands seeking to differentiate themselves and capture the imagination, data seems likely to offer a slew of new production tools.

The benefits of data are also in its malleability vs traditional footage. Not only could this help address some of the production issues around the shift towards more varied, targeted communication (mentioned earlier), but also encourage consumer engagement. Radiohead's second piece of genius was to release their data as open-source code that fans could play with and remix to their heart's content.[34]

'But that's the flashy end of data', you may say. 'What about the practical side? How about data analysis?' Well, the good news is there's a revolution happening there too.

Analysis is the new storytelling

The new art of data analysis

Thankfully, while we've been carving up our pie charts, a new breed of computer scientist/artist hybrid has been pioneering new ways of presenting data, to expose the beauty and life that lies beneath the world's information.

After all, while we human beings like to think we're rational and verbal, the truth is we're emotional and visual.[35] So, as *Information Is Beautiful* author David McCandless says, it's no surprise that 'We don't want to read information any more. We want to see it. Feel it.'[36]

Visualizations turn data into pictures (or 'infographics'), so that we can explore, understand and engage with even highly complicated information. See Figure 16.1 for one of my favourites, which speaks volumes about the United States's relationship with the Middle East.

The best visualizations turn the data into an involving and engaging story – and the very best help us to reveal the humanity behind it. After all, as our industry becomes more and more data driven, we must be careful not to exchange our sense of empathy for a fetishistic fascination with numbers and information. As computer scientist, artist and anthropologist Jonathan Harris says, 'Really, the data is just part of the story. The human stuff is the main stuff, the data should enrich it.'[38]

In the next section we explore how to apply these thoughts to the ongoing evaluation of a brand.

Learnings for evaluation: from scoreboards to storybooks

One of the big pushes throughout the business world is the creation of marketing dashboards that bring together key data sets, so that organizations can assess their ongoing performance. So far, most of these are fairly dry affairs, featuring basic bar charts, line graphs and tables.[39]

Just presenting the numbers is not good enough. Emotional data is powerful data. Better presented information makes for better decisions. A dashboard should be an engaging and inspirational tool where a rich narrative about a brand's progress can be told and learned from. Not a scoreboard, but a storybook.

FIGURE 16.1 An infographic showing who has the world's oil – and who needs it[37]

Who has the oil?

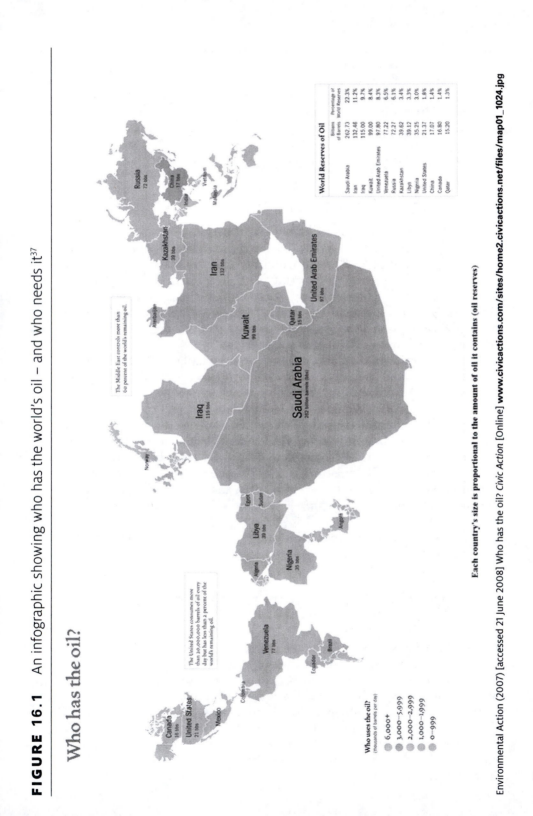

Each country's size is proportional to the amount of oil it contains (oil reserves)

Environmental Action (2007) [accessed 21 June 2008] Who has the oil? *Civic Action* [Online] www.civicactions.com/sites/home2.civicactions.net/files/map01_1024.jpg

FIGURE 16.2   Mock-up of a Carling Evaluation Storybook, where themed widgets present live qualitative and quantative data in an emotionally engaging, interactive way

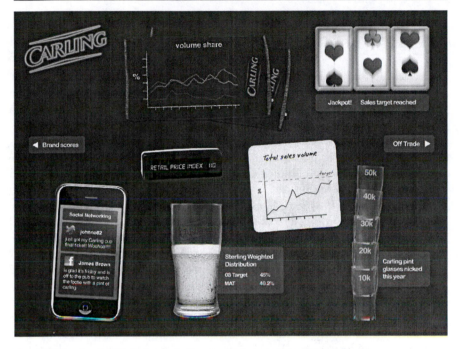

Euro RSCG London (2008) *Carling evaluation storybook*, commissioned by Sadler, M

In order to tell a story, we need to dramatize the ongoing 'who, what, where, when, why and how' of a brand in a way that has feeling and humanity.

Brands should express themselves in everything they do – and bring as much of their personality and style to the way they evaluate themselves as they do in their advertising. I briefed my agency to create an example 'Evaluation Storybook' for Carling and the result is shown in Figure 16.2.

It's time to see things differently

Hans Rosling, Professor of International Health at the Karolinska Institute in Sweden, uses interactive, animated charts to bring world poverty, money and health data to life. As he explains 'few people will appreciate the music if I just show them the notes. Most of us need to listen to the music to understand how beautiful it is. But often it's how we present statistics: we just show the notes and don't play the music'.[40]

Surely there are symphonies hiding inside every company's data, if only we can find the right instruments to reveal them? Far from being purely cosmetic, making data warm, entertaining and inspiring is vital for cultural change. Only when we can engage the whole of the client–agency world with our information will everyone truly benefit from it.

Conclusion: the age of infomagination welcomes you

So concludes our whirlwind tour of the Age of Infomagination.

First, we looked at consumers and saw how data is bringing power to the people. While personalization and relevance are propelling the data revolution forward, carelessness and distrust are causing people to rise up and take control of the data they've created. The democratization of information is shifting the balance of power further, as consumers use data to their advantage throughout their lives, including their relationship with brands. Brands need to open up and get involved.

Next, we looked at how breakthroughs in analytics offer brands new depths of understanding. The companies leading the charge have developed huge competitive advantages through using data to better understand people and deliver on their needs. Most companies, however, are trapped in a data tidal wave – and need partners to help them surf. New technologies, new capabilities and new connections are needed to succeed. It's a mixture of brains *and* balls that will define the next creative hotshops.

After that, we saw how data is driving more creative conversations with consumers – and how the leaders of the future will use on-the-fly analysis to talk to people like people. Next, I demonstrated why brands should mashup datasets to create new tools and ways of thinking, because using data to your customers' advantage is the best way of turning it to your own.

I then showed how data is giving us new and original ways of storytelling; be it through dramatic production techniques or dramatic analytics. These tools have a vital role to play in touching the humanity beneath the information, by visualizing data in a way that moves and inspires people emotionally. As an industry that thrives on creativity, making data entertaining and accessible is vital for integrating it into our culture. Once our information becomes warmer, more inclusive and more fluid, then so can our ways of working. Ultimately, data should be an inspirational resource and creative tool for all, not just the insights or planning department.

In the future, marketing will operate at the crossroads of information and imagination. To succeed we need to embrace both, equally. Now is not a time for fear, but fascination; not a time for restriction but liberation; and not a time for data to replace humanity but enhance it. In the age of infomagination, the data punks rule. Now it's time for you to decide if you'd like to come join them.

Notes

1 Field, P *et al* (2011) The link between creativity and effectiveness: 2011 update, IPA.

2 Keller, H (1957) *The Open Door*, Doubleday.

3 Gray, R (2008) How 'Big Brother' watches your every move, *Sunday Telegraph* [Online] www.telegraph.co.uk/news/uknews/2571041/How-Big-Brother-watches-your-every-move.html

4 Kanse, P (2008) We can be heroes, *Viewpoint*, 22.

5 Kelly, K (December 2007) Predicting the next 5,000 days of the web, *TED entertainment gathering*, Los Angeles [Online] www.ted.com/index.php/talks/kevin_kelly_on_the_next_5_000_days_of_the_web.html

6 Yakob, F and Brier, N (2008) Ways of seeing, *Contagious*, (15) [Online] http://farisyakob.typepad.com/blog/files/ways_of_seeing.pdf

7 Sifry, D (2007) [accessed 18 August 2008] The state of the live web, *Technorati* [Online] http://technorati.com/weblog/blogosphere

8 IDC (2007) Taming information chaos, *IDC*, sponsored by Teradata [Online] http://www.financialtech-mag.com/_docum/141_Estudios_de_Mercado_04.pdf

9 Hayward, M (2006) How to be a customer champion: Turning insight into action, *Market Leader* (34).

10 Slack, J (August 2008) Danger criminal files go missing, *Daily Mail*.

11 IIPS (2008) The 'quid pro quo' relationship of personal information provision, *The Futures Company* [Online] http://blog.thefuturescompany.com/2008/05/

12 Kelly, K (December 2007) Predicting the next 5,000 days of the web, *TED entertainment gathering*, Los Angeles [Online] www.ted.com/index.php/talks/kevin_kelly_on_the_next_5_000_days_of_the_web.html

13 Pick, M (2008) DataPortability: connect, control, share, remix, *Dataportability.org* [online] www.vimeo.com/610179

14 Hayward, M (2006) How to be a customer champion: Turning insight into action, *Market Leader* (34).

15 Gordon, W (2002) Brands on the Brain, in *Brand New Brand Thinking: Brought to life by 11 experts who do*, ed M Baskinand M Earls, Kogan Page, London.

16 Ayres, I (2007) *Super Crunchers: Why thinking-by-numbers is the new way to be smart*, Bantam Dell, New York.

17 Kiss, J (September 2008) Google puts papers' archives online, *The Guardian* [Online] www.guardian.co.uk/media/2008/sep/09/googlethemedia.digitalmedia

18 Walmsley, A (September 2008) The sparkle of Chrome, *Marketing*.

19 Millward Brown Optimor (2008) Top 100 most powerful brands 08, *Millward Brown Optimor* [Online] www.millwardbrown.com/docs/default-source/global-brandz-downloads/global/2008_BrandZ_Top100_PressRelease.pdf

20 White, D (August 2007) Last.fm charts to reveal next big things, *Daily Telegraph*.

21 Hayward, M (2006) How to be a customer champion: Turning insight into action, *Market Leader* (34).

22 Humby, C, Hunt, T and Phillips, T (2007) *Scoring Points: How Tesco continues to win customer loyalty*, Kogan Page, London.

23 Taylor, J (2005) *Space Race: An inside view of the future of communications planning*, John Wiley & Sons.

24 IDC (2007) Taming information chaos, *IDC*, sponsored by Teradata [Online] www.financialtech-mag.com/_docum/141_Estudios_de_Mercado_04.pdf

25 Landry, E, Ude, C and Vollmer, C (2008) HD marketing 2010: Sharpening the conversation, *Booz Allen Hamilton* [Online] www.boozallen.com/media/file/HD_Marketing_2010.pdf

26 Davenport, T H (January 2006) Competing on analytics, *Harvard Business Review.*

27 Taylor, J (2005) *Space Race: An inside view of the future of communications planning*, John Wiley & Sons.

28 Sadler, M (August 2008) A two-minute survey about data, based on employees at communications agencies in London [*n* = 122] Conducted via [Online] www.surveymonkey.com

29 Bernbach, B (1947) in *Bill Bernbach's Book: A history of the advertising that changed the history of advertising*, Villard Books, New York.

30 2 Many DJs, Nirvana & Destiny's Child (2002) Smells like Teen Booty, Soulwax Bootleg Remix [Online] www.youtube.com/watch?v=CLqqTHAizts

31 Taylor, T (2008) [accessed 7 August 2008] Delighting with data, *Oxford geek night 7* [Online] www.tomtaylor.co.uk/talks/delighting-with-data

32 Show us a better way (2008) [Online] http://webarchive.nationalarchives.gov.uk/20100402134053/showusabetterway.com

33 Morrissey, B (June 2008) Why Nike embraces brand utility, *Adweek* [Online] www.adweek.com/aw/content_display/news/client/e3i58d6cda1cb00deaf721a366dbc00ec4a

34 Radiohead and Google (2008) [accessed 18 August 2008] *The making of House of Cards* [Online] http://code.google.com/creative/radiohead

35 2 Many DJs, Nirvana & Destiny's Child (2002) Smells like Teen Booty, Soulwax Bootleg Remix [Online] www.youtube.com/watch?v=CLqqTHAizts

36 McCandless, D (2008) [accessed 23 June 2008] You are the future, *Under the influence*, London [Online] www.irisnation.com/undertheinfluence/videohtml/dip_mcandless.html

37 Civic Actions (2005) Who has the oil? Civic Actions, licensed under CC BY-SA 3.0.

38 Harris, J in Danzico, L (March 2008) Telling stories using data: an interview with Jonathan Harris, Adobe Design Centre [Online] http://web.archive.org/web/20120105154107/http://www.adobe.com/designcenter/thinktank/danzico2.html

39 Scanmar (2006) in Wise, L (January 2008) Marketing dashboards, *Dashboard Insight* [Online] www.dashboardinsight.com/articles/business-verticals/marketing-dashboards.aspx

40 Rosling, H (2007) [accessed 14 August2008] Unveil the beauty of statistics, OECD World Forum, Istanbul [Online] www.depthreporting.com/2007/07/hans-rosling-beauty-of-statistics.html

I believe brands need to adopt an outside-in brand management approach

17

2005/06

SAM D'AMATO
Chief Strategy Officer, M2M

I believe Successful brands will place customers, not shareholders, at the heart of business and the brands that access customers' own networks, pulling the outside in to work for them, will succeed. It is an essay inspired by the fan-driven rise of Arctic Monkeys that caught the music industry on the back foot.

Editor's therefore, for your brand...

Your brand thinking

Your brand engagement

Your brand organization & capability

Your brand thinking:
How does your brand bring the consumer 'inside'?

Your brand engagement:
Do you build communication and content with shareability built in?

Your brand organization & capability:
Does your whole company feel they work for your brand? Is every employee a brand evangelist?

...and author's personal therefore

My work: bringing the customer inside

In 2010, Richard Martin of the Harvard Business School evaluated the financial return to shareholders of companies adopting a shareholder-value model versus customer capitalism.[1] Those that focused on customers first had consistently delivered higher returns over the previous 80 years. This, along with UGC, co-creation, transmedia, big data, real-time, engagement planning, and paid, owned, earned, have all reinforced my belief in outside-in thinking.

My first step into the theory focused on projects, employing customers in departments. Here are a few examples.

- **Marketing.** Working with Paddy Power during the 2012 Ryder Cup, we got fans to tweet support to the Europeans. As the home crowd chanted 'USA, USA' on the course and the Europeans were crumbling, seven planes, miles above, translated their support into 'skytweets' the world saw on air. It was a campaign that truly gave power to the punter and the comeback became known as 'The Miracle at Medinah'.

FIGURE 17.1   'Do us a flavour'

- **NPD.** We convinced Walkers to discard their 12-month product, marketing and sales cycle, and let the public invent and market six new flavours in three months (Figure 17.1). 'Do us a flavour' remains one of their most successful campaigns ever. The client even paid 1 per cent of sales to the winning family.

- **Creative.** Be it Doritos that ran our UGC ad on TV for years; *The Raid* which saw a fan remake the film in Claymation for us; or the film *Sinister* where we hooked cinemagoers up to heart rate, sweat and temperature monitors, triangulating a fear factor, we continue to recruit customers into the creative process.
- **Corporate social responsibility.** Realizing that there was not one openly gay professional footballer in the UK, and finding that punters questioned this, we recently worked with Paddy Power to launch the 'Right Behind Gay Footballers' #RBGF campaign. We sent rainbow laces to every professional in the United Kingdom, asking them to show support, and then delivered worldwide coverage, harvesting and responding to people as it played out in the news and social media. Fifty-four professional clubs got involved. We appeared in over 400 news stories, had a motion passed in Parliament and elevated an issue to new heights.

My career: driving the outside in human agenda

In 2009 I joined M2M, a company with an entrepreneurial heart and culture I believed in. With the founder leaving though, the agency needed renewed direction.

Crystallizing the company's essence, Think Human became the operating system we live by, and it is exciting how being human has spread throughout the industry since. For us it is not simply a planning process, but the next step in outside-in thinking; giving a career purpose. One underpinned with principles:

- Place yourself in other people's shoes: get away from your desk and speak to people, test and live their perspective. We call it people watching.
- Seek the truth behind behaviour: what makes us human is our ability to ask questions.[2] We leverage the five whys to get to the root cause of people's actions.
- Don't sell, help people buy better: no one likes to be sold to, but we love to buy. Always be interesting, useful, entertaining or relevant.
- Ground everything in the purpose: people don't buy what you do; they buy why you do it.[3] Just as we join a company because we believe in it, so customers follow brands with purpose.
- Promote interaction and collaboration throughout: if your colleagues, clients or customer are invested in the solution you will better succeed.
- Make it simple: Our job is to help brands put the right content in front of the right people, in the right context, in the right manner, with the right purpose at heart, and in the most simple and inspiring way possible.
- Keep inspired and moving forward: Bernard Shaw said 'the reasonable man adapts himself to the world; the unreasonable one persists in trying to adapt the world to himself. Therefore all progress depends on the unreasonable man'. His assertion was that in our

FIGURE 17.2   Simon Sinek's 'Golden Circle'. 'Why' you do something sits at the heart, with 'how' and 'what' you sell outside

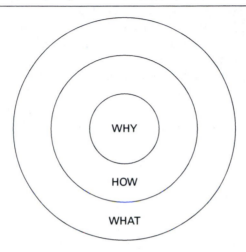

ever-changing, uncertain world, the greatest limitation on our capacity to innovate is reasonable people. It is our job to strive for the unreasonable; hence we have 'Moonshots' and 'Nudge' programmes at our company, fostering entrepreneurialism.

My life: making life work for me

The Sigmoid Curve (Figure 17.3) depicts my thoughts well. The curve represents life. It could be a product, businesses or relationship lifecycle. We start

FIGURE 17.3   The Sigmoid Curve

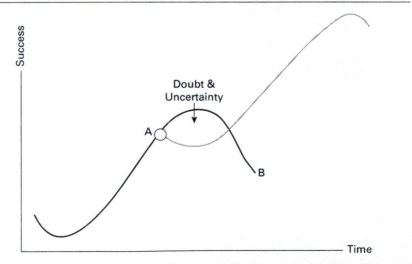

As depicted in *The Empty Raincoat: Making sense of the future*, by Charles Handy, 1994

slowly, learning. We then grow fast before a decline. At point A it is hard to see the oncoming decent. As a result, change only tends to happen at B when it is too late. To 'Think Human' is to recognize the cycle, yet understand that the greatest among us are not bound to it. Life for me is about letting outside possibilities in. Navigating doubt and uncertainty and seeking new curves not just for clients, colleagues and customers, but myself and family too.

With this in mind, companies should not just foster success in work; they should foster happiness in life. Our company has introduced a raft of outside-in initiatives that include flexible working; passion days; no one being 100 per cent assigned to clients; investing in personal projects and businesses of colleagues; guest speakers; and a 'Get out More' initiative to keep inspired.

In conclusion

The outside-in theory (Figure 17.4) is greater than employing customers today; it is about a better career and life. Given happiness and creativity are a collision of influences, we have to open up to the world and make it 'work' for us. It is about being more unreasonable!

FIGURE 17.4   'Outside-in' thinking

I believe brands need to adopt an outside-in brand management approach

Standing outside their gig, the excitement around Arctic Monkeys was palpable. I began researching the band, even accosting fans at a gig, when I discovered they were taking the UK by storm with a rise to fame championed not through traditional music industry means, but their fans. Fans that took CDs the band gave out at gigs loaded them up online and fuelled a frenzy of excitement by sharing files, writing blogs and singing their praises in chat rooms before they were signed.

Music fans will know they went on to win the Best British Breakthrough Act Brit Award. As *The Guardian* put it, 'the simple fact that the internet allows fledgling bands' music to be heard without label assistance has heralded a joyous new musical socialism'.[4] And as Laurence Bell of Domino Records who signed them later said, 'I think that bands are in a stronger position, as they are not so desperate for the record company to magic up the numbers. They come with an audience.'[5]

While considering Arctic Monkeys' case and the parallels it held with the marketing world in general, my theory formed: *Successful brands of the future will utilize an outside-in approach. They will access consumers' 'own networks' and get them to work for them.*

It's an approach that does not fear the rising power of consumers, it embraces it. To explain how, I have structured this paper as follows:

- Why consumers are forming their own networks.
- Outside-in brand management – an approach to gain control by giving it away.
- What it means for channel planning and creative.
- What it means for research and measurement.
- How the outside-in agency of the future will be structured.

Why consumers are forming their 'own' networks and 'working' for brands

Technology is giving people control over message reception

Be it TV, radio or online, more and more you can screen out messages so that nothing comes to you unless you choose it to. The implication of this is a radical increase in consumer sovereignty.[6] Consumers are becoming their own DJs, schedulers and programmers.

Consumers are finding new ways to get content

Today content is being sold direct to consumers, or pirated free. In fact, once consumers get online, they don't want to pay for anything.[7] While gate-keepers, like Sky and iTunes (see Figure 17.5) can build their relationship with consumers,[8] advertisers are losing their route to market.

Consumers want and feel they can have 'their 15 minutes of fame'

People are creating blogs, websites or even TV shows on YouTube. People want and believe they can build fame on their own terms.

FIGURE 17.5 As a consumer, which information do you usually consult prior to purchase? Do you often, sometimes or never consult?

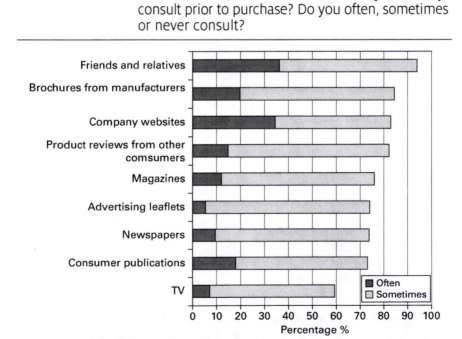

SOURCE: OMD Snapshots consumer panel

FIGURE 17.6 In relation to brands, have you ever done any of the following?

SOURCE: OMD Snapshots consumer panel. Base: 816 aged 16+, March 2006

We trust each other first

As Mark Earls says, we are 'herd animals'[9], and through word of mouth, consumers instinctively create the most powerful communication channel there is, one capable of rapid spread of ideas, products and behaviour.[10]

In summary, the challenge is how we embrace consumers' desire to take control and actually get them to want to 'work' for brands. Fortunately it would seem people are already happy to do so (see Figures 17.5 and 17.6).

Why consumers are willing to work for brands

Buyer-centric marketing gives people a better, customized deal

Alan Mitchell, in *Right Side Up*,[11] speaks of the high and wasteful go-to-market costs of traditional 'just-in-case' production, describing his view that the future is in matching supply to demand, not demand to supply. As soon as people start telling companies the exact design, price, features and benefits they want, the 'consumer employee' is acting as the company research, marketing and NPD department all in one. They are telling us they want to be partners, not pawns.[12]

FIGURE 17.7 The evolution of marketing

What it has (features)	What it does (benefits)	What you'll feel (experience)	Who you are (identification)	To	Who you'll work for (Consumer employee)
1990	1925	1950	2000		2006+

Adapted from Neumeier, M (2005) *The Brand Gap: How to bridge the distance between business strategy and design*, New Riders, California

Branded experiences offer richer involvement

As brands focus on the full 'experience engagement process',[13] companies set the stage and give people the props, but consumers are the actors who ultimately bring the experience to life. The 'consumer employee' is completing the brand experience.

Corporate social responsibility has increased

No longer can a company simply bring a product to market, consumers want brands to be 'citizens'.[14] If they are to trust and work with a brand, the 'consumer employee' wants emotional and societal benefits as well.

Consumers want things in their own time

No longer do we visit our local bank, instead we go online and do it ourselves, both saving time and reducing a company's payroll costs, because the 'consumer employee' happily does the administration for companies.

We stick together in tribes

People balance conflicting desires to be individuals, with the desire to fit in.[15] Nature leads us to segment ourselves into groups through our preferences, and when this happens the 'consumer employee' is doing the marketing job once again.

The more you look, the more you notice the work consumers are now doing, often through networks they are creating. It is why I believe marketing has moved on a step from that which Marty Keumeier describes in *The Brand Gap*.

The consumer is the new channel planner and we need to embrace them. Meabh Quoirin touched on this in a recent nVision study when he said: 'rather than worrying that marketers may be a dying breed, companies should be looking to the potential for enlisting consumers to the marketing effort.'[16]

Outside-in brand management: An approach to gain control by giving it away

Agencies need to think like recruitment consultants and consider how they can encourage consumers to work for them. All brands can benefit, because consumers can be employed in every department.

Marketing department

Brand managers need to consider how they can get consumers to aid the marketing process and market products to other consumers for them. We recently ran a campaign for Furby (Hasbro Toys) employing consumers within marketing. We realized that kids would want to work with us if we gave them the opportunity to use their imaginations and actually influence the campaign story. To do this, we partnered with Nickelodeon and Capital Radio, and built a campaign in which different Furby characters competed for the prize of 'Furby Star' (Figure 17.8). Having followed the characters' development on air, online and on the radio, through interviews and singing performances, more than 30,000 kids voted for their favourite Furby.

FIGURE 17.8   Three Furbys record their songs, as they battle for the prize of 'Furby Star'

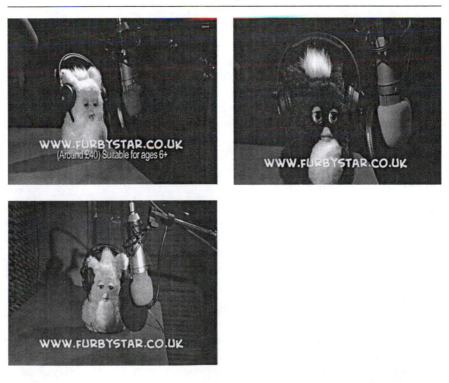

Following the announcement of the winner, we went on to release the 'single' as a ringtone, and a Furby movie.

Furby became the No 1 toy in its category for Christmas 2005. Kids had dictated the creative by voting, encouraged their friends to get involved by discussing and sharing the site online, and then downloaded ringtones that marketed the product once the campaign finished.

Trade sales department

With the rising power of the trade, particularly in the FMCG market, companies are often forced to offer discounts and promotions, devaluing their brands, while the retailer compounds their problem by producing own-label competitors. We need the consumer to work for us by requesting brands. By giving consumers a reason, such as loyalty programmes, to actively request products, you limit retailer dominance.

Administration department

A simple way to employ the consumer and reduce costs is to encourage consumers to fill in information online, place orders, and complete the job previously fulfilled by others themselves.

Corporate social responsibility department

Working with brands like Esso and Walkers, you realize the importance of CSR, and if the government's White Paper and PR around snack foods, kids and health say anything, it is that the issue is not going away. Companies like Walkers need to face the problem head on. They should move the debate away from their products alone, towards the real issue; the need for a more balanced diet in combination with an active lifestyle. They should get consumers to work for their CSR department by getting them involved with the campaign, by associating themselves with sport, the Olympic bid, or by running a yearly 'Walkerthon' in conjunction with the marathon.

These examples show what Hamish Pringle describes as 'corporate social leadership', and demonstrate a genuine partnership with consumers, towards the co-creation of a healthier lifestyle.

NPD Department

The online bank, for example, recruited consumers to design the original brand strategy for the company.[17] Similarly, I believe that my client Hasbro could encourage people to work for their NPD department. What kid, if we ran a competition, wouldn't want to be the designer of the next Action Man or My Little Pony?

Creative department

The 'Star Wars Kid' is an example of consumer-created content that further built the Star Wars brand. With this in mind, and embracing the incredible explosion in consumer creativity arising from digital photography and video technology,[18] Hasbro have recently partnered with *Empire* magazine to deliver a competition in which people have to spoof a scene from the movies using their action figures. In this case, the customer is Hasbro's new creative.

Senior management

Taking the idea a step further, we could metaphorically 'sell the company' to the consumer,[19] by asking them what they would do if they owned it. I wouldn't be surprised if swapitshop.com, a site that allows kids to swap their toys online, did just this. Ultimately the consumer could evolve brands for us.

PR department

Because the press monitor popular culture and consumers are embracing non-traditional information sources, we should encourage customers to seed news to the press, or just help them be the press, by giving influential consumers access to our thoughts first.

IT department

For years Microsoft received criticism from technicians picking faults in their software. By allowing the same people to beta test products, they have been able to solve complex problems quickly, achieving substantial cost savings before the product goes to market. Similarly, by harvesting site usage patterns and feedback, companies can resolve issues. As Danny Van Emden of EMI Records put it: 'what a good website repays a brand and a label in knowing who their audience are and where they are coming from, is incomparable in terms of any other marketing and research channel.'[20]

Research department

The interesting thing about the rise of the Arctic Monkeys is how the record companies missed it coming. Hitwise.com explained that it could have been predicted if they had been monitoring search activity, blogs, chat rooms and online communities.[21] I believe all brands will be doing just this in future. Data management will be central to an outside-in approach.

The idea I am proposing fits the old saying that 'a company is only as good as its employees'. It will be those that manage the consumer employee most efficiently that stand out in an environment where consumers are keen to take control.

Having discussed how companies can apply the outside-in approach by thinking of it in terms of different departments, I will first share how this approach influences channel planning and creative, secondly research and measurement, and lastly agencies.

Outside-in channel planning and creative

To get consumers to work for us, we need to learn from consumers' use of channels. To be welcomed to their network, media and creative needs to evolve as follows.

Less business to consumer, more consumer to consumer

Every one of us has purchased goods they otherwise wouldn't have because of a recommendation. With this in mind we need to think of 'consumers as media' and do all we can to facilitate word of mouth between influencers. With a client like Bridgestone for example, why not let aspiring racing drivers test their new tyres, not just Jenson Button.

Less 'finished', and more 'unfinished' marketing

The industry treats consumers like 'targets to hit, not people to persuade'.[22] If consumers are to embrace advertising, accepting their employment, we have to give them more control. Let them co-create, re-shape and add layers to the story.

Why couldn't Walkers run a national campaign to find the nation's favourite crisp and then celebrate it, for example? Doing so would deliver a richer brand experience, one people actually feel a part of.

Less advertising, more brands as media (content and dialogue)

Consumers tend to have a stronger relationship with programmes than ads, so we should start to look at 'the trinity that is content, media and marketing'.[23] Learn from the fact that people are building their own sites and blogs. In the past we targeted passive consumers, now we need to work through audiences and communities of interest.[24] We need to provide media they don't just choose to consume, but media they want to watch, would even be willing to pay for. The approach calls for a rise in advertiser-funded content and a better management of brands' own media. It is important because how we remember things depends on how they are encoded. The more vivid, emotional and original an event the more likely it is to be recalled.[25]

To summarize, we need to remember what we all want from our employers – recognition; reward; involvement; respect; development; responsibility; a better way of life; and not forgetting fun. Through this process we can be welcomed to consumers' networks in a way that makes them willing employees of our brands. And in this environment, 'share of employment' will be key, not just 'share of voice'.

Research and measurement: becoming an 'investor in people'

All too often agencies' measure of campaign success encompasses an inadequate 'basket of metrics' they feel confident they can influence, rather than those most relevant.[26] Agencies need to think like the brand's recruitment consultant and understand the client's needs alongside the full value the employees add. It is my proposal that agencies partake in the following strategies.

Understand how well your campaign employs the consumer

Understanding where, and how efficiently, we are employing the consumer into departments is crucial. An outside-in agency needs to be listening to consumers, working on and monitoring every recruitment opportunity the brand has.

Become a 'Citizen Brand'[27]

We need to monitor and research the trends, habits and feelings of 'employees'. A brand confident enough to engage in debate and speak freely with consumers will gain their respect. Good examples include Dove with their campaignforrealbeauty.com site and AOL's discuss.aol.co.uk.

Research employees in their own environment

As Martin Raymond argues in *The Tomorrow People*,[28] we should monitor consumers in their own environment, as this will uncover what we all know, but often neglect: that people rarely say what they mean, or do as they say.

Use the technology available to you

We can now monitor hundreds of millions of natural discussions from blogs, chat rooms, e-mail groups and product feedback sites. This allows companies to identify those individuals who most effectively spread buzz and trends among consumers.[29] As Nancy Vonk, Co-Chief Creative Officer of Ogilvy Toronto, recently said, 'With the right blogger at the wheel, bad moments can be addressed quickly and with admired transparency. You have a chance to beat the press to the message, and take control of your response.'[30]

Think 'customer resource', not just 'customer research'

In a recent *Campaign* supplement, 'The world's leading independent agencies', James Mackay of Belgiovane Williams Mackay said 'as our focus has moved away from ad-centric outcomes towards idea-centric ones, we have found that the more eclectic our creative department's talent, the higher the level of creative challenge achieved'.[31] This was a common theme amongst the independents covered, but none mentioned the consumer as a potential source. By whatever means we can, we should be giving consumers the opportunity to feedback and get involved.

Integrate research and retail

Esso has its garages; Walkers could have convenience stores and Hasbro a toy shop. The stores would help keep a constant tab on trends and needs, test new products, monitor behaviour first hand, POS and promotions.

Understand the full value of your consumer employees

Agencies can be slow to measure their impact on the bottom line, preferring to 'put a stick in the ground' and measure marketing's 'magic numbers' (awareness scores, relative price, loyalty).[32] We need to be able to demonstrate the return our employees add to the business, quantify results against true intentions, and keep raising the bar to deliver better results.[33]

In summary, we need to establish a shared understanding of the objectives our marketing is to address; ensuring that everyone understands what success looks like up-front.[34] Following this, we will want to take a holistic customer approach and evaluate the full returns resulting from their 'employment': 'the longer and broader, as well as the short-term effects.'[35] Taking this approach gives agencies more credibility. It makes agencies truly accountable for their work.

By making the customer, not shareholders, the measurement focus, agencies can better position and justify their contribution. It will help agencies push for fair payment by results too.

The structure of an outside-in agency

Just as we all want to work with inspiring people we respect and believe in, so consumers want to work with brands they respect and believe in. With this in mind, outside-in agencies will need the following.

Strong leadership

To help agencies 'employ the consumer' and become more accountable requires training of, and the buy-in, from all involved. To win the internal and outside-in respect of 'employees' agencies and brands need genuine purpose.

Flexible and varied teams

At a recent IPA debate, Jonathan Mildenhall of Mother said, 'I don't know if agencies will be ad agencies, production agencies or brand content agencies in the future, but what I do know is that it's all about the talent. You need to go where the talent is.'[36] Agencies of the future will need to be able to pool all the creativity at their fingertips, and appreciate that ideas can come from anywhere. This includes a closer, more holistic and ongoing approach with consumers, even having them in-house.

Greater HR-centred remuneration measures

The focus of an outside-in approach is the 'consumer employee', and likewise the consumer should be the focus of agency remuneration. Just as a manager is rewarded for the success of his internal staff, so agencies should be rewarded for the profit and productivity of their 'consumer employees'. However, just as that same manager is rewarded for the success of his employees, so the manager needs a basic wage to survive as well. Likewise, I believe remuneration needs to be two-fold:

- The Basic – agencies should first charge a fee that reflects their basic resource cost.
- Employee performance-related pay – having covered costs, the main profit driver becomes the delivery of the strongest idea possible to maximize the efficiency and profitability of your 'employees'. You should be rewarded relative to the success of your campaign.

By demonstrating we get a client's customer better than they do, I believe we will be able to state our case for a new form of remuneration. A case that reflects the effectiveness of our brand management. A case that will inspire agency staff to both measure and develop the strongest ideas possible – ideas that will encourage us to escape the 'shackles of craft creativity and create media-neutral ideas that transcend advertising and address all brand stake-holders'.[37] It is a route that would deliver a win–win for both agency and client.

Conclusion

Jim Stengel of Procter & Gamble wrote an article titled 'Consumers are reinventing marketing', in which he asked the reader: 'Will the consumer be your boss, your coach, your inspiration, or will you be out of touch and out of business?'[38] It is my proposal that the consumer should be our inspiration, but that we need to think of them as brand 'employees' so that we do not simply 'keep in touch', we move ahead.

Marketers need to find ways to make consumers willing to 'work' with them. A brand is only as strong as its 'consumer employees'. If the 'employees' do not enjoy, or feel rewarded for working with us, natural selection will occur via the vote of the wallet, negative word of mouth, and more. They will look for 'employment' elsewhere.

With this in mind, I have identified three key areas of outside-in brand management to aid the process. First, the successful agencies will be those that get consumers to work for their brands in the right mix of roles. Second, companies will need to take a more inclusive and holistic approach to research. Last, they need to make sure their agencies are set up to deliver, and be rewarded, for this approach.

And as a final point, I obviously bought the Arctic Monkeys album, and I can't get the song 'I bet you look good on the dance floor' out of my head, so recommend you buy it. If you like it too, why not recommend it to all your friends; write your own blog about them; buy their T-shirt and walk proudly around town singing their songs; suggest some ideas for their next album; tell your local shop they should stock it; sign up for band updates on their site; or even contact their record company, buy the albums in bulk and become a retailer yourself. You might just make employee of the month!

Notes

1 Martin, R (January 2010) The Age of Customer Capitalism, *Harvard Business Review.*

2 Jane Goodall, quoted in Morell, V (March 2007) The Discover interview: Jane Goodall, *Discover Magazine.*

3 Sinek, S (September 2009) How great leaders inspire actions, *TED* [Online] www.ted.com/talks/simon_sinek_how_great_leaders_inspire_action

4 Barton, L (October 2005) The question: Have the Arctic Monkeys changed the music business?, *The Guardian.*

5 (January 2006) Rockers Seeking Fame Online, *Wired* [Online] http://archive.wired.com/culture/lifestyle/news/2006/01/70054

6 Naughton, J (March 2006) The age of permanent net revolution, *The Observer.*

7 Johnson, L (June 2005) The mad media party is over, *Sunday Telegraph.*

8 Curry, A (2004) The branding bubble, extract from The New Medium of Television, *Interactive Digital Sales* [Online] www.re-thinkingtv.com/pdf/Curry.pdf

9 Earls, M (2007) *Herd: How to change mass behaviour by harnessing our true nature*, John Wiley & Sons.

10 Gladwell, M(2002) *The Tipping Point: How little things can make a big difference*, Abacus.

11 Mitchell, A (2002) *Right Side Up: Building brands in the age of the organized consumer*, HarperCollins.

12 Solomon, M R (2003) *Conquering Consumerspace: Marketing strategies for a branded world*, Amacom, US.

13 LaSalle, D and Britton, T A (2003) *Priceless: Turning ordinary products into extraordinary experiences*, Harvard Business Review Press.

14 Gobe, M (2002) *Citizen Brands: 10 commandments for transforming brands in a consumer democracy*, Allworth Press, New York.

15 Levy, S J (1999) *Brands, Consumers, Symbols and Research*, Sage Publications, California.

16 Quoirin, M (January 2006) Marketing in the Information Economies of Europe, nVision.

17 Sherrington, M (2003) *Added Value: The alchemy of brand-led growth*, Palgrave Macmillan.

18 Naughton, J (March 2006) The age of permanent net revolution, *The Observer*

19 Morgan, A (2004) *The Pirate Inside: Building a challenger brand culture within yourself and your organization*, John Wiley & Sons.

20 Keating, M (January 2006) Marketing music on the web, *The Guardian.*

21 Hopkins, H (November 2005) Arctic Monkeys: Viral Marketing Success, *Hitwise UK* [Online] www.hostmybb.com/phpbb/viewtopic.php?mforum=arctic&p=85281

22 Collin, W (2003) How better media strategy leads to greater business success, in *AdValue: Twenty ways advertising works for business*, ed L Butterfield, pp141–56, Butterworth-Heinemann.

23 Hayer, S (February 2005) Keynote speech at *Advertising Age Madison & Vine conference*, California [Online] http://adage.com/article/news/steve-heyer-s-manifesto-a-age-marketing/36777/

24 Grant, J (2000) *The New Marketing Manifesto: The 12 rules for building successful brands in the 21st century*, Texere Publishing.

25 Schacter, D (1997) *Searching for Memory: The brain, the mind, and the past*, Basic Books, New York.

26 Shaw, R and Merrick, D (2005) *Marketing Payback: Is your marketing profitable?*, Financial Times/Prentice Hall.

27 Gobe, M (2002) *Citizen Brands: 10 commandments for transforming brands in a consumer democracy*, Allworth Press, New York.

28 Raymond, M (2003) *The Tomorrow People: Future consumers and how to read them today*, Financial Times/Prentice Hall.

29 Carson, J (October 2005) Word-of-mouth marketing: A new mandate? *Admap*, Issue 465.

30 Vonk, N (February 2006) A blogger's guide to blogging, *Campaign* [Online] www.campaignlive.co.uk/news/541823/bloggers-guide-blogging

31 Mackay, J (February 2006) The world's leading independent agencies, *Campaign* [Online] www.campaignlive.co.uk/news/541860/Worlds-Leading-Independent-Agencies-Belgiovane-Williams-Mackay/

32 Shaw, R and Merrick, D (2005) *Marketing Payback: Is your marketing profitable?*, Financial Times/Prentice Hall.

33 Tim Ambler quoted in: Shaw, Prof R and Merrick, D (2005) *Marketing Payback: Is your marketing profitable?*, Financial Times/Prentice Hall, Harlow.

34 Ambler, T and Broadbent, S (July 2000) A dialogue on advertising effectiveness and efficiency, *Admap*.

35 Broadbent, T quoted in (2007) *Evaluation: A best practice guide to evaluating the effects of your campaigns*, IPA.

36 Mildenhall, J (2006) Module 6 training centre, *IPA Excellence Diploma*.

37 Rainey, M T (December 1997) In the wrong business, or getting the business wrong?, *Admap*.

38 Stengel, J (2003) *Consumers are reinventing marketing – will you be in touch or left behind?* Presentation given at World Federation of Advertisers Conference, Brussels.

I believe we must manage brand ideas from the bottom up
2005/06

18

TOM ROACH

Strategy Director and Partner, BBH London

I believe Technological developments will mean that in the future, one-way, mass communications designed to interrupt consumers will cease to be effective. The best brand ideas will have to be effective memes. And the most effective, long-lasting and well-adapted memes will emerge from the bottom up: the control model will be replaced with the bottom-up model.

Editor's therefore, for your brand...

Your brand thinking:
What memes surround your market? Who are your brand's creative consumers? Do you have a process to harvest their creativity?

Your brand engagement:
How much of your work is created with the built-in capability to be copied and go viral?

Your brand organization & capability:
Do you develop work in 'collaboration' with your audience (or simply test them)?

...and author's personal therefore

When Nick told us our essays were to be published and asked us to contribute something to this book about them, my feelings were complicated. Yes, there was some pride, but there was also a good slug of embarrassment about my youthful meanderings once again being exposed to the world.

But in re-reading it for the first time since 2006 in preparation for writing this, I've decided to put aside any embarrassment. To focus on the more original bits, to explore which of my predictions have come true since I wrote it, to build on what it can teach us about the future.

My essay was founded on the following belief: 'I believe the future needs a new breed of communications idea: one that evolves from the bottom up rather than being imposed on consumers from the top down.' It explored the theory of memes and memetics, and how we in the marketing communications world could exploit the principles behind them to develop better brand and communications ideas. It envisioned a future where marketers would fully co-opt consumers into the creation of ideas, using them in the evolution of new, stronger communications ideas, better suited to long-term survival in the digital world.

If you're thinking memes are old-hat now, you might be right. In fact, memes have become a permanent feature of mainstream internet culture since I wrote my piece (see the Google Trends chart, Figure 18.1, above) below showing the exponential increase in searches for the term 'memes' which kicked off around 2011).

In late 2005 to early 2006, many of the platforms that have since allowed memes to go mainstream weren't available to us: YouTube wasn't quite a year old, Facebook was only available to students at a handful of UK universities, the arrival of Twitter was a few months away, and the iPhone hadn't yet launched.

FIGURE 18.1

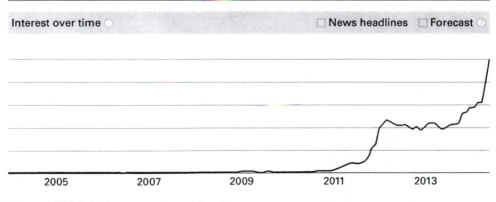

| Interest over time ⓘ | ☐ News headlines ☐ Forecast ⓘ |

| 2005 | 2007 | 2009 | 2011 | 2013 |

[Accessed 2014, Online] **www.google.co.uk/trends**

But in comparison to the somewhat limited role memes play in marketing today, my grand vision for the role they might play in the future turned out to be rather idealistic.

This is partly semantic: the word meme itself has come to be very narrowly used, and for most people means nothing more than the funny little videos, animated gifs and images overlaid with text found on meme-specific sites and shared on social networks, often intended as humorous commentaries on events in popular culture.

And, while my piece imagined a future world where marketers would employ the services of communities of creative consumers to build and shape brands over the longer term using memes, the truth of how marketers actually now use memes is pretty lightweight, and mostly limited to jumping on the bandwagon of the latest internet meme to help their brand ride the zeitgeist.

The use of user-generated content in marketing has become extremely widespread, and UGC is now a well-established part of the modern communications landscape. There have been some notable successes – Sainsbury's 'Christmas in a Day', the long-running Doritos UGC campaigns, and Burberry's 'Art of the Trench' to name just a few.

But it's hard to see yet another hashtag campaign, selfie competition or film featuring a singing cat (purpose-built to prompt people to make their own parodies) as much more than just yet another slightly lazy deployment of the latest faddy marketing tactic.

Comparing how I imagined we'd engage our consumers' creativity to how it's turned out in reality, I can't help thinking user-generated content campaigns tend towards the superficial. There just don't seem to be many marketers using consumers to help build their brands in the longer term.

I suspect the truth is that my essay probably overestimated consumers' desire to get involved in creating brand communications, but underestimated their desire to get far more deeply involved in businesses in other, perhaps more influential, ways.

Consumers, it turns out, are up for a limited amount of co-creation when it comes to communications, but are seriously keen to help brands out in a range of other ways – some of which go well beyond marketing.

For example, the Lego brand has been reinvented as a content brand in recent years, partly through its astonishingly active community of amateur film-makers, many of whose films have received millions of views in their own right. The T-shirt designs of fashion brand Threadless are all user-generated, with 1,374 designers having submitted over 250,000 T-shirt designs since its inception. Fan Fiction has become a fundamental component of a range of media and entertainment brands and properties – from *Harry Potter* to *Star Wars* to *50 Shades of Grey*.

Consumers have also developed a taste for helping fund other people's ideas via crowd-funding platforms. Some even want to actively help run companies on an ongoing basis – for example, the UK mobile network Giff Gaff ('the mobile network run by you') whose customer service is facilitated by consumers, leading to it having one of the highest Net Promoter Scores of any company anywhere.

So, while my original belief and the essay founded on it wasn't exactly laden with chillingly prescient predictions of how the relationship between brands, consumers and marketing would evolve – on re-reading it a few years on, it turns out it wasn't entirely inaccurate either.

And therefore?

My work: none of us is as good as all of us

This is probably the most fundamental basic principle underpinning my Diploma essay – great work is the result of collaboration not lone genius. It's a principle that's true of all the work I'm most proud of. Simple and obvious, but easy to forget.

My career: careers are stories written in chapters

The year I spent doing the IPA Excellence Diploma, and the months spent writing my final essay, were a distinct and major chapter in my career. Writing the essay directly helped prepare me for future chapters – specifically the next one, which was defined by my writing of IPA Effectiveness Awards cases.

My life: career is wonderful, but you can't curl up with it on a cold night

In the time since the course I have got married, and now have two wonderful sons. No diplomas or awards can compare to them.

I believe we must manage brand ideas from the bottom up

In 1859, Charles Darwin single-handedly had The Greatest Idea in the World Ever™. The theory of natural selection instantly imposed from above an entirely new way of thinking on everyone below.

Well, no he didn't actually. Darwin's ideas built on the work of many others before him and, far from instantly causing a paradigm shift in scientific thought, his big idea competed with other ideas from many other thinkers, and needed to be improved upon by several generations of others in order to survive as the fittest idea in a fiercely fought struggle.

In our business, we tend to believe in the power of the individual creative genius and the primacy of originality in the creation of these ideas. We try to impose these ideas on consumers from the top-down through a communications model based on interrupting consumers with one-way communications.

But the world is changing, from a place where we have total control over how our ideas are delivered, received and interpreted, to a world where advances in technology mean consumers have total control over our ideas and can simply ignore anything imposed on them from above. So, we need to develop a better understanding of how ideas work in this environment and adapt a new breed of ideas to suit. Then, and only then, can we generate ideas that can be unleashed on the world and set free to create the impact we need them to have.

In this paper I borrow from the principles of evolution to set out a new model for communications ideas, the 'meme', that involves consumers in idea evolution. A new way of thinking that would result in communications ideas that evolve and improve from the bottom-up.

It's time we stopped trying to control consumers from the top down

My agency was responsible for creating the idea 'Make Poverty History'. It started life as an endline on some outdoor advertising, but its true power was only really unleashed once people took it on as their own and it entered the chaotic and unpredictable world outside of controlled, paid-for communication – once it started appearing on people's wrists, in speeches by Nelson Mandela, and in print everywhere, from newspaper headlines to church notice boards.

We need to think harder about how to create ideas that have this potential, work out how best to facilitate people's engagement with them, and make it easy for them to be passed on.

The traditional advertising model of attempting to control what people think by interrupting them with one-way communications is looking extremely out dated. People's time and attention is an increasingly precious commodity – and one that they're getting more protective of. Our response to this has largely been to push ever more attention-grabbing mass communications on mass audiences. Unfortunately, as Seth Godin has pointed out, 'the cost to the consumer of wasting their time on irrelevant interruption advertising is too high.'[1] In this context, the fact that 'to deal with the clutter and the diminished effectiveness of Interruption Marketing, we're interrupting them even more'[2] is beginning to look rather absurd. The facts of ad avoidance are also well-established: people are increasingly taking measures to avoid our top-down communications.

The end of the control model means we need a new breed of communications idea

This new world is a difficult and quite scary place for most marketers, who tend to only want to think about managed communications – the things they can control.

And control is exactly what brand management has traditionally been about. But when you admit that the stuff we can control, the paid-for advertising, pales into insignificance next to all the other factors (Mark Earls quotes a study that suggests word of mouth already accounts for 80 per cent of the influence on an individual's purchasing behaviour)[3], the 'control model' begins to look rather inadequate. Wendy Gordon writes that 'the brand-centric control model is anachronistic...Yes, the brand is responsible for sending out cues. But ordinary people are responsible for creating meaning, choosing whether or not to engage with the brand'.[4] The great thing about embracing this is that it allows us to take advantage of a world of unpredictable and powerful forces beyond our control – where much more powerful forces like word of mouth and other viral communications hold the key to success. As communications professionals, we need to stop thinking only about the messages we can control and think about the enormous rewards of creating ideas that we can't.

Memes – a new breed of communications idea

Richard Dawkins coined the term 'meme' in his 1976 book *The Selfish Gene*, to describe the cultural equivalent of the gene. He defined it as a 'unit of cultural transmission'.[5]

A number of other academics subsequently took up the challenge of turning memetics into a fully fledged branch of science. Aaron Lynch defines them as 'self-propagating ideas',[6] while the psychologist Susan Blackmore defines them as 'instructions for carrying out behaviour, stored in brains (or other objects) and passed on by imitation'[7].

Central to an individual meme's success is its ability to self-replicate, often a process of manipulating its hosts' communication and imitation skills. Blackmore believes that humans make great meme machines because we have evolved powers of imitation unparalleled in the natural world, writing that 'unlike any other animals we readily imitate almost everything and anything and seem to take pleasure in doing so'.[8] We love copying things we've seen and heard and we're hard-wired to do so.

Richard Dawkins listed three very simple characteristics of any successful replicator, and these would apply to genes, memes, or indeed any other thing with the ability to self-replicate:[9]

- Fidelity: the more faithful the copy, the more will remain of the initial pattern.
- Fecundity: the faster the rate of copying the more the replicator will spread.
- Longevity: the longer any instance of the replicating pattern survives the more copies can be made of it.

Memetics provides us with an intellectual framework to help us think about how human culture and ideas are passed on and evolve, using Darwin's 'Big Idea' about natural selection as its basis. At their simplest, the principles of memetics are that good ideas get themselves replicated and survive in the long term, while bad ideas don't and die out.

The Nike 'Just do it' meme is an excellent example that forces its own replication by being such an appealing belief. It encourages people to replicate it by wearing sports clothes emblazoned with it (and latterly by its shorthand, the 'swoosh'), as well as living by it. Running the Nike 10K is essentially 'just doing it', a highly visible re-enactment of the idea.

Powerful memes are like MRSA super-bugs compared to the average 'viral'

Richard Dawkins famously believes world religions to be the result of memes. Individual religions tend to have a network of memes working in harmony to further their own existence, resulting in powerful beliefs capable of self-replicating over millennia. Two examples from Christianity are the heaven meme that inspires Christians to do good works, working in perfect unison with the hell meme that inspires them to try and save others from eternal damnation by spreading 'the word', and therefore spreading the meme.

A theory that can help explain the evolution and survival of ideas as big and as seemingly permanent as these has got to be one that can help us create lasting ideas. We have got pretty good at creating fun, novel, ideas and content that will very quickly make its way around the internet virally, but we haven't yet thought enough about how we can use the new environment to create communications ideas which work for our brands in the longer term, and which have the power to create powerful long-term positionings.

Partly, this is because there is a contemporary obsession with 'faster/ cheaper', of which every marketer's current flirtation with buzz is symptomatic. We need deep ideas, ideas that are 'longer/better', that can penetrate and be internalized. As Stephen Downes, a commentator on new media has written: 'mere transference is not sufficient, for an idea to take hold in another person it must be internalized.'[10]

We need to think of ourselves as being an industry that can genuinely work at the level of culture rather than the level of fashion. We need to create ideas that can have a cultural legacy as lasting as those created by scientists, novelists and artists. Our ads and ideas can genuinely be cultural artefacts. This is not a new idea – every time a Guinness ad is in development the team involved are absolutely aware of the weight of history behind it, but I suspect this is a rare case, and is more about the weight of expectation rather than a desire to leave 'good memes' for future generations of Guinness creatives to play with.

So how are memes created?

Kate Distin, author of *The Selfish Meme*, believes that innovation in memes is due to two factors, recombination and mutation: 'in recombination, existing memes are appropriately recombined in new situations creating new ways of thought and novel effects.'[11] Mutation is the other, far more random way that new memes can be generated. They are created by combining two or more old ones, or by applying random mutations to existing memes. Unfortunately, as in nature, random mutation can lead to pitiful creatures ill-adapted to their environment.

Great memes are evolutions of existing memes

Applying theories of re-combination and mutation to our business would lead you to favour re-combination over mutation every time as the strategy most likely to result in effective and long-lasting creative ideas. Our industry prides itself on utter originality – but meme theory would suggest that combining pre-existing ideas leads to a far higher success rate, whilst an obsession with novelty and originality is both unrealistic and likely to result in a far higher number of mutations, and therefore failures. Kate Distin illustrates this point with the example of adding salt to a chocolate brownie: a random mutation that in no way adds to the survival rate of the new recipe.[12] An example of a highly successful re-combination of existing ideas from advertising would be the Guinness 'Extra Cold' campaign. Taking well-loved Guinness ads, such as 'Surfer', and building in the additional idea of coldness created successful, new ideas out of an idea that had already been selected by its audience, supporting Kate Distin's assertion that 'in order to be accepted, an idea usually has to be compatible with those already in existence'.[13]

We need to end the myth of the creative genius and begin to accept ideas from anywhere

Memetics suggest that the true creative genius is not necessary for the creation of great ideas. I believe we need to end the myth of the creative genius and learn to embrace other people's ideas with relish. It may be more noble to adopt Herman Melville's dictum that 'it is better to succeed in originality than to fail in imitation', but it doesn't necessarily make sense from the point of view of meme theory.

The truth is that what we term creativity isn't really about creating 100 per cent new ideas, so much as having brains that are able to re-combine existing ones into novel forms. The more ideas a creative has access to, the larger the meme pool and the more likely it is that they will be able to generate long-lasting ideas for our brands. Nothing new here you may think, but extending the accessible meme pool available could lead us to an entirely different agency model.

For the discipline of planning, given the current trend for reductionism, this would suggest there's a need for a counter revolution and a serious need for planners to create a quantity as well as a quality of ideas. Evolutionary principles suggest variety to be a good thing that allows quicker evolution of a well-adapted solution.

Abandoning the concept of the creative genius would also mean we should accept ideas from anywhere, and could mean abandoning small, elite creative departments altogether.

The best ideas emerge from the bottom up

The author Stephen Johnson believes 'emergent intelligence' is the way idea revolutions take place, and that emergence, or change that occurs from the bottom up, will increasingly hold sway in an increasingly complex, networked world.[14]

Emergence, according to Johnson, is the phenomenon which explains how complex systems such as ant colonies, internet communities and cities appear to behave as single organisms, despite having no central, top-down controlling force.

The analogy to which Johnson repeatedly returns is that of ant colonies that, he says, 'display some of nature's most mesmerising de-centralised behavior: intelligence, personality and learning that emerges from the bottom up'.[15] He goes on to write about developments in artificial intelligence, which started with early computer scientists trying to write software to teach computers how to think, and resulted in them recognizing that evolution could create far more intelligent software if you create a huge pool of relatively stupid, but competing programs, which are programmed to replicate and mutate in order for them to evolve artificial intelligence from the bottom up.

Johnson would recognize bottom-up principles in the increasingly common idea of getting consumers to 'co-create' our brands and ideas, and would certainly recognize them in the following excerpt from a recent *Campaign* article by Russell Davies:

> It's obvious that in the modern world ideas aren't really had by lone geniuses. They don't come from a clever planner in an ivory tower or a genius creative team in a black box. The modern brand world is too complex for that. Ideas are turning up through teamwork, conversation and iteration. And that team includes the client, agency people, other partners and all sorts of random people like consumers.[16]

Naresh Ramchandani is a creative with a seriously good grasp of how technological developments are changing the way consumers interact with content. Writing in *The Guardian* he points out the difference between the shift in consumer media behaviour from passive TV consumption to active internet participation: 'On the internet, I can seek out content, consume content, consume related content, add to content, rate content, subvert content or create content of my own. Think of it like this: TV equals inactivity, but the internet equals interactivity.'[17] He sees a future where we allow consumers to edit and improve on our ideas through the use of interactive media, and envisages a world where, again, bottom-up principles appear to be at work: 'What about a poster campaign that is re-shot and re-posted three times over three weeks, each time modified by the calls or emails from people who have seen it?'[18]

The beginnings of a bottom-up revolution are also already clearly evident for all to see in terms of the generation of entertainment content. Current TV is an online TV channel, 30 per cent of whose content is currently 'viewer-created'; Google video and YouTube have also both recently emerged as seriously interesting developments in terms of video content.

I believe it's only a matter of time before it's the norm for brand communications to be developed this way too.

We live in the age of the creative consumer

John Kao has written that we live in a creative age, the age of the creative consumer.[19] Thanks to companies like Apple taking the lead in bringing creative tools to the mainstream, people increasingly have the technology to allow an outlet for their natural creativity. Anyone who has the slightest urge to share their creativity with the world can now do so in an instant, whether through the written word, through music, video, photography, illustration or animation.

Consumers have long since shown the desire to use whatever technology they can to spontaneously generate their own versions of internet jokes, movies and virals – all effective memes – in the desire to make versions that are even better at replicating themselves than the originals. We all remember the endless variations of the 'Dancing Baby' from Ally McBeal, the 'Dancing Hamsters', or the spoof 'I Kiss You' websites that appeared within days of the originals spreading around the internet. This desire and ability to imitate and refresh ideas will be what we need to exploit in the creation of bottom-up ideas in the future.

The blogger Hugh MacLeod, recently suggested that brands will increasingly become involved in 'meme endorsement' – marketing people scouring the net for appropriate memes like the above that they want to put their brand's name to. This may well happen, but it does feel like a rather shallow attempt to pay lip-service to the idea of 'co-creation': I believe the real future for brands lies in pure bottom-up brand ideas which are created for the brand rather than just badged by it.

In fact 'co-creation' is really just a kind of half-way house between the current top-down communications model and the new world of bottom-up brand communications creation. It may be a leap into the unknown, but it's not impossible to imagine a world in which brand communications are created by consumers and emerge from the bottom up just as purely as content is now doing.

But why would consumers help generate ideas for a commercial enterprise like a brand?

Howard Rheingold (an authority on the social and cultural implications of technology) writes insightfully on what happens when people are hooked up to everyone else through peer-to-peer networks. One effect is that they'll happily get involved in all sorts of peer-to-peer computing and networked experiments with no commercial incentive: 3 million people currently devote their computing power to SETI (the Search for Extra Terrestrial Intelligence); 200,000 have just signed up in the United Kingdom to help the BBC work out the effects of climate change; countless others globally are currently involved with similar networked research experiments – seemingly just for the thrill of being involved and participating in a cause. 'A great deal of peer-to-peer technology was created for fun – the same reason why the PC and the web first emerged from communities of amateur enthusiasts… venture capitalists would never have paid attention to the web in the first place if a million people hadn't created web pages because it was a cool thing to do.'[20]

Rheingold also sheds light on the connection between hacking and a more creative act such as making amendments to a piece of open-source software like Linux: 'It's the same old hacker intoxication of getting a buzz from giving tools away and then coming back to find that someone else has made the tool even more useful.'[21]

This feeling is what the anthropologist Robert Wright calls 'non-zero-sumness', which he defines as 'the unique human power and pleasure that comes from doing something that enriches everyone, a game where nobody has to lose for everyone to win'.[22] To me this sounds like a modern definition of an age-old human urge: to *create*.

The future: anthills of creative consumers evolving brand memes?

So, the conditions seem to be set for brand owners to take advantage of consumers by co-opting them into the creation of their brand communications. Consumers increasingly have the means (via technology) to help us generate our brands' ideas, and they have the motivations to start creating ideas. All it will take is for brand owners and agencies to begin to take advantage of the situation.

Given the right brand, one that consumers feel is a worthy enough cause, is cool enough, fun enough, or that they believe in enough, consumers won't take much persuading to get involved. Brands not in this position may have to kick-start the process by bribing consumers. However, paying creative consumers small amounts to contribute communications ideas may be a small price to pay for the added benefits that generating ideas from a wider meme pool might bring.

The brand owners would play the part of 'God' in the process – setting up the memetic algorithm and stepping back to let increasingly better adapted memes evolve from the bottom up. The principles of emergence suggest that it may be enough for the brand leader to simply set the stage by establishing a few simple evolutionary ground rules (in the form of a basic brand idea, or maybe some other memetic material for the meme pool such as historical communications ideas). Then, having recruited enough creative consumers to create enough variety in the meme pool, they will begin, like worker ants in one of Steve Johnson's ant colonies, re-combining, mutating, *evolving*, brand memes from the bottom up.

So how will memes be transmitted?

The standard model adopted by marketers to think about the transmission of ideas has become the 'Two Step Flow' model, which in itself was something of an evolution of the previous 'Magic Bullet' model, where communications were simply fired into consumers' brains and were assumed to have an impact[23] (Figure 18.2). In the 'Two Step Flow' model, marketers seed ideas with small groups of consumers who they know to be exceptionally good transmitters of ideas (and tend to be called different things by different

FIGURE 18.2 'Magic bullet' model vs 'two step flow' model

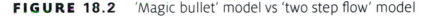

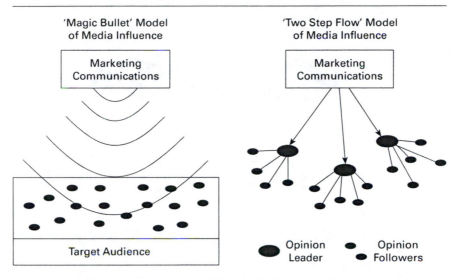

Marsden, P and Kirby, J (2005) *Connected Marketing: The viral, buzz and word of mouth revolution,* Butterworth-Heinemann, Oxford (page 8)

commentators – such as connectors, transmitters, sneezers, etc) in order to spread them, virus-like, to the broader population.

The 'bottom-up model' I've created (Figure 18.3) builds on the 'two step flow' model but focuses on ideas, not consumers, and builds in the evolution of the idea (rather than assuming the idea to be fixed) which is the key driver of the idea's flow from niche to mainstream.

So what would the agency of the future's role be in all this?

Clearly in this kind of world, where brand ideas are being generated from the bottom up by consumers who are part of the process, advertising agencies would have to play a different role from today. Having given up the responsibility of generating communications ideas we would need to find other ways to make money from our clients.

- Brand god: setting the basic rules for the brand that help guide the evolution of memes in the right direction for the brand owners' business objectives.
- Product design could become a key role: great brands will still need to start with a great product (although in time emergence could occur here too).
- Meme production facility: for any brand memes that have been generated conceptually but which still need to be executed in-house.

FIGURE 18.3   The 'bottom-up' model of memetic evolution and flow

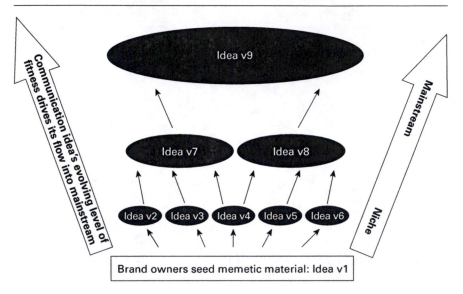

- Meme therapy: adapting memes that have been generated for one audience, but that have not been able to flow to another audience. This could be as a result of cultural barriers such as differences in language (analogous to when Hollywood re-makes foreign language films), or aesthetic ones (such as when Hollywood re-makes an indie film for a mainstream audience).

In conclusion

Technological developments will mean that in the future, one-way, mass communications designed to interrupt consumers will cease to be effective. We will therefore need to evolve a new breed of communications idea with the ability to cope with this new environment – a type of idea that can travel far from its original source without additional help from the brand owner. And where better to look than to evolution for clues about how to evolve something new?

Memes provide us with the perfect model for this new breed of idea: not only do their powers of self-replication give them the ability to leap 'from brain to brain',[24] but their ability to re-combine and mutate could also give them the power to evolve and improve as they do so – consumers will build on them, adapt them, play with them and pass them around without any additional help.

And if we are to look for alternatives to the top-down communications model, why not take the idea of 'co-creation' of brands and brand ideas by consumers to the next level and get them to create and transmit ideas from the bottom up? In this way the future creation of brand memes could lie in the co-option of creative consumers as the generators of our brand ideas, who will compete to evolve more and more effective memes which will spread from them and into the mainstream.

The best brand ideas will have to be effective memes. And the most effective, long-lasting and well-adapted memes will emerge from the bottom up: the control model will be replaced with the bottom-up model.

Notes

1 Godin, S (1999) *Permission Marketing: Turning strangers into friends, and friends into customers*, Simon & Schuster.

2 *ibid.*

3 Earls, M (2003) Advertising to the herd, *International Journal of Market Research*, 45 Quarter 3, Market Research Society.

4 Gordon, W (2002) 'Brands on the Brain' in ed M Baskin and M Earls, *Brand New Brand Thinking*, Kogan Page, London.

5 Dawkins, R (1976) *The Selfish Gene*, Oxford University Press.

6 Lynch, A (1996) *Thought Contagion: How belief spreads through society*, Basic Books, New York.

7 Blackmore, S (1999) *The Meme Machine*, Oxford University Press.

8 *ibid.*

9 Dawkins, R (1976) *The Selfish Gene*, Oxford University Press, Oxford.

10 Downes, S (October 1999) Hacking Memes, *First Monday*, 4 (10).

11 Distin, K (2005) *The Selfish Meme*, Cambridge University Press.

12 *ibid.*

13 *ibid.*

14 Johnson, S (2001) *Emergence: The connected lives of ants, brains, cities and software*, Allen Lane The Penguin Press.

15 *ibid.*

16 Davies, R (September 2005) Speech at UK Planning Awards.

17 Ramchandani, N (March 2006) Interactive marketing beats putting lipstick on a pig, *The Guardian*.

18 *ibid.*

19 Kao, J (1997) *Jammin: The Art & Discipline of Business Creativity*, HarperCollins Business, New York.

20 Rheingold, H (2002) *Smart Mobs: The next social generation*, Basic Books, Cambridge MA.

21 *ibid.*

22 Wright, R (2000) *Nonzero: The logic of human destiny*, Vintage.

23 Marsden, P and Kirby, J (2005) *Connected Marketing: The viral, buzz and word of mouth revolution*, Butterworth-Heinemann.

24 Dawkins, R (1989) *The Selfish Gene*, Second edition, Oxford University Press.

I believe it's time for a new system for leading beliefs

2011/12

19

ROSS FARQUHAR
Partner, 101

I believe Marketers need to improve the results of what we do and form a better contract with society. Change will require a positive alternative advocated by The Unit, an industry practice institute. This paper outlines 10 touchstones of this new movement and how the institute would work.

Editor's therefore, for your brand...

Your brand thinking:
What principles of brand building are you consciously or unconsciously acting on? Does everyone know and agree on them? How much are 'old woman's tales' dominant vs new learning?

Your brand engagement:
What percentage of your budget is focused on doing new things based on new learning?

Your brand organization & capability:
What is your system for creating or injecting new learning and new thinking into the team? Do you have a Brand School or Brand Training?

...and author's personal therefore

Two years on from writing a piece calling for a new system for leading beliefs, a rather more significant debate on the way we organize ourselves has reached a major milestone. Back in my native Scotland, people have contemplated whether they're better off as a part of the United Kingdom, or set apart from it. I take comfort from the fact it took 47 years from the Scottish National Party winning its first parliamentary seat to this monumental change in national discourse being realized, as by comparison two years isn't a very long time at all.

I originally believed that a rallying cry might lead to the establishment of an industry-wide body in pursuit of marketing best practice, bridging academia and action. It would be the physical manifestation of my belief, the very public 'and therefore' that stemmed from a kind of 'marketing progressivism'. I now understand that such a degree of change, not to mention finding a building with affordable rents in which to house it, is going to take a little longer. So I'm going to start bottom up instead.

Or as Gandhi says: 'If we could change ourselves, the tendencies in the world would also change. As a man changes his own nature, so does the attitude of the world change towards him... We need not wait to see what others do.'[1] And Gandhi can't be wrong. Hopefully it won't take 47 years. I'd best get going.

The three ways in which I'll be my own little marketing progressive all stem from the three themes I now recognize in my original essay.

My work: with collaboration comes credibility

I strongly believe that our industry needs to come together to find a consensus around best practice, because it's only when the various stakeholder groups agree on a new system of leading beliefs that we will start to have greater credibility in the eyes of those holding the purse strings (be they CFOs or CEOs).

Although I am yet to realize my dream, I've become even more evangelical about the principle that underpins it. So perhaps by being an evangelical collaborator in my work, I'll encourage our industry to adopt the same behaviour.

I'm lucky enough to have enjoyed the benefits of 'team' in the last two years. I've been part of the one that, over the course of 18 months, developed a struggling liqueur concept into Diageo's biggest ever launch in Western Europe. I've also played a role in successfully re-launching one of financial services' most iconic brand icons, the Scottish Widow, in 18 weeks. Neither would have succeeded had they not been influenced by a variety of great clients, great agencies and great researchers.

And yet our industry conspires against this kind of teamwork. Clients slice and dice their agency arrangements against executional imperatives rather than seeking out meaningful partnership. Agencies too often behave like scope defenders and turf marauders all at once. Researchers increasingly attempt to occupy the murky waters of 'brand consultancy'. These are not the conditions from which a higher order of collaboration and consensus will emerge.

I believe that none of us are as good as all of us, and until we work better together we have little chance of appearing credible. Therefore, my mini ministry will start at the start – investing more time in collaboration upfront, contracting on the brand we want to build and the idea we need to do it.

My career: be better informed

My starter-for-ten 'manifesto for heretics' expresses my hunger for us all to be better informed. To take advantage of all the knowledge we now have access to, to not accept common sense as the best way, and to forge better work out the back of it.

I've felt the benefits of that in my career, and I now believe it's the key to enhancing the fortunes of the industry at large.

When I first started the IPA Excellence Diploma, I was a client. It was only halfway through that I made the jump to a small start-up agency, run by some incredible people with equally incredible pedigrees in demonstrating the power of creativity. Now that small start-up agency has become bigger and stronger, I can see how our ever-growing band of heretics strengthens the cause overall.

I can encourage others to start with context, or to treat the audience as people not consumers. I can suggest we side-step the rationality vs emotion debate given the truth involves both, or that we think more deeply about whether more people, or more often, is a better path to brand growth. I can demand we measure *whether* something worked through business effects, judging effectiveness in a more balanced way.

I believe that we're *all* better off when we're *all* better informed, and the imperative is for us to spread the heretic's manifesto far and wide. Therefore, my mini ministry will be on a constant recruitment drive, doors always open for those who want to join me in learning more.

My life: offer a positive alternative

> Any fool can criticize, condemn and complain and most fools do.
>
> (Benjamin Franklin, 2014[2])

It's too easy to destroy, more challenging to construct.

My final theme is possibly the most important 'and therefore' that I've taken from the experience of writing my final piece. It was only in investigating and researching the characteristics of heresy, and understanding how paradigms are shifted, that I came to realize that nothing changes when all you offer is a rejection of the status quo, or single-issue criticism. Pulling things apart piece by piece is unlikely to be fruitful.

If there's one thing I've been able to apply in my life more broadly, it's more often trying to offer a positive rather than a negative judgement. Perhaps we'd be better off as an industry if we suggested 'what if...?' more frequently than we attempted to tear down.

I believe we'll never see change through complaint and condemnation – we should be the apostles of a positive alternative. Therefore, in my mini ministry I will make being constructive a condition of any team I work on, or any life endeavour I undertake.

I believe it's time for a new system for leading beliefs

This paper argues that marketing practice is ruled by a misleading *common sense orthodoxy*, and there's a burning need to improve the results of what we do and form a better contract with wider society. That change will require heresy, a positive and total alternative (Marketing Progressivism) advocated by a single voice (The Unit: The Marketing Industry's Thinking and Practice Institute). It outlines the 10 Touchstones of this new, progressive movement, and how the institution itself would function.

Introduction

We've all experienced the slightly awkward moment where we're told what we do is 'just common sense, though, isn't it?' Awkward, perhaps, because it's not without an iota of truth – vast swathes of our practice appears to conform to certain intuitive rules:

- Advertising exists to increase sales.
- Advertising works by communicating messages about products/services.
- To be effective, you must get people to sit up and take notice.
- Differentiation at a product level (leading to a USP) is critical.
- Etc.

These rules have remained in place despite significant headwinds for the output they produce – accusations ranging from ineffectiveness to subversion and manipulation, and pertinently varied and plentiful evidence from academics and practitioners that they are *fundamentally flawed or misleading* (for example, Binet[3] and Sharp[4]).

The doctrine remains in place for two reasons: because innovators in academia and practice have concentrated their efforts on *disproving* its principles (being characterized by what they don't believe, rather than what they do); and because the approach to date has been *piecemeal* (attacking individual strands instead of the whole).

Thus, the last thing we need is another paper that demonstrates why the orthodoxy is wrong. We need a new belief system, a total (viable) alternative projected through a new system of leadership. *We need heresy.*

I believe that the future of brands requires heresy – it's time for a new system for leading beliefs.

The problem with common sense

Common sense marketing has been the de facto guiding light for decades. Its assumptions underpin both what we make and how we measure it, creating a self-supporting industry.

These intuitive assumptions have several consequences:

- The orthodoxy becomes a *rule-based comfort blanket* that drives behaviour – we allow our common sense to rule our decision making, rather than learning from the past and making a reasoned judgement.
- The orthodoxy becomes *self-reinforcing* – it drives objective setting, which drives measurement, which drives the work produced (a circular production line, regardless of genuine performance).
- The orthodoxy becomes *dogma* – so established and ingrained that, despite not having a figurehead or institution, it is almost impossible to dislodge.

Why is there a need for a better option?

The ineffectiveness of what we do

Half my advertising works, I just don't know which half. Actually, it's closer to 1% of your advertising that works, at the most. Your billboard reaches 100,000 people and if you're lucky, it gets you a hundred customers... (Seth Godin)[5]

While UK adspend continues to rise,[6] so does the investment in research.[7] We suffer from an unbearable tension between insecurity over effectiveness, and rising stakes in having to spend more to achieve our goals.

Worse still, the research we are increasingly investing in appears not to mitigate the risk. Godin concludes pre-testing is 'not an objective, predictive measure of the effectiveness of the advertising' (given the myriad of biases introduced), results corroborated quantitatively by analysis of the IPA Databank.[8]

We're caught in a vicious cycle. To articulate what we do (particularly to those who hold the purse strings), we reduce our discipline down to common sense rules and pre-test by them. This results in below-par real performance and increased pressure on the next round of investment.

A destabilising public contract

> Advertising, [this report] suggests, harms society and the planet by increasing consumerism, manipulating cultural values and intruding into all aspects of our lives. (Caroline Lucas, Leader of the Green Party of England and Wales[9])

Advertising's uneasy relationship with wider society has simmered for decades – see *The Hidden Persuaders*[10] through to *No Logo*,[11] and more recently 2011's 'Think of me as evil?'[12]

A new orthodoxy alone is not likely to resolve the question of brands' and advertising's wider role within society, but it *would* contribute to resolving the increasing theme of mistrust – the common sense model is akin to our industry saying it's doing one thing (behaving with rationality and reason in the stimulus we create) while doing a variety of others. A new system needs to create better transparency.

In conclusion, the need for a new orthodoxy relies on two drivers: the hunger from within our industry for something *more effective to work to*, and the hunger from wider society for *greater honesty and transparency*.

The time for heresy

Why does this sub-optimal orthodoxy (fuelled by common sense) survive, and what will it take to dislodge it?

Why have we failed thus far?

There are two facets of the problem that keep the common sense orthodoxy in place.

Atheism – a negative approach

The common sense orthodoxy, it could be argued, came to prominence by inductive reasoning (from observing individual cases and extrapolating their results to universal truths). To change this, we've behaved like proper scientists, and employed a deductive method of interrogation – subjected hypotheses to tests designed to *disprove* their robustness. The difficulty here is that 'non-belief' is rarely ever a majority opinion – no population in Europe is more than one third atheist.[13]

Crises without paradigm shift – a piecemeal approach

Several academics and practitioners have challenged individual component parts of the orthodoxy – see Heath and Feldwick,[14] Sharp[15] or Field and Binet.[16] Unfortunately, paradigms are not shifted by mere crises of accuracy.[17] Instead, they take a better alternative to come along and replace them.

Thus, we need to behave like heretics, because heresy is the only way to address these complaints:

- By definition it starts with an *opinion at odds with current dogma*.
- It is about *compelling people to follow you* as much as it is about 'being right'.
- It leads to paradigm shifts: 'Heresies bring paradigm shifts when they catalyse new ways of understanding old fields of knowledge. Galileo and Darwin belong to the select set of paradigm shifters, revolutionaries and heretics all.'[18]

Characteristics of heresy

Heresy often starts in the way our own has thus far: 'Beliefs are most clearly and systematically articulated when they are formed via negative.'[19]

It's now time to create a new dominant ideology through an active and coherent movement. To do so, Kurtz[20] suggests four characteristics that define a heresy.

Intense union of nearness and remoteness

What separates a heretic from an infidel is that they sit *within the orthodoxy to start with* – they are close enough to be threatening, but distant enough to be discounted as being 'in error'.

Socially constructed

Heresy is socially divisive – it starts from a different place to the accepted wisdom, and asks followers to choose a side – but its proponents have the interests of the institution at heart.

Social consequences

Heresy has consequences for the distribution of power, causing new societal lines to be drawn. It is less about intellectual content and more about social outcomes.

Doctrinal consequences

Heresy is an emotive concept, and it makes it increasingly difficult to adopt a compromised position.

Our breed of heresy

In conclusion, we need a very specific breed of heresy that:

- Clearly *states a case* (a better alternative) built from within the current discipline.
- Works *in the interests of the industry* – progressive not abolitionist.
- Fills the *institution vacuum* and is pragmatic in setting parameters for how it will work, tackling the social context by demonstrating *clear leadership*.

- Has *doctrinal qualities* (a belief system to follow), but is characterized by a *flexible, evolutionary approach* as opposed to rigid rules.

The 10 touchstones of a new belief system

The essence of heresy is standing for something, albeit in opposition to current dogma. I believe this heretical movement should go by the name *marketing progressivism*.

1. Brands exist to speed up decision making

The first touchstone serves as a timely reminder of where brands came from. Feldwick[21] offers five functions that brands have historically served:

- a badge of origin/guarantee of authenticity;
- a promise of performance;
- the value of reassurance;
- differentiation or distinctiveness;
- transformation of experience.

Four out of the five functions he observes lead you to one conclusion – brands are there simply to *make our decisions easier*.

This may not sound like ground-breaking information, but given the common sense orthodoxy appears to be gravitating towards 'engagement', 'dialogue' and 'participation', it seems appropriate that we heretics should start with a timely reminder that *all* interventions a brand makes should be designed to create new associations or strengthen existing ones.

This also lends itself to a more acceptable contract with society – it is *helpful* rather than *manipulative*.

2. Start with context, not rules

This is not an appeal to abandon the notion of a framework for marketing decision making – rather, it's an appeal to start with robust situation analysis.

Duckworth[22] provides a useful analogy – if we think of a brand as a patient (whose health is multi-faceted), then as marketers we are the medical practitioners making interventions. Those interventions must be *specific* to the patient's circumstances and *directional* to improve their health – there is no 'one prescription fits all', a diagnosis must first be made.

So, contrary to the orthodoxy, we cannot blindly apply common sense rules of thumb to improve the health of our brands.

3. Treat people as people, not 'consumers'

The norm of approaching the public as 'consumers' is bordering on destructive, for the term has three negative implications:

- an *empty vessel*, waiting to be filled with whatever the brand owner wants;
- a *homogenous* group of people;
- a *primary purpose* of consumption.

Rather, to the suggestion of Gordon and Valentine,[23] we should see consumers not as a fixed point, but as a 'temporary, precarious point of identity, which is ever-changing, ambiguous and unpredictable'. Or in other words, we need to stop using proxies that imply people are *fixed* in order to target them, and start using common characteristics *when they consider buying us.*

4. Focus on creating, building and reinforcing memories (not messages)

The mystery that surrounds neuroscience means this may well be the touchstone that advances the most over the next decade.

What we do know is that the representation of a brand at a neuronal level is called a *brand engram* – the permanent change in the brain as a result of learning something.[24]

Accordingly, our relationship with brands cannot be linear in nature if brands are stored as multi-sensorial memories – like any other memory, our recall can be triggered as much by a smell, sight, taste or sound.

To prioritize 'message' above all else in our marketing communications closes us off to a world of ways in which we can create or strengthen associations in the brain.

In practice, we might therefore open ourselves up to a wider world of brand behaviour – and consider *how* we speak more than *what* we say.

5. Respect the role of both rationality and emotion, not either/or

It seems odd that our industry has divided on an issue like 'rationality vs emotion'. We heretics will take a more balanced view.

First, the evidence that rationality and emotion are profoundly (and neurologically) connected is overwhelming (for example, McGilchrist[25] and Franzen and Bouwman[26]).

Second, the notion that emotion and reason are in a winner-takes-all battle in the way marketing communications are processed is misplaced – while one may take a front seat depending on the media used (a logical conclusion from the work of Heath and Feldwick[27]), no action happens without a degree of both.

So our heresy adopts the position that the better question is – which sits in the front seat in any given circumstance? And to answer that question, the better determinant might be the proximity of the stimulus to the desired behaviour change.

6. Find our connections, not just our (individual) motivations

The orthodoxy has developed with a view that our audience is individual and rational.

In contrast, Christakis and Fowler[28] present compelling evidence that:

- We shape our network (often unconsciously, by gravitating to those similar to us).
- Our network shapes us (where we sit in it significantly impacts who we are).
- Our friends affect us (what we do, what we buy...).
- Our friends' friends' friends affect us (hyperdyadic spread – like Chinese whispers).

So there is a web – sometimes loose and unconscious, sometimes tight and in the foreground – which profoundly influences our behaviour.

Thus, to know our audience, we must know their connections, and more practically we should research accordingly (for example, Kearon and Earls[29] effectively demonstrate we are unreliable witnesses to our own motivations, but excellent amateur ethnographers).

7. Significant growth does not come from frequency alone

Common sense would dictate that there are two ways to grow a brand – get more people buying it, or get the people already buying it to do so more often.

Unfortunately, the evidence doesn't support the notion that both penetration and loyalty are equally valid paths. Sharp[30] illustrates that, across categories and markets, the frequency to value curve is always broadly similar. In fact, the distinguishing factor between big and small brands is not how often they're purchased, but how many (light) buyers they have.

However, the heretic's stance is not simply that 'penetration is the only valid goal', but rather that significant growth without it is highly unlikely. Sharp's assertion that this is a 'law-like pattern' is dangerous: 'Rule-based knowledge is not complete without the "user's manual" that specifies the domain of applicability. By contrast, case-based knowledge allows for greater flexibility, separating the "hard" knowledge of cases from the "soft" judgement of similarity' (Gilboa *et al*, 2012[31]).

For example, it does not take account of a circumstance in which a brand is able to reframe its product offer in a different context (eg a broader category) in order to generate greater frequency.

The touchstone for our heresy is therefore to remember that frequency is unlikely to generate significant brand growth alone, instead it is likely to be outpaced by penetration.

8. Value fans for quality, not quantity

To the evidence in the last touchstone, if the shape of the frequency curve is predictable and common across categories,[32] attempting to grow fan numbers would appear to be a fool's errand.

But that is not to dismiss the role of fans in our new orthodoxy. They have three purposes:

1 To make up a respectable chunk of value/volume (a given).
2 To advocate on our behalf (as we are all connected, see Touchstone 6).
3 To do interesting things that draw interest to the brand.

We should always remember that we are primarily in the business of 'nudging the behaviour of the largely indifferent',[33] and so the primary focus of what we do with our fans should be on points 2 and 3. A platform for creativity, and willing participants when we need them.

9. Prejudice in planning media is the enemy of effectiveness

TV has received a somewhat bad rap of late in orthodox marketing thinking, while media that promotes dialogue with brands (eg social) has been given its time in the sun. It seems somewhat unfair, given the evidence:

- Over 10 years of data, TV returned the highest sales ROI of any medium, and had significant longevity in subsequent years after use.[34]
- The effectiveness of TV is getting better with time: campaigns from the IPA Databank that used TV as the lead medium saw greater market share gains decade on decade from the 80s, 90s and 2000s.[35]

Reports of TV's death may have been greatly exaggerated. The delivery mechanism may evolve, but the concept of recorded film is highly unlikely to falter.[36]

I use TV to illustrate the dangers of allowing prejudice to dictate media planning – whether positively ('it worked for us before...') or negatively ('it's on the way out...'). Our heresy will be guided by the need for an open mind combined with sound judgement.

10. *Set business objectives, and measure success against them alone*

The notion of a new orthodoxy is pointless if it is accompanied by the kind of self-supporting industry of evaluation the current model operates by. We must divorce our way of measurement from our current best thinking, such that it allows evolution in best practice to be judged on the right (discrete) criteria.

The only way to achieve this is for us heretics to believe wholeheartedly in business objectives, and to clearly delineate between measuring *whether* something worked and *how* it worked.

Following that line of thought through, this relies on having set a business objective in the first place. As an added benefit, marketing communications that follow this have been shown to be more effective than those that set behavioural or attitudinal objectives.[37]

This is not to discount the value of intermediate measures but, as Field and Binet themselves advocate, only as part of a balanced scorecard that is of a more diagnostic nature (*how* something worked).

The heretic's (first) manifesto

In summary, these new 10 Touchstones form the start of the *Marketing Progressivism* movement – both a new, positive set of beliefs and a departure from the assumptions that underpin the common sense orthodoxy (Table 19.1).

An idea for an industry

To be true heretics, we must turn our manifesto ('Marketing Progressivism') into something much more active, a revolution of thinking into practice. A new system of *leading* beliefs. To do so, I believe we need four things:

A new setting

I earlier touched on the current orthodoxy having one peculiar characteristic – the lack of an institution holding it up. Heretics usually come from within an institution, rejecting its teachings. We have none.

I believe this institutional vacuum is, in fact, part of the problem. Thus, I propose *a new institution for marketing, built in the model of a modern-day Royal Society/Missional Church hybrid.*

The Royal Society

Formed by followers of Sir Francis Bacon (himself a heretic of sorts through the scientific revolution) in 1660, the Royal Society founded modern

TABLE 19.1

Common sense orthodoxy	New marketing progressivism orthodoxy
Brands form the basis for interaction	Brands exist to speed up decision making
Start with rules from the past	Start with context we find ourselves in
The public as consumers	The public as diverse and temporary identities
Send messages	Create, build and reinforce memories
Decision making a product of rationality	Decision making a product of reason and emotion
Decision makers as individuals	Decision makers within connected networks
Grow through penetration or frequency	Significant growth without penetration is unlikely
Grow fan numbers	Grow fan quality (and use them to influence the indifferent)
Plan media based on experience	Plan media based on the connections to be made
Measure intermediate effects	Measure business effects

science.[38] Today its core purpose is to 'recognise, promote, and support excellence in science and to encourage the development and use of science for the benefit of humanity'.[39]

A Missional Church

The Missional Church movement formed in response to a perception that the Christian church had become too internally focused (maintaining their cultural privilege in society).[40] Carlson defines a Missional Church as one which 'directs its ministry focus outward toward the context in which it was located and to the broader world beyond'.[41]

A hybrid for heresy

I believe that an institution that draws from both of these (in the scientific rigour of the Royal Society and the external-focus of the Missional Church) would benefit the marketing industry and would be the catalyst for displacing the common sense orthodoxy. I suggest the name for this institution, the banner under which heresy will thrive, should be 'The Unit: The Marketing Industry's Thinking & Practice Institute'.

The next three points will detail its function, but in essence it would serve as a central body funded and managed jointly by the organizations charged with representing clients (ISBA), agencies (IPA) and researchers (MRS).

A new leadership

The Unit would operate as a fellowship – electing a set number of new fellows each year from academia and practice (across clients, agencies and researchers).

In addition, a democratically elected council responsible for setting the overall policy direction of the body would then lead the institution. Within the council, one president would be elected by the membership who could serve a maximum of four years (consecutively or otherwise) at the helm. For balance, no one organisation could elect two consecutive presidents.

Accordingly, The Unit will be highly democratic and extremely balanced across the discipline.

A set purpose

The Unit would exist with a very clear purpose – 'in pursuit of marketing best practice, bridging academia and action'.

Its activities would focus on interrogating the broad range (and quality) of thinking that currently exists, and setting new standards for study that lead to adoption and practice. By setting a clear policy, academics and practitioners across the industry will have a fixed point to refer to, challenge and advance, but in a more positive way than we've been characterized by thus far.

A defined output

Finally, The Unit will have a defined output that begins with the heretical behaviour we urgently need but which quickly moves into a better marketing orthodoxy.

It will start with the 10 Touchstones outlined in this paper, and will have a constitutional obligation to set up policy units that continually investigate and review their validity.

Accordingly, the output of The Unit will be characterized by the notion I advocated for earlier – 'a strong view, lightly held'. The rigour to support the policy held by the council, but an obligation and desire to continually better it.

Replacing the orthodoxy – taking the first steps

Finally, while The Unit would be extremely beneficial to our industry in the medium and long term, getting to it will require some concrete first steps that tie back in with the manifesto of our successful heresy.

State a case from within

The most critical thing to spread our breed of heresy is that it comes from within our industry – accordingly it must start with a gathering of like-minded individuals to quickly form a working party.

In the interests of the industry

The first heretics must present themselves to the industry in a progressive and positive manner. We are doing this to improve the industry's output and to create greater transparency in what we do.

Fill the institutional vacuum with clear leadership

Setting up The Unit will, in itself, create a leadership body that the industry currently lacks. It is our division as an industry that has prevented us from making the meaningful impact needed. By signalling our intent to create a new, cross-party institution, we will both build momentum within the industry and increase our effectiveness externally.

Create doctrine with evolutionary ambitions

In beginning with the 10 Touchstones, our new heresy is setting itself up for the doctrinal qualities we've thus far lacked. In the early days, what's critical is that the 10 Touchstones are presented to the industry as a 'complete picture' and not a 'pick and mix' of thoughts on the industry. They are not there to be picked off one by one, but rather represent a view on the discipline of marketing characterized by balance, rigour and a desire for progression – the Marketing Progressivism movement.

Conclusion

In this paper, I've outlined an industry-wide problem that needs to be resolved. The common sense orthodoxy is prevalent but ineffective, intuitive but dishonest. Failure to dislodge it will result in serious questions being raised over the value of our discipline and the future of our practice over the coming two decades.

We need to act now. Credible and compelling lone voices for change are not enough. We need to stop behaving like quarrelling laissez-faire atheists, attempting to disprove component parts of the status quo and appearing like disparate troublemakers. We need to start behaving like heretics, united behind a better alternative belief system and an infrastructure that will revolutionize the way we go about our practice and the contract we form with society at large.

By starting with the 10 Touchstones outlined ('Marketing Progressivism'), working towards a new institution in the mould of the Royal Society and a Missional Church ('The Unit'), and taking the first steps through a working party of like-minded heretics, I believe the time has come for a shift to a new orthodoxy.

I believe that the future of brands lies in heresy – it's time for a new system for leading beliefs.

Notes

1 Morton, B (29 August 2011) Falser words were never spoken. Retrieved 17 July 2014 [Online] www.nytimes.com/2011/08/30/opinion/falser-words-were-never-spoken.html?_r=2&nl=todaysheadlines&emc=tha212&

2 Franklin, B, Famous Philadelphians – Benjamin Franklin. Retrieved 17 July 2014 [Online] http://philadelphia.about.com/cs/history/a/ben_franklin.htm

3 Binet, L (2009, Quarter 3) The Dangers of Common Sense, *Market Leader*, pp 55–57.

4 Sharp, B (2010) *How Brands Grow: What marketers don't know*, Oxford University Press.

5 Godin, S (24 October 2006) *Five common clichés (done wrong)*. Retrieved 30 May 2012 from Seth Godin's blog: http://sethgodin.typepad.com/seths_blog/2006/10/five_common_cli.html

6 Parsons, R (17 December 2010) UK ad spend up 6.6% in 2010, *Marketing Week*.

7 Market Research Society (2011) *2010 Industry League Tables*. Retrieved 30 May 2012 from Market Research Society: www.mrs.org.uk/intelligence/industry_statistics

8 Field, P (2010) The IPA Effectiveness Awards at 30, *Measuring Advertising Performance 2010*, World Advertising Research Centre, London.

9 Alexander, J, Crompton, T and Shrubsole, G (2011) Think of me as evil? Opening the ethical debates in advertising. October: Public Interest Research Centre (PIRC) & WWF-UK.

10 Packard, V (1957) *The Hidden Persuaders*, Longman.

11 Klein, N (1999) *No Logo*, Knopf Canada & Picador, Toronto.

12 Alexander, J, Crompton, T and Shrubsole, G (2011) Think of me as evil? Opening the ethical debates in advertising. October: Public Interest Research Centre (PIRC) & WWF-UK.

13 European Commission (2005) *Special Eurobarometer: Social values, science and technology*, Directorate General Press and Communication, Brussels.

14 Heath, R and Feldwick, P (2007) 50 years of the wrong model of TV advertising, *Working Paper Series 3*, University of Bath School of Management, Bath.

15 Sharp, B (2010) *How Brands Grow: What marketers don't know*, Oxford University Press.

16 Field, P and Binet, L (2007) *Marketing in the Era of Accountability*, Institute of Practitioners in Advertising, World Advertising Research Centre, London.

17 Godin, S (24 October 2006) *Five common clichés (done wrong)*. Retrieved 30 May 2012 from Seth Godin's blog: http://sethgodin.typepad.com/seths_blog/2006/10/five_common_cli.html

18 Bartley, G (July/August 2006) The truth about heresy?, *Philosophy Now* (56).

19 Kurtz, L R (1983) The Politics of Heresy, *American Journal of Sociology*, 88 (6), pp1085–1115.

20 *ibid.*

21 Feldwick, P (2002) *What is Brand Equity Anyway?*, World Advertising Research Centre, London.

22 Duckworth, G (1996) Brands and the role of advertising, in *Understanding Brands: By 10 people who do*, D Cowley (ed), pp58–81, Kogan Page.

23 Gordon, W and Valentine, V (2000) The 21st century consumer – a new model of thinking, MRS Conference, pp 1–35, Market Research Society, London.

24 Kearon, J and Earls, M (2009) Me-to-we research – From asking unreliable witnesses about themselves to asking people what they notice, believe and predict about others, ESOMAR Congress, Montreux.

25 McGilchrist, I (21 October 2011) *The Divided Brain* (Royal Society for the Encouragement of Arts, Producer) Retrieved 31 May 2012 from RSA Animate: http://comment.rsablogs.org.uk/2011/10/24/rsa-animate-divided-brain/

26 Kearon, J and Earls, M (2009) Me-to-we research – From asking unreliable witnesses about themselves to asking people what they notice, believe and predict about others, ESOMAR Congress, Montreux.

27 Feldwick, P (2002) *What is Brand Equity Anyway?*, World Advertising Research Centre, London.

28 Christakis, N A and Fowler, J H (2009) *Connected: The surprising power of our social networks and how they shape our lives*, Little, Brown.

29 Kearon, J and Earls, M (2009) Me-to-we research – From asking unreliable witnesses about themselves to asking people what they notice, believe and predict about others, ESOMAR Congress, Montreux.

30 Sharp, B (2010) *How Brands Grow: What marketers don't know*, Oxford University Press.

31 Gilboa, I, Postlewaite, A, Samuelson, L and Schmeidler, D (29 January 2012) Economic models as analogies. Department of Economics, University of Pennsylvania.

32 Sharp, B (2010) *How Brands Grow: What marketers don't know*, Oxford University Press.

33 Weigel, M (21 May 2012) *Love, Friendship and Brands: The inadequacy of metaphor*. Retrieved 22 May 2012 from Canalside View [Online] http://mweigel.typepad.com/canalside-view/2012/05/love-friendship-and-brands-the-inadequacy-of-metaphor.html

34 Thinkbox (April 2007) *Discover the Power of TV Advertising*. Retrieved 31 May 2012 from Thinkbox [Online] www.thinkbox.tv/server/show/nav.1345

35 Klein, N (1999) *No Logo*, Knopf Canada & Picador, Toronto.

36 Jenkins, H (2006) *Convergence Culture: Where old and new media collide*, New York University Press.

37 Duckworth, G (1996) Brands and the role of advertising, in *Understanding Brands: By 10 people who do*, D Cowley (ed), pp 58–81, Kogan Page.

38 The Economist (7 January 2010) The establishment of science: Celebrating the 350th anniversary of the birth of modern science. Retrieved 1 June 2012 from *The Economist* [Online] www.economist.com/node/15214028

39 The Royal Society (1 June 2012) About us. Retrieved 1 June 2012 from The Royal Society (Online) http://royalsociety.org/about-us/

40 Billings, J (3 May 2008) What makes a church missional? Freedom from cultural captivity does not mean freedom from tradition, *Christianity Today*.

41 Carlson, R (2007) *Six Characteristics of a Missional Church*, National Ministries/American Baptist Churches of the USA, Valley Forge, PA.

I believe brands must shift from vanity to value

2013/14

20

MATTHEW PHILIP
Strategy Director, Manning Gottlieb OMD

I believe I believe that brand communications agencies are out of touch with the ideas that underpin modern business, leading brand communications to be treated as an accounting cost rather than an investment. By embracing Brand Value Analysis – a way of thinking about where brand communications can create real difference to businesses – we can uncover new opportunities for planners, agencies and marketing as a whole, safeguarding a bright future for brands.

Editor's therefore, for your brand...

Your brand thinking: What are the three big brand 'value' opportunities in your market? What is the size of the prizes and the investment worth making?

Your brand engagement: Do your briefs always start with a clear articulation of the value-based objectives?

Your brand organization & capability: Is your team rewarded by the value they create or the hours they put in?

...and author's personal therefore

It's perhaps a touch unfair asking the current cohort of delegates to write this. Our results have only just been made public, yet we're being asked to reflect on how the IPA Excellence Diploma – and our beliefs – has influenced our work, our careers, even our lives.

As ever, context is everything. Just a matter of months since putting my belief to paper – why we should move from vanity to value – I seem (through no action on my part) to be at the centre of an industry-wide debate. Heather Alderson, the outgoing managing partner at BBH has fired a broad-shot to an advertising industry obsessed with vanity proxies. Laurence Green of 101 is warning about the dangers of a myopic focus on short-term communications effects. Even the *FT* is running detailed investigations into the scale of online ad fraud. And at the other end, the incumbent IPA President, Ian Priest, is kicking off his agenda about the value of agencies and how we deserve to be remunerated. Beyond this, clients are asking questions about their marketing and advertising budgets like never before. Difficult questions about the very reason and purpose of what we do as communications professionals can stand up to business scrutiny.

It might be that my belief isn't as personal as I thought. Perhaps we're on the cusp of something bigger, some miraculous shift in our industry's priorities from vanity to value...

Or perhaps not. If the IPA Excellence Diploma teaches you anything, it's that most of the great ideas have already happened. We've just conspired to collectively forget, misplace, misinterpret or staunchly ignore them.

History suggests that we can't rely on the industry to do what's best for itself and the change has to come from individuals. In which case 'What effect will the IPA Excellence Diploma – and your belief – have on your work, career and life?' might be the most appropriate and important question that can be asked at this juncture. Given the decade advantage some in this book have had to turn their belief into reality, let's look at what I need to do over the next 10 years to be a bit more valuable and a little less vain.

Moving my work from vanity to value

Too often, the role of a strategy in the communications industries is one of vanity – to be the smart-arse in the room. (If you don't believe me, have a quick search for a YouTube video from the IPA about the planner with a brain the size of a planet. Overcompensating for something, surely.)

It often feels great, but it needs to change. Smart creates a snappy sound-bite, an intriguing insight, a probing proposition, but ultimately gets us nowhere most of the time. We need to constantly challenge our output, and for me this means bringing every piece of work I do back to the business reality and opportunity that's there.

Therefore: I believe I need to kick the smart-arse and get serious about the commercial opportunity of communications.

Moving my career from vanity to value

Will I be a fully-fledged chartered brand planner in 10 years' time? I really hope so. Just imagine the kudos of others understanding what it means to be a brand planner – the graft, the knowledge, the appreciation of a refined craft... pure vanity of course, but at least I'd be able to articulate exactly how those three letters after my name help create astonishing value for my clients.

The reality is that this might be a step too far. Way back in 1958, Martin Meyer attributed the advertising industry's 'endless confusion of purpose, function, organization and status',[1] to a lack of professional standing. In the proceeding half-century countless others such as Paul Feldwick and Stephen Woodfood have renewed the call to professionalize, but we've seen scant improvement.

But what should be grasped is the power of the Diploma. As it rolls out wider (and the alumni in this book continue to champion it) I can see the start of a virtuous circle – as more talented young planners do it, more clients will experience first-hand the advantages it brings and demand more of their account teams be trained this way. Perhaps at that point, when the majority rather than the few are committed to understanding more about our craft and our practice, we can start to think about being a profession.

That's why I'm taking part in this book. And why I'd recommend every planner who believes that this industry can add value should do the Diploma. What emerges might very well not be my view of a professional industry, but we'll be a whole host better than we are now for sure.

Therefore: I believe in championing a more professional approach to our craft, both in my approach and how I can inspire others.

Moving my life from vanity to value

This is a more fundamental issue. How do you orient your life around value rather than vanity? Is it a philosophy you can successfully apply to life?

The core thesis of my piece is about ditching the short-term outlook, weaning ourselves off instant gratification. I think we can apply this to life. Like our campaigns, perhaps we're guilty of living our lives in cyclical periods, expecting the results of our actions to occur immediately and getting the urge to move on every year when they don't materialize on schedule.

So perhaps it's time to slow down and take stock of the bigger picture. Don't expect to master things overnight (one Instagram filter does not the new David Bailey make). Plan more for where I want to be in seven years, not seven months. Learn an instrument (properly this time). Train for something that will truly stretch me. But above all, invest more in the people around me, in their trust, their humour and their belief. With time I'll hopefully create a lot more value for myself than a series of short-term fixes.

Therefore: I'll just have to wait and see...

I believe brands must shift from vanity to value

The marketing millstone

I'd rather take my money and set fire to it. (James Watt, Founder of BrewDog[2])

We should be enjoying a golden age of marketing and branding

Today's companies are more consumer-centric than they have ever been.[3] Revolutions in data, production and supply mean that we can understand and fulfil customer needs like never before.

But, if anything, the influence of marketers and branding is waning. Only 17 per cent of FTSE 100 CEOs have marketing experience and just 14 per cent of companies have marketers represented at board level.[4] Put simply, it's because the marketing and branding community has a massive lack of credibility when it comes to business; marketing departments are routinely seen as 'unaccountable, expensive and slippery' with poor commercial and financial understanding.[5]

Marketing assets are seldom, if ever, recorded on the balance sheet[6] and thus brand building expenditure is seen by many companies as a cost rather than an investment. The industry has tried to counter this by showing how communications can increase a company's earnings based on ratios such as return on investment, but the logic of 'return' makes this approach invariably unproductive, as cutting (rather than increasing) communications spend will almost always boost short-term profits.[7] This might explain the increasing importance of procurement departments in our industry as clients ask how they can strip out uneconomical costs from the bottom line.

But I believe that brand communication is an essential, and even under-used, investment for a company. And because it's commonly treated as an accounting cost rather than an investment, we could even be spending too little on brand communications. If we stop thinking about how we can strip spend and start thinking about where brand communications can create real value, I believe that we can uncover new opportunities for planners, agencies and marketing as a whole. Specifically, greater understanding of the business of brand communications will help us:

- understand and exploit the greater value that brands can create for companies;
- recognize the importance of brand building as an investment and convince CEOs of the effect it can have on other elements of a company;
- safeguard, and even increase, brand communications investment;
- make brand planning a more professional, accountable and valuable discipline; and
- build and maintain profitable long-term relationships with clients.

This essay examines this problem in three chapters:

- **Part I** looks at where we should be aiming to create value in the modern business world, and how brands can make an enormous contribution.
- **Part II** analyses where we've lost our way and the bad habits we need to break.
- **Part III** introduces *brand value analysis*, a new way of thinking about brand communications to get us back on track.

Part I

Where we should be aiming

> Revenue is vanity, profit is sanity, cash is reality.
>
> (Hilary Devey, *Dragons' Den*)[8]

Company managers are putting less importance on absolute revenue as a measure of success. A greater focus is being put on profitability. Good, solid and sustainable profits give access to the capital required to grow and sustain businesses.[9] But profit is susceptible to short-term distortion, and is most easily increased by manipulating costs. Aggressively upselling existing customers, reducing product quality or even reducing product size can all drastically increase profit.[10] So, it's no surprise that the easiest way to make marketing appear more profitable is by slashing communications budgets.

Beyond this, a focus on profitability leads us to worry about more marginal, tactical issues in brand communications – such as shifting campaign timings to periods where media is slightly cheaper (suggested by James

Dyson as one of the greatest drivers of campaign profitability![11]) – instead of the bigger questions of how brands drive business success.

Free cash flow – the cash generated by a company after it has paid for ongoing operations and growth – is a much better focus to gauge business performance than profit, as it's more difficult to manipulate for accounting purposes.[12] Indeed, cash is the life-blood of any organization: decent cash reserves or access to cheaper credit and equity are essential to growth and provide a significant competitive advantage against the sector.[13]

The central task of those running a company is to drive *sustainable* profit growth.[14] This is best done by increasing the discounted value of its future free cash flows, a concept known as Net Present Value (NPV), which is calculated by taking the stream of expected cash flows and estimating their current value by applying a discount factor. Because we're looking at cash flows realized over an extended time period (often 10 or more years), the discount factor is vital to account for:

- the time-value of money, as a pound received today is worth more than a pound tomorrow;
- the opportunity cost of capital; and
- the risk attached to the certainty of return.[15]

The Net Present Value of cash flows can be expressed as the following formula (Figure 20.1).

What's apparent is that the majority of a company's value will come from profitable sales made in the future. From a financial point of view, even if the payback will take many years, it's worth making an investment if it increases NPV. This explains why many companies are valued at well in excess of 20 times their annual earnings.[16]

But in brand communications agencies, we're a long way off reflecting this in our work. Even among the very best examples, too few show a link between communication activity and business effects; fewer than 5 per cent of IPA Effectiveness Awards case histories show a validated return on investment.[17] Beyond this, the overwhelming business effect claimed is based on sales or revenue. Even the most stand-out brand campaigns show an unhealthy focus on short-term revenue return on investment, and little understanding or analysis of how communications drive *cash flow*. In many ways, we're stuck in the past with our thinking and analysis – even the IPA admit that many Effectiveness Awards authors seem confused about the difference between revenue and profit![18]

Like it or not, our continued focus on revenue means we're a vanity industry. No wonder we've lost a degree of credibility.

If cash is king, brand is the kingmaker

If this business were to be split up, I would take the brands... and you could have the bricks and mortar – and I would fare better than you.

(John Stuart, Chairman of Quaker Oats[19])

FIGURE 20.1 Simplified fomula for working out Net Present Value (NPV) of a company or investment

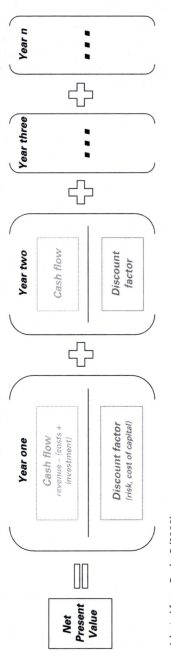

Adapted from: Doyle, P (2000)

Over the past four decades, the intangible assets of the world's biggest firms have grown exponentially.[20] Brand Finance estimate that intangible assets make up more than 70 per cent of the value of some of the world's biggest businesses.[21]

If we can have a business where significant value can be robustly attributed to intangible assets like these, we have to conclude that it is the brand that is responsible for a vast amount of this future value. This isn't an asset bubble that's set to burst, as Gerzema and Lebar suggest,[22] but a growing realization of the power of brands to drive future cash flow. But our existing approach to brand communications massively underplays the contribution that brand building can have in securing and growing this cash.

As we've seen, brand communication investment can increase the value of a company when it creates assets that generate future cash flows with a positive Net Present Value. Our NPV formula (Figure 20.1) gives us an expanded view of how brands can create value and shows that there are four principle ways that they can help deliver significant cash flow changes for a company[23]:

- *Increasing the level of cash flow now* – raising revenues, cutting costs or reducing investments. Brands can help by obtaining higher prices,[24] stimulating higher volume growth, reducing costs[25] or enabling higher asset utilization.[26]

- *Accelerating cash flows* – because cash has a time value, NPV is increased if cash flows can be generated sooner. Brands can help by stimulating higher initial demand and faster access to distribution channels.[27]

Generating cash flows sooner than otherwise:

Audi might be launching a new small car. The cost of bringing a new vehicle to market stretches into the 100s of millions of pounds – an investment that has to be borrowed at a cost. If sales build slowly, the cost of borrowing the cash increases.

However, Audi could invest in heavyweight brand communications (featuring a halo model such as their R8 supercar) for two years prior to launch to create desire among a new target group. If this resulted in an increased rate of sales for the new launch, the money saved from interest payments could boost the profitability of the investment well above the cost of the campaign.

- *Increasing the continuing value of cash flow* – the residual values of a company (the returns projected outside of the current planning period, typically five years) account for in excess of 70 per cent of a company's total worth.[28] Thus brands can play a key role in increasing the continuing value of cash flows by boosting longevity,[29] loyalty, and habit; increasing the success rates of brand extensions and NPD,[30] encouraging greater recommendation and earned media,[31] engaging staff,[32] establishing enduring owned platforms and appealing to future category buyers.[33]

- *Reducing risk* – lowering the firm's cost of capital by reducing the risks and volatility of the projected cash flows. Managing risk is as important as managing return for a business.[34] A Harvard Business School study found that strong brands not only generated significantly greater returns, but reduced risk by 20 per cent.[35] They can help in a number of ways, from creating a barrier to competitor entry[36] to lessening the effect of negative communications.[37]

Creating a barrier to competitors:

Specsavers dominate the optical category, having consistently spent over £40 million per year in above-the-line communications over the past decade. This equity creates a huge deterrent for anyone looking to expand in the market and almost certainly creates a barrier for category killers such as supermarkets to take market share. The importance of this to long-term success should not be underestimated – ASDA's parent company Walmart are massive players in the US optical category – anyone looking to expand would likely have to overinvest significantly for a period of many years before seeing a reasonable return, increasing their risk and potentially their cost of capital. Other investment opportunities might be more attractive to them and helps Specsavers retain their category leadership.

As brand communications practitioners, we put far too much focus on a narrow part of the first area; seeking to boost sales and increase value.

To illustrate the opportunities that we might be overlooking as brand planners, I set up an experiment, showing some recent communications campaigns to a group of brand planners and a group of fund managers and investors, asking how they felt the campaigns might help increase company value (Figure 20.2).

FIGURE 20.2   Summary of a brand planner vs fund manager's view of communications campaigns

'How do might these communications campaigns increase company value?'		
Brand planner view:		**Fund manager view:**
'Typical halo strategy – increases perception of Audi being a sporty brand against premium competitors and helps justify a hefty price premium' [Command price premium]	**Audi R8 TV ad**	'Probably setting the scene to launch a new car or two' [Accelerates rate of sales of new launches]
'It's about knocking people out of their routine and persuading them to cross the street to see how much better Starbucks is than their usual coffee' [Increase sales]	**Starbucks free latte offer**	'I guess they want a short-term spike – maybe the demand will give them a better negotiating position with the supermarkets' [Reduces cost of extending distribution]
'Creates buzz and controversy to persuade people to tune in' [Increase programme viewers]	**Channel 4 'Bigger. Fatter. Gypsier.' outdoor ad**	'It shows that they're a champion of risqué programming... maybe it makes them more attractive for out-there programme makers' [Increase continuing value/ reduces risk]
'Typical end of pathway stuff – tries to get those in-market to consider a Dacia Duster rather than the 4x4 they're thinking about' [Increases sales]	**Dacia Duster press ad**	'It makes them feel more legitimate, more like a reliable car marque. That will help the other models they're launching' [Accelerates speed of cash flow]

Perhaps we should start thinking more like investors and focus our energy around the areas where brand can deliver the biggest business results?

From this mindset, the control that brand communications gives us makes it a vital tool; we can determine weight, timing and message, and increasingly the context of reception, in addition to who and where. There are few comparable inputs into the business system that a company can treble or quadruple overnight.

It's the brand that drives a large proportion of valuable future cash flows, and investment in brand communications is one lever that we can reliably pull. Given this understanding, we can propose a wider definition of brand based on its contribution to business: 'A brand is a set of intangible perceptions and assets designed to drive future cash flows.'

So if we are brand planners, by default we're business planners and our central task is to maximize the NPV of those future cash flows.

Part II

Why we fall short

> Every form of addiction is bad, no matter whether the narcotic be alcohol, morphine or idealism.
>
> (Carl Jung, 1989[38])

Brands are a phenomenally powerful tool to drive long-term value for a business, but there's a lack of understanding and practical application of this in marketing and branding. For the most part, we're stuck in an antiquated way of looking at things; Peter Doyle describes how accounting earnings (focused on the short-term revenue or profit on the balance sheet) still form the basis for valuing intangible business strategies.[39] Nowhere is this more present than with marketing and advertising budgets.

Stephen King lamented this approach as accountants' marketing.[40] In simple terms, it looks at brand communication expenditure's relationship with business success in a linear way within a very limited window of incremental sales and profits. It's this mindset that leads us to commit four cardinal sins that undermine the value communications can create.

Brand communications should drive immediate sales

Our industry has an overriding interest in tweaking communication's ability to create short-term interest. It explains our continued reliance on pre-testing. While pre-tested campaigns tend to perform better in the short term (under six months), they lose out dramatically over non-pre-tested campaigns over time[41] – this may be a clear indication that focusing on communications that is meant to elicit a sales reaction destroys value.

The fundamental job of brand communication is to create value, and simply increasing sales in a short-term window appears to be a very ineffective way of doing this. Shifting our thinking to embrace the numerous ways of increasing cash flow is essential.

The brand exists as a series of dials

'Management,' writes Paul Feldwick, 'demands measurement',[42] but too often we measure precisely the wrong things. While traditional models such as AIDA have been widely discredited,[43] we are still guilty of treating the customer relationship with brands as a series of dials to turn up – a kind of graphic equalizer marketing.

Most of our measures of brand strength might actually be tautologies for brand size. Just as Andrew Ehrenberg described the 'double-jeopardy' effect of greater penetration boosting loyalty,[44] there might be a triple-jeopardy effect where usage also drives positive attitudes.[45] Therefore bigger brands will naturally appear better in the eyes of the public.

This isn't to underplay the effect of brand and preference on purchase, but it may suggest that explicitly measuring brand perceptions might tell us more about the size of our brand than the efficacy of our communications strategy. Therefore, simply focusing on improving brand perceptions might not be the best objective.

But, instead of dispensing with these dials and returning to vital business measures, the recent data and communications revolutions have given us a whole host of new intermediate metrics to explain the success of communications and obsess over, from click-through rates to Facebook 'likes'.

Brand communications should solve a problem

Most planning processes hinge on a problem to be solved.[46] In practice, this is usually a business problem (such as dropping sales) or a customer barrier to overcome. It's not limited to short-term campaigns either – a quarter of IPA Effectiveness Awards winners tell a turnaround story.[47] While it certainly helps us tell a good tale (something we love as an industry)[48] it focuses our attention, resources and understanding of communication around short-term issues and sources of value, not the long-term gains that could be made. We should set up our thinking to spot these opportunities instead. Refocusing our approach on the advantages and opportunities that brand building can provide could help safeguard our client relationships and brands at the same time.

Communications works in discrete campaign periods

It might be, as Tim Ambler suggests, that our annual cycle of brand communications planning is so embedded into our processes that it attracts no real critical review.[49] But this implies that the brand is a cyclical entity, where we build and see returns over a certain period, reinforcing the notion that brand communications should show specific short-term returns. Again, most IPA Effectiveness Awards entries cover a single campaign, or merely a few years.[50] But the best brands are enduring, are built over time, and as we've shown create business value far into the future.

As the most valuable aspects of a brand are only apparent in the long run, we should adjust our thinking to look at brand as a structural entity, with a distinct past and future, and build according to a long-term strategy.

But accountant's marketing is addictive. It justifies spending on communication in the short term (even if it will rarely create value) and it allows us to think we're constantly doing something, hooking us on instant gratification.

And our addiction is only getting worse. Online now accounts for 30 per cent of ad revenue in the UK,[51] with the majority going straight to optimized search advertising.[52] Outside search, the picture is getting more pronounced: sources suggest that by 2017, over 80 per cent of online display spend (including the fast-growing markets of online video and mobile) will be automatically bought and optimized to response.[53]

Beyond this, seismic shifts in more traditional media channels, such as increased migration of print media onto tablets and addressable TV advertising, will appeal directly to accountants' marketing, promising to cut wastage and speak to those just in marketing. And it's not just media buying; marketers are showing an increased appetite to bring a programmatic approach to everything from audience segmentation to insights and content.[54]

Back in the 1960s and 70s, company managers were driven by a mandate of growth for growth's sake, chasing market share through unprofitable customers and launching products that were doomed to fail.[55] Companies saw customer bases grow quickly, but failed to create value. We're making similar mistakes today; searching for immediate justification of our activity at the expense of the value that brands can really create.

If we truly believe in the value that brands can create for a company, we should be taking the lead and championing this approach to brand communications, *brand value analysis*. Therefore, we first need to shift our thinking, from vanity to value (Figure 20.3).

FIGURE 20.3   The shift from traditional planning to brand value analysis

Traditional planning		Brand Value Analysis
Sales, revenue, profit payback	⟶	Sources of cash flow
Immediate accountability	⟶	Long-term effectiveness
Problem solving	⟶	Spotting opportunities
Cyclical campaigns	⟶	Structural brand

Part III

How we can get there

A shift to brand value analysis (BVA) has sizable implications for the way we structure our industry, planning process and relationships. To get there, we need a roadmap for a brand communications industry that looks to builds value (Figure 20.4).

FIGURE 20.4 Roadmap for building confidence in a brand planning rooted in financial understanding

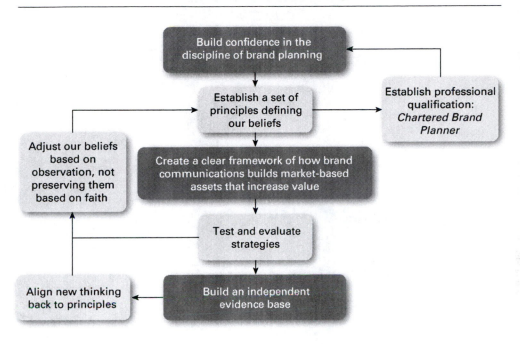

Brand value analysis (BVA) should be a professional discipline

The key aim of BVA is establishing brand planning as a professional discipline, the Chartered Brand Planner (CBP). This certification will cover the core knowledge base, essential skills and techniques needed to build valuable brands, in addition to a code of ethics and beliefs.

At the heart would be a solid grasp of the true nature of finance and growth for our clients, in addition to the key measurement techniques, econometric analysis and core craft skills gained during a comprehensive study course and assessment.

The brand value analysis planning process

For this to be successful, it's clear that we need to rework major elements of our approach to planning in line with brand value analysis thinking. Figure 20.5 summarizes some of the significant changes to current wisdom that BVA will necessitate.

FIGURE 20.5   Major shifts between current planning approach and brand value analysis planning approach

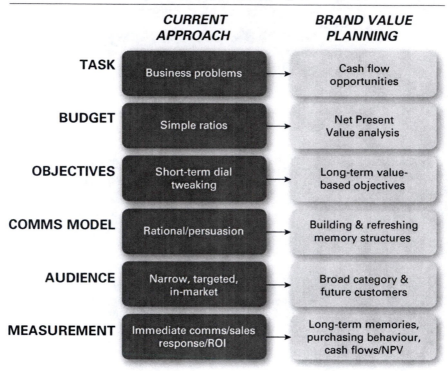

	CURRENT APPROACH	BRAND VALUE PLANNING
TASK	Business problems	Cash flow opportunities
BUDGET	Simple ratios	Net Present Value analysis
OBJECTIVES	Short-term dial tweaking	Long-term value-based objectives
COMMS MODEL	Rational/persuasion	Building & refreshing memory structures
AUDIENCE	Narrow, targeted, in-market	Broad category & future customers
MEASUREMENT	Immediate comms/sales response/ROI	Long-term memories, purchasing behaviour, cash flows/NPV

Defining the task

Principle: brand value analysis looks for opportunities to maximize cash flow, not business problems to solve.

To help define the task we create a brand value hypothesis (BVH), which lists out where we believe brand investment can increase NPV and where the greatest opportunities are. The key to this is a subtle shift from thinking like an ad man to thinking like an investor. But financial acumen is just the starting point – this technique, if anything, should allow for greater creative input, spotting new opportunities where brand communications can build value.

Once the potential sources of value have been established, existing econometric techniques could be easily adapted around the NPV equation (Figure 20.1) to identify their potential to create value, forecasting the potential cash flow from each area and creating a discount rate from the associated risks and cost of capital.

Setting the budget

Principle: budgets should be set according to the available opportunity not simple ratios, shifting to long-term, task-based investment.

If we treat brand communications as an investment, it means that expenditure on developing brand assets through communications makes sense if the sum of the discounted cash flows they generate is positive. Valuing the aspects of the brand value hypothesis allows us to do this and compare potential return to other investments, as well as analysing the effect brand building can have on other capital projects.

If we understand the true value of brand communications as an investment, it may tell us that greater value can be created by spending more.

Setting objectives

Principle: the brand value hypothesis should lead directly to clear value-based objectives.

Effective brand value hypotheses should be translated into clear objectives. For example, Specsavers may bet that growth of their hearing centres might be a significant business opportunity. The BVH might suggest that the best way to increase the NPV of the investment is to increase the speed of distribution, by getting more partners to sign up to offer hearing services in addition to optics. The most valuable objective for communications in this case could be to demonstrate to potential partners that Specsavers will dominate the hearing-aid landscape, as they have done in the optician market, by significantly over-investing – a hypothesis that could be supported by econometric modelling from the growth of their opticians. Whilst they may not see a profitable return for many years, brand value analysis might show it to be an effective strategy.

Communications model

Principle: brand communications is a comparatively weak but pervasive force.

Martin Weigel equates it to gravity[56] – gently pushing us towards an increased likelihood of purchase through building and refreshing appropriate memory structures, creating what Byron Sharp terms 'distinctive market based assets'.[57] It is the quantity and quality of these assets in people's minds that allow increased, faster and continual cash flows, in addition to creating a substantial barrier that reduces risk.

Audience

Principle: target everyone in a category – potentially even future customers – rather than those currently 'in-market'.

Les Binet and Peter Field's findings support this, showing that a broad approach to targeting generates greater efficiency and effectiveness.[58] This insight could liberate us from a myopic focus on over-defined target audiences and allow us more resource to focus on the best long-term direction to create value.

It also has a distinct impact on the way we plan media. While individual and in-market targeting may be in vogue, brand value analysis would suggest that the volume of impacts created by broad, traditional channels are key to successful communications, and our biggest area for concern is how we continue to use these channels to successfully build and refresh our market-based assets.

Measurement

Principle: test hypotheses and learn about strategy.

Different tasks and objectives will require different approaches to measurement. However, I would suggest measurement frameworks take a hierarchical approach linking changes in mental structures through to individual behavioural shifts (by analysing single-source purchase data) to increased business value.

Brand value analysis aligns all our thinking back to core ideas

Beyond our internal planning process, there are certain shifts we need to make within the industry in order for this approach to gain recognition.

Awards

Principle: celebrate the true value of brands, not an agency.

Too few awards celebrate the true value of brands; most are focused on a very limited period and promote the short-term value that a new agency can create. The IPA Effectiveness Awards should take the lead and establish a category immediately that seeks to recognize the value that long-term brand building creates, focusing specifically on quantifying the longer and broader effects.

Crucially, these award entries would supplement existing long-term studies and marketing science in our evidence bank, to help us understand sources of value created by brands, better forecast cash flows and adjust our approaches accordingly.

Remuneration

Principle: fee structures based on long-term business contribution.

Brand value analysis would suggest that remuneration should be weighted towards value created over the long term. I propose that we focus on two core elements to agree compensation.

1 *Cash flows relating to brand activity* – the agency would take an agreed commission on cash realized from communications activity. As cash flows increase, so too would the agency's remuneration.

2 *Incremental future flows created* – the agency would take a commission based on the increase in net present value from communications activity, encouraging the agency to identify new areas where brand activity can build value.

In the first year of the contract, an agreed base fee would cover basic expenses (staffing costs, overheads, etc). As the incremental effects were being felt in year two, the base fee would drop and the agency would take a commission based on the cash flow attributable to the communications activity. In subsequent years, the base fee would be phased out and a long-term incentive introduced based on the incremental future flows created.

Clearly this approach needs stable, trusting clients in addition to a patient, focused agency. However, if followed correctly, this process could foster longer, deeper and more collaborative relationships where all parties are seeking to maximize the same objectives.

New thinking

Brand value analysis gives us a framework to test hypotheses and ideas, allowing us to objectively weigh up the value of new ideas before embracing them.

But this shouldn't be seen as a barrier to creativity. Creativity remains enormously, overwhelmingly important in the creation and curation of brands. What BVA can do is help aim it in a better direction so we can create a genuine difference to our clients' businesses.

Conclusion

I believe that as brand planners, our focus is too often in the wrong place. Pandering to the accountant's view of marketing leads us to position brand communications as a cost to be minimized rather than an investment to be maximized.

Therefore, we need to shift our focus to understanding, and exploiting, the longer and broader contribution that brands make to a business. We need to root our planners' thinking in the value that can be created and embrace brand value analysis; teach our industry to be fully fluent in the language and concepts that drive companies forwards in the modern world, and create a revolution in the way brands are built.

This shouldn't, however, be perceived as anything new. Stephen King imagined his planners as 'almost *economists*' (emphasis added).[59] What we might be painting a picture of here is his original grand strategist, with the financial foresight to look beyond the immediate to see the myriad potential in brands and root their thinking in the value that can be created. But to paraphrase the great man, perhaps brand planning hasn't failed, we just haven't really tried it yet...

Notes

1 Mayer, M (1958) *Madison Avenue USA*, Cardinal, US.

2 Charles, G (January 2013) BrewDog founder on advertising, *Marketing Magazine*.

3 Doyle, P (2000) *Value-Based Marketing: Marketing strategies for corporate growth and shareholder value*, John Wiley & Sons.

4 *ibid.*

5 Shaw, R and Merrick, D (2005) *Marketing Payback: Is your marketing profitable?*, Financial Times Prentice Hall.

6 Doyle, P (Spring 2000) How shareholder analysis re-defines marketing, *Market Leader*, 8.

7 Agres, S, Daiberl, S, Moult, B and Spaeth, J (2003) Maximising shareholder value by bridging the metrics of finance and marketing, ESOMAR Congress 2003. Agres suggested that a pound spent on communications often generates less than a pound in intermediate sales; any short-term analysis of communications – no matter how comprehensive – is likely to deem it unprofitable.

8 *Dragons' Den*, BBC2 programme, 30 September 2012.

9 Doyle, P (2000) *Value-Based Marketing: Marketing strategies for corporate growth and shareholder value*, John Wiley, Chichester.

10 Agres, S, Daiberl, S, Moult, B and Spaeth, J (2003) Maximising shareholder value by bridging the metrics of finance and marketing, ESOMAR Congress 2003.

11 Dyson, P and Weaver, K (2006) Advertising's greatest hits: profitability and brand value, *Admap*.

12 Jones, R A D (2012)) One-day MBA, *ICSA Information & Trading*.

13 Doyle, P (2000) *Value-Based Marketing: Marketing strategies for corporate growth and shareholder value*, John Wiley & Sons.

14 Agres, S, Daiberl, S, Moult, B and Spaeth, J (2003) Maximising shareholder value by bridging the metrics of finance and marketing, ESOMAR Congress 2003.

15 Doyle, P (2000) *Value-Based Marketing: Marketing strategies for corporate growth and shareholder value*, John Wiley & Sons.

16 Deboo, M (June 2007), Ad metrics and stock markets: how to bridge the yawning gap, *Admap*. Many companies have even changed their financial processes to take account of this long-term view: Unilever, for instance, has stopped providing quarterly reports to the market as they are too sensitive to short-term fluctuations in revenue and profits, with CEO Paul Polman (2011) The Remedies for Capitalism, *McKinsey* [Online] www.mckinsey.com/features/capitalism/paul_polman knowing that building sustainability necessitates a long-term approach.

17 In *Marketing in the Era of Accountability* Les Binet and Peter Field (2008) found that out of 880 cases, just 39 showed a validated return on investment, where a conclusive return on communications expenditure had been demonstrated.

18 IPA (2014) IPA Effectiveness Awards Writing Pack, IPA.

19 Feldwick, P (1996) Do we really need 'brand equity?', ESOMAR Congress, September.

20 Gerzema, J and Lebar, E (2009) The danger of a 'brand bubble', *Market Leader*, Q4.

21 Brand Finance (2014) Brand Finance US 500: The Billion Dollar Brands Club 2014, *Brand Finance* [Online] http://brandfinance.com/images/upload/brand_finance_us500_infographic_embargoed_03172014_final.pdf

22 Gerzema, J and Lebar, E (2009) The danger of a 'brand bubble', *Market Leader*, Q4.

23 Doyle, P (2000) *Value-Based Marketing: Marketing strategies for corporate growth and shareholder value*, John Wiley & Sons.

24 Miller, J and Muir, D (2004) *The Business of Brands*, John Wiley & Sons.

25 Agres, S, Daiberl, S, Moult, B and Spaeth, J (2003) Maximising shareholder value by bridging the metrics of finance and marketing, ESOMAR Congress 2003.

26 Binet, L and Field, P (2008) *Marketing in the Era of Accountability*, IPA.

27 Shaw, R and Merrick, D (2005) *Marketing Payback: Is your marketing profitable?*, Financial Times Prentice Hall, London. Sharp, B (2010) *How Brands Grow: What marketers don't know*, Oxford University Press, also discusses how increases in physical distribution are one of the biggest drivers of brand growth. Strong brands can provide extra benefits and growth options: for example, franchised brands such as Dominoes may get greater numbers of enquiries from interested franchisees, helping them to expand quicker or recruit franchisees in more desirable locations.

28 Doyle, P (Spring 2000) How shareholder analysis re-defines marketing, *Market Leader*, 8.

29 Agres, S, Daiberl, S, Moult, B and Spaeth, J (2003) Maximising Shareholder Value by Bridging the Metrics of Finance & Marketing, ESOMAR Congress 2003. In light of revelations from Andrew Ehrenberg (Sharp, B (2010) *How Brands Grow: What marketers don't know*, Oxford University Press) we need to look at loyalty measures across much longer periods – perhaps stretching from a typical one-year period to a decade or more. In some categories, looking at the long-term potential of a customer is vital in realizing value. High-street banks typically make little money on a current account, but see the life-time value of existing customers taking out new financial products – from credit cards to mortgages – at different life-stages, not convenient campaign windows.

30

31 Keller, E and Fay, B (2012) Word-of-mouth advocacy: a new key to advertising effectiveness, *Journal of Advertising Research*, 52 (4).

32 Miller, J and Muir, D (2004) *The Business of Brands*, John Wiley. This area is particularly relevant to service brands where perceptions are overwhelmingly driven by experience – a piece of communications may indirectly nudge you towards trying it, but your experience as a customer may determine your long-term value. So communications that motivate employees might be a much bigger driver of value than ones that seek to recruit new customers; Doyle, P (Broadening the concept of account planning, *Admap* March 1986) suggests that British Rail's ads of the time might have been aimed as much at staff as passengers, designed to motivate them to improve the quality of their passengers' experience.

33 Binet, L and Field, P (2012) *The Long and the Short of It*, IPA.

34 McDonald, M (July/August 2012) Marketing for share price effect, Warc Best Practice.

35 Agres, S, Daiberl, S, Moult, B and Spaeth, J (2003) Maximising shareholder value by bridging the metrics of finance and marketing, ESOMAR Congress 2003.

36 *ibid*.

37 See the example of British Gas in Goodlad, N and Jamieson, C (2012) British Gas: Taking British Gas back to the future, IPA Effectiveness Awards.

38 Jung, C G (1963/1989) *Memories, Dreams, Reflections*, Random House.

39 Doyle, P (2000) *Value-Based Marketing: Marketing strategies for corporate growth and shareholder value*, John Wiley & Sons.

40 King, S (1985) Has marketing failed, or was it never really tried?, in (2007) *A Master Class in Brand Planning: The timeless works of Stephen King*, J Lannon and M Baskin (eds), John Wiley & Sons.

41 Binet, L and Field, P (2012) *The Long and the Short of It*, IPA.

42 Feldwick, P (2002) How should you research brands?, in *What Is Brand Equity, Anyway?*, Warc.

43 See Heath, R and Feldwick, P (2008) Fifty years using the wrong model of advertising, *International Journal of Market Research*, 50 (1) for an introduction to low-involvement processing, a much more sensible way of thinking about how communications works.

44 Sharp, B (2010) *How Brands Grow: What marketers don't know*, Oxford University Press.

45 Sharp, B and Romaniuk, J (2000) Using known patterns in image data to determine brand positioning, *International Journal of Market Research*, 42 (2).

46 For example, the process Leslie Butterfield (1997) suggests in Strategy Development in *Excellence in Advertising: the IPA Guide to Best Practice*, ed L Butterfield.

47 IPA Effectiveness Awards Search Engine [Online] www.ipa.co.uk/ease

48 Shaw, R and Merrick, D (2005) *Marketing Payback: Is your marketing profitable?*, Financial Times Prentice Hall, London. They discuss how marketing likes to surround itself with 'damn good stories about its successful track record'.

49 Ambler, T (2003) *Marketing and the Bottom Line: The new metrics of corporate wealth*, Financial Times Prentice Hall.

50 69 per cent of IPA Effectiveness Awards entries cover a period of less than two years (Binet, L and Field, P, 2012).

51 (2013) Communications Market Report 2013, Ofcom.

52 (2014) IAB/PwC Digital Adspend Study H1 2013, IAB/PwC.

53 Admap (January 2014) Adstats: Programmatic buying, *Admap*.

54 (November 2013) Programmatic everywhere? Data, technology and the future of audience engagement, *Winterberry Group*.

55 Doyle, P (2000) (Spring 2000) How shareholder analysis re-defines marketing, *Market Leader*, 8.

56 Weigel, M [accessed 8 April 2013] Weakness with consequence: Why marketing is like gravity, *Canalside View Blog*, [Online] http://martinweigel.org/2013/04/08/weakness-with-consequence-why-marketing-is-like-gravity/

57 Sharp, B (2010) *How Brands Grow: What marketers don't know*, Oxford University Press.

58 Binet, L and Field, P (2012) *The Long and the Short of it*, IPA.

59 King, S (1988) Strategic Development of Brands in (2007) *A Master Class in Brand Planning: The timeless works of Stephen King*, J Lannon and M Baskin (eds), John Wiley & Sons.

Outro
I believe that the IPA Excellence Diploma transforms careers

PATRICK MILLS
Director of Professional Development, IPA

I believe that the IPA Excellence Diploma transforms careers, agencies and brands.

The contents of this book would vouch for that.

It is hugely gratifying that so much of what has been written is now current thinking and has come about through participation in the IPA's industry leading education programme.

We need to keep stoking the fires of invention, so if you have enjoyed the essays in this book and have a strong opinion about the future of brands then this course is for you.

To apply for our scholarship, simply write an 'I believe... therefore' in 500 words about a strongly held belief and the impact it has had on you and send it to me at **Patrick@ipa.co.uk**.

We award one scholarship every year at the end of October for the following year's course.

INDEX